The Global
Resurgence of
Democracy

The Global Resurgence of Democracy

Edited by Larry Diamond
and Marc F. Plattner

The Johns Hopkins University Press
Baltimore and London

The Johns Hopkins University Press
2715 North Charles Street
Baltimore, Maryland 21218-4319
The Johns Hopkins Press Ltd., London

Chapters in this volume appeared in the following issues of the *Journal of Democracy:*
Winter 1990: chapters 9 and 29; Spring 1990: 5 and 26; Summer 1990: 8; Fall 1990: 10, 11, and 12; Winter 1991: 4, 6, 13, 22, and 23; Spring 1991: 1; Summer 1991: 3, 14, 15, 16, 24, and 27; and Fall 1991: 2, 7, 17, 18, 19, 20, 21, 25, and 28.

Library of Congress Cataloging-in-Publication Data
The Global resurgence of democracy / edited by Larry Diamond and Marc F. Plattner.
   p.   cm.
   Articles originally published in the quarterly Journal of democracy, 1990–1991.
   Includes bibliographical references and index.
   ISBN 0-8018-4564-5 (hard : alk. paper). —ISBN 0-8018-4565-3 (pbk. : alk. paper)
   1. Democracy. 2. World politics—1989–   I. Diamond, Larry Jay.
   II. Plattner, Marc F., 1945– .
JC421.G58   1993
321.8—dc20   92-26344

A catalog record for this book is available from the British Library

CONTENTS

PREFACE AND ACKNOWLEDGMENTS

This volume is composed of a selection of essays originally published in the *Journal of Democracy*. A quarterly publication launched in January 1990, the *Journal* seeks to examine all aspects of the struggle to achieve and maintain democracy around the world. It features an unusual blend of scholarly analysis by leading social scientists, reflective essays by prominent intellectuals, reports from democratic activists in developing and postcommunist countries, and news and information about key developments in the study and practice of democracy. In the few short years since its founding, the *Journal* has become a leading worldwide forum for serious discussion of the problems and prospects of democracy.

For this volume, we have chosen essays from the *Journal* that address broad issues relating to the establishment and consolidation of democracy. Most of the contributions come from political scientists, but also represented are such outstanding figures as philosopher Leszek Kolakowski, novelist and Peruvian presidential candidate Mario Vargas Llosa, and former Uruguayan president Julio María Sanguinetti. We have organized the 29 essays reprinted here into four sections: (I) The Democratic Moment; (II) Problems of Democratic Institutionalization; (III) Political Corruption and Democracy; and (IV) The Global Democratic Prospect. The detailed introduction both elucidates the rationale underlying this arrangement and sketches out some of the central points raised by our authors.

Despite the astonishing pace of political change in recent years, the essays in this collection remain both timely and enduring. Indeed, we believe that this volume constitutes the best available guide—both for general readers and for teachers and students of political science—to understanding the opportunities and challenges that currently confront supporters of democracy around the world.

The *Journal* is published under the sponsorship of the National Endowment for Democracy, a private, nonprofit corporation that receives an annual appropriation from the United States Congress for a grant-making program to strengthen democratic institutions abroad. The *Journal*, which has largely been supported by private funds, has an independent editorial board that advises its editors in setting editorial policy. In August 1991, the Endowment entered into an agreement with the Johns Hopkins University Press, which now publishes the *Journal* on its behalf.

As we have come to learn from our experience as coeditors, publishing a journal is a complex and difficult operation that requires a great deal of effort and assistance. We are very pleased to have this opportunity to acknowledge the support of those institutions and individuals whose contributions have been indispensable to our work. First, we wish to thank the Board of Directors of the National Endowment for Democracy and especially the Endowment's president, our good friend Carl Gershman. Carl helped to conceive the idea of the *Journal,* and he has given it his unflagging support, while scrupulously respecting its editorial integrity.

We are equally grateful to the members of our editorial board, who have generously volunteered their time to provide us both with overall editorial guidance and with evaluations of particular manuscripts. No less essential has been the financial assistance provided by a number of private foundations, above all the Lynde and Harry Bradley Foundation. Other important contributors have been the Smith Richardson, William H. Donner, John M. Olin, and Joyce Foundations, and Pfizer, Inc.

The *Journal* has also been blessed with a first-rate staff. The fine editorial hand of our senior editor Phil Costopoulos is in evidence throughout this volume. Our production editor Debra Liang provided essential assistance in the preparation both of the original essays and of this volume. Our editorial intern Kathy Vitz did a super job of compiling the index. Thanks are also due to former managing editor Peter Pavilionis and editorial interns Gary Rosen and Juliet Johnson, as well as to our unfailingly helpful colleagues at the Johns Hopkins University Press.

Whatever merit this volume possesses is, of course, ultimately due to the arguments and insights of the authors whose essays are collected here. We are enormously grateful to them for their willingness to contribute to what was still a new publication, and thus to help it become an established presence on the international scene.

Finally, we wish to take note of the extraordinary efforts to secure and strengthen democracy made by men and women from every region of the globe. It is due to their courage and dedication that the international study of democracy has now become so rich a field for inquiry and reflection.

INTRODUCTION

Larry Diamond and Marc F. Plattner

When historians look back on the twentieth century, they may well judge its last quarter as the greatest period of democratic ferment in the history of modern civilization. As Samuel P. Huntington observes in the essay that opens this volume, some 30 countries made transitions to democracy between 1974 and 1990. During 1991 and 1992 a number of other democratic transitions were initiated or completed. Depending on how rigorously "democracy" is defined, the list of new democracies by mid-1992 could be considered to include virtually all of the former communist dictatorships of Eastern Europe, and much of the former Soviet Union, including Russia. Moreover, as Richard Joseph details later in this volume, numerous African countries have reached varying stages of transition to democracy.

In its 1992 annual survey of "Freedom in the World," Freedom House judged that 75 countries were politically "free" at the end of 1991, 10 more than the previous year. By a somewhat more generous standard, it counted 89 democracies—roughly half the (growing number of) independent countries in the world, and twice the number 20 years ago. Clearly, to use Huntington's term, democracy has been "snowballing," and the powerful demonstration and spillover effects generated by the very momentum of its expansion partly account for its growth.

As Marc F. Plattner observes in his contribution to this collection, this global democratic resurgence has also occurred on the plane of ideology, with the utter "self-discrediting" of communist systems and of such other dictatorial regimes as "African socialism" and "bureaucratic authoritarianism." As a result, antidemocratic forces (especially on the left) have been weakened throughout the world, democracy has been left "with no serious geopolitical or ideological rivals," and democrats have regained their self-confidence. In fact, Plattner argues, liberal democracies today are widely regarded as "the only truly and fully modern societies."

In a formulation that has greatly influenced contemporary analyses, Huntington maintains that this current period of democratic growth—dating from the breakdowns of authoritarianism in Portugal, Spain, and

Greece in 1974–75—represents a "third wave" of global democratic expansion. Both the first "long" wave from the 1820s to 1926 and the second wave from 1945 to 1962 gave way to "reverse waves" that significantly reduced both the number of democracies in the world and the sense of hope about the global prospects for democracy. As Plattner notes, prominent democratic intellectuals were led, in the depths of the second reverse wave in the early 1970s, to lament that "liberal democracy . . . has simply no relevance to the future. It is where the world was, not where it is going."[1]

The question that preoccupies Huntington is also the central issue of this book: Can democracy's third wave be sustained indefinitely, or will it ebb into a third reverse wave of democratic breakdowns at some point during the 1990s?

With the ordeals that infant democracies are undergoing in Eastern Europe, Russia, and other postcommunist states, and with the coups against democracy in Haiti, Thailand, and Peru (and the military uprising in Venezuela) during 1991 and 1992, some might ask whether a third reverse wave has not already begun. If one is inclined toward economic determinism, democracy's prospects might appear gloomy. Most of the upper- and upper-middle-income countries had already become democratic by 1990, and most of those that remained in the upper reaches of Huntington's "political zone of transition" (as indicated by per capita GNP) were states whose predominant cultural orientations—Confucian or Islamic—are often regarded as inhospitable toward democracy. Moreover, as Huntington notes, democratic breakdowns in previous reverse waves owed much to poor regime performance—severe economic setbacks, intensified social conflict, the breakdown of law and order. In their essay, Peter Hakim and Abraham F. Lowenthal show that most of the newly restored democracies in Latin America suffer from these problems to one degree or another—indeed, as their analysis could be seen to have anticipated, Peruvian democracy finally bowed to them, at least temporarily, in 1992. And none of the new postcommunist democracies is yet out of danger.

While remaining skeptical about the universal viability of liberal democracy, Huntington cautions against cultural or economic determinism. Cultural legacies can gradually soften and change with time, and most great cultural traditions are "highly complex bodies of ideas . . . and beliefs," some of which may be compatible with democracy and some not. A more likely prospect than authoritarianism in much of rapidly developing East Asia, he suspects, is a "distinctly East Asian" form of democracy, akin to the Japanese dominant-party system, offering "competition for power but not alternation in power." More generally, he argues, the two most important factors determining the likelihood of democracy will be economic development and political leadership.

Many observers question the democratic credentials of a system like Japan's, which has conducted free and fair elections under constitutional rule for almost half a century without any change in the governing party. This raises the crucial question of what democracy is and is not, the issue addressed by Philippe C. Schmitter and Terry Lynn Karl in chapter 3. Schmitter and Karl stress that there is no one form of democracy, and that Americans should be careful not to identify the concept of democracy too closely with their own institutions. Democracies can differ greatly in the degree in which they encourage consensus versus competition, shared power versus majoritarian rule, and public authority versus private action. Democratic regimes may be parliamentary or presidential, and federal or unitary. Contemporary democracies also vary widely in their levels of citizen participation, access to power, checks and balances, governmental responsiveness, party strength, and political pluralism. These variations, particularly in constitutional design and electoral systems, may have far-reaching implications for the quality and stability of democracy (as Juan J. Linz and his critics and Arend Lijphart and his critics debate later in this volume) but, provided certain minimum criteria are met, they do not bear on whether democracy exists.

For Schmitter and Karl, "modern political democracy is a system of governance in which rulers are held accountable for their actions in the public realm by citizens, acting indirectly through the competition and cooperation of their elected representatives." This implies criteria very similar to Robert A. Dahl's conception of polyarchy[2]—extensive competition for power through regular, free, and fair elections; highly inclusive citizenship conferring rights of participation on virtually all adults; and, implicitly, extensive civil and political liberties to allow for pluralism of information and organization. But to this now conventional understanding Schmitter and Karl add some important qualifications. Between elections, citizens must be able to influence public policy through various nonelectoral means, like interest-group associations and social movements, which inevitably involve cooperation as well as competition among citizens. Popularly elected governments must be able to exercise their powers without obstruction or control by unelected officials (e.g., the military). And the polity must be self-governing.

The question of how democracy comes into being is the focus of chapter 4 by Julio María Sanguinetti and chapter 5 by Alfred Stepan. Sanguinetti writes from a unique vantage point, as the first president of Uruguay following its return to democracy in 1985 and a key player in the transition process. Emphasizing the critical role of political leadership and practice in producing democracy, Sanguinetti draws several lessons from the Uruguayan experience. First, "a transition requires the constant management of two emotions: fear and impatience"—fear on the part of the deposed (military) leaders that they or their institution may be victimized by the new regime, and impatience on the part of democratic forces to exercise their new-found liberties. Second, democratic stability depends on economic progress; new democracies must put a high priority on rekindling economic growth (while keeping control of inflation) if they are eventually to be able to meet long-deferred social expectations. Third, Sanguinetti emphasizes the value of gradualism and dialogue, negotiation and compromise, which can narrow the huge chasm of mistrust and misunderstanding between the military and civilian politicians. Fourth, new democracies must seek to build a very broad base of legitimacy. This requires a high degree of tolerance and inclusiveness, and sometimes extraordinary acts of reconciliation, bringing together old political enemies and granting amnesty even to terrible human rights violators. The latter issue can pose a painful conflict, he concedes, between "the ethics of conviction" (or morality) and "the ethics of responsibility" ("always strive to ensure that your actions do not produce consequences which contradict your good intentions"). It is the pragmatism of the latter, Sanguinetti concludes, that must take precedence if a democratic transition is to succeed.

Stepan views the challenge of democratic transition from the perspective of democratic oppositions. These formations, sometimes merely small bands of determined and courageous activists, perform several tasks that are crucial to democratization. To begin with, merely by surviving as an opposition force they can deny an authoritarian regime its goal of complete hegemony over society. This then enables them to move on to the next task of maintaining some zones of autonomy in which various organizations in civil society (parties, trade unions, religious and cultural groups) can continue to operate independently of the regime. "The larger and stronger these various non- or anti-authoritarian subsystems grow, the more effectively they can perform the other tasks of democratic opposition: contesting the legitimacy of the authoritarian regime, raising the costs of maintaining it, and generally grinding it down while building support for a democratic alternative."

As Claude Ake explains in chapter 6, the quest for a democratic alternative to authoritarian misrule has become increasingly widespread in Africa in recent years. To some extent, this responds to international pressures, which have been growing as the end of the Cold War and the marginalization of Africa have "given the West more latitude to conduct its relations with Africa in a principled way." Ake applauds this democratic concern (however belated), and welcomes economic sanctions against antidemocratic regimes. He believes, however, that it is primarily indigenous democratic forces that have put democracy on the agenda in Africa, and that these forces must be strengthened if the democracy movement is to succeed. Arguing passionately that Africa needs democracy in order to develop, Ake refutes a number of myths: that democracy contradicts traditional African cultures; that it would cause ethnic rivalries to erupt into conflict; and that it must take second place to the needs of development. Ake shows that many traditional African polities "were infused with democratic values," that ethnic conflict has intensified with 30 years of authoritarian rule, and that the notion of a choice between democracy and development is both morally and empirically false. Postponing democracy has not promoted development in Africa; indeed, there is a growing consensus in Africa that the absence of democracy is the chief cause of the continent's developmental crisis. "The primary issue," Ake argues, "is not *whether* it is more important to eat well than to vote, but *who* is entitled to decide which is more important."

Choosing democracy, even at some cost and risk, is part of what Mario Vargas Llosa identifies in chapter 7 as "The Culture of Liberty." Rejecting all determinist conceptions, including the notion of the "end of history," Vargas Llosa argues that the recent victories over communism "were hard-won by the stubborn resistance of victims, sometimes aided by the desperation of communist oligarchs." Their efforts were an important step in building a "culture of liberty," without which democracy cannot be secure. For Vargas Llosa, this culture is multidimensional. Central to it is a "sense of individual responsibility" that no longer looks to the state to solve all problems and fulfill all desires, but rather accepts the discipline, rules, risks, and initiative required for a successful market economy. Such a culture, he argues, rejects not only statism and collectivism but also nationalism and mercantilism. The latter two have been the bane of development and democracy in Latin America, he asserts, warping productive incentives and strangling individual initiative. The culture of liberty values "a free economy that banishes monopolies and guarantees everyone access to markets governed by simple, clear, and equitable rules." At the same time, however, it requires, if it is to be sustained, support for the weak and infirm and widespread access to cultural activity, which is an important antidote to the materialism, selfishness, and cynicism that tend to afflict capitalist society.

Problems of Democratic Institutionalization

The challenge of maintaining and institutionalizing democracy, one of the principal concerns of this volume, is addressed in the essays in sections II and III. In chapter 8, Larry Diamond explores this challenge by analyzing three tensions or "paradoxes" intrinsic to all democracies and particularly troubling for new ones. The first is the tension between conflict and consensus. By its very nature, democracy is a system of institutionalized competition for power, but if competition becomes too intense, the system can break down entirely. Democracies must therefore find mechanisms to mitigate conflict and cleavage with consensus. This may happen in the long run through the emergence of a civic culture. Along the way, democracies must take the initiative to reduce socioeconomic inequality through an incremental process of reform, and to institute appropriate structures and agreements, such as federalism and power-sharing "pacts," to manage ethnic and party cleavage. A second tension sets representativeness against governability. The former involves dispersing power and holding it accountable, while the latter requires "sufficient concentration and autonomy of power to choose and implement policies with energy and dispatch." Parliamentary rule with proportional representation (PR) may be admired for ensuring widespread representation in government, but it may also so fragment the political party structure as to make the system ungovernable. In such cases, reducing representativeness (e.g., by modifying pure PR) may strengthen democracy. Finally, Diamond identifies a contradiction between consent and effectiveness, in that electorates tend to judge government performance on short-run criteria while countries may only truly be able to improve their economic performance with structural reforms that may take many years to bear fruit. Getting public consent for these structural, market-oriented reforms, Diamond suggests, may require both short-term external aid and the negotiation of a broad agreement or pact among contending parties and social forces on the overall outlines of economic policy.

In chapter 9, Juan J. Linz argues that a key problem with democracy in Latin America and other developing regions has been a misguided choice of presidential rather than parliamentary government. In this widely cited essay that has occasioned extensive debate among political thinkers and practitioners worldwide, Linz identifies a number of "perils of presidentialism." Because of their direct election by the people, presidents tend to make strong claims to democratic legitimacy that can assume a "plebiscitarian" and undemocratic character. When a president is elected with much less than a majority of the vote, as Salvador Allende was in Chile in 1970, the result can be a dramatic conflict between the president and a legislature opposed to his policies, each claiming legitimacy based on the expression of the popular will. The potential for deadlock is exacerbated by the president's relatively fixed term of office, which leaves "no room for the continuous readjustments that events may demand." A related problem is the greater difficulty of selecting a legitimate and effective successor in presidential systems. In general, Linz argues, "while parliamentarism imparts flexibility to the political process," permitting a change of leaders or reorganization of government in midterm, "presidentialism makes it rather rigid."

Another dimension of this rigidity is the absence of a constitutional monarch or ceremonial president who can act as a "moderating power" and provide "moral ballast" in times of crisis. In addition, presidentialism is poorly suited to the kind of coalition government that may be necessary to govern effectively in multiparty systems. Indeed, because of the "winner-take-all" character of presidential elections, presidentialism is much more likely to produce political polarization both during and after the election. The fact that "losers must wait at least four or five years without any access to executive power and patronage" further heightens the zero-sum character of presidential systems. This is a particularly dangerous feature for deeply divided societies, especially those with grave social and economic problems and significant extremist parties, because it raises even higher the electoral stakes and the potential for confrontation and polarization. For these and other reasons, Linz suggests that presidentialism is especially poorly suited for new and unconsolidated democracies, such as those emerging in Latin America, Asia, Eastern Europe, and Africa.

In the debate that follows in chapters 10 and 11, Donald L. Horowitz and Seymour Martin Lipset challenge Linz's broad conclusion about the advantages of parliamentary over presidential government. Horowitz, a leading scholar of ethnic conflict, observes that the Westminster version of parliamentary democracy also has winner-take-all features, and that postcolonial Africa and Asia (in contrast to Latin America) witnessed the breakdown primarily of parliamentary, not presidential, democracies. Coalition governments and power-sharing can occur under presidentialism, Horowitz maintains, noting not only the semi-consociational systems in Colombia and Venezuela that Linz acknowledges as "exceptions," but also the presidential system in Nigeria's Second Republic. Horowitz argues that most of Linz's complaints about presidentialism derive from the assumption that the president will be elected on a plurality or majority-runoff basis. However, different electoral rules—like the Nigerian requirement for a broad ethnic distribution of the vote for any presidential winner, or the Sri Lankan alternative-vote system—can avoid narrowly based outcomes and induce major presidential contenders to build broad ethnic coalitions. Linz's real quarrel, Horowitz suggests, "is not with the presidency, but with two features that epitomize the Westminster version of democracy: first, plurality elections that produce a majority of seats by shutting out third-party competitors; and second, adversary democracy, with its sharp divide between winners and losers, government and opposition."

Lipset takes an even more skeptical stance, questioning the importance of institutional choices altogether. The chief reason for the relative instability of democracy in Latin America, he suggests, is not presidentialism but economic and cultural factors that historically have rendered Latin, Catholic, and poorer countries more prone to authoritarianism. He claims that the same holds true today for Islamic countries, no matter what political institutions they adopt. The fact that the British colonial legacy is one of the most powerful correlates of democracy in the world today points up the salience of the cultural variable.

In his response, Linz acknowledges Horowitz's point about the importance of the way the constitutional system (parliamentary or presidential) interacts with the electoral system, as well as Lipset's point that a majoritarian parliamentary system like Britain's can give a prime minister more effective power than the typical president in a presidential system. Linz underscores, however, the plebiscitarian style and inflated expectations that tend more often to be associated with presidentialism, as well as the potential for conflict and even contested legitimacy between executive and legislature. Further, he questions the degree to which Horowitz's cases of Nigeria and Sri Lanka can be considered examples of successful presidentialism, and calls attention to another peril of presidential government: the weakening of political parties that comes with the ability of a president, as in Brazil, to constitute a government without systematically involving the parties that back him (including his own). Even the U.S. example of "successful presidentialism," Linz suggests, is increasingly dubious given the costs and problems of divided government in recent years. "The American system works or has worked in spite of, rather than because of, the presidential constitution," he maintains. Conceding the importance of culture, he emphasizes Lipset's own observation that political institutions are the only variables open to relatively rapid and deliberate manipulation. This makes "the search for those political institutions that will best suit the circumstances in this or that particular country . . . a modest quest, but a worthy one."

This quest also occupies Arend Lijphart in his analysis in chapter 13 of "constitutional choices for new democracies." Endorsing Linz's arguments in favor of parliamentary government, he suggests that the type of electoral system is a no less important institutional choice, and he points to the advantages of PR, especially for new democracies and deeply divided societies. Drawing upon and extending his previous work,[3] Lijphart rejects majoritarian democracy in favor of the consensus model, which "tries to limit, divide, separate, and share power," and features multiple parties, coalition governments, and more equal executive-legislative power relations. By promoting a multiparty system, PR (combined with parliamentarism) is a key device for structuring democracy in this consensual way. But in addition to ensuring minority representation and so better managing ethnic conflict, PR, Lijphart argues, is preferable because it is intrinsically more democratic. Moreover, his data from the Western democracies suggest that parliamentary-PR systems have a higher quality of democracy, including higher rates of voter turnout, without the diminished governability and economic performance that many critics allege to be the "cost" of PR systems. Moderate PR systems, like those in Germany and Sweden, which give rise to a moderate number of parliamentary parties, seem to offer the best combination of power sharing and governability for new democracies.

In the debate in chapters 14 and 15, both Guy Lardeyret and Quentin L. Quade argue strongly for the advantages of majoritarian democracy. Indeed, Lardeyret favors the most majoritarian system possible, which (as Lijphart indicates) is not presidentialism but rather parliamentary government combined with the single-member-district plurality method of election—i.e., the Westminster system. Because such plurality elections for the legislature tend to give rise to a two-party or two-party-dominant system, they create strong parliamentary governments, free of the need for coalitions, that fuse executive and legislative power. Although Linz inclines to the same moderate, multiparty system that Lijphart favors and Lardeyret dislikes, Lardeyret does share Linz's concern about the potential for legislative-executive deadlock in presidential systems. He believes, however, that the greatest danger lies in the fragmentation associated with parliamentary-PR systems, such as the Fourth Republic that faltered in his native France. Quentin L. Quade also cites this example, as well as pre-Mussolini Italy and Weimar Germany, to show how PR can foster not conciliation and compromise but fragmentation, extremism, and governmental paralysis. Like most critics of the consensus model, Quade focuses attention on the inherently greater fragility of coalition government.

Precisely because it gives such wide scope to the representation of "minorities," and thereby encourages polarization and party fragmentation, Lardeyret maintains that PR "is dangerous for countries faced with ethnic or cultural divisions." By contrast, "parties in plurality systems tend to be moderate because most votes are to be gained among the undecided voters of the center." Ethnic moderation will be greatest when members of the same ethnic group must compete against one another in single-member-districts along cross-cutting political and ideological lines of cleavage. Lardeyret not only prefers plurality electoral systems for the stronger, more stable, and more decisive governments they produce, but (like Quade) also believes that they are "more democratic as well as more efficient." Unlike PR, plurality systems lock out extremist parties, marginalize small parties, and give the choice of who will govern to the voters, rather than to party elites negotiating in secret after the election, sometimes for weeks or even months. Quade writes that "plurality voting encourages the competing parties to adopt a majority-forming attitude . . . to be moderate, to seek conciliation . . . —in short, to do *before* the election, in the public view, the very tasks that Lijphart applauds PR systems for doing *after* the election."

The institutional choice between PR (with parliamentary government) and plurality elections (whether in a presidential or parliamentary system) involves more than the empirical and analytical debate joined in chapters 14 and 15. At play here as well is a tension between competing values. As Diamond shows in chapter 8, in democracies there is a certain inherent contradiction between representativeness and governability. PR systems risk some sacrifices in decisive governance and clear alternation of majorities in order to maximize representativeness. Opponents of PR put a higher priority on governability than on directly representing the many elements in society in the legislature. To be fair, however, few prominent students of democracy would advocate the kind of extreme PR–with virtually no minimum threshold of the vote necessary for entry into parliament—that exists today in Italy and Israel. As Lijphart emphasizes, there are many types and degrees of PR, and moderate PR with thresholds like the 5-percent minimum in Germany tends to give rise to only a moderate number of parties. In responding to Lardeyret and Quade in chapter 16, Lijphart not only

defends his comparative analysis of the performance of PR and majoritarian systems; he also reiterates the normative case for PR—namely, "that
disproportional election results are inherently unfair and undemocratic"—
and notes that none of Britain's postwar governing parties carried a majority of the vote (a fact that has held true for all of India's one-party governments as well).

Whatever the type of electoral system, however, elections must be free
and fair and credible if the regime is to be considered democratic. In the
circumstances in which many new democracies come into being, after
many years of repression, polarization, and civil strife, administering democratic elections is a daunting challenge. In chapter 17, Jennifer McCoy,
Larry Garber, and Robert Pastor, writing in part from their extensive direct
experience, show how international pollwatching and mediation efforts
can help to assist the conduct of effective founding elections for new
democracies. An important landmark in this regard was the Nicaraguan
election of February 1990, in which "groups of international observers
helped both to negotiate the rules of the electoral 'game' and to implement
a collectively guaranteed democratization process arising from a regional
peace plan." There, and subsequently in Haiti, El Salvador, Namibia, and
other conflict-ridden countries in political transition, collective international efforts to promote national reconciliation and guarantee the integrity
of the electoral process have overcome traditional concerns about "foreign
intervention."

In such circumstances, where suspicion and mistrust run deep, international observers enhance the legitimacy of the electoral process in two crucial ways: in advance, by helping to keep all significant parties in the race;
and during and after the voting and counting, "by ensuring that the election will either be fair or else be denounced as fraudulent." International
observers can legitimize a genuine ruling-party victory that might not otherwise be credible (as in South Korea in 1987); they can certify an opposition victory and persuade the incumbents to accept defeat, as in Nicaragua
and Chile; and they can expose the fraud of a government that tries to rig
itself back into power, as in the Philippines and Panama. Their mere presence tends to increase confidence in the process and to deter fraud. But to
be effective, observers (whether domestic or foreign) must mount a sustained and active presence, ideally with a sufficiently skilled and comprehensive organization to execute a parallel vote count.

Political Corruption and Democracy

The abuse of public office for private gain afflicts all forms of government, including communist, military, and personalistic dictatorships. Yet
political corruption poses particularly serious dangers for democracy, because it is more likely to be exposed under conditions of constitutionalism
and press freedom, and because this exposure can do great damage to

political legitimacy, on which democracies depend for their survival much more than authoritarian regimes.

During the 1960s, some theories viewed corruption as useful for economic and political development because it enables entrepreneurs to get around bureaucratic logjams and helps to distribute resources widely through party machines and patron-client networks. But development and wider distribution of resources have not been the primary consequences of the large-scale political corruption that has prevailed in many developing countries over the past 30 years. Instead, rampant corruption, typically accompanied by incompetent and arrogant governance, has tended to disillusion ordinary citizens and alienate them from the political process. At its worst, it can so enervate the capacity of government to deliver development and even basic services that it may totally destroy the legitimacy of a putatively democratic regime. Corruption frequently gives rise to sudden accumulations of massive personal wealth and growing inequalities that fuel social resentment and political anger. Often it distorts the structure of economic incentives in ways that discourage and undermine genuine capitalism. In fact, rent seeking is less likely to facilitate productive enterprise than to pervert the entrepreneurial spirit and drive it into unproductive activity. In many (but not all) countries, corruption also drains the economy of capital as elites transfer their huge illicit fortunes abroad. Regime legitimacy is further eroded by the instability, violence, fraud, bribery, and contempt for the rules of the game that characterize political competition in a system where election to office is the ticket to instant personal fortune. In many developing countries—including two that are examined in case studies here, Nigeria and Thailand—corruption has been a central factor in the breakdown of democracy.

It is important, however, to view the problem of corruption in historical and comparative perspective. Political corruption is hardly unique to the politics of "Third World" democracies. As Michael Johnston shows in the essay that introduces this section, the use of public office for private gain was so embedded in the custom and practice of European regimes prior to the nineteenth century that it did not constitute an "abuse" of laws or norms, and hence was not technically corruption. Even when laws and norms did emerge to constrain public behavior in office in the world's two oldest democracies, Britain and the United States, serious problems of political corruption persisted. In each case, corruption only receded gradually through a protracted process of political conflict and reform. Indeed, conflicts over the meaning of corruption, along with major scandals involving violations of standards, continue to this day, particularly in the United States. Such scandals and conflicts should not necessarily be dismissed as signs of political decay, but "may indeed be steps toward new and lasting settlements between social values and legal institutions."

Catharin E. Dalpino argues in chapter 19 that in Thailand the "perception of unabashed and mounting corruption in high government circles" was a major source of the public discontent with the parliamentary system that provided an opportunity for the February 1991 military coup. A particular feature of political corruption in Thailand is its intimate relationship with the weak and fragmented party system. Due in part to frequent military intervention, Thai political parties have been poorly developed, with little in the way of broad and lasting grassroots support or coherent policy perspectives. "Parties tried to compensate for all of their institutional weaknesses through vote-buying." And party leaders and Members of Parliament then sought to make good on their financial investments once they had captured political office. Thailand's "fluid, diffuse, and personalistic party system lent itself easily to the aspirations of new actors" able to finance campaigns, and the party system became more and more factionalized and corrupt.

If Thailand is to make real progress toward consolidating democracy in the future, Dalpino suggests, it must enhance accountability. Some promising developments interrupted by the coup included proposals for a parliamentary ombudsman to monitor and investigate corruption and a number of steps to strengthen and professionalize the parliamentary committee system. The latter would contribute to the overall deepening of Thailand's democratic institutions, which Dalpino believes is an important requirement for accountability. Among the highest priorities, she suggests, is strengthening the political and financial autonomy of local government, which would stimulate political participation and party development at the local level in Thailand's traditionally highly centralized system. No less important for accountability is the potential of the nongovernmental sector, which has grown rapidly since the student revolution of 1973 to encompass some 3,000 nongovernmental organizations, including a growing number of public advocacy groups. Such groups not only provide an additional channel of representation but also can help to educate, inform, and mobilize citizens for accountable government.

In Nigeria, democracy has twice been overturned because of public cynicism, economic mismanagement, and political turmoil due in large measure to pervasive political corruption; the already turbulent politics of the emerging Third Republic show no signs of being any different. Like Dalpino, Larry Diamond in his study of Nigeria in chapter 20 sees improved accountability as a critical condition for democratic progress. This will require more than the usual words and gestures in Nigeria. Corruption has seeped deeply into the political culture of the country, Diamond argues, but it is not a *product* of the culture. Rather, it results from an incentive structure in which political corruption has become the easiest, fastest, and least risky way for public officials and the politically well-connected at all levels to accumulate sizable personal wealth. If corruption is to be significantly reduced, the costs and risks of engaging in corrupt conduct must increase; corrupt officials must regularly be exposed, tried, and punished. The means for doing so have existed on paper since the Second Republic in the form of a Code of Conduct Bureau and Tribunal, and these structures have even been reactivated by the military regime during the current transition to civilian rule. But unless this institutional apparatus is given vigorous leadership and real power and autonomy, there is little hope that deeply entrenched patterns of corruption can be altered—and probably little hope for Nigeria's Third Republic.

Strategies for combatting corruption constitute the focus of Robert Klitgaard's innovative analysis in chapter 21. While the global trends toward democracy and free markets will help to increase accountability and transparency and to reduce rent seeking, they will not in themselves be sufficient: "Whatever size and type of state a country chooses, the threat of bribery, extortion, influence peddling, kickbacks, fraud, and other illicit activities remains." Like Diamond, Klitgaard argues that reform must directly target the structure of incentives rather than seeking first a transformation in values. To reduce corruption to manageable levels that do not threaten democracy, a country needs political and institutional leaders committed to reform, and those leaders must follow a comprehensive strategy for altering the structure of incentives. This involves not only increasing the legal, bureaucratic, and informal penalties for corruption, and improving information and auditing to detect corruption more reliably, but also enhancing rewards for law-abiding and effective public officials. Limiting the discretion and monopoly power of public officials and agencies, rotating officials, and inducing competition in the provision of public services can also reduce the scope for rent seeking. Only as part of such a broader strategy can an effort to raise the "moral costs" of corruption be effective. In the fight against corruption, democracy, with its free flow of information and capacity for citizen mobilization, can itself be an important tool.

The Global Democratic Prospect

Can the third global wave of democratic expansion be sustained, and if so, how? These are the key questions democrats the world over must confront in the remainder of this century, and they occupy the concluding eight chapters of this volume. Certainly, there are reasons to be hopeful. As Plattner notes in chapter 2, authoritarian regimes seem doomed ultimately both by economic failure and by economic success, and in a rapidly integrating, increasingly information-intensive world economy, "only democracy seems compatible with economic success in the advanced nations." Inevitably, Plattner concedes, some of the new democracies of recent years will "sink back into authoritarianism." Both he and Huntington expect that the current wave of democratic expansion will probably pause or come to an end at some point in the coming years, but for Plattner this does not necessarily portend another "reverse wave" or a serious challenge to the overall strength of democracy in the world: "Democracy's preeminence can be seriously challenged only by an ideology with universalist aspirations that proves capable of coming to power in an economically advanced or militarily powerful nation." For this reason, Russia and China may be the most important countries for democrats to watch in the coming years, along with the possibility of a successful and attractive nondemocratic model emerging in East Asia.

For Ken Jowitt, the threat to democracy need not come from some coherent and widely appealing ideological rival to democracy. It may rather emanate from what he terms in chapter 22 "the new world disorder" that has emerged with the end of the Cold War and the "mass extinction of Leninist regimes." Criticizing Francis Fukuyama's thesis of the "end of history," Jowitt argues that the coming years will feature acute "territorial, ideological, and political confusion," in which boundaries, identities, and the control of regimes will be vigorously contested. Amidst the turbulence, "leaders will matter more than institutions," and "new ways of life" may emerge, offering new ideologies that militantly reject existing institutions and beliefs, including liberal democracy. The prospects for democratic consolidation in the post-Leninist states are clouded by the Leninist legacy of pervasive distrust of the state and fellow citizens and by lack of experience with the values and habits of democratic politics. More generally, liberal capitalist democracy will remain vulnerable to challenge from movements and ideologies that scorn its "inordinate emphasis on individualism, materialism, technical achievement, and rationality." At best, the global progress of democracy is likely to be slow, painful, and conflict-ridden.

A more hopeful prognosis is offered by Giuseppe Di Palma in chapter 23. Writing about the new democracies of Eastern Europe, with the lessons of previous democratic transitions in mind, Di Palma notes that the old order has been more thoroughly discredited and rejected in the post-communist states than in many postauthoritarian situations. More generally, he argues that the requisites for democratic consolidation have been overstated. "Genuine democrats need not precede democracy"; democratic attitudes and beliefs can develop after political actors have embraced democracy for largely instrumental reasons. Recent transitions to democracy, like that in Spain, show "the rapidity and eagerness with which political actors seem to have learned the ropes of the democratic game." Moreover, since the democratic revolution in Eastern Europe was in large part a quest for "political dignity," the fate of the new democracies will not be simply linked to material performance, and "extreme discontent about economic hardships . . . will not normally be enough to turn people against democratization." Ultimately, a viable market economy will be necessary to sustain democracy in Eastern Europe, but a broad consensus for creating a market economy now exists. And while democratic culture may be thin, East European countries can benefit from their legacies of anticommunist dissent, which will help "to make civil society, rather than the state, the force behind Eastern Europe's regeneration."

Yet there is reason to be concerned about the "postrevolutionary hang-over" that has settled on Eastern Europe. This, writes Leszek Kolakowski in chapter 24, is inevitable in the aftermath of any revolution, because inflated expectations are necessary to mobilize people sufficiently to topple the old order. In this sense, the many divisions now emerging within the former broad democratic fronts represent the beginning of a return to normal politics. Kolakowski is more impressed than Di Palma with the difficulty of the transition to a market economy. The very concept of money must be rediscovered, and measures to free prices and rationalize industry and taxation cause extensive unemployment and pain. This provides "fertile ground . . . for all sorts of demagogues," and many of the hard steps of privatization and liberalization still remain to be tackled. Economic reform must also overcome the cultural and psychological legacy of communism, which accustomed people of all classes to patronage and protection from the state. Particularly in Poland, Hungary, and Czechoslovakia, political vitality is "too widely dispersed" to make a return to dictatorship likely, but the process of democratic and economic reform will continue to be painful and difficult.

If Plattner is right that Russia and China will be two of the key countries to watch with respect to the future of democracy in the world, readers of this volume may take special interest in the chapters by Charles H. Fairbanks, Jr., and Andrew J. Nathan addressing the future of those great nations. Each essay was written in the aftermath of a crucial moment for democracy: the failed August 1991 coup that brought down communism in Russia, and the crushing of the democracy movement in Tiananmen Square that halted China's democratic progress in June 1989. Fairbanks writes in chapter 25 that "the coup made clear that the outwardly imposing political structure being renovated by Gorbachev was already rotting away beneath the surface." By the time of the coup, the communist state had essentially disintegrated, and democracy-building must now proceed in this context of administrative chaos. This imposes especially difficult challenges on Russia, which, even after the breakup of the Soviet Union, contains many peoples and autonomous regions that may seek to break away from Moscow. Russia also inherits notably weaker democratic traditions than its East European neighbors. Fortunately, as in Eastern Europe, the communist legacy and party apparatus have been smashed (in part through the opportunity provided by the coup). Yet the old *apparatchiki* themselves and the army remain to cast a shadow over the nascent democracy, and democratic parties and culture remain very weak and fragmented. These obstacles only underscore how much the fate of democracy rests on the ability of the Yeltsin government to implement economic reform and regenerate economic growth.

In contrast to the Soviet Union under Gorbachev, China under Deng Xiaoping experienced economic liberalization and growth but with only very slight political reform. The 1989 demonstrations in Tiananmen

Square sought to cleanse and open up (but not necessarily democratize in the Western sense) the Chinese political system. Had Deng chosen the path of political opening and reform in response, Nathan argues in chapter 26, he might have solved the immediate crisis of political legitimacy as well as the succession problem, while establishing a framework for peaceful and gradual political evolution and continued economic reform. Instead, the repression of the prodemocracy demonstrations "has left in its wake a regime that is the weakest in PRC history." This very weakness has induced the regime to fall back on authoritarian policies for both economic and political management. Such policies, however, cannot restore the dwindling legitimacy of the Chinese Communist Party, and the party's effective control over the country continues to erode. At the same time, economic growth and industrialization, and the consequent spread of mass literacy and communications, are thrusting China toward a level of development where democracy is increasingly feasible. These two facts—the decay of communist control and socioeconomic change—make likely a new attempt at democratization later in this decade, triggered perhaps by the death of Deng or new factional rivalry within the regime. But because the communist regime remains entrenched, "the transition to democracy is likely to come from above when it comes, and to be hard, prolonged, complex—and inconclusive."

Latin America is the region where democratic progress has been most extensive during the "third wave," with most of the region now having popularly elected civilian regimes. But as Peter Hakim and Abraham F. Lowenthal explain in chapter 27, "democracy in Latin America is far from robust. It is nowhere fully achieved, and it is perhaps most firmly established in those few countries where it was already deeply rooted and vibrant a generation ago." Outside those few countries—Costa Rica, Chile, Uruguay (and much of the Caribbean, including Jamaica)—democracy faces a number of serious threats. In several countries (Peru, Colombia, Guatemala), extensive violence by drug traffickers, guerrillas, and repressive and poorly disciplined militaries "is undermining the institutions, procedures, and values essential to democracy." Since their essay was first published, violence has yielded to a democratic settlement in El Salvador, but it has only intensified in Peru, contributing to the suspension of democracy there. In the violence-ridden countries and many others, democratic rule is challenged and threatened "by armed forces that are not effectively subordinated to civilian control" and that may even influence and constrain most aspects of government policy. The military overthrow of President Aristide in Haiti during 1991 is one indication of how precarious some of these civilian regimes are.

In many of Latin America's new democracies, political institutions—parties, legislatures, judicial systems, and so on—are poorly developed, poorly funded, poorly staffed, and generally ineffective, "plagued by rampant corruption, political polarization, and growing public skepticism about government and politics." This skepticism has been deepened by the profound economic depression in the region, which has seen per capita income fall by more than 10 percent for the region as a whole since 1982 while poverty and unemployment have sharply increased. The situation is not hopeless, but Hakim and Lowenthal argue forcefully that if democracy is to become stable in Latin America, these problems must be urgently addressed. Market-oriented reforms must begin to attract investment and restore growth. The autonomy, resources, and capacity of democratic institutions must be greatly strengthened. Settlements to the region's debilitating internal wars must be negotiated. The role of the military in many countries must be reshaped to remove it from the political arena and subordinate it to civilian control. And the rights of political dissidents, minorities, and other vulnerable groups must be better protected by strengthening legal systems and human rights efforts.

In Africa, progress toward democracy rests at a much earlier and even more fragile stage. As Richard Joseph details in chapter 28, Africa is now in the midst of a rebirth of freedom, a "second independence" that has generated significant pressure for democratic change in about half the states of the continent. While this democratic trend has been stimulated by international factors, it springs primarily from the pervasive failures of authoritarian regimes in Africa and the courageous mobilization of indigenous associations, parties, and movements. Africa is proving, in Richard Sklar's words, "a workshop of democracy," and some notable innovations are emerging, such as the model of transition via a "national conference," first implemented in Benin. But as Joseph shows, numerous African transitions have been coopted or controlled from above, if not aborted altogether. In most of the continent, democratic transitions have yet to be completed, and daunting challenges await the new regimes. In many respects, these challenges overlap with those identified by Hakim and Lowenthal for Latin America: reconciling democratization with the pain of economic stabilization and structural adjustment policies, and finding a way for those policies to rekindle growth; redressing longstanding social injustices; deepening new and fragile democratic institutions; settling violent civil conflicts; and institutionalizing new protections for human rights. "Above all," writes Joseph, "Africa needs peace. If peace is shown to be one of the first fruits of the democratic movement, many others will follow in time."

What, then, is the democratic prospect in the final decade of this extraordinary century? We conclude this volume with reflections on this question by one of the outstanding democratic thinkers of our time, Leszek Kolakowski. "We had better not imagine," Kolakowski cautions in chapter 29, "that the cause of freedom is now safe and its victory imminent." Several factors will threaten democracy in the foreseeable future, he argues. One is "the growth of malignant nationalism all over the world." Patriotism, in the sense of "attachment to national cultural heritage," may be quite compatible with democracy, but a chauvinistic belief in the superiority of one's own people and culture is not. A related danger is posed by "religious intolerance and theocratic aspirations" that would abolish the separation of religion and state and establish "an ideological despotism." This threat is most apparent in various Islamic fundamentalist movements but visible as well in other religions. Terrorism and criminal violence also threaten democracy, not with direct conquest but through the danger that democratic governments might be driven to combat them with undemocratic means—a phenomenon that, as Hakim and Lowenthal observe, has been particularly corrosive to democracy in Latin America. A more diffuse danger, Kolakowski believes, stems from the threats to human welfare presented by overpopulation, shrinking resources, and actual or potential ecological catastrophes, which will necessarily dampen hopes for material progress. "Widespread misery is fertile ground for the successful demagogy of totalitarian movements and for the temptation to 'solve' social problems by means of military dictatorship."

These dangers do not mean, in our view, that democracy is doomed to recede at any time soon into a "third reverse wave." The Leninist extinction and the dizzying pace of international change that it has initiated offer great opportunities to shape the prospects for democracy and enhance the possibility of a substantially democratic world. Those opportunities are greater today than at any time since the end of World War I, and perhaps than ever before in modern history. Wise leadership and intelligent institution-building can consolidate tentative and fragile democracies around the world. But time is of the essence. As many of the essays in this volume show, democracy has many intrinsic vulnerabilities and requires well-chosen and deeply rooted institutions to be secure. With the exception of Spain, Portugal, and Greece, the new democracies of the third wave have yet to be consolidated. In Latin America, the Philippines, South Korea, and elsewhere, the political turbulence of the past five to ten years has exposed their very real frailties. The established democracies have much to contribute in experience, expertise, and resources that can help the newer regimes to develop enduring democratic institutions, if they have the will and imagination to make them available. In shaping a democratic world, as in building a democratic nation, there is, as Samuel P. Huntington notes, no substitute for skilled and determined political leadership.

NOTES

1. The specific quote, as Plattner indicates, was from a 1975 article by Daniel Patrick Moynihan, "The American Experience," in *The Public Interest* 41 (Fall 1975), 6.

2. Robert A. Dahl, *Polyarchy* (New Haven: Yale University Press, 1971).

3. Arend Lijphart, *Democracies: Patterns of Majoritarian and Consensus Government in Twenty-one Countries* (New Haven: Yale University Press, 1984).

I.
The Democratic Moment

1.
DEMOCRACY'S THIRD WAVE

Samuel P. Huntington

Samuel P. Huntington *is Eaton Professor of the Science of Government and director of the John M. Olin Institute for Strategic Studies at Harvard University. This article is based upon the 1989 Julian J. Rothbaum Lectures at the Carl Albert Center of the University of Oklahoma,* which were published as The Third Wave: Democratization in the Late Twentieth Century. *Copyright © 1991 by Samuel P. Huntington. Published by the University of Oklahoma Press.*

Between 1974 and 1990, at least 30 countries made transitions to democracy, just about doubling the number of democratic governments in the world. Were these democratizations part of a continuing and ever-expanding "global democratic revolution" that will reach virtually every country in the world? Or did they represent a limited expansion of democracy, involving for the most part its reintroduction into countries that had experienced it in the past?

The current era of democratic transitions constitutes the third wave of democratization in the history of the modern world. The first "long" wave of democratization began in the 1820s, with the widening of the suffrage to a large proportion of the male population in the United States, and continued for almost a century until 1926, bringing into being some 29 democracies. In 1922, however, the coming to power of Mussolini in Italy marked the beginning of a first "reverse wave" that by 1942 had reduced the number of democratic states in the world to 12. The triumph of the Allies in World War II initiated a second wave of democratization that reached its zenith in 1962 with 36 countries governed democratically, only to be followed by a second reverse wave (1960-1975) that brought the number of democracies back down to 30.

At what stage are we within the third wave? Early in a long wave, or at or near the end of a short one? And if the third wave comes to a halt, will it be followed by a significant third reverse wave eliminating many of democracy's gains in the 1970s and 1980s? Social science cannot provide reliable answers to these questions, nor can any social scientist. It may be possible, however, to identify some of the factors that will affect the future expansion or contraction of democracy in the world and to pose the questions that seem most relevant for the future of democratization.

One way to begin is to inquire whether the causes that gave rise to the third wave are likely to continue operating, to gain in strength, to weaken, or to be supplemented or replaced by new forces promoting democratization. Five major factors have contributed significantly to the occurrence and the timing of the third-wave transitions to democracy:

1) The deepening legitimacy problems of authoritarian regimes in a world where democratic values were widely accepted, the consequent dependence of these regimes on successful performance, and their inability to maintain "performance legitimacy" due to economic (and sometimes military) failure.

2) The unprecedented global economic growth of the 1960s, which raised living standards, increased education, and greatly expanded the urban middle class in many countries.

3) A striking shift in the doctrine and activities of the Catholic Church, manifested in the Second Vatican Council of 1963-65 and the transformation of national Catholic churches from defenders of the status quo to opponents of authoritarianism.

4) Changes in the policies of external actors, most notably the European Community, the United States, and the Soviet Union.

5) "Snowballing," or the demonstration effect of transitions earlier in the third wave in stimulating and providing models for subsequent efforts at democratization.

I will begin by addressing the latter three factors, returning to the first two later in this article.

Historically, there has been a strong correlation between Western Christianity and democracy. By the early 1970s, most of the Protestant countries in the world had already become democratic. The third wave of the 1970s and 1980s was overwhelmingly a Catholic wave. Beginning in Portugal and Spain, it swept through six South American and three Central American countries, moved on to the Philippines, doubled back to Mexico and Chile, and then burst through in the two Catholic countries of Eastern Europe, Poland and Hungary. Roughly three-quarters of the countries that transited to democracy between 1974 and 1989 were predominantly Catholic.

By 1990, however, the Catholic impetus to democratization had largely exhausted itself. Most Catholic countries had already democratized or, as in the case of Mexico, liberalized. The ability of Catholicism to promote further expansion of democracy (without expanding its own ranks) is limited to Paraguay, Cuba, and a few

Francophone African countries. By 1990, sub-Saharan Africa was the only region of the world where substantial numbers of Catholics and Protestants lived under authoritarian regimes in a large number of countries.

The Role of External Forces

During the third wave, the European Community (EC) played a key role in consolidating democracy in southern Europe. In Greece, Spain, and Portugal, the establishment of democracy was seen as necessary to secure the economic benefits of EC membership, while Community membership was in turn seen as a guarantee of the stability of democracy. In 1981, Greece became a full member of the Community, and five years later Spain and Portugal did as well.

In April 1987, Turkey applied for full EC membership. One incentive was the desire of Turkish leaders to reinforce modernizing and democratic tendencies in Turkey and to contain and isolate the forces in Turkey supporting Islamic fundamentalism. Within the Community, however, the prospect of Turkish membership met with little enthusiasm and even some hostility (mostly from Greece). In 1990, the liberation of Eastern Europe also raised the possibility of membership for Hungary, Czechoslovakia, and Poland. The Community thus faced two issues. First, should it give priority to broadening its membership or to "deepening" the existing Community by moving toward further economic and political union? Second, if it did decide to expand its membership, should priority go to European Free Trade Association members like Austria, Norway, and Sweden, to the East Europeans, or to Turkey? Presumably the Community can only absorb a limited number of countries in a given period of time. The answers to these questions will have significant implications for the stability of democracy in Turkey and in the East European countries.

The withdrawal of Soviet power made possible democratization in Eastern Europe. If the Soviet Union were to end or drastically curtail its support for Castro's regime, movement toward democracy might occur in Cuba. Apart from that, there seems little more the Soviet Union can do or is likely to do to promote democracy outside its borders. The key issue is what will happen within the Soviet Union itself. If Soviet control loosens, it seems likely that democracy could be reestablished in the Baltic states. Movements toward democracy also exist in other republics. Most important, of course, is Russia itself. The inauguration and consolidation of democracy in the Russian republic, if it occurs, would be the single most dramatic gain for democracy since the immediate post-World War II years. Democratic development in most of the Soviet republics, however, is greatly complicated by their ethnic heterogeneity and the unwillingness of the dominant nationality to allow equal rights to ethnic minorities. As Sir Ivor Jennings remarked years ago, "the people cannot decide until somebody decides who are the people." It may take years if not decades to resolve the latter issue in much of the Soviet Union.

During the 1970s and 1980s the United States was a major promoter of democratization. Whether the United States continues to play this role depends on its will, its capability, and its attractiveness as a model to other countries. Before the mid-1970s the promotion of democracy had not always been a high priority of American foreign policy. It could again subside in importance. The end of the Cold War and of the ideological competition with the Soviet Union could remove one rationale for propping up anti-communist dictators, but it could also reduce the incentives for any substantial American involvement in the Third World.

American will to promote democracy may or may not be sustained. American ability to do so, on the other hand, is limited. The trade and budget deficits impose new limits on the resources that the United States can use to influence events in foreign countries. More important, the ability of the United States to promote democracy has in some measure run its course. The countries in Latin America, the Caribbean, Europe, and East Asia that were most susceptible to American influence have, with a few exceptions, already become democratic. The one major country where the United States can still exercise significant influence on behalf of democratization is Mexico. The undemocratic countries in Africa, the Middle East, and mainland Asia are less susceptible to American influence.

Apart from Central America and the Caribbean, the major area of the Third World where the United States has continued to have vitally important interests is the Persian Gulf. The Gulf War and the dispatch of 500,000 American troops to the region have stimulated demands for movement toward democracy in Kuwait and Saudi Arabia and delegitimized Saddam Hussein's regime in Iraq. A large American military deployment in the Gulf, if sustained over time, would provide an external impetus toward liberalization if not democratization, and a large American military deployment probably could not be sustained over time unless some movement toward democracy occurred.

The U.S. contribution to democratization in the 1980s involved more than the conscious and direct exercise of American power and influence. Democratic movements around the world have been inspired by and have borrowed from the American example. What might happen, however, if the American model ceases to embody strength and success, no longer seems to be the winning model? At the end of the 1980s, many were arguing that "American decline" was the true reality. If people around the world come to see the United States as a fading power beset by political stagnation, economic inefficiency, and social chaos, its perceived failures will inevitably be seen as the failures of democracy, and the worldwide appeal of democracy will diminish.

Snowballing

The impact of snowballing on democratization was clearly evident in 1990 in Bulgaria, Romania, Yugoslavia, Mongolia, Nepal, and Albania. It also affected movements toward liberalization in some Arab and African countries. In 1990, for instance, it was reported that the "upheaval in Eastern Europe" had "fueled demands for change in the Arab world" and prompted leaders in Egypt, Jordan, Tunisia, and Algeria to open up more political space for the expression of discontent.[1]

The East European example had its principal effect on the leaders of authoritarian regimes, not on the people they ruled. President Mobutu Sese Seko of Zaire, for instance reacted with shocked horror to televised pictures of the execution by firing squad of his friend, Romanian dictator Nicolae Ceauşescu. A few months later, commenting that "You know what's happening across the world," he announced that he would allow two parties besides his own to compete in elections in 1993. In Tanzania, Julius Nyerere observed that "If changes take place in Eastern Europe then other countries with one-party systems and which profess socialism will also be affected." His country, he added, could learn a "lesson or two" from Eastern Europe. In Nepal in April 1990, the government announced that King Birendra was lifting the ban on political parties as a result of "the international situation" and "the rising expectations of the people."[2]

If a country lacks favorable internal conditions, however, snowballing alone is unlikely to bring about democratization. The democratization of countries A and B is not a reason for democratization in country C, unless the conditions that favored it in the former also exist in the latter. Although the legitimacy of democratic government came to be accepted throughout the world in the 1980s, economic and social conditions favorable to democracy were not everywhere present. The "worldwide democratic revolution" may create an external environment conducive to democratization, but it cannot produce the conditions necessary for democratization within a particular country.

In Eastern Europe the major obstacle to democratization was Soviet control; once it was removed, the movement to democracy spread rapidly. There is no comparable external obstacle to democratization in the Middle East, Africa, and Asia. If rulers in these areas chose authoritarianism before December 1989, why can they not continue to choose it thereafter? The snowballing effect would be real only to the extent that it led them to believe in the desirability or necessity of democratization. The events of 1989 in Eastern Europe undoubtedly encouraged democratic opposition groups and frightened authoritarian leaders elsewhere. Yet given the previous weakness of the former and the long-term repression imposed by the latter, it seems doubtful that the East European example will actually produce significant progress toward democracy in most other authoritarian countries.

By 1990, many of the original causes of the third wave had become significantly weaker, even exhausted. Neither the White House, the Kremlin, the European Community, nor the Vatican was in a strong position to promote democracy in places where it did not already exist (primarily in Asia, Africa, and the Middle East). It remains possible, however, for new forces favoring democratization to emerge. After all, who in 1985 could have foreseen that Mikhail Gorbachev would facilitate democratization in Eastern Europe?

In the 1990s the International Monetary Fund (IMF) and the World Bank could conceivably become much more forceful than they have heretofore been in making political democratization as well as economic liberalization a precondition for economic assistance. France might become more active in promoting democracy among its former African colonies, where its influence remains substantial. The Orthodox churches could emerge as a powerful influence for democracy in southeastern Europe and the Soviet Union. A Chinese proponent of *glasnost* could come to power in Beijing, or a new Jeffersonian-style Nasser could spread a democratic version of Pan-Arabism in the Middle East. Japan could use its growing economic clout to encourage human rights and democracy in the poor countries to which it makes loans and grants. In 1990, none of these possibilities seemed very likely, but after the surprises of 1989 it would be rash to rule anything out.

A Third Reverse Wave?

By 1990 at least two third-wave democracies, Sudan and Nigeria, had reverted to authoritarian rule; the difficulties of consolidation could lead to further reversions in countries with unfavorable conditions for sustaining democracy. The first and second democratic waves, however, were followed not merely by some backsliding but by major reverse waves during which most regime changes throughout the world were from democracy to authoritarianism. If the third wave of democratization slows down or comes to a halt, what factors might produce a third reverse wave?

Among the factors contributing to transitions away from democracy during the first and second reverse waves were:

1) the weakness of democratic values among key elite groups and the general public;

2) severe economic setbacks, which intensified social conflict and enhanced the popularity of remedies that could be imposed only by authoritarian governments;

3) social and political polarization, often produced by leftist governments seeking the rapid introduction of major social and economic reforms;

4) the determination of conservative middle-class and upper-class groups to exclude populist and leftist movements and lower-class groups from political power;

5) the breakdown of law and order resulting from terrorism or insurgency;

6) intervention or conquest by a nondemocratic foreign power;

7) "reverse snowballing" triggered by the collapse or overthrow of democratic systems in other countries.

Transitions from democracy to authoritarianism, apart from those produced by foreign actors, have almost always been produced by those in power or close to power in the democratic system. With only one or two possible exceptions, democratic systems have not been ended by popular vote or popular revolt. In Germany and Italy in the first reverse wave, antidemocratic movements with considerable popular backing came to power and established fascist dictatorships. In Spain in the first reverse wave and in Lebanon in the second, democracy ended in civil war.

The overwhelming majority of transitions from democracy, however, took the form either of military coups that ousted democratically elected leaders, or executive coups in which democratically chosen chief executives effectively ended democracy by concentrating power in their own hands, usually by declaring a state of emergency or martial law. In the first reverse wave, military coups ended democratic systems in the new countries of Eastern Europe and in Greece, Portugal, Argentina, and Japan. In the second reverse wave, military coups occurred in Indonesia, Pakistan, Greece, Nigeria, Turkey, and many Latin American countries. Executive coups occurred in the second reverse wave in Korea, India, and the Philippines. In Uruguay, the civilian and military leadership cooperated to end democracy through a mixed executive-military coup.

In both the first and second reverse waves, democratic systems were replaced in many cases by historically new forms of authoritarian rule. Fascism was distinguished from earlier forms of authoritarianism by its mass base, ideology, party organization, and efforts to penetrate and control most of society. Bureaucratic authoritarianism differed from earlier forms of military rule in Latin America with respect to its institutional character, its presumption of indefinite duration, and its economic policies. Italy and Germany in the 1920s and 1930s and Brazil and Argentina in the 1960s and 1970s were the lead countries in introducing these new forms of nondemocratic rule and furnished the examples that antidemocratic groups in other countries sought to emulate. Both these new forms of authoritarianism were, in effect, responses to social and economic development: the expansion of social mobilization and political participation in Europe, and the exhaustion of the import-substitution phase of economic development in Latin America.

Although the causes and forms of the first two reverse waves cannot generate reliable predictions concerning the causes and forms of a possible third reverse wave, prior experiences do suggest some potential causes of a new reverse wave.

First, systemic failures of democratic regimes to operate effectively could undermine their legitimacy. In the late twentieth century, the major nondemocratic ideological sources of legitimacy, most notably Marxism-Leninism, were discredited. The general acceptance of democratic norms meant that democratic governments were even less dependent on performance legitimacy than they had been in the past. Yet sustained inability to provide welfare, prosperity, equity, justice, domestic order, or external security could over time undermine the legitimacy even of democratic governments. As the memories of authoritarian failures fade, irritation with democratic failures is likely to increase. More specifically, a general international economic collapse on the 1929-30 model could undermine the legitimacy of democracy in many countries. Most democracies did survive the Great Depression of the 1930s; yet some succumbed, and presumably some would be likely to succumb in response to a comparable economic disaster in the future.

Second, a shift to authoritarianism by any democratic or democratizing great power could trigger reverse snowballing. The reinvigoration of authoritarianism in Russia or the Soviet Union would have unsettling effects on democratization in other Soviet republics, Bulgaria, Romania, Yugoslavia, and Mongolia; and possibly in Poland, Hungary, and Czechoslovakia as well. It could send the message to would-be despots elsewhere: "You too can go back into business." Similarly, the establishment of an authoritarian regime in India could have a significant demonstration effect on other Third World countries. Moreover, even if a major country does not revert to authoritarianism, a shift to dictatorship by several smaller newly democratic countries that lack many of the usual preconditions for democracy could have ramifying effects even on other countries where those preconditions are strong.

If a nondemocratic state greatly increased its power and began to expand beyond its borders, this too could stimulate authoritarian movements in other countries. This stimulus would be particularly strong if the expanding authoritarian state militarily defeated one or more democratic countries. In the past, all major powers that have developed economically have also tended to expand territorially. If China develops economically under authoritarian rule in the coming decades and expands its influence and control in East Asia, democratic regimes in the region will be significantly weakened.

Finally, as in the 1920s and the 1960s, various old and new forms of authoritarianism that seem appropriate to the needs of the times could emerge. Authoritarian nationalism could take hold in some Third World countries and also in Eastern Europe. Religious fundamentalism, which has been most dramatically prevalent in Iran, could come to power in other countries, especially in the Islamic world. Oligarchic authoritarianism could develop in both wealthy and poorer countries as a reaction to the leveling tendencies of democracy. Populist dictatorships could emerge in the future, as they have in the past, in response to democracy's protection of various forms of economic privilege, particularly in those countries where land tenancy is still an issue. Finally, communal dictatorships could be imposed in democracies with two or more distinct ethnic, racial, or religious groups, with one group trying to establish control over the entire society.

All of these forms of authoritarianism have existed in the past. It is not beyond the wit of humans to devise new ones in the future. One possibility might be a technocratic "electronic dictatorship," in which authoritarian rule is made possible and legitimated by the regime's ability to manipulate information, the media, and sophisticated means of communication. None of these old or new forms of authoritarianism is highly probable, but it is also hard to say that any one of them is totally impossible.

Obstacles to Democratization

Another approach to assessing democracy's prospects is to examine the obstacles to and opportunities for democratization where it has not yet taken hold. As of 1990, more than one hundred countries lacked democratic regimes. Most of these countries fell into four sometimes overlapping geocultural categories:

1) Home-grown Marxist-Leninist regimes, including the Soviet Union, where major liberalization occurred in the 1980s and democratic movements existed in many republics;

2) Sub-Saharan African countries, which, with a few exceptions, remained personal dictatorships, military regimes, one-party systems, or some combination of these three;

3) Islamic countries stretching from Morocco to Indonesia, which except for Turkey and perhaps Pakistan had nondemocratic regimes;

4) East Asian countries, from Burma through Southeast Asia to China and North Korea, which included communist systems, military regimes, personal dictatorships, and two semidemocracies (Thailand and Malaysia).

The obstacles to democratization in these groups of countries are political, cultural, and economic. One potentially significant political obstacle to future democratization is the virtual absence of experience with democracy in most countries that remained authoritarian in 1990. Twenty-three of 30 countries that democratized between 1974 and 1990 had had some history of democracy, while only a few countries that were nondemocratic in 1990 could claim such experience. These included a few third-wave backsliders (Sudan, Nigeria, Suriname, and possibly Pakistan), four second-wave backsliders that had not redemocratized in the third wave (Lebanon, Sri Lanka, Burma, Fiji), and three first-wave democratizers that had been prevented by Soviet occupation from redemocratizing at the end of World War II (Estonia, Latvia, and Lithuania). Virtually all the 90 or more other nondemocratic countries in 1990 lacked significant past experience with democratic rule. This obviously is not a decisive impediment to democratization—if it were, no countries would now be democratic—but it does make it more difficult.

Another obstacle to democratization is likely to disappear in a number of countries in the 1990s. Leaders who found authoritarian regimes or rule them for a long period tend to become particularly staunch opponents of democratization. Hence some form of leadership change within the authoritarian system usually precedes movement toward democracy. Human mortality is likely to ensure such changes in the 1990s in some authoritarian regimes. In 1990, the long-term rulers in China, Côte d'Ivoire, and Malawi were in their eighties; those in Burma, Indonesia, North Korea, Lesotho, and Vietnam were in their seventies; and the leaders of Cuba, Morocco, Singapore, Somalia, Syria, Tanzania, Zaire, and Zambia were sixty or older. The death or departure from office of these leaders would remove one obstacle to democratization in their countries, but would not make it inevitable.

Between 1974 and 1990, democratization occurred in personal dictatorships, military regimes, and one-party systems. Full-scale democratization has not yet occurred, however, in communist one-party states that were the products of domestic revolution. Liberalization has taken place in the Soviet Union, which may or may not lead to full-scale democratization in Russia. In Yugoslavia, movements toward democracy are underway in Slovenia and Croatia. The Yugoslav communist revolution, however, was largely a Serbian revolution, and the prospects for democracy in Serbia appear dubious. In Cambodia, an extraordinarily brutal revolutionary communist regime was replaced by a less brutal communist regime imposed by outside force. In 1990, Albania appeared to be opening up, but in China, Vietnam, Laos, Cuba, and Ethiopia, Marxist-Leninist regimes produced by home-grown revolutions seemed determined to remain in power. The revolutions in these countries had been nationalist as well as communist, and hence nationalism reinforced communism in a way that obviously was not true of Soviet-occupied Eastern Europe.

One serious impediment to democratization is the absence or weakness of real commitment to democratic values among political leaders in Asia, Africa, and the Middle East. When they are out of power, political leaders have good reason to advocate democracy. The test of their democratic commitment comes once they are in office. In Latin America, democratic regimes have generally been overthrown by military coups d'état. This has happened in Asia and the Middle East as well, but in these regions elected leaders themselves have also been responsible for ending democracy: Syngman Rhee and Park Chung Hee in Korea, Adnan Menderes in Turkey, Ferdinand Marcos in the Philippines, Lee Kwan Yew in Singapore, Indira Gandhi in India, and Sukarno in Indonesia. Having won power through the electoral system, these leaders then proceeded to undermine that system. They had little commitment to democratic values and practices.

Even when Asian, African, and Middle Eastern leaders have more or less abided by the rules of democracy, they often seemed to do so grudgingly. Many European, North American, and Latin American political leaders in the last half of the twentieth century were ardent and articulate advocates of democracy. Asian and African countries, in contrast, did not produce many heads of government who were also apostles of democracy. Who were the Asian, Arab, or African equivalents of Rómulo Betancourt, Alberto Llera Camargo, José Figueres, Eduardo Frei, Fernando Belaúnde Terry, Juan Bosch, José Napoleón Duarte, and Raúl Alfonsín? Jawaharlal Nehru and Corazon Aquino were, and there may have been others, but they were few in number. No Arab leader comes to mind, and it is hard to identify any Islamic leader who made a reputation as an advocate and supporter of democracy while in office. Why is this? This question inevitably leads to the issue of culture.

Culture

It has been argued that the world's great historic cultural traditions vary significantly in the extent to which their attitudes, values, beliefs, and related behavior patterns are conducive to the development of democracy. A profoundly antidemocratic culture would impede the spread of democratic norms in the society, deny legitimacy to democratic institutions, and thus greatly complicate if not prevent the emergence and effective functioning of those institutions. The cultural thesis comes in two forms. The more restrictive version states that only Western culture provides a suitable base for the development of democratic institutions and, consequently, that democracy is largely inappropriate for non-

Western societies. In the early years of the third wave, this argument was explicitly set forth by George Kennan. Democracy, he said, was a form of government "which evolved in the eighteenth and nineteenth centuries in northwestern Europe, primarily among those countries that border on the English Channel and the North Sea (but with a certain extension into Central Europe), and which was then carried into other parts of the world, including North America, where peoples from that northwestern European area appeared as original settlers, or as colonialists, and laid down the prevailing patterns of civil government." Hence democracy has "a relatively narrow base both in time and in space; and the evidence has yet to be produced that it is the natural form of rule for peoples outside those narrow perimeters." The achievements of Mao, Salazar, and Castro demonstrated, according to Kennan, that authoritarian regimes "have been able to introduce reforms and to improve the lot of masses of people, where more diffuse forms of political authority had failed."[3] Democracy, in short, is appropriate only for northwestern and perhaps central European countries and their settler-colony offshoots.

The Western-culture thesis has immediate implications for democratization in the Balkans and the Soviet Union. Historically these areas were part of the Czarist and Ottoman empires; their prevailing religions were Orthodoxy and Islam, not Western Christianity. These areas did not have the same experiences as Western Europe with feudalism, the Renaissance, the Reformation, the Enlightenment, the French Revolution, and liberalism. As William Wallace has suggested, the end of the Cold War and the disappearance of the Iron Curtain may have shifted the critical political dividing line eastward to the centuries-old boundary between Eastern and Western Christendom. Beginning in the north, this line runs south roughly along the borders dividing Finland and the Baltic republics from Russia; through Byelorussia and the Ukraine, separating western Catholic Ukraine from eastern Orthodox Ukraine; south and then west in Romania, cutting off Transylvania from the rest of the country; and then through Yugoslavia roughly along the line separating Slovenia and Croatia from the other republics.[4] This line may now separate those areas where democracy will take root from those where it will not.

A less restrictive version of the cultural obstacle argument holds that certain non-Western cultures are peculiarly hostile to democracy. The two cultures most often cited in this regard are Confucianism and Islam. Three questions are relevant to determining whether these cultures now pose serious obstacles to democratization. First, to what extent are traditional Confucian and Islamic values and beliefs hostile to democracy? Second, if they are, to what extent have these cultures in fact hampered progress toward democracy? Third, if they have significantly retarded democratic progress in the past, to what extent are they likely to continue to do so in the future?

Confucianism

Almost no scholarly disagreement exists regarding the proposition that traditional Confucianism was either undemocratic or antidemocratic. The only mitigating factor was the extent to which the examination system in the classic Chinese polity opened careers to the talented without regard to social background. Even if this were the case, however, a merit system of promotion does not make a democracy. No one would describe a modern army as democratic because officers are promoted on the basis of their abilities. Classic Chinese Confucianism and its derivatives in Korea, Vietnam, Singapore, Taiwan, and (in diluted fashion) Japan emphasized the group over the individual, authority over liberty, and responsibilities over rights. Confucian societies lacked a tradition of rights against the state; to the extent that individual rights did exist, they were created by the state. Harmony and cooperation were preferred over disagreement and competition. The maintenance of order and respect for hierarchy were central values. The conflict of ideas, groups, and parties was viewed as dangerous and illegitimate. Most important, Confucianism merged society and the state and provided no legitimacy for autonomous social institutions at the national level.

In practice Confucian or Confucian-influenced societies have been inhospitable to democracy. In East Asia only two countries, Japan and the Philippines, had sustained experience with democratic government prior to 1990. In both cases, democracy was the product of an American presence. The Philippines, moreover, is overwhelmingly a Catholic country. In Japan, Confucian values were reinterpreted and merged with autochthonous cultural traditions.

Mainland China has had no experience with democratic government, and democracy of the Western variety has been supported over the years only by relatively small groups of radical dissidents. "Mainstream" democratic critics have not broken with the key elements of the Confucian tradition.[5] The modernizers of China have been (in Lucian Pye's phrase) the "Confucian Leninists" of the Nationalist and Communist parties. In the late 1980s, when rapid economic growth in China produced a new series of demands for political reform and democracy on the part of students, intellectuals, and urban middle-class groups, the Communist leadership responded in two ways. First, it articulated a theory of "new authoritarianism," based on the experience of Taiwan, Singapore, and Korea, which claimed that a country at China's stage of economic development needed authoritarian rule to achieve balanced economic growth and contain the unsettling consequences of development. Second, the leadership violently suppressed the democratic movement in Beijing and elsewhere in June of 1989.

In China, economics reinforced culture in holding back democracy. In Singapore, Taiwan, and Korea, on the other hand, spectacular growth created the economic basis for democracy by the late 1980s. In these countries, economics clashed with culture in shaping political development. In 1990, Singapore was the only non-oil-exporting "high-income" country (as defined by the World Bank) that did not have a democratic political system, and Singapore's leader was an articulate exponent of Confucian values as opposed to those of Western democracy. In the 1980s, Premier Lee Kwan Yew made the teaching and promulgation of Confucian values a high priority for his city-state and took vigorous measures to limit and suppress dissent and to prevent media criticism of the government and its policies. Singapore was thus an authoritarian Confucian anomaly among the wealthy countries of the world. The interesting question is whether it will remain so now that Lee, who created the state, appears to be partially withdrawing from the political scene.

In the late 1980s, both Taiwan and Korea moved in a democratic direction. Historically, Taiwan had always been a peripheral part of China. It was occupied by the Japanese for 50 years, and its inhabitants rebelled in 1947 against the imposition of Chinese control. The Nationalist government arrived in 1949 humiliated by its defeat by the Communists, a defeat that made it impossible "for most Nationalist leaders to uphold the posture of arrogance associated with traditional Confucian notions of authority." Rapid economic and social development further weakened the influence of traditional Confucianism. The emergence of a substantial entrepreneurial class, composed largely of native Taiwanese, created (in very un-Confucian fashion) a source of power and wealth independent of the mainlander-dominated state. This produced in Taiwan a "fundamental change in Chinese political culture, which has not occurred in China itself or in Korea or Vietnam—and never really existed in Japan."[6] Taiwan's spectacular economic development thus overwhelmed a relatively weak Confucian legacy, and in the late 1980s Chiang Ching-kuo and Lee Teng-hui responded to the pressures produced by economic and social change and gradually moved to open up politics in their society.

In Korea, the classical culture included elements of mobility and egalitarianism along with Confucian components uncongenial to democracy, including a tradition of authoritarianism and strongman rule. As one Korean scholar put it, "people did not think of themselves as citizens with rights to exercise and responsibilities to perform, but they tended to look up to the top for direction and for favors in order to survive."[7] In the late 1980s, urbanization, education, the development of a substantial middle class, and the impressive spread of Christianity all weakened Confucianism as an obstacle to democracy in Korea. Yet it remained unclear whether the struggle between the old culture and the new prosperity had been definitively resolved in favor of the latter.

The East Asian Model

The interaction of economic progress and Asian culture appears to have generated a distinctly East Asian variety of democratic institutions. As of 1990, no East Asian country except the Philippines (which is, in many respects, more Latin American than East Asian in culture) had experienced a turnover from a popularly elected government of one party to a popularly elected government of a different party. The prototype was Japan, unquestionably a democracy, but one in which the ruling party has never been voted out of power. The Japanese model of dominant-party democracy, as Pye has pointed out, has spread elsewhere in East Asia. In 1990, two of the three opposition parties in Korea merged with the government party to form a political bloc that would effectively exclude the remaining opposition party, led by Kim Dae Jung and based on the Cholla region, from ever gaining power. In the late 1980s, democratic development in Taiwan seemed to be moving toward an electoral system in which the Kuomintang (KMT) was likely to remain the dominant party, with the Democratic Progressive Party confined to a permanent opposition role. In Malaysia, the coalition of the three leading parties from the Malay, Chinese, and Indian communities (first in the Alliance Party and then in the National Front) has controlled power in unbroken fashion against all competitors from the 1950s through the 1980s. In the mid-1980s, Lee Kwan Yew's deputy and successor Goh Chok Tong endorsed a similar type of party system for Singapore:

> I think a stable system is one where there is a mainstream political party representing a broad range of the population. Then you can have a few other parties on the periphery, very serious-minded parties. They are unable to have wider views but they nevertheless represent sectional interests. And the mainstream is returned all the time. I think that's good. And I would not apologize if we ended up in that situation in Singapore.[8]

A primary criterion for democracy is equitable and open competition for votes between political parties without government harassment or restriction of opposition groups. Japan has clearly met this test for decades with its freedoms of speech, press, and assembly, and reasonably equitable conditions of electoral competition. In the other Asian dominant-party systems, the playing field has been tilted in favor of the government for many years. By the late 1980s, however, conditions were becoming more equal in some countries. In Korea, the government party was unable to win control of the legislature in 1989, and this failure presumably was a major factor in its subsequent merger with two of its opponents. In Taiwan, restrictions on the opposition were gradually lifted. It is thus conceivable that other East Asian countries could join Japan in providing a level playing field for a game that the government party always wins. In 1990 the East Asian dominant-party systems thus spanned a continuum between democracy and authoritarianism, with Japan at one extreme, Indonesia at the other, and Korea, Taiwan, Malaysia, and Singapore (more or less in that order) in between.

Such a system may meet the formal requisites of democracy, but it differs significantly from the democratic systems prevalent in the West, where it is assumed not only that political parties and coalitions will freely and equally compete for power but also that they are likely to *alternate* in power. By contrast, the East Asian dominant-party systems seem to involve competition for power but not alternation in power, and participation in elections for all, but participation in office only for those in the "mainstream" party. This type of political system offers democracy without turnover. It represents an adaptation of Western democratic practices to serve not Western values of competition and change, but Asian values of consensus and stability.

Western democratic systems are less dependent on performance legitimacy than authoritarian systems because failure is blamed on the incumbents instead of the system, and the ouster and replacement of the incumbents help to renew the system. The East Asian societies that have adopted or appear to be adopting the dominant-party model had unequalled records of economic success from the 1960s to the 1980s. What happens, however, if and when their 8-percent growth rates plummet; unemployment, inflation, and other forms of economic distress escalate; or social and economic conflicts intensify? In a Western democracy the response would be to turn the incumbents out. In a dominant-party democracy, however, that would represent a revolutionary change. If the structure of political competition does not allow that to happen, unhappiness with the government could well lead to demonstrations, protests, riots, and efforts to mobilize popular support to overthrow the government. The government then would be tempted to respond by suppressing dissent and imposing authoritarian controls. The key question, then, is to what extent the East Asian dominant-party system presupposes uninterrupted and substantial economic growth. Can this system survive prolonged economic downturn or stagnation?

Islam

"Confucian democracy" is clearly a contradiction in terms. It is unclear whether "Islamic democracy" also is. Egalitarianism and voluntarism are central themes in Islam. The "high culture form of Islam," Ernest Gellner has argued, is "endowed with a number of features—unitarianism, a rule-ethic, individualism, scripturalism, puritanism, an egalitarian aversion to mediation and hierarchy, a fairly small load of magic—that are congruent, presumably, with requirements of modernity or modernization." They are also generally congruent with the requirements of democracy. Islam, however, also rejects any distinction between the religious community and the political community. Hence there is no equipoise between Caesar and God, and political participation is linked to religious affiliation. Fundamentalist Islam demands that in a Muslim country the political rulers should be practicing Muslims, *shari'a* should be the basic law, and *ulema* should have a "decisive vote in articulating, or at least reviewing and ratifying, all governmental policy."[9] To the extent that governmental legitimacy and policy flow from religious doctrine and religious expertise, Islamic concepts of politics differ from and contradict the premises of democratic politics.

Islamic doctrine thus contains elements that may be both congenial and uncongenial to democracy. In practice, however, the only Islamic country that has sustained a fully democratic political system for any length of time is Turkey, where Mustafa Kemal Ataturk explicitly rejected Islamic concepts of society and politics and vigorously attempted to create a secular, modern, Western nation-state. And Turkey's experience with democracy has not been an unmitigated success. Elsewhere in the Islamic world, Pakistan has made three attempts at democracy, none of which lasted long. While Turkey has had democracy interrupted by occasional military interventions, Pakistan has had bureaucratic and military rule interrupted by occasional elections.

The only Arab country to sustain a form of democracy (albeit of the consociational variety) for a significant period of time was Lebanon. Its democracy, however, really amounted to consociational oligarchy, and 40 to 50 percent of its population was Christian. Once Muslims became a majority in Lebanon and began to assert themselves, Lebanese democracy collapsed. Between 1981 and 1990, only two of 37 countries in the world with Muslim majorities were ever rated "Free" by Freedom House in its annual surveys: the Gambia for two years and the Turkish Republic of Northern Cyprus for four. Whatever the compatibility of Islam and democracy in theory, in practice they have rarely gone together.

Opposition movements to authoritarian regimes in southern and eastern Europe, in Latin America, and in East Asia almost universally have espoused Western democratic values and proclaimed their desire to establish democracy. This does not mean that they invariably would introduce democratic institutions if they had the opportunity to do so, but at least they articulated the rhetoric of democracy. In authoritarian Islamic societies, by contrast, movements explicitly campaigning for democratic politics have been relatively weak, and the most powerful opposition has come from Islamic fundamentalists.

In the late 1980s, domestic economic problems combined with the snowballing effects of democratization elsewhere led the governments of several Islamic countries to relax their controls on the opposition and to attempt to renew their legitimacy through elections. The principal initial beneficiaries of these openings were Islamic fundamentalist groups. In Algeria, the Islamic Salvation Front swept the June 1990 local elections, the first free elections since the country became independent in 1962. In the 1989 Jordanian elections, Islamic fundamentalists won 36 of 80 seats in parliament. In Egypt, many candidates associated with the Muslim Brotherhood were elected to parliament in 1987. In several countries, Islamic fundamentalist groups were reportedly plotting insurrections. The strong electoral showings of the Islamic groups partly reflected the absence of other opposition parties, some because they were under government proscription, others because they were boycotting the elections. Nonetheless, fundamentalism seemed to be gaining strength in Middle Eastern countries, particularly among younger people. The strength of this tendency induced secular heads of government in Tunisia, Turkey, and elsewhere to adopt policies advocated by the fundamentalists and to make political gestures demonstrating their own commitment to Islam.

Liberalization in Islamic countries thus enhanced the power of important social and political movements whose commitment to democracy was uncertain. In some respects, the position of fundamentalist parties in Islamic societies in the early 1990s raised questions analogous to those posed by communist parties in Western Europe in the 1940s and again in the 1970s. Would the existing governments continue to open up their politics and hold elections in which Islamic groups could compete freely and equally? Would the Islamic groups gain majority support in those elections? If they did win the elections, would the military, which in many Islamic societies (e.g., Algeria, Turkey, Pakistan, and Indonesia) is strongly secular, allow them to form a government? If they did form a government, would it pursue radical Islamic policies that would undermine democracy and alienate the modern and Western-oriented elements in society?

The Limits of Cultural Obstacles

Strong cultural obstacles to democratization thus appear to exist in Confucian and Islamic societies. There are, nonetheless, reasons to doubt whether these must necessarily prevent democratic development. First, similar cultural arguments have not held up in the past. At one point many scholars argued that Catholicism was an obstacle to democracy. Others, in the Weberian tradition, contended that Catholic countries were unlikely to develop economically in the same manner as Protestant countries. Yet in the 1960s, 1970s, and 1980s Catholic countries became democratic and, on average, had higher rates of economic growth than Protestant countries. Similarly, at one point Weber and others argued that countries with Confucian cultures would not achieve successful capitalist development. By the 1980s, however, a new generation of scholars saw Confucianism as a major cause of the spectacular economic growth of East Asian societies. In the longer run, will the thesis that Confucianism prevents democratic development be any more viable than the thesis that Confucianism prevents economic development? Arguments that particular cultures are permanent obstacles to change should be viewed with a certain skepticism.

Second, great cultural traditions like Islam and Confucianism are highly complex bodies of ideas, beliefs, doctrines, assumptions, and behavior patterns. Any major culture, including Confucianism, has some elements that are compatible with democracy, just as both Protestantism and Catholicism have elements that are clearly undemocratic. Confucian democracy may be a contradiction in terms, but democracy in a Confucian society need not be. The real question is which elements in Islam and Confucianism are favorable to democracy, and how and under what circumstances these can supersede the undemocratic aspects of those cultural traditions.

Third, cultures historically are dynamic, not stagnant. The dominant beliefs and attitudes in a society change. While maintaining elements of continuity, the prevailing culture of a society in one generation may differ significantly from what it was one or two generations earlier. In the 1950s, Spanish culture was typically described as traditional, authoritarian, hierarchical, deeply religious, and honor-and-status oriented. By the 1970s and 1980s, these words had little place in a description of Spanish attitudes and values. Cultures evolve and, as in Spain, the most important force bringing about cultural changes is often economic development itself.

Economics

Few relationships between social, economic, and political phenomena are stronger than that between the level of economic development and the existence of democratic politics. Most wealthy countries are democratic, and most democratic countries—India is the most dramatic exception—are wealthy. The correlation between wealth and democracy implies that transitions to democracy should occur primarily in countries at the mid-level of economic development. In poor countries democratization is unlikely; in rich countries it usually has already occurred. In between there is a "political transition zone": countries in this middle economic stratum are those most likely to transit to democracy, and most countries that transit to democracy will be in this stratum. As countries develop economically and move into the transition zone, they become good prospects for democratization.

In fact, shifts from authoritarianism to democracy during the third wave were heavily concentrated in this transition zone, especially at its upper reaches. The conclusion seems clear. Poverty is a principal—probably *the* principal—obstacle to democratic development. The future of democracy depends on the future of economic development. Obstacles to economic development are obstacles to the expansion of democracy.

The third wave of democratization was propelled forward by the extraordinary global economic growth of the 1950s and 1960s. That era of growth came to an end with the oil price increases of 1973-74. Between 1974 and 1990, democratization accelerated around the world, but global economic growth slowed down. There were, however, substantial differences in growth rates among regions. East Asian rates remained high throughout the 1970s and 1980s, and overall rates of growth in South Asia increased. On the other hand, growth rates in the Middle East, North Africa, Latin America, and the Caribbean declined sharply from the 1970s to the 1980s. Those in sub-Saharan Africa plummeted. Per capita GNP in Africa was stagnant during the late 1970s and declined at an annual rate of 2.2 percent during the 1980s. The economic obstacles to democratization in Africa thus clearly grew during the 1980s. The prospects for the 1990s are not encouraging. Even if economic reforms, debt relief, and economic assistance materialize, the World Bank has predicted an average annual rate of growth in per capita GDP for Africa of only 0.5 percent for the remainder of the century.[10] If this prediction is accurate, the economic obstacles to democratization in sub-Saharan Africa will remain overwhelming well into the twenty-first century.

The World Bank was more optimistic in its predictions of economic growth for China and the nondemocratic countries of South Asia. The current low levels of wealth in those countries, however, generally mean that even with annual per capita growth rates of 3 to 5 percent, the economic conditions favorable to democratization would still be long in coming.

In the 1990s, the majority of countries where the economic conditions for democratization are already present or rapidly emerging are in the Middle East and North Africa (see Table 1). The economies of many of these countries (United Arab Emirates, Kuwait, Saudi Arabia, Iraq, Iran,

Table 1 — Upper and Middle Income Nondemocratic Countries - GNP Per Capita (1988)

INCOME LEVEL	ARAB-MIDDLE EAST	SOUTHEAST ASIA	AFRICA	OTHER
Upper Income (>$6,000)	(UAE) (Kuwait) (Saudi Arabia)	Singapore		
Upper Middle Income ($2,000- 5,500)	(Iraq) (Iran) (Libya) (Oman)* Algeria*		(Gabon)	Yugoslavia
Lower Middle Income ($500-2,200) $1,000	Syria Jordan* Tunisia*	Malaysia* Thailand*	Cameroon*	Paraguay
	Morocco* Egypt* Yemen* Lebanon*		Congo* Côte d'Ivoire Zimbabwe Senegal* Angola	

Note: ( ) = major oil exporter
       * = average annual GDP growth rate 1980-1988 > 3.0%

Source: World Bank, *World Bank Development Report 1990* (New York: Oxford University Press, 1990), 178-181.

Libya, Oman) depend heavily on oil exports, which enhances the control of the state bureaucracy. This does not, however, make democratization impossible. The state bureaucracies of Eastern Europe had far more power than do those of the oil exporters. Thus at some point that power could collapse among the latter as dramatically as it did among the former.

In 1988 among the other states of the Middle East and North Africa, Algeria had already reached a level conducive to democratization; Syria was approaching it; and Jordan, Tunisia, Morocco, Egypt, and North Yemen were well below the transition zone, but had grown rapidly during the 1980s. Middle Eastern economies and societies are approaching the point where they will become too wealthy and too complex for their various traditional, military, and one-party systems of authoritarian rule to sustain themselves. The wave of democratization that swept the world in the 1970s and 1980s could become a dominant feature of Middle Eastern and North African politics in the 1990s. The issue of economics versus culture would then be joined: What forms of

politics might emerge in these countries when economic prosperity begins
to interact with Islamic values and traditions?

In China, the obstacles to democratization are political, economic, and
cultural; in Africa they are overwhelmingly economic; and in the rapidly
developing countries of East Asia and in many Islamic countries, they
are primarily cultural.

Economic Development and Political Leadership

History has proved both optimists and pessimists wrong about
democracy. Future events will probably do the same. Formidable
obstacles to the expansion of democracy exist in many societies. The
third wave, the "global democratic revolution" of the late twentieth
century, will not last forever. It may be followed by a new surge of
authoritarianism sustained enough to constitute a third reverse wave.
That, however, would not preclude a fourth wave of democratization
developing some time in the twenty-first century. Judging by the record
of the past, the two most decisive factors affecting the future
consolidation and expansion of democracy will be economic development
and political leadership.

Most poor societies will remain undemocratic so long as they remain
poor. Poverty, however, is not inevitable. In the past, nations such as
South Korea, which were assumed to be mired in economic
backwardness, have astonished the world by rapidly attaining prosperity.
In the 1980s, a new consensus emerged among developmental economists
on the ways to promote economic growth. The consensus of the 1980s
may or may not prove more lasting and productive than the very
different consensus among economists that prevailed in the 1950s and
1960s. The new orthodoxy of neo-orthodoxy, however, already seems to
have produced significant results in many countries.

Yet there are two reasons to temper our hopes with caution. First,
economic development for the late, late, late developing
countries—meaning largely Africa—may well be more difficult than it
was for earlier developers because the advantages of backwardness come
to be outweighed by the widening and historically unprecedented gap
between rich and poor countries. Second, new forms of authoritarianism
could emerge in wealthy, information-dominated, technology-based
societies. If unhappy possibilities such as these do not materialize,
economic development should create the conditions for the progressive
replacement of authoritarian political systems by democratic ones. Time
is on the side of democracy.

Economic development makes democracy possible; political leadership
makes it real. For democracies to come into being, future political elites
will have to believe, at a minimum, that democracy is the least bad form

of government for their societies and for themselves. They will also need the skills to bring about the transition to democracy while facing both radical oppositionists and authoritarian hard-liners who inevitably will attempt to undermine their efforts. Democracy will spread to the extent that those who exercise power in the world and in individual countries want it to spread. For a century and a half after Tocqueville observed the emergence of modern democracy in America, successive waves of democratization have washed over the shore of dictatorship. Buoyed by a rising tide of economic progress, each wave advanced further—and receded less—than its predecessor. History, to shift the metaphor, does not sail ahead in a straight line, but when skilled and determined leaders are at the helm, it does move forward.

NOTES

1. *New York Times*, 28 December 1989, A13; *International Herald Tribune*, 12-13 May 1990, 6.

2. *The Times* (London), 27 May 1990; *Time*, 21 May 1990, 34-35; *Daily Telegraph*, 29 March 1990, 13; *New York Times*, 27 February 1990, A10, and 9 April 1990, A6.

3. George F. Kennan, *The Cloud of Danger* (Boston: Little, Brown, 1977), 41-43.

4. See William Wallace, *The Transformation of Western Europe* (London: Royal Institute of International Affairs-Pinter, 1990), 16-19.

5. See Daniel Kelliher, "The Political Consequences of China's Reform," *Comparative Politics* 18 (July 1986): 488-490; and Andrew J. Nathan, *Chinese Democracy* (New York: Alfred A. Knopf, 1985).

6. Lucian W. Pye with Mary W. Pye, *Asian Power and Politics: The Cultural Dimensions of Authority* (Cambridge: Harvard University Press, 1985), 232-236.

7. *New York Times*, 15 December 1987, A14.

8. Goh Chok Tong, quoted in *New York Times*, 14 August 1985, A13.

9. Ernest Gellner, "Up from Imperialism," *The New Republic*, 22 May 1989, 35-36; R. Stephen Humphreys, "Islam and Political Values in Saudi Arabia, Egypt, and Syria," *Middle East Journal* 33 (Winter 1979): 6-7.

10. World Bank, *World Development Report 1990* (New York: Oxford University Press, 1990), 8-11, 16, 160; and *Sub-Saharan Africa: From Crisis to Sustainable Growth* (Washington: World Bank, 1990).

2.
THE DEMOCRATIC MOMENT

Marc F. Plattner

Marc F. Plattner is coeditor of the Journal of Democracy *and counselor at the National Endowment for Democracy. He is the author of* Rousseau's State of Nature *(1979), and the editor of* Human Rights in Our Time *(1984). His essay is an updated version of an April 1991 lecture at the John M. Olin Center for Inquiry into the Theory and Practice of Democracy at the University of Chicago.*

The dramatic events of August 1991 in Moscow should convince any remaining skeptics that the democratic revolutions of 1989 indeed marked a watershed in world history. The sudden downfall that year of long-entrenched Communist regimes throughout Eastern Europe dramatically transformed the face of world politics. Together with the remarkable changes that had already taken place in both the foreign and domestic policies of the Soviet Union, this development effectively brought to an end the period, beginning in 1945, that has generally been labeled the postwar or Cold War era. Yet despite the general consensus that we have now entered the post-Cold War era, there is sharp disagreement about what the nature and characteristics of this new period will be.

Before addressing this central question, it is worth briefly reviewing the Cold War era and the dynamics that brought it to a close. In the years following the Second World War, the militarily strongest and economically most advanced nations of the world became divided into two sharply opposed camps headed by two superpowers, the United States and the Soviet Union. The division of the world into East and West was marked by the "Iron Curtain" that ran through the middle of Germany and the heart of Central Europe. But the split between East and West was not only geopolitical; it was also a conflict between two fundamentally opposed ideologies—Leninist communism and liberal democracy. Many countries sought to maintain varying degrees of neutrality in this struggle, styling themselves as the Nonaligned Movement or the Third World, but they remained more an arena for superpower competition than a potent independent force in global politics. It is hard to quarrel with the characterization of the international system during the Cold War era as a bipolar world.

Although there was great immobility in this system from 1949 on, the changes that did take place generally seemed to strengthen the Soviet camp. It is now apparent to almost everyone that the communist regimes had long been disintegrating from within, but during most of the Cold War period communism seemed to be enjoying a slow but steady ascendancy. It gradually brought a number of additional non-European countries into its orbit; during the 1970s alone, new procommunist regimes emerged in some dozen nations. Even more significant was the seeming irreversibility of such gains. In fact, until the U.S. intervention in Grenada in 1983, not a single consolidated communist regime had ever been displaced.

Meanwhile, democracy, after receiving a brief ideological boost from the establishment of new democratic regimes during the wave of decolonization, seemed to be in deep trouble. The postcolonial democracies almost all soon failed, giving way to regimes that were authoritarian and generally "nonaligned," though with a strong admixture of hostility toward the West. The imposition of dictatorial rule in India by Indira Gandhi in 1975, seemingly bringing to an end the largest and most important democracy in the non-Western world, marked a low point for democratic fortunes. At that very moment, Daniel Patrick Moynihan, a staunch champion of liberal democracy, despairingly wrote:

> Liberal democracy on the American model increasingly tends to the condition of monarchy in the nineteenth century: a holdover form of government, one which persists in isolated or peculiar places here and there, and may even serve well enough for special circumstances, but which has simply no relevance to the future. It is where the world was, not where it is going.[1]

Although the late 1970s witnessed transitions to democracy in Spain and Portugal and its restoration in India, only in the 1980s did it become clear that Moynihan's pessimism was unfounded and that democracy was experiencing a true resurgence. The democratic tide swept through most of Latin America, reached such key Asian countries as the Philippines, Korea, Taiwan, and Pakistan, and by decade's end was beginning to make ripples in sub-Saharan Africa and even the Middle East. Moreover, the 1980s saw such Third World alternatives to democracy as African socialism and bureaucratic authoritarianism in Latin America revealed as political and economic failures.

Most dramatic, of course, was the growing crisis—and in some places the sudden collapse—of communism. Not only did the 1980s witness no new communist gains, but existing communist regimes were suddenly thrown on the defensive. Relatively new pro-Soviet regimes were challenged by U.S.-backed anticommunist insurgencies in Afghanistan, Angola, and Nicaragua. Yet while these armed resistance movements may have taken a physical, economic, and psychological toll on communist governments, it is noteworthy that so far they have nowhere come to power. Except for the cases of Romania and Ethiopia (where the victorious insurgent movements were Marxist in origin), East European and Third World communist regimes have ceded power largely through negotiations, elections, and other peaceful means.

This peaceful denouement was made possible, of course, by the internal crisis of communism at its very core in the Soviet Union. We are still very far from having an adequate understanding of how this once seemingly impregnable regime could crumble so quickly, or of the motives and strategies of the chief architect of its undoing, Mikhail Gorbachev. What does seem clear is that by the 1980s, Soviet communism faced a choice between continuing socioeconomic stagnation and reform. But modest reform proved incapable of overcoming stagnation, and more thoroughgoing reform proved impossible without decisively undermining the communist system. In the formulation of one of communism's most acute analysts, the Yugoslav dissident Milovan Djilas, the liberalization of communism turned out to be identical with the crisis of communism.

Even more damaging to communism than its economic failures and foreign policy reverses was its ideological self-discrediting. By attributing their system's shortcomings to its lack of economic markets and political democracy, the Soviet leaders effectively conceded the ideological struggle to the West, and dealt communism's worldwide appeal a mortal blow. Who wants to devote oneself to a cause that has been repudiated by its own most prominent spokesmen? Today's international political heroes are no longer leftist revolutionaries, but the peaceful protesters demanding democracy who were so brutally crushed in Tiananmen Square or who triumphed in Wenceslas Square (and, most recently, at the barricades surrounding the Russian Parliament). In this context, let us also note what may be viewed as a coda to the revolutions of 1989: the peaceful rejection of the Sandinistas at the polls by the people of Nicaragua, which ended the last pro-Soviet Third World regime still capable of eliciting passionate support in the West.

The Post-Cold War World

We thus find ourselves living in the new post-Cold War world—a world with one dominant principle of political legitimacy, democracy, and only one superpower, the United States. But how long can this, the democratic moment, last? Is democracy's unchallenged preeminence, with no serious geopolitical or ideological rivals, only transitory, a momentary worldwide "era of good feelings" that will soon give way to bitter new divisions? Or does it signal a lasting victory due either to democracy's own inherent strengths or to the shortcomings of antidemocratic regimes and ideologies?

The most forceful statement of the latter view, of course, is to be found in Francis Fukuyama's now famous article on "The End of History," where he asserts that we may be witnessing "the end point of man's ideological evolution and the universalization of Western liberal democracy as the final form of human government." While there is reason to be dubious about the metaphysical trappings and sweeping conclusions of Fukuyama's thesis, he was absolutely right with respect to what may be considered the essential premise of his essay—namely, "the total exhaustion of viable systematic alternatives to Western liberalism."[2]

The collapse of communism and the manifest failure of various authoritarian brands of Third Worldism have resulted in the absence of a single nondemocratic regime in the world with wide appeal. They have also led to a drastic weakening of openly antidemocratic forces within democratic regimes. Just as the defeat of fascism led to the virtual disappearance of the antidemocratic right in the West, so the downfall of communism seems to be causing the withering away of the antidemocratic left.

Moreover, it is not solely the extreme or antidemocratic left that has suffered from the crisis of "really existing socialism." For example, Miklós Haraszti, a former underground writer who is now a member of the Hungarian parliament, describes the current political spectrum in his country as follows:

> All in all what we have here is a quite classic European feature: a conservative and liberal side to modern society, where in conformity with the political reality of postcommunist democracy there is no left as such. . . . In postcommunist societies, you see, the left is dead. . . . So the structure we have now is an American kind of political split, and in that sense East European politics is closer to the U.S. rather than the West European model."[3]

Yet to some extent the development Haraszti describes in Eastern Europe can also be observed in Western Europe (and even Latin America), as socialist parties continue to move toward the center.[4] Without too much exaggeration, one might say that today there is no Left left. Everywhere in the more advanced countries, politics is tending to move closer to the U.S. model—not only in being influenced by American campaign and media techniques, but in the more important respect of being dominated by moderate center-left and center-right parties united in agreement on fundamental democratic principles and procedures, and increasingly on an acceptance of the market economy as well.

Even before the collapse of communism, the 1980s had witnessed a remarkable rehabilitation of free-market economics in the West. Not only had capitalism gained a new intellectual respectability, but the successful entrepreneur once again became an object of admiration. By contrast, state ownership of the means of production came to be identified not with economic progress but with stagnation. The eagerness of communist and especially postcommunist countries to transform themselves into market economies dramatically reinforced this trend.

The discrediting of traditional socialist economics contributed significantly to restoring the self-confidence of liberal democracy. It helped bring to an end a long-established tendency in the West to view modern democracy as moving "progressively" in the direction of an ever greater role for the state, and even to see socialism as the logical culmination of liberal democracy. From this perspective, no matter how retrograde communist states may have seemed with respect to their denial of civil and political liberties, they nonetheless had some claim to be more "modern," to represent the wave of the future. The evidence and testimony that have recently emerged from Eastern Europe and the Soviet Union have utterly undermined this way of thinking.

Rejoining World Civilization

Indeed, today it is the liberal democracies that are widely regarded as the only truly and fully modern societies. This sentiment is reflected in the often expressed desire on the part of Soviets and East Europeans to live in a "normal society." It is a sentiment that was shared not only by dissident intellectuals but also by many representatives of the ruling elites—especially by those who had traveled abroad—and it played a critical role in the demise of communist regimes.

These regimes founded their legitimacy on an ideology that claimed that its adherents constituted the vanguard of a new world. Yet the people living under these regimes came to realize that they were drifting into backwardness and stagnation, that the world was passing them by, that they were laboring under what Milan Šimečka called "the burden of wasted time."[15] In a speech to the Russian parliament, Boris Yeltsin blamed the socialist experiment for leaving the people of the Soviet Union "at the tail end of world civilization."[6]

When they speak of rejoining world civilization, Soviets and East Europeans mean that they want to return to "Europe"—to a market economy and to political democracy. Václav Klaus, the finance minister of Czechoslovakia and the elected leader of Civic Forum, recently stated in answer to a question about his country's economic policies: "We are absolutely not interested in a 'third way' solution. I believe that 'the third way' is the fastest way to the Third World."[7] Many others, both in the West and in the Third World itself, have now come to identify statist economies and nondemocratic polities with corruption and retrogression. Third World intellectuals whose greatest worry once was that their countries would be dominated by Western capital now voice the fear that Latin America or Africa will become "marginalized" from the world economy.

It is true, of course, that not all nondemocratic Third World regimes have been economic failures. In fact, some authoritarian regimes with relatively open, market-oriented economies—Taiwan, Korea, Chile—have achieved extraordinary economic success. Yet that very success, by fostering and augmenting the power of a self-reliant and outward-looking middle class, has raised popular demands for democratic government that have led to significant political transformations in all of these countries. Authoritarian rulers in developing countries seem to face a kind of Catch-22: they are undermined by both economic failure and economic success.

These economically successful Third World authoritarian regimes have held some attraction for certain communist reformers. This has led to the curious spectacle of Taiwan becoming a model in some quarters in Beijing and Pinochet becoming a hero in some quarters in Moscow. The arguments of many of those in both countries attracted by this "neoauthoritarian" model are similar: The premature introduction of political democracy, they assert, will allow popular opposition to forestall the painful measures necessary to introduce a market economy. A strong hand, à la Pinochet, is needed to implement the economic reforms, which will in turn lay the basis for the gradual transition to democracy. It is interesting to note that the strongest argument in favor of authoritarianism today is its alleged ability to dismantle a socialist economy. But even this neoauthoritarian doctrine seems to acknowledge the ultimate superiority of liberal democracy as the eventual goal toward which it aims.

While there may be room for debate about the relative capacity of democracies and market-oriented authoritarian regimes to achieve economic growth in developing countries, only democracy seems compatible with economic success in the advanced nations. Soviet-style command economies may have achieved substantial gains at an earlier phase of industrialization, but building more and bigger steel mills is no longer the measure of economic progress. In the era of computers and instant worldwide telecommunications, innovation, adaptability, and openness to the world economy are essential to maintaining economic competitiveness. And it is difficult for these characteristics to persist for long where political freedom is seriously curtailed.

Democracies also appear to enjoy a comparable advantage with respect to military power. Despite their generally pacific character, they are more capable of producing and operating the weapons that are essential to victory on the battlefield. As Adam Smith had already observed two centuries ago: "In modern war the great expense of firearms gives an evident advantage to the nation which can best afford that expense."[8] Today, as the war against Iraq has underlined, technological superiority is as essential as the ability to equip, deploy, and maintain a large force in the field. It would be rash, given the evidence of past Nazi and Soviet military achievements, to be overconfident about the inability of totalitarian powers to compete militarily with democracies. Yet it does seem that a growing sense of being unable to keep pace economically and technologically in their military competition with the United States was crucial in persuading the Soviet elite to embark on the path of reform.

Democracy seems, then, to enjoy superiority not merely in popular legitimacy and ideological appeal, but also in economic and military strength. And it is difficult to discern any powerful new nondemocratic ideological, economic, or military challengers on the horizon. All this would appear to suggest that, if we have not yet arrived at Fukuyama's "end of history," we may at least be entering a sustained period of peaceful democratic hegemony—a kind of "Pax Democratica."

A New Ideology?

Perhaps the most compelling counterargument to this view of democracy triumphant has been presented by Ken Jowitt.[9] Although writing in explicit opposition to Fukuyama, Jowitt agrees with him that the collapse of communism has resulted in a situation where "liberal capitalism is now the only politically global civilization." For Jowitt, however, this is only an initial and temporary effect of what he calls "the Leninist extinction." He argues that the sudden demise of one of the two camps long engaged in a comprehensive global struggle will lead not to the easy and unchallenged ascendancy of its rival but to a radical reshaping of all the previously fixed boundaries of international politics.

In the first place, this refers to the territorial borders that separate sovereign states. The Leninist extinction not only has fostered the breakup of the Soviet Union but is likely to unleash more open ethnic conflict and the redrawing of national borders among peoples who were previously restrained by Soviet imperial power. There is ample historical precedent for believing that the breakup of empires can lead to new eruptions of long-dormant conflicts between previously subject peoples. Brian Urquhart, who served for several decades as UN undersecretary general for special political affairs, has said that most of his professional life was spent dealing with the problems that the British Empire left in its wake—the Arab-Israeli conflict, the Indo-Pakistani conflict, the Nigerian civil war, the Cyprus dispute. (If Urquhart had stayed on the job a bit longer, he could have added the Iraq-Kuwait conflict to the list.) It would not be surprising if UN officials in the decades ahead were to find themselves similarly preoccupied with crises arising from conflicts between Armenians and Azeris, Hungarians and Romanians, or Croats and Serbs.

But Jowitt argues that the disorder spawned by the Leninist extinction will not be confined to the peoples who once lived under the Leninist yoke. During the Cold War, the superpowers' influence over their client states and their fear of a wider conflict helped to maintain the territorial status quo. Today superpower rivalry is much diminished as a source of Third World conflict, but by the same token it no longer serves to restrain the ambitions of local rulers. Saddam Hussein's invasion of Kuwait is a dramatic example of how the diminution of Soviet power might lead to new regional instability. To be sure, Saddam's expulsion from Kuwait has sent a most salutary message to Third World dictators contemplating territorial aggression. Yet there is reason to doubt that the West would respond so resolutely to aggression in a strategically less critical area of the world.

Jowitt's argument goes beyond asserting that the Leninist extinction will lead to an increase in local wars and a redrawing of territorial boundaries. For he asserts that the vacuum left behind by the "clearing away" of communism may well be filled by the emergence of new ideologies. Liberal democracy, he argues, cannot hold the field to itself because, in "its elevation of rational impersonality as the organizing principle of social life," it fails to satisfy certain basic human longings. Therefore, the West, in his words, "will regularly witness the rise of both internal and external movements dedicated to destroying or reforming it—movements that in one form or another will stress ideals of group membership, expressive behavior, collective solidarity, and heroic action."

Fukuyama might actually agree with a surprisingly large part of Jowitt's argument. For far from predicting the end of international conflict, Fukuyama envisages "a high and perhaps rising level of ethnic and nationalist violence," as well as the continuation of terrorism and wars of national liberation. Nor would he necessarily dispute Jowitt's prediction that we will see the emergence of what the latter calls "movements of rage" in the Third World—"nihilistic backlashes" against political and economic failure such as are embodied in groups like the Khmer Rouge or Peru's Sendero Luminoso. In a sense Fukuyama responds in advance to possible developments of this kind by stating: "Our task is not to answer exhaustively the challenges to liberalism promoted by every crackpot messiah around the world, but only those that are embodied in important social or political forces and movements, and which are therefore part of world history."

This finally brings us to the heart of the disagreement between these two authors. Fukuyama seems to contend that the liberal democratic idea has definitively triumphed among the advanced nations of the world, and thus that there will not again arise a major power animated by an antidemocratic ideology. Jowitt, by contrast, can envisage the emergence of a new ideology capable of generating a new "way of life"—an ideology whose power to move great nations would be comparable to that of Catholicism, liberal democracy, fascism, or Leninism.

Of course, one can only speculate about whether a potent and attractive new ideology will emerge to challenge democracy. Fukuyama persuasively points to the widespread appeal of liberal democracy, its ability to penetrate diverse cultures and win adherents around the world, and the absence of plausible contenders to dethrone it from its current hegemony. Much less convincing, however, is his suggestion that modern liberalism has resolved all the fundamental "contradictions" in human life. As Jowitt argues, liberalism will always leave many human beings unsatisfied and hence will generate powerful antiliberal movements. The real question is whether any such movement can succeed in attaining the economic success and broad appeal necessary to compete successfully with liberalism. The answer, which only the future can reveal, will be decisive for the fate of democracy.

Challenges and Competitors

Despite its broad popular appeal, democracy is not an easy form of government to maintain, especially in poorer countries that lack an educated populace, a substantial middle class, and a democratic culture. The events of the past decade and a half may have exploded the view that democracy can be sustained only in rich Western countries, but they should not give rise to an unwarranted optimism that expects democracy to be quickly achieved and uninterruptedly preserved throughout the world.

It is remarkable how few breakdowns of democracy there have been in the past few years, even under conditions as adverse as those in Peru or the Philippines. Some of the countries that have more recently installed freely elected governments—Nicaragua, Haiti, and Benin, for example—face still more daunting challenges in trying to create stable democratic institutions. Even the formerly communist countries, despite their European heritage and relatively higher levels of economic development, confront an enormously difficult task in seeking simultaneously to introduce market economies and to consolidate democratic political systems. All these experiments currently benefit both from the extraordinary worldwide momentum and prestige of democracy, and from still vivid memories of the tyrannical and unsuccessful regimes that they supplanted. Yet as these memories fade and the new democracies encounter the inevitable difficulties that lie ahead, it is only to be expected that some of them will sink back into authoritarianism.

Such backsliding would undoubtedly be a great misfortune for the people of these countries, and it could very easily create some serious economic and foreign policy problems for the established democracies. Yet its impact on the overall fortunes of democracy in the world would not be all that great, so long as no weighty new ideological rival to democracy appears on the scene. If the majority of the new democracies fail and revert to various local brands of authoritarianism, the view might once again become current that democracy is an unworkable or inappropriate system for developing countries, but the presumption would remain that it is the only form of government suitable for advanced and economically successful nations.

We would then have a kind of two-tier world, with the top tier consisting of a global democratic civilization and an integrated world economy, and the bottom tier occupied by backward, failed, or otherwise marginalized nations. In many ways this would be an ugly world to live in, and the plight of the bottom tier would have ramifications that could not be wholly and neatly sealed off and kept beyond the confines of the democratic countries. There would be problems of access to raw materials, illegal immigration, refugee flows, famine, terrorism, drug trafficking, and a host of other difficulties to contend with—many of which we are already facing. The problems would become even more acute if major economic or political breakdowns were to afflict such strategically located countries as Algeria or Mexico. Yet none of this by itself would pose a mortal threat to democratic hegemony.

Democracy's preeminence can be seriously challenged only by an ideology with universalist aspirations that proves capable of coming to power in an economically advanced or militarily powerful nation. Though there are no convincing signs of the emergence of such an ideology at this time, it is worth taking a brief look at the major alternatives often cited as competitors to democracy.

The first of these is nationalism, which is clearly enjoying a resurgence in many parts of the world, even as its influence appears to be waning elsewhere. Nationalism, however, is not a universalist ideology, but a category that embraces a myriad of particularisms. Serbian nationalism and Croatian nationalism may share many formal similarities, but the former will have no appeal to Croats and the latter no appeal to Serbs. Moreover, nationalism as such does not mandate any particular kind of political order. One can find Russian nationalists, for example, who are Communists, fascists, monarchists—or democrats. Nationalist passions may indeed threaten democracy in many specific circumstances, and ethnic strife can be a serious problem for established as well as new democracies. But in principle nationalism is by no means incompatible with democracy. In fact, as the case of the Baltic peoples makes clear, nationalist movements are often strongly democratic.

Turning next to religious doctrines, it is clear that radical or fundamentalist Islam is by far the most formidable competitor to democracy. Indeed, it is probably the most vital alternative to democracy to be found anywhere today. Only among Islamic peoples does opposition to dictatorial regimes frequently express itself in nondemocratic forms; in fact, in some Islamic countries free elections might well bring Islamicist rather than democratic oppositions to power. Yet it is doubtful that fundamentalist Islam can pose a serious global challenge to democracy.

Although Islam holds the allegiance of more than 800 million people who dominate a wide area stretching from West Africa to Southeast Asia, it does not appear to be attracting many adherents outside the Islamic world. Moreover, it is highly questionable whether Islamic fundamentalism can become the basis for economically or militarily successful regimes. When it burst upon the scene a little over a decade ago, the Ayatollah Khomeini's Iran seemed to have tremendous revolutionary élan. Yet it proved incapable of winning a bitter war against a much smaller neighbor, of exporting the revolution to other Islamic countries, or of running a modern economy. It now appears to be following more moderate policies that may help to improve the economy and to stabilize the regime, but it no longer seems to represent even the Islamic wave of the future.

Countries to Watch

Another possible competitor to democracy would be a reinvigorated communism, but the events of August 1991 in the Soviet Union show how unlikely it is that the remaining communist regimes can regain their former vitality. Particularly telling was the fact that the coup plotters made no reference at all to communism in justifying their actions. Even in China, whose octogenarian rulers remain committed communists, knowledgeable observers say that hardly anyone under the age of 40 still believes in Marxism-Leninism. Especially for an ideology oriented toward the future, the failure to attract the young is an unmistakable sign of decay. Communism today appears to be doomed to the fate that Moynihan foresaw for democracy in 1975: it is "a holdover form of government . . . which has simply no relevance to the future. It is where the world was, not where it is going."

The nature and the fate of the successor regimes in the Soviet Union and China will be of decisive importance for the future of democracy—not just because of their size and power but also because of the influence they can exert over Eastern Europe and East Asia respectively. If both these countries were successfully to follow the democratic path, the world might indeed approach Fukuyama's vision of an enduringly triumphant liberal democracy. But if they do not, they offer the most likely seedbeds for the birth of a new antidemocratic ideology.

Democrats have just gained the ascendancy in the Soviet Union, and the passing of Deng Xiaoping may open the way for a revival of the Chinese democratic movement that was so harshly repressed in Tiananmen Square. Yet there are also other important political currents and forces in both countries, including powerful military establishments. The emergence of a military-backed neoauthoritarian regime, possibly after a period of chaos or even civil war, may be as likely an outcome as a stable democracy in both Russia and China. Though a regime of this type might initially claim to be a temporary stop on the road toward democracy, it could easily wind up evolving in unpredictable and antidemocratic directions. And if such a regime were economically or militarily successful, it could quickly become an attractive model for other countries in its region and in the world.

Another possible source for a future alternative to liberal democracy may be Japan and the other noncommunist countries of East Asia. These countries have achieved spectacular economic progress through a synthesis of elements drawn from Confucian and other traditional influences, market economics, and democratic politics. The stability of democracy in Japan and the recent democratic openings in Korea and Taiwan could be taken as evidence of the triumph of liberal democracy in the region. Yet the political systems of these countries operate rather differently from those in the West. As Samuel P. Huntington has pointed out, "the East Asian dominant-party systems seem to involve competition for power but not alternation in power, and participation in elections for all, but participation in office only for those in the 'mainstream' party."[10]

It is not a foregone conclusion that the future will bring East Asia toward a greater convergence with Western-style liberal democracy; it might instead lead to an increased emphasis on those features that distinguish East Asian societies from the West. In that case, East Asia might gradually evolve a new ideology, which, given the extraordinary economic and technological dynamism of the region, could become extremely attractive to other nations as well.

Let us return, then, to the question with which we began: How long will the democratic moment last? I venture to predict that it will endure at least for the remainder of this century. Some recently established democracies will almost certainly fail during the coming decade, but other countries that are now under authoritarian or communist rule are likely to move toward democracy. Though it would be hazardous to forecast beyond that, the three key countries to watch in assessing the longer-term prospects for democracy in the world are Russia, China, and Japan.

There is one other key country, however, that has not yet been mentioned—the United States. If in 1980 a political analyst had sought to predict the future of communism on the basis of a survey of the international scene, he almost certainly would have gotten things very wrong; for he would have missed the most important factor—the largely hidden internal decay of the Soviet Union. This is certainly not meant to imply that the United States today is in an analogous situation. Yet as observers on all points of the U.S. political spectrum seem to agree, there are many reasons to worry about the political, economic, and cultural health of American democracy. A serious social or economic crisis in the United States would not only be terrible for Americans, it would have a devastating effect on the fortunes of democracy worldwide. Thus the highest priority for Americans must be to repair the fabric of our own democratic order.

That is not to advocate, however, that America "come home" and turn its back on its international responsibilities as the world's leading democracy. It is true that the energies and resources of the United States are not unlimited, but if properly directed, they are sufficient for both its domestic and international needs. There is no real conflict between improving democracy at home and supporting its spread and consolidation abroad. Just as the model provided by a healthy United States enhances the aspiration for democracy elsewhere, so the progress of the struggle for democracy around the world can give Americans renewed appreciation of the principles on which our country was founded and on which its future success depends.

NOTES

1. Daniel P. Moynihan, "The American Experiment," *The Public Interest* 41 (Fall 1975), 6.

2. Francis Fukuyama, "The End of History," *The National Interest* 16 (Summer 1989), 3-18.

3. Miklós Haraszti, "A Choice Between Resolution and Emotion," *East European Reporter*, Spring-Summer 1990, 76.

4. See Seymour Martin Lipset, "The Death of the Third Way," *The National Interest* 20 (Summer 1990), 25-37.

5. Milan Šimečka, "The Restoration of Freedom," *Journal of Democracy* 1 (Summer 1990): 3-12.

6. *Washington Post*, 31 March 1991, A23.

7. Interview with Václav Klaus, *NFF Update*, Winter 1991, 2.

8. Adam Smith, *The Wealth of Nations*, 2 vols. (Chicago: University of Chicago Press, 1976), 2:230.

9. Ken Jowitt, "The New World Disorder," *Journal of Democracy* 2 (Winter 1991): 11-20.

10. Samuel P. Huntington, "Democracy's Third Wave," *Journal of Democracy* 2 (Spring 1991): 27.

3.
WHAT DEMOCRACY IS
. . . AND IS NOT

Philippe C. Schmitter & Terry Lynn Karl

Philippe C. Schmitter *is professor of political science and director of the Center for European Studies at Stanford University.* **Terry Lynn Karl** *is associate professor of political science and director of the Center for Latin American Studies at the same institution. The original, longer version of this essay was written at the request of the United States Agency for International Development, which is not responsible for its content.*

For some time, the word democracy has been circulating as a debased currency in the political marketplace. Politicians with a wide range of convictions and practices strove to appropriate the label and attach it to their actions. Scholars, conversely, hesitated to use it—without adding qualifying adjectives—because of the ambiguity that surrounds it. The distinguished American political theorist Robert Dahl even tried to introduce a new term, "polyarchy," in its stead in the (vain) hope of gaining a greater measure of conceptual precision. But for better or worse, we are "stuck" with democracy as the catchword of contemporary political discourse. It is the word that resonates in people's minds and springs from their lips as they struggle for freedom and a better way of life; it is the word whose meaning we must discern if it is to be of any use in guiding political analysis and practice.

The wave of transitions away from autocratic rule that began with Portugal's "Revolution of the Carnations" in 1974 and seems to have crested with the collapse of communist regimes across Eastern Europe in 1989 has produced a welcome convergence towards a common definition of democracy.[1] Everywhere there has been a silent abandonment of dubious adjectives like "popular," "guided," "bourgeois," and "formal" to modify "democracy." At the same time, a remarkable consensus has emerged concerning the minimal conditions that polities must meet in order to merit the prestigious appellation of "democratic." Moreover, a number of international organizations now monitor how well these standards are met; indeed, some countries even consider them when formulating foreign policy.[2]

What Democracy Is

Let us begin by broadly defining democracy and the generic *concepts* that distinguish it as a unique system for organizing relations between rulers and the ruled. We will then briefly review *procedures*, the rules and arrangements that are needed if democracy is to endure. Finally, we will discuss two operative *principles* that make democracy work. They are not expressly included among the generic concepts or formal procedures, but the prospect for democracy is grim if their underlying conditioning effects are not present.

One of the major themes of this essay is that democracy does not consist of a single unique set of institutions. There are many types of democracy, and their diverse practices produce a similarly varied set of effects. The specific form democracy takes is contingent upon a country's socioeconomic conditions as well as its entrenched state structures and policy practices.

Modern political democracy is a system of governance in which rulers are held accountable for their actions in the public realm by citizens, acting indirectly through the competition and cooperation of their elected representatives.[3]

A *regime or system of governance* is an ensemble of patterns that determines the methods of access to the principal public offices; the characteristics of the actors admitted to or excluded from such access; the strategies that actors may use to gain access; and the rules that are followed in the making of publicly binding decisions. To work properly, the ensemble must be institutionalized—that is to say, the various patterns must be habitually known, practiced, and accepted by most, if not all, actors. Increasingly, the preferred mechanism of institutionalization is a written body of laws undergirded by a written constitution, though many enduring political norms can have an informal, prudential, or traditional basis.[4]

For the sake of economy and comparison, these forms, characteristics, and rules are usually bundled together and given a generic label. Democratic is one; others are autocratic, authoritarian, despotic, dictatorial, tyrannical, totalitarian, absolutist, traditional, monarchic, oligarchic, plutocratic, aristocratic, and sultanistic.[5] Each of these regime forms may in turn be broken down into subtypes.

Like all regimes, democracies depend upon the presence of *rulers*, persons who occupy specialized authority roles and can give legitimate commands to others. What distinguishes democratic rulers from nondemocratic ones are the norms that condition how the former come to power and the practices that hold them accountable for their actions.

The *public realm* encompasses the making of collective norms and choices that are binding on the society and backed by state coercion. Its content can vary a great deal across democracies, depending upon preexisting distinctions between the public and the private, state and society, legitimate coercion and voluntary exchange, and collective needs and individual preferences. The liberal conception of democracy advocates circumscribing the public realm as narrowly as possible, while the socialist or social-democratic approach would extend that realm through regulation, subsidization, and, in some cases, collective ownership of property. Neither is intrinsically more democratic than the other—just *differently* democratic. This implies that measures aimed at "developing the private sector" are no more democratic than those aimed at "developing the public sector." Both, if carried to extremes, could undermine the practice of democracy, the former by destroying the basis for satisfying collective needs and exercising legitimate authority; the latter by destroying the basis for satisfying individual preferences and controlling illegitimate government actions. Differences of opinion over the optimal mix of the two provide much of the substantive content of political conflict within established democracies.

Citizens are the most distinctive element in democracies. All regimes have rulers and a public realm, but only to the extent that they are democratic do they have citizens. Historically, severe restrictions on citizenship were imposed in most emerging or partial democracies according to criteria of age, gender, class, race, literacy, property ownership, tax-paying status, and so on. Only a small part of the total population was eligible to vote or run for office. Only restricted social categories were allowed to form, join, or support political associations. After protracted struggle—in some cases involving violent domestic upheaval or international war—most of these restrictions were lifted. Today, the criteria for inclusion are fairly standard. All native-born adults are eligible, although somewhat higher age limits may still be imposed upon candidates for certain offices. Unlike the early American and European democracies of the nineteenth century, none of the recent democracies in southern Europe, Latin America, Asia, or Eastern Europe has even attempted to impose formal restrictions on the franchise or eligibility to office. When it comes to informal restrictions on the effective exercise of citizenship rights, however, the story can be quite different. This explains the central importance (discussed below) of procedures.

Competition has not always been considered an essential defining condition of democracy. "Classic" democracies presumed decision making based on direct participation leading to consensus. The assembled citizenry was expected to agree on a common course of action after listening to the alternatives and weighing their respective merits and demerits. A tradition of hostility to "faction," and "particular interests" persists in democratic thought, but at least since *The Federalist Papers* it has become widely accepted that competition among factions is a necessary evil in democracies that operate on a more-than-local scale. Since, as James Madison argued, "the latent causes of faction are sown into the nature of man," and the possible remedies for "the mischief of faction" are worse than the disease, the best course is to recognize them and to attempt to control their effects.[6] Yet while democrats may agree on the inevitability of factions, they tend to disagree about the best forms and rules for governing factional competition. Indeed, differences over the preferred modes and boundaries of competition contribute most to distinguishing one subtype of democracy from another.

> *"However central to democracy, elections occur intermittently and only allow citizens to choose between the highly aggregated alternatives offered by political parties..."*

The most popular definition of democracy equates it with regular *elections*, fairly conducted and honestly counted. Some even consider the mere fact of elections—even ones from which specific parties or candidates are excluded, or in which substantial portions of the population cannot freely participate—as a sufficient condition for the existence of democracy. This fallacy has been called "electoralism" or "the faith that merely holding elections will channel political action into peaceful contests among elites and accord public legitimacy to the winners"—no matter how they are conducted or what else constrains those who win them.[7] However central to democracy, elections occur intermittently and only allow citizens to choose between the highly aggregated alternatives offered by political parties, which can, especially in the early stages of a democratic transition, proliferate in a bewildering variety. During the intervals between elections, citizens can seek to influence public policy through a wide variety of other intermediaries: interest associations, social movements, locality groupings, clientelistic arrangements, and so forth. *Modern democracy, in other words, offers a variety of competitive processes and channels for the expression of interests and values—associational as well as partisan, functional as well as territorial, collective as well as individual. All are integral to its practice.*

Another commonly accepted image of democracy identifies it with *majority rule*. Any governing body that makes decisions by combining the votes of more than half of those eligible and present is said to be democratic, whether that majority emerges within an electorate, a parliament, a committee, a city council, or a party caucus. For exceptional purposes (e.g., amending the constitution or expelling a member), "qualified majorities" of more than 50 percent may be required, but few would deny that democracy must involve some means of aggregating the equal preferences of individuals.

A problem arises, however, when *numbers* meet *intensities*. What happens when a properly assembled majority (especially a stable, self-perpetuating one) regularly makes decisions that harm some minority (especially a threatened cultural or ethnic group)? In these circumstances, successful democracies tend to qualify the central principle of majority rule in order to protect minority rights. Such qualifications can take the form of constitutional provisions that place certain matters beyond the reach of majorities (bills of rights); requirements for concurrent majorities in several different constituencies (confederalism); guarantees securing the autonomy of local or regional governments against the demands of the central authority (federalism); grand coalition governments that incorporate all parties (consociationalism); or the negotiation of social pacts between major social groups like business and labor (neocorporatism). The most common and effective way of protecting minorities, however, lies in the everyday operation of interest associations and social movements. These reflect (some would say, amplify) the different intensities of preference that exist in the population and bring them to bear on democratically elected decision makers. Another way of putting this intrinsic tension between numbers and intensities would be to say that "in modern democracies, votes may be counted, but influences alone are weighted."

Cooperation has always been a central feature of democracy. Actors must voluntarily make collective decisions binding on the polity as a whole. They must cooperate in order to compete. They must be capable of acting collectively through parties, associations, and movements in order to select candidates, articulate preferences, petition authorities, and influence policies.

But democracy's freedoms should also encourage citizens to deliberate among themselves, to discover their common needs, and to resolve their differences without relying on some supreme central authority. Classical democracy emphasized these qualities, and they are by no means extinct, despite repeated efforts by contemporary theorists to stress the analogy with behavior in the economic marketplace and to reduce all of democracy's operations to competitive interest maximization. Alexis de Tocqueville best described the importance of independent groups for democracy in his *Democracy in America*, a work which remains a major source of inspiration for all those who persist in viewing democracy as something more than a struggle for election and re-election among competing candidates.[8]

In contemporary political discourse, this phenomenon of cooperation and deliberation via autonomous group activity goes under the rubric of "civil society." The diverse units of social identity and interest, by remaining independent of the state (and perhaps even of parties), not only can restrain the arbitrary actions of rulers, but can also contribute to forming better citizens who are more aware of the preferences of others, more self-confident in their actions, and more civic-minded in their willingness to sacrifice for the common good. At its best, civil society provides an intermediate layer of governance between the individual and the state that is capable of resolving conflicts and controlling the behavior of members without public coercion. Rather than overloading decision makers with increased demands and making the system ungovernable,[9] a viable civil society can mitigate conflicts and improve the quality of citizenship—without relying exclusively on the privatism of the marketplace.

Representatives—whether directly or indirectly elected—do most of the real work in modern democracies. Most are professional politicians who orient their careers around the desire to fill key offices. It is doubtful that any democracy could survive without such people. The central question, therefore, is not whether or not there will be a political elite or even a professional political class, but how these representatives are chosen and then held accountable for their actions.

As noted above, there are many channels of representation in modern democracy. The electoral one, based on territorial constituencies, is the most visible and public. It culminates in a parliament or a presidency that is periodically accountable to the citizenry as a whole. Yet the sheer growth of government (in large part as a byproduct of popular demand) has increased the number, variety, and power of agencies charged with making public decisions and not subject to elections. Around these agencies there has developed a vast apparatus of specialized representation based largely on functional interests, not territorial constituencies. These interest associations, and not political parties, have become the primary expression of civil society in most stable democracies, supplemented by the more sporadic interventions of social movements.

The new and fragile democracies that have sprung up since 1974 must live in "compressed time." They will not resemble the European democracies of the nineteenth and early twentieth centuries, and they cannot expect to acquire the multiple channels of representation in gradual historical progression as did most of their predecessors. A bewildering array of parties, interests, and movements will all simultaneously seek political influence in them, creating challenges to the polity that did not exist in earlier processes of democratization.

Procedures that Make Democracy Possible

The defining components of democracy are necessarily abstract, and may give rise to a considerable variety of institutions and subtypes of democracy. For democracy to thrive, however, specific procedural norms must be followed and civic rights must be respected. Any polity that fails to impose such restrictions upon itself, that fails to follow the "rule of law" with regard to its own procedures, should not be considered democratic. These procedures alone do not define democracy, but their presence is indispensable to its persistence. In essence, they are necessary but not sufficient conditions for its existence.

Robert Dahl has offered the most generally accepted listing of what he terms the "procedural minimal" conditions that must be present for modern political democracy (or as he puts it, "polyarchy") to exist:

1) Control over government decisions about policy is constitutionally vested in elected officials.

2) Elected officials are chosen in frequent and fairly conducted elections in which coercion is comparatively uncommon.

3) Practically all adults have the right to vote in the election of officials.

4) Practically all adults have the right to run for elective offices in the government. . . .

5) Citizens have a right to express themselves without the danger of severe punishment on political matters broadly defined. . . .

6) Citizens have a right to seek out alternative sources of information. Moreover, alternative sources of information exist and are protected by law.

7) . . . Citizens also have the right to form relatively independent associations or organizations, including independent political parties and interest groups.[10]

These seven conditions seem to capture the essence of procedural democracy for many theorists, but we propose to add two others. The first might be thought of as a further refinement of item (1), while the second might be called an implicit prior condition to all seven of the above.

8) Popularly elected officials must be able to exercise their constitutional powers without being subjected to overriding (albeit informal) opposition from unelected officials. Democracy is in jeopardy if military officers, entrenched civil servants, or state managers retain the capacity to act independently of elected civilians or even veto decisions made by the people's representatives. Without this additional caveat, the militarized polities of contemporary Central America, where civilian control over the military does not exist, might be classified by many scholars as democracies, just as they have been (with the exception of Sandinista Nicaragua) by U.S. policy makers. The caveat thus guards against what we earlier called "electoralism"—the tendency to focus on the holding of elections while ignoring other political realities.

9) The polity must be self-governing; it must be able to act independently of constraints imposed by some other overarching political system. Dahl and other contemporary democratic theorists probably took

this condition for granted since they referred to formally sovereign nation-states. However, with the development of blocs, alliances, spheres of influence, and a variety of "neocolonial" arrangements, the question of autonomy has been a salient one. Is a system really democratic if its elected officials are unable to make binding decisions without the approval of actors outside their territorial domain? This is significant even if the outsiders are themselves democratically constituted and if the insiders are relatively free to alter or even end the encompassing arrangement (as in Puerto Rico), but it becomes especially critical if neither condition obtains (as in the Baltic states).

Principles that Make Democracy Feasible

Lists of component processes and procedural norms help us to specify what democracy is, but they do not tell us much about how it actually functions. The simplest answer is "by the consent of the people"; the more complex one is "by the contingent consent of politicians acting under conditions of bounded uncertainty."

In a democracy, representatives must at least informally agree that those who win greater electoral support or influence over policy will not use their temporary superiority to bar the losers from taking office or exerting influence in the future, and that in exchange for this opportunity to keep competing for power and place, momentary losers will respect the winners' right to make binding decisions. Citizens are expected to obey the decisions ensuing from such a process of competition, provided its outcome remains contingent upon their collective preferences as expressed through fair and regular elections or open and repeated negotiations.

The challenge is not so much to find a set of goals that command widespread consensus as to find a set of rules that embody contingent consent. The precise shape of this "democratic bargain," to use Dahl's expression,[11] can vary a good deal from society to society. It depends on social cleavages and such subjective factors as mutual trust, the standard of fairness, and the willingness to compromise. It may even be compatible with a great deal of dissensus on substantive policy issues.

All democracies involve a degree of uncertainty about who will be elected and what policies they will pursue. Even in those polities where one party persists in winning elections or one policy is consistently implemented, the possibility of change through independent collective action still exists, as in Italy, Japan, and the Scandinavian social democracies. If it does not, the system is not democratic, as in Mexico, Senegal, or Indonesia.

But the uncertainty embedded in the core of all democracies is bounded. Not just any actor can get into the competition and raise any issue he or she pleases—there are previously established rules that must be respected. Not just any policy can be adopted—there are conditions that must be met. Democracy institutionalizes "normal," limited political uncertainty. These boundaries vary from country to country. Constitutional guarantees of property, privacy, expression, and other rights are a part of this, but the most effective boundaries are generated by competition among interest groups and cooperation within civil society. Whatever the rhetoric (and some polities appear to offer their citizens more dramatic alternatives than others), once the rules of contingent consent have been agreed upon, the actual variation is likely to stay within a predictable and generally accepted range.

This emphasis on operative guidelines contrasts with a highly persistent, but misleading theme in recent literature on democracy—namely, the emphasis upon "civic culture." The principles we have suggested here rest on rules of prudence, not on deeply ingrained habits of tolerance, moderation, mutual respect, fair play, readiness to compromise, or trust in public authorities. Waiting for such habits to sink deep and lasting roots implies a very slow process of regime consolidation—one that takes generations—and it would probably condemn most contemporary experiences *ex hypothesi* to failure. Our assertion is that contingent consent and bounded uncertainty can emerge from the interaction between antagonistic and mutually suspicious actors and that the far more benevolent and ingrained norms of a civic culture are better thought of as a *product* and not a producer of democracy.

How Democracies Differ

Several concepts have been deliberately excluded from our generic definition of democracy, despite the fact that they have been frequently associated with it in both everyday practice and scholarly work. They are, nevertheless, especially important when it comes to distinguishing subtypes of democracy. Since no single set of actual institutions, practices, or values embodies democracy, polities moving away from authoritarian rule can mix different components to produce different democracies. It is important to recognize that these do not define points along a single continuum of improving performance, but a matrix of potential combinations that are *differently* democratic.

1) *Consensus*: All citizens may not agree on the substantive goals of political action or on the role of the state (although if they did, it would certainly make governing democracies much easier).

2) *Participation*: All citizens may not take an active and equal part in politics, although it must be legally possible for them to do so.

3) *Access*: Rulers may not weigh equally the preferences of all who come before them, although citizenship implies that individuals and groups should have an equal opportunity to express their preferences if they choose to do so.

4) *Responsiveness*: Rulers may not always follow the course of action preferred by the citizenry. But when they deviate from such a policy, say on grounds of "reason of state" or "overriding national interest," they must ultimately be held accountable for their actions through regular and fair processes.

5) *Majority rule*: Positions may not be allocated or rules may not be decided solely on the basis of assembling the most votes, although deviations from this principle usually must be explicitly defended and previously approved.

6) *Parliamentary sovereignty*: The legislature may not be the only body that can make rules or even the one with final authority in deciding which laws are binding, although where executive, judicial, or other public bodies make that ultimate choice, they too must be accountable for their actions.

7) *Party government*: Rulers may not be nominated, promoted, and disciplined in their activities by well-organized and programmatically coherent political parties, although where they are not, it may prove more difficult to form an effective government.

8) *Pluralism*: The political process may not be based on a multiplicity of overlapping, voluntaristic, and autonomous private groups. However, where there are monopolies of representation, hierarchies of association, and obligatory memberships, it is likely that the interests involved will be more closely linked to the state and the separation between the public and private spheres of action will be much less distinct.

9) *Federalism*: The territorial division of authority may not involve multiple levels and local autonomies, least of all ones enshrined in a constitutional document, although some dispersal of power across territorial and/or functional units is characteristic of all democracies.

10) *Presidentialism*: The chief executive officer may not be a single person and he or she may not be directly elected by the citizenry as a whole, although some concentration of authority is present in all democracies, even if it is exercised collectively and only held indirectly accountable to the electorate.

11) *Checks and Balances*: It is not necessary that the different branches of government be systematically pitted against one another, although governments by assembly, by executive concentration, by judicial command, or even by dictatorial fiat (as in time of war) must be ultimately accountable to the citizenry as a whole.

While each of the above has been named as an essential component of democracy, they should instead be seen either as indicators of this or that type of democracy, or else as useful standards for evaluating the performance of particular regimes. To include them as part of the generic definition of democracy itself would be to mistake the American polity for the universal model of democratic governance. Indeed, the parliamentary, consociational, unitary, corporatist, and concentrated arrangements of continental Europe may have some unique virtues for guiding polities through the uncertain transition from autocratic to democratic rule.[12]

What Democracy Is Not

We have attempted to convey the general meaning of modern democracy without identifying it with some particular set of rules and institutions or restricting it to some specific culture or level of development. We have also argued that it cannot be reduced to the regular holding of elections or equated with a particular notion of the role of the state, but we have not said much more about what democracy is not or about what democracy may not be capable of producing.

There is an understandable temptation to load too many expectations on this concept and to imagine that by attaining democracy, a society will have resolved all of its political, social, economic, administrative, and cultural problems. Unfortunately, "all good things do not necessarily go together."

First, democracies are not necessarily more efficient economically than other forms of government. Their rates of aggregate growth, savings, and investment may be no better than those of nondemocracies. This is especially likely during the transition, when propertied groups and administrative elites may respond to real or imagined threats to the "rights" they enjoyed under authoritarian rule by initiating capital flight, disinvestment, or sabotage. In time, depending upon the type of democracy, benevolent long-term effects upon income distribution, aggregate demand, education, productivity, and creativity may eventually combine to improve economic and social performance, but it is certainly too much to expect that these improvements will occur immediately—much less that they will be defining characteristics of democratization.

Second, democracies are not necessarily more efficient administratively. Their capacity to make decisions may even be slower than that of the regimes they replace, if only because more actors must be consulted. The costs of getting things done may be higher, if only because "payoffs" have to be made to a wider and more resourceful set of clients (although one should never underestimate the degree of corruption to be found within autocracies). Popular satisfaction with the new democratic government's performance may not even seem greater, if only because necessary compromises often please no one completely, and because the losers are free to complain.

Third, democracies are not likely to appear more orderly, consensual, stable, or governable than the autocracies they replace. This is partly a byproduct of democratic freedom of expression, but it is also a reflection of the likelihood of continuing disagreement over new rules and institutions. These products of imposition or compromise are often initially quite ambiguous in nature and uncertain in effect until actors have learned how to use them. What is more, they come in the aftermath of serious struggles motivated by high ideals. Groups and individuals with recently acquired autonomy will test certain rules, protest against the actions of certain institutions, and insist on renegotiating their part of the bargain. Thus the presence of antisystem parties should be neither surprising nor seen as a failure of democratic consolidation. What counts is whether such parties are willing, however reluctantly, to play by the general rules of bounded uncertainty and contingent consent.

"...democracies will have more open societies and polities than the autocracies they replace, but not necessarily more open economies."

Governability is a challenge for all regimes, not just democratic ones. Given the political exhaustion and loss of legitimacy that have befallen autocracies from sultanistic Paraguay to totalitarian Albania, it may seem that only democracies can now be expected to govern effectively and legitimately. Experience has shown, however, that democracies too can lose the ability to govern. Mass publics can become disenchanted with their performance. Even more threatening is the temptation for leaders to fiddle with procedures and ultimately undermine the principles of contingent consent and bounded uncertainty. Perhaps the most critical moment comes once the politicians begin to settle into the more predictable roles and relations of a consolidated democracy. Many will find their expectations frustrated; some will discover that the new rules of competition put them at a disadvantage; a few may even feel that their vital interests are threatened by popular majorities.

Finally, democracies will have more open societies and polities than the autocracies they replace, but not necessarily more open economies. Many of today's most successful and well-established democracies have historically resorted to protectionism and closed borders, and have relied extensively upon public institutions to promote economic development. While the long-term compatibility between democracy and capitalism does not seem to be in doubt, despite their continuous tension, it is not clear whether the promotion of such liberal economic goals as the right of individuals to own property and retain profits, the clearing function of markets, the private settlement of disputes, the freedom to produce without government regulation, or the privatization of state-owned enterprises necessarily furthers the consolidation of democracy. After all, democracies do need to levy taxes and regulate certain transactions, especially where private monopolies and oligopolies exist. Citizens or their representatives may decide that it is desirable to protect the rights of collectivities from encroachment by individuals, especially propertied ones, and they may choose to set aside certain forms of property for public or cooperative ownership. In short, notions of economic liberty that are currently put forward in neoliberal economic models are not synonymous with political freedom—and may even impede it.

Democratization will not necessarily bring in its wake economic growth, social peace, administrative efficiency, political harmony, free markets, or "the end of ideology." Least of all will it bring about "the end of history." No doubt some of these qualities could make the consolidation of democracy easier, but they are neither prerequisites for it nor immediate products of it. Instead, what we should be hoping for is the emergence of political institutions that can peacefully compete to form governments and influence public policy, that can channel social and economic conflicts through regular procedures, and that have sufficient linkages to civil society to represent their constituencies and commit them to collective courses of action. Some types of democracies, especially in developing countries, have been unable to fulfill this promise, perhaps due to the circumstances of their transition from authoritarian rule.[13] The democratic wager is that such a regime, once established, will not only persist by reproducing itself within its initial confining conditions, but will eventually expand beyond them.[14] Unlike authoritarian regimes, democracies have the capacity to modify their rules and institutions consensually in response to changing circumstances. They may not immediately produce all the goods mentioned above, but they stand a better chance of eventually doing so than do autocracies.

NOTES

1. For a comparative analysis of the recent regime changes in southern Europe and Latin America, see Guillermo O'Donnell, Philippe C. Schmitter, and Laurence Whitehead, eds., *Transitions from Authoritarian Rule*, 4 vols. (Baltimore: Johns Hopkins University Press, 1986). For another compilation that adopts a more structural approach see Larry Diamond, Juan Linz, and Seymour Martin Lipset, eds., *Democracy in Developing Countries*, vols. 2, 3, and 4 (Boulder, Colo.: Lynne Rienner, 1989).

2. Numerous attempts have been made to codify and quantify the existence of democracy across political systems. The best known is probably Freedom House's *Freedom in the World: Political Rights and Civil Liberties*, published since 1973 by Greenwood Press and since 1988 by University Press of America. Also see Charles Humana, *World Human Rights Guide* (New York: Facts on File, 1986).

3. The definition most commonly used by American social scientists is that of Joseph Schumpeter: "that institutional arrangement for arriving at political decisions in which individuals acquire the power to decide by means of a competitive struggle for the people's vote." *Capitalism, Socialism and Democracy* (London: George Allen and Unwin, 1943), 269. We accept certain aspects of the classical procedural approach to modern democracy, but differ primarily in our emphasis on the accountability of rulers to citizens and the relevance of mechanisms of competition other than elections.

4. Not only do some countries practice a stable form of democracy without a formal constitution (e.g., Great Britain and Israel), but even more countries have constitutions and

legal codes that offer no guarantee of reliable practice. On paper, Stalin's 1936 constitution for the USSR was a virtual model of democratic rights and entitlements.

5. For the most valiant attempt to make some sense out of this thicket of distinctions, see Juan Linz, "Totalitarian and Authoritarian Regimes" in *Handbook of Political Science*, eds. Fred I. Greenstein and Nelson W. Polsby (Reading, Mass.: Addision Wesley, 1975), 175-411.

6. "Publius" (Alexander Hamilton, John Jay, and James Madison), *The Federalist Papers* (New York: Anchor Books, 1961). The quote is from Number 10.

7. See Terry Karl, "Imposing Consent? Electoralism versus Democratization in El Salvador," in *Elections and Democratization in Latin America, 1980-1985*, eds. Paul Drake and Eduardo Silva (San Diego: Center for Iberian and Latin American Studies, Center for US/Mexican Studies, University of California, San Diego, 1986), 9-36.

8. Alexis de Tocqueville, *Democracy in America*, 2 vols. (New York: Vintage Books, 1945).

9. This fear of overloaded government and the imminent collapse of democracy is well reflected in the work of Samuel P. Huntington during the 1970s. See especially Michel Crozier, Samuel P. Huntington, and Joji Watanuki, *The Crisis of Democracy* (New York: New York University Press, 1975). For Huntington's (revised) thoughts about the prospects for democracy, see his "Will More Countries Become Democratic?," *Political Science Quarterly* 99 (Summer 1984): 193-218.

10. Robert Dahl, *Dilemmas of Pluralist Democracy* (New Haven: Yale University Press, 1982), 11.

11. Robert Dahl, *After the Revolution: Authority in a Good Society* (New Haven: Yale University Press, 1970).

12. See Juan Linz, "The Perils of Presidentialism," *Journal of Democracy* 1 (Winter 1990): 51-69, and the ensuing discussion by Donald Horowitz, Seymour Martin Lipset, and Juan Linz in *Journal of Democracy* 1 (Fall 1990): 73-91.

13. Terry Lynn Karl, "Dilemmas of Democratization in Latin America," *Comparative Politics* 23 (October 1990): 1-23.

14. Otto Kirchheimer, "Confining Conditions and Revolutionary Breakthroughs," *American Political Science Review* 59 (1965): 964-974.

4.
PRESENT
AT THE TRANSITION

Julio María Sanguinetti

*As president of Uruguay from 1985 to 1990, **Julio María Sanguinetti** played a critical role in guiding his country back to democratic rule after 12 years of military government. A lawyer, journalist, and avid soccer fan, President Sanguinetti is a leader of the Colorado Party and a likely candidate in the 1994 presidential race. He is currently the president of the PAX Institute of Uruguay. The following remarks are taken from his keynote address to the International Workshop on Democratic Governability in Latin America, organized by the Center for Latin American Studies at Georgetown University on 8-9 October 1990 with the support of the Tinker Foundation.*

Not long ago we marked the two hundredth anniversary of the French Revolution, and we are about to celebrate the five hundredth anniversary of the discovery of the Americas, our New World and unfinished adventure. These celebrations seem to be coinciding with the death of the postwar world and the birth of a new era.

Consider all the momentous changes that are now taking place: the progress of European unity; the surmounting of the East-West conflict and the easing of Soviet-American tensions; the waning of the East-East conflict as both China and the Soviet Union become preoccupied with internal problems and reforms and find that they no longer have the energy to be rivals. And there is also, of course, the democratization of Eastern Europe and Latin America. These are all, without a doubt, historic developments; they all combine to show us a different picture of the world. We might say that the twentieth century is now essentially completed and that these events, which undoubtedly define a new historical era, are the dawn of the twenty-first.

This is the broader context in which we must view the decade of democratic transitions that has brought such rapid and surprising changes to Latin America. In the early 1980s, three different roads carried Argentina, Brazil, and Uruguay toward democracy. In Argentina the debacle of the Malvinas War led directly to the breakup of the military regime; the democratic opening arrived suddenly without the ground first being prepared by a process of negotiations. In Uruguay, by contrast, there were four years of negotiations, beginning with the plebiscite proposed by the military government in 1980 and ending with national elections in 1984. In Brazil, democracy came by way of an indirect democratic election, the groundwork for which had been laid by the military government as part of its plan for a gradual transition back to civilian rule. Adroit political maneuvering permitted opposition leader Tancredo Neves to team up with parliamentary leader José Sarney to pave the way for democracy's return.

The economic paths of Argentina, Brazil, and Uruguay have been as disparate as their roads to democracy. Brazil enjoyed very strong, export-led growth, but its economy was unstable and finally succumbed to hyperinflation. The Argentine economy lacked Brazil's dynamism, but it too fell into hyperinflation at the same time as Brazil. In Uruguay we managed to get our economy growing again and inflation never got out of control, despite the influence that our two big neighbors, Argentina and Brazil, have on a smaller economy like ours.

The situation regarding the military in each country has been different as well. Brazil's armed forces have been fairly placid, and there were no explosive questions concerning possible legal claims against the military services or their personnel for misconduct during the period of military rule. The Uruguayan military showed proper deference to civilian authority throughout the five-year-long democratic transition (1985-1989). The military remained quiescent as civilian supremacy was reasserted in part because this reassertion took place within a climate of free debate and peaceful discussion that ultimately reached a resolution through popular elections. Argentina's military, by contrast, was very turbulent. Along with economic upheaval, Argentina suffered constant military agitation throughout this whole period. The beleaguered government of President Raúl Alfonsín had scarcely a day of peace while it struggled to preserve democratic institutions, and finally had to hand over power to Carlos Menem ahead of schedule.

The most recent transitions—those in Chile, Nicaragua, and Paraguay in 1989 and 1990—differ both from the earlier transitions and from one another. Chile's free elections were the result of a more or less negotiated evolution within the regime. Nicaragua also had a relatively free election after negotiations; the result there was, paradoxically, both analogous in form to that in Chile, and at the opposite ideological remove from it. In both countries the forces of the old and new regimes presently coexist, and civilian presidents must govern with military commanders-in-chief who are representatives of the old regime and its still very active and numerous partisans.

Paraguay experienced a surprising internal coup against the 30-year-old military dictatorship of General Alfredo Stroessner. General Andrés Rodríguez, the coup's leader, seemed likely to extend military rule but defied expectations by engineering a political opening and a possible transition to full-fledged democracy. (To these three transitions may soon be added that of Haiti. The first independent black republic in the world and the second independent republic in the Americas, this unfortunate land has never yet, in 186 years of independent existence, succeeded in establishing democracy.)

Like Argentina, Uruguay, and Brazil before them, Chile, Nicaragua, and Paraguay also face widely varying economic outlooks as their democratic transitions proceed. Chile inherits a strong fiscal position and vigorous growth led by exports. Chile still has unmet social needs, but also displays an economic dynamism unparalleled on the continent. Nicaragua's outlook, on the other hand, is grim on all fronts. Inflation is high, growth is virtually nonexistent, and the social situation is explosive. Paraguay is somewhere in between, with an air of stability typical of an economy that is opening up as it follows the path to modernization.

The Uruguayan Experience

Having suggested some ways in which to characterize and classify the variety of transitions that have taken place throughout Latin America, I now want to focus more directly on the case of Uruguay. My reflections on my own country are shaped not by any particular methodological approach, but by my actual experiences in living through and helping to direct a democratic transition. I cannot offer clear-cut lessons, because experiences are not transferable, but there may be some value in the conclusions drawn by someone who has viewed a transition from the inside.

Let us consider first the psychological element. A transition requires the constant management of two emotions: fear and impatience. Transition periods create expectations. The rebirth of liberty can unleash new or long-dormant forces, all of which generate very strong emotions. The deposed leaders fear that they may become targets of retaliation; in the case of a military dictatorship, they may fear that the military as an institution will itself come under assault.

At the same time, there is the impatience of those who have come to power. The fledgling democracy wants to spread its wings and show off all its plumage. Recently acquired rights all at once seek an outlet and an occasion to be exercised. Liberty is not just enjoyed, it is shouted. The management of emotions—the fear of some, the impatience of others—is essential if we are to push forward the effort to restore order and direction to the segments of society that are most unsettled by the experience of democratic transition.

The quelling of what I call "now-ism" is also a major psychological task. During times of transition, there is a tendency for all claims to become urgent. I remember Brazilians' cries of "Direct elections, NOW!"; and in my own country, "General and unlimited amnesty, NOW!" "Now-ism" is quite understandable, of course, but the energy it signals must be harnessed if a lapse into conflict and revenge is to be avoided. In addition, nostalgia must not be allowed to fester, but must be transformed into hope and thus be able to bar the way to intolerance and the spirit of retaliation.

"In our countries, no one becomes famous for his economic policies, but he can certainly perish because of them."

Peace in transitions is not mere abstention from war. Peace cannot be simply the supervention of old conflict, because the old conflict remains. Those who have previously had confrontations must learn to live together as members of the same society. Peace must be transformed into a value in its own right if we are to build a stable democracy. The key is inclusion. As the seventeenth-century Spanish liberal thinker Don Mateo de López Bravo reminds us: "From all those who are excluded, enemies are made." Everyone must somehow be made to feel like a part of the new democratic process; no one must be denied the right to speak out, to compete politically, and to have influence.

The peace "project" requires precisely that even those who are locked in heated debate should think of themselves as collaborators in the same project, even as they are questioning it. We achieved this in Uruguay as we argued about what kind of transition we would have. Our goal was that there be no excluded sector outside the democratic process pelting it with stones.

Another key factor in transitions is economics. In our countries, no one becomes famous for his economic policies, but he can certainly perish because of them. Latin America has never been an economic success. We paint the best pictures, we write the best novels, but we still do not have a clear understanding of our budget deficits. We are beginning to improve in this regard, but our culture is still inhospitable to economic thinking.

When our democratically elected government took power, Uruguay had sagging economic growth and employment, mounting inflation, and low wages and exports. We needed to make an adjustment in order to bring our macroeconomic indicators back into balance. Faced with the choice of an adjustment aimed primarily at taming inflation or at boosting growth, we chose the latter. This signaled our rejection of orthodox adjustment programs of the sort favored by the International Monetary Fund, which seek to stabilize inflation even at the expense of economic activity. (Lately, however, the IMF's attitude has become more flexible.) It seemed to us that growth had to be our priority in order to avoid jeopardizing the entire transition process. If the country's economy did not grow and unemployment continued to rise, we would find ourselves with an unmanageable social situation with ominous political implications.

The divisions that we posit between politics, economics, sociology, and law are less a reflection of reality than a consequence of our own intellectual limitations. We lack a method for assimilating all of the facts at once, so we must segment them. When someone goes into a store and buys a pair of pants, a lawyer sees a purchase agreement, an economist a demand phenomenon, and a sociologist a fashion statement. Nevertheless, it is the same pair of pants. An economic phenomenon can also have a great political impact, one that may destabilize the whole democratic process.

For example, Chile's new democratic government inherited a certain prosperity. Now it must manage the tensions raised by deferred social claims, but without weakening the economy, because a fall in growth could put democracy at risk. Uruguay's democrats, on the other hand, inherited a situation of economic decline that had to be reversed. Fortunately, our adjustment program was successful—in five years we grew by 16 percent; lowered our unemployment rate from over 14 percent to about 8 percent; increased our exports by 60 percent; and boosted real wages by 30 percent.

Another significant element is the mechanics of the transition process itself. In Uruguay there was a gradual transition through negotiations, which was very important. Why? Because the dialogue between the political and military leaders permitted us to get to know each other. The politicians learned to understand military reasoning, and the military learned to negotiate and compromise. From 1980 to 1984 we talked, argued, left the negotiating table, returned again, and finally agreed to hold elections. This was a very significant asset for us in our transition process, one which was lacking in countries like Argentina, where democracy was restored with no period of debate or negotiation.

National democratic traditions also influence transitions. Constructing a democracy is not the same as reconstructing one. Chile and Uruguay are old democracies with a history of stability and only occasional authoritarian interruptions. The people have a democratic culture. In Nicaragua, however, it is not a question of reviving traditions or revitalizing institutions. In order to establish democracy, they must form democrats, which is more a cultural than a political task.

Then, there is the issue of legitimacy. The people must view the transition as legitimate. Indeed, legitimacy is a crucial consideration for every government. I do not know of any dictator who has said, "I am illegitimate." No! He has searched for his own legitimacy. Even Napoleon strove to legitimize himself by holding several referendums and coercing the Pope into presiding at an imperial coronation ceremony (at which Napoleon wound up placing the crown on his own head). A democratic government, especially, wants not only its own people but the whole world to perceive it as legitimate.

In Uruguay this legitimacy was fully attained only after four popular votes in the space of nine years. The military government proposed a constitutional reform in 1980, only to have it rejected in a plebiscite. Dialogue was soon resumed, but the military insisted that the old political leaders could not be regarded as legitimate party representatives. In 1982, therefore, the political parties simultaneously held internal elections in which voters chose party representatives to discuss the terms of the transition with the military government.

> *"From a political standpoint... the transition cannot be considered complete as long as the problems associated with the previous regime remain unresolved."*

National elections for a new government took place two years later. Of course, there were imperfections in these elections: some significant party leaders were proscribed, and the Communist Party, unable to participate under its own name, called itself Advanced Democracy. Still, all the parties participated; the people chose a Parliament, I was elected president, and a democratic era was ushered in.

Yet the legacy of the past is not so easily overcome. A transition, after all, is a passage from one situation to another. A constitutional lawyer might consider the transition as taking place at a single point in time—the moment when a de facto government is replaced by a democratically elected one. From a political standpoint, however, the transition cannot be considered complete as long as the problems associated with the previous regime remain unresolved.

Soon after the 1984 election there arose a debate over the issue of amnesty. In 1985 Parliament granted amnesty not only to political prisoners and to those detained without trial, but also to those who were prosecuted for committing outrages against democracy prior to 1973, the Tupamaro guerrillas. I was not a supporter of general amnesty at the time; I favored a restricted amnesty instead. When Parliament voted overwhelmingly for general amnesty, however, I thought the matter through again and realized that vetoing the law would make a significant group of people feel excluded, and that it was ultimately better to concede the point.

Later, the explosive subject of human rights charges against the military came up. The threat of violence—perhaps from a fearful military, perhaps from its most vociferous opponents—was in the air. I proposed to extend the general amnesty to the military. After a long period of negotiation the Parliament, by a significant majority, passed a law granting amnesty to the military. Opposition forces marshalled enough support to force a referendum on the issue by acquiring the signatures of 10 percent of the citizens of Uruguay. In April 1989, we held a referendum on amnesty for the military, and the country voted in favor of it. This act of reconciliation, I believe, completed the transition process in Uruguay. We can sum up this chapter of Uruguayan history by drawing its most important lesson—that the ballot box is the most powerful source of legitimacy.

Finally, I want to touch upon the ethical aspects of transitions. When an institutional collapse occurs, profound moral issues come into play. It is not just a question of individual moral behavior. Also at stake is the enormous ethical value of establishing democratic institutions, preserving liberty, and affirming peace. Max Weber said that "in all societies which desire to be guided by an ethical principle, there are always two ethics in conflict: the ethics of conviction and the ethics of responsibility." The ethics of conviction tells the religious man to "act according to what you believe is right and leave the consequences to God," while the ethics of responsibility says "always try to do good, but never forget the logical and foreseeable consequences of your actions." Political leaders must be especially attentive to consequences, for we have no right to wash our hands of them.

This is for me the great theme, the very crux of the ethics of transitions: always strive to ensure that your actions do not produce consequences which contradict your good intentions. Otherwise, democratic idealism may degenerate into a dream and then give rise to a nightmare, when instead it should be transformed, through the medium of politics, into the moral substance of a real working democracy.

What will be the legacy of these transitions, not just in Uruguay but in all of the Americas? Stable regimes? Perpetual democracy? Have we entered a stage of consolidation? The Europeans asked themselves the same questions at the end of World War II. Who could guarantee that there would never again be a dictatorship in Germany? After all, the land of Goethe had given us Hitler. Who could guarantee that Italy—where Mussolini had coexisted with Benedetto Croce—would never revert to authoritarianism? Nevertheless, through a plan of integration, a great economic transformation, and successful national political programs, Europe arrived at a stage of consolidation.

We in Latin America now face a somewhat similar challenge. Our success or failure will depend on us. At times we remain skeptical, as when we see social groups making unrealistic demands, parties splitting up, leaders assuming messianic pretentions, and drug dealers challenging the state itself. Yet we are also optimistic, because we feel that as a hemisphere born for liberty, we are not condemned to a lesser share of stability and prosperity than the rest of the world.

So much has already been attained. In this hemisphere we have not only the modern dynamism represented by great cities like Rio de Janeiro, Caracas, and São Paulo; but also historic vigor of the sort typified by Nazca ceramics, Paracas weavings, and Mayan pyramids. All these testify that Latin American civilization is a flourishing precinct within the larger civilization of the West. Even the United States now looks on Latin America with a new respect. A new generation has taken Latin America's destiny in its hands. Abbé Raynal said two centuries ago that the human species will be what we make of it. We may add that Latin America too will be what we make of it.

5.
ON THE TASKS OF A DEMOCRATIC OPPOSITION

Alfred Stepan

Alfred Stepan, *Burgess Professor of Political Science and Dean of the School of International and Public Affairs at Columbia University, is widely known for his writings on civil-military relations, authoritarian regimes, and democratic transitions. An expert on Latin America, he serves on the National Executive Committee of the human rights organization Americas Watch. His study* The Military in Politics: Changing Patterns in Brazil *became a best seller in Brazil despite government attempts to censor it. His most recent book,* Rethinking Military Politics: Brazil and the Southern Cone, *was reviewed in the Winter 1990 issue of the* Journal of Democracy.

While democracy as a form of government has long been a staple concern of social science, the question of the genesis of democracy has been largely neglected. Moreover, until very recently, most studies of the growth of democracy have restricted their focus to its emergence from traditional oligarchies or absolute monarchies over the last two centuries in Europe, or to the problem of democracy in the context of decolonization.

This is unfortunate because much of the current theoretical and political concern with democracy centers on countries that have already had some experience with it, and where what is at stake is not the original establishment of popular government but its restoration as a successor to nontraditional authoritarian regimes. Active democratic opposition movements play a particularly important role in such countries, a role that deserves more sustained attention than it has so far received. Although this essay is based primarily on the experience of authoritarian regimes in countries like Chile, Brazil, Uruguay, South Korea, and the Philippines, I believe that the analysis also applies in substantial part to the recent breakdowns of communist regimes in Eastern Europe, most notably in Poland. What must be studied in all these cases is not merely the final collapse or overthrow of authoritarian regimes, but the incremental process of "authoritarian crosion" and the opposition's contribution to it. This in turn requires a dynamic analysis both of relationships within the authoritarian regime and of the multiple functions or tasks of the opposition.

Although the installation of a democratic regime scarcely heralds the end of political struggle, it does provide a new procedural setting for political life. This setting is not only more just in itself, but in most cases also offers the great masses of the people better opportunities than does authoritarianism to pursue such other goals as economic equality, social justice, and political participation.

In order to understand how a democratic opposition can attenuate the bonds of authoritarianism, we must first consider where the opposition stands in relation to the other components of the regime. Our analysis should emphasize not governmental *structures* but rather the overall *relationships* of domination. Generally speaking, the principal parties to such relationships are: 1) the core group of regime supporters (who find that their political, economic, or institutional interests are best served under the status quo); 2) the coercive apparatus that maintains the regime in power; 3) the regime's passive supporters; 4) the active opponents of the regime; and, 5) the passive opponents of the regime.

While structural or institutional studies place the coercive elite on center stage, an analysis of power relations within the authoritarian regime gives a fuller picture by examining the interactions among these five groups. The task of the active democratic opposition is to change the relations among all the component parts of the authoritarian system in such a way as to weaken authoritarianism while simultaneously improving the conditions for democratization.

Eroding Authoritarianism

In order to understand how these power relations may change in ways that affect the prospects for a democratic transition, it is useful to consider how each group will tend to perceive its situation and possible courses of action at different stages of authoritarian rule. For illustrative purposes, we will select for comparison two positions from opposite ends of the continuum of changing relationships that characterize authoritarian systems: the first involving a strong regime ruling in an atmosphere of widespread fear, and the second a weakened and eroding regime.

In the first case, the existence of a strong regime will tend to coincide with certain attitudes on the part of both its supporters and its opponents. Its core supporters, for example, will quite likely be gripped by something on the order of a siege mentality. To them, authoritarian rule is a ready help in time of trouble and a shield against clear and present danger. They will think it in their interest actively to help the regime and will not shrink from supporting even harshly repressive measures.

Like the core supporters, the military and security officials who wield the regime's coercive power will tend strongly to identify the interests of their organizations with those of the regime. This group may even conclude that considerations of national security positively require that the armed forces run the government.

Faced with a strong regime enjoying the allegiance of these two formidable groups, the third group—the passive supporters—will submit to authoritarian hegemony. They will remain quiescent and pliable, even to the point of participating in the institutions that serve as the regime's indirect, noncoercive bulwarks. Thus a cohesive and self-confident authoritarianism can enlist numerous middle-class intellectuals, clergymen, journalists, and other professionals on its side.

Among the opposition, the activists will be virtually demobilized by the massive coercion the regime is willing to use against them. The passive opposition is likely to be relatively small in this scenario, and almost certainly will hold itself aloof from those who actively oppose the regime.

In the regime-erosion situation, on the other hand, all these groups will be found thinking and acting differently. With the fear that holds the regime together subsiding, the core group of regime supporters will start to fragment as doubts arise concerning the wisdom and expediency of authoritarian policies. Some core supporters will decide that the perpetuation of authoritarianism is not in their interest, and will go over to passive—or sometimes even active—opposition. Such a shift would reflect their unwillingness to continue abdicating their political power and judgment to the government, and might also signal a newfound appreciation of democracy as a peaceful and predictable method for settling social and political conflicts.

Given the divisions among core supporters—and probably a corresponding resurgence among the active opposition as well—direct physical coercion will become even more important for the maintenance of the regime. But unless the military officers who command the means of coercion perceive severe domestic threats to the military itself, their resolve too may weaken. Some among them will then come to suspect that the continuation of the military-as-government (as in Brazil), or continued military support of an increasingly despised regime (as in Romania), may be inimical to the interests of the military as a national institution.

At these signs of weakening among the forces of authoritarianism, most of the passive supporters will quietly shift to passive opposition. It may also be expected that parts of key groups such as the clergy, the press, and the intellectual classes generally will place themselves under the banner of active opposition. Such passive supporters as do remain will no longer allow themselves to be incorporated into the institutions of the authoritarian regime.

With their ranks bolstered by growing numbers of defectors from authoritarianism, the active regime opponents will find their days of paralysis at an end. They will be able to undertake a broad array of activities to pressure the regime and publicly state their case for change. The passive opposition will grow much larger as people no longer need constantly to fear savage repression. Passive opponents will also lose some of their passivity as they become willing to participate in antiregime actions orchestrated by the active opposition. Under the right conditions, the passive and active opposition will coalesce and expand to the point where the idea of redemocratization wrests hegemony away from authoritarianism.

Although authoritarian regimes may buckle because of external setbacks like military defeat, foreign occupation, or international economic reversals, they are more likely to collapse under the strain of conflicts and contradictions that are purely internal. If it performs its multiple functions well, the active democratic opposition can exacerbate discord among the authoritarians, as well as prepare the indispensable political foundations for a democratic successor regime.

Priorities for the Opposition

What then are the multiple functions or tasks of democratic opposition movements in authoritarian regimes? In roughly ascending order of complexity (but not necessarily temporal sequence), the five key opposition functions are: 1) resisting integration into the regime; 2) guarding zones of autonomy against it; 3) disputing its legitimacy; 4) raising the costs of authoritarian rule; and 5) creating a credible democratic alternative. Analytically, the degree to which the opposition can perform these functions is a useful indicator of the severity of authoritarian control. The less the opposition is able to carry out any of these tasks, the more effective the regime's control of the polity is shown to be.

The first of the functions, resistance to integration, is the sine qua non for an opposition in the first place. If the cadre of the active opposition allows itself to become effectively demobilized and co-opted into authoritarian institutions, then the active opposition—for the time being at least—will have ceased to exist. On the other hand, if the active opposition maintains some independent ideological, cultural, and above all institutional existence, it will remain able to carry out its other tasks. Indeed, its prospects will be promising, for the total elimination of all opposition requires extremely effective mobilization and the full integration of all institutions and social groups into the structures of the regime, a project of surpassing difficulty at which no modern authoritarian government has ever succeeded.

If the active opposition can remain independent, its next task (in order of survival imperatives) is to encourage the growth of passive opposition. There are two good ways to do this. One is to contest the government's claim to legitimacy. The other and more important way is to maintain some zones of autonomy in which nonregime organizations can operate.

If, for instance, there are political parties or trade unions that predate the authoritarian regime, every effort must be made to sustain them, if necessary from exile (although to be effective, the exiled leaders must maintain national roots). If the coalition of active and passive supporters of the coercive elite is strong, the institutions of civil society most likely to retain some autonomy are those with some claim to extrapolitical legitimacy, such as religious or cultural associations. Religious bodies, especially, can lend tremendous weight to human rights or basic needs claims and can also provide an umbrella under which the active opposition can help furnish community services such as food distribution, health clinics, and missing-persons centers. In Poland, Brazil, and Chile, the Catholic Church played this crucial role.

The more that new or preexisting democratic trade unions, parties, or community movements take root and flourish, the less space is left for the implantation of new-model authoritarian institutions. The larger and stronger these various non- or anti-authoritarian subsystems grow, the more effectively they can perform the other tasks of democratic opposition: contesting the legitimacy of the authoritarian regime, raising the costs of maintaining it, and generally grinding it down while building support for a democratic alternative. This sort of grassroots campaigning to create non- or antiregime subsystems—and not direct assaults on the coercive elite—should be the active opposition's main order of business.

According to the definition given by the Italian Marxist theoretician Antonio Gramsci, a regime has attained *hegemony* when there is "consent given by the great masses of the population to the general direction imposed on social life by the dominant social groups."[1] The more a regime rules by hegemony, the less it has to rely on coercion. The greater the degree of hegemony or tacit consent an authoritarian regime can acquire, the less pressure will be felt by its coercive elite. Hence one of the active opposition's central tasks is to make the costs that the regime's policies impose on society so clear to the initially passive opposition that the achievement of authoritarian hegemony is rendered impossible.

In addition, since the international climate can be a support or an obstacle to an authoritarian regime, the active opposition should appeal to world opinion by documenting and publicizing the regime's most flagrant violations of civilized standards of conduct. If the regime's accession was especially violent (as in Chile in 1973, for instance) and the violence is well documented, this can create well-nigh insurmountable international opprobrium. The stronger such repugnance becomes, the higher the costs of rule mount. The more serious the domestic and international challenges to the legitimacy of the new regime, the greater the likelihood that the coercive elite and its core supporters will be thrown on the defensive and forced to justify their rule as a mere "temporary exception" rendered "indispensable" by the absence of a viable alternative. The "temporary exception" argument plays right into the hands of the democratic opposition by making it more difficult for the regime permanently to institutionalize its rule. The claim to indispensability, on the other hand, presents more of a challenge—but also more of an opportunity—to the active democratic opposition. For the best response to this claim is to create a viable democratic alternative.

Much of the support or acquiescence enjoyed by nontraditional authoritarian regimes comes from passive supporters and passive, demoralized opponents who all believe that the coercive elite is securely in control of the political system. If the active opposition can encourage activities—such as strikes, slowdowns, widespread protests, samizdat-style publications, "flying" university classes, and noncooperation generally—that give the lie to this belief, it will have increased the costs of rule yet again.

If such costs are raised high enough, they can rob the government of much of its legitimacy in the eyes of both its active and passive supporters. Some among those active supporters whose adherence springs from their belief in the efficacy of the authoritarian government may shift to merely passive support, either because they have lost confidence in the regime itself or because they find the costs of active identification with an unpopular regime too great. Also, some original active supporters may even make the leap over to passive or even active opposition if they begin to feel that their interests dictate such a move.

The danger lurking in this strategy should be apparent. If the opposition raises the costs of authoritarian rule too high, the coercive elite may lash back with heightened repression. Yet such a backlash would carry its own risks, and the coercive elite must assess the probable net effect on the regime before deciding between suppression and toleration. Under some conditions the coercive elite—especially if its own vital organizational interests are not directly threatened—may opt for toleration. As Robert Dahl has argued, "The likelihood that a government will tolerate an opposition increases as the expected costs of suppression increase."[2]

In most contemporary authoritarian governments, the core of the coercive elite is a military bureaucracy. Although some scholars accord little in the way of independent value to this circumstance, my studies of military organizations in the United States, Peru, and Brazil have led me to conclude otherwise. The internally perceived requirements of complex military bureaucracies, it would seem, do possess a weight and significance all their own. Not surprisingly, this is especially so when the military's vital organizational interests are at stake. The continuation of rule by the "military-as-government" imposes costs on the "military-as-institution." If key officers conclude that these institutional costs outweigh the costs of relinquishing military rule, and if other conditions are right, then—regardless of the interests of the regime's active supporters—the military's withdrawal from power will become a serious possibility. By the same token, intensified repression will grow less likely.

Creating a Democratic Alternative

The redemocratization of an authoritarian regime must combine erosion and construction. The kinds of things that effectively eat away at an authoritarian regime (labor unrest, widespread passive resistance, stubbornly autonomous social groups) are not necessarily the same things needed to lay the procedural foundations for democracy. Indeed, groups such as community-based religious organizations might have developed such independent casts of mind and such maximalist goals that they will balk at integration into broader democratic parties. A crucial task of the active opposition is to integrate as many antiauthoritarian movements as possible into the institutions of the emerging democratic majority. Failure in this task strengthens the authoritarian regime's claim to be the only alternative. If the opposition attends only to the task of erosion, as opposed to that of construction, then the odds are that any future change will merely be a shift from one authoritarian government to another, rather than a change from authoritarianism to democracy.

What type of alternative should the democratic opposition pursue? There is a temptation to respond to this question with calls for a viable shadow government. That temptation should be resisted for two reasons. First, it is likely that the increasing autonomy of subsystems will have enlarged both the number of interests and the means available to advance them. Second, we can also assume that after years of authoritarian rule by a narrow elite, there will be numerous contentious issues of policy to be debated, with a great variety of solutions proposed. Common sense says that under these conditions it will be exceedingly difficult, if not impossible, to get all prodemocratic forces to agree upon the kind of unified, detailed platform that a shadow government would require.

Absent such a platform, of what should the democratic alternative consist? At first, all that would be needed is some kind of broadly agreed-upon formula for the conduct of democratic contestation. A formula like this would serve to begin, not end, peaceful democratic struggles over other issues such as social or economic equality. In effect, a consensus would be reached about the rules of the game, though not about its results.

Focusing on procedure rather than policy serves an important goal of the democratic opposition. Premature wrangling over substantive issues could not only divide democrats, but could do so in a dangerously polarizing fashion. If, for instance, the authoritarian regime were to be so tactically astute as to take up a relatively centrist stance, part of the democratic opposition could well find itself to the right of the government on policy while another part stood to the left. In this case, both poles of the democratic opposition would stand closer—on substantive policy grounds—to the authoritarian regime than to each other. The authoritarians would then enjoy a strategic advantage over their badly divided opponents. If, however, the opposition concentrates on procedure, then all democratic forces can act as one to extract democratic procedural guarantees from the regime.

A broad procedural consensus among all democratic groups would alter the relationships of domination within the authoritarian regime in several crucial ways. The presentation of a clear alternative would undermine one of the authoritarian regime's central self-justifications, namely, its claim to be indispensable.

To the extent that fair democratic procedures would offer guarantees to the former supporters of the authoritarian regime, such procedures would accord them the possibility of continuing to pursue their interests under the new institutional arrangements. Thus, to the extent that the regime's initial supporters come to see democratic contestation as a serious alternative, their fears concerning the costs of democratic reform will diminish. By the same token, the growing power and cohesiveness of the forces of democracy will boost the expected cost of repression, including the prospect that it might ignite a revolutionary upheaval. Should something like this happen, then an important change favoring democratization will have occurred within the authoritarian regime itself. More precisely, the power relations among the regime's five components will have begun to approximate Robert Dahl's axiom: "the more the costs of suppression exceed the costs of toleration, the greater the chance for a competitive regime."[3]

The active supporters of the authoritarian regime and the members of the coercive elite themselves are often the major agents of this change; except in very rare cases of successful democratic revolution, crucial decisions favoring democratization are usually made by those who had previously been counted among the pillars of the authoritarian regime. We have recently seen this in cases such as Spain, Brazil, Chile, South Korea, Poland, and Hungary.

This is not, of course, to say that these decisions will be made gladly, freely, or out of disinterested good will. And there will always be those within the authoritarian regime who will dig in their heels and call for resistance to reform. Intense pressure from below by the active opposition and its allies is almost always the initial reason why liberalization is contemplated. The expected consequences of resisting such pressure figure heavily in the power struggle within the coercive elite and the ranks of its active supporters when they make their final decisions about democratization.

The ways in which democratic opposition movements go about their tasks can and should vary greatly, as prudence and circumstances dictate. Thus the purpose of this essay has not been to set forth a deterministic model describing the manner in which the democratic reform of authoritarian regimes must proceed. My goal, rather, has been a far more modest one. It has been simply to show that a richer understanding of how authoritarian regimes become democratized can be achieved if less attention is paid to the structures forged by the coercive elite, while more is accorded to the relationships of domination that pervade such regimes. In particular, it is important that scholars learn to identify the major parties to these relationships, and to analyze those processes that might serve not only to cut the ground out from under authoritarian modes and orders, but to lay the basis for a securely democratic future.

NOTES

1. Antonio Gramsci, *Selections from the Prison Notebooks*, eds. Quintin Hoare and Geoffrey Nowell Smith (New York: International Publishers Co., 1971), 12; see also pp. 57-59 and 260-61. Gramsci, *The Modern Prince and Other Writings*, trans. Louis Marks (New York: International Publishers Co., 1970), 164-88.

2. Robert A. Dahl, *Polyarchy: Participation and Opposition* (New Haven: Yale University Press, 1971), 15.

3. Ibid., 15.

6.
RETHINKING AFRICAN DEMOCRACY

Claude Ake

Claude Ake, *a Nigerian political economist, is currently a visiting fellow at the Brookings Institution in Washington, D.C. Formerly professor of political science and dean of the faculty of social sciences at the University of Port Harcourt, Nigeria, he has served as president of the Nigerian Political Science Association and of the Council for Development of Economic and Social Research in Africa (CODESRIA). He is the author of numerous books and articles on politics and political economy in Africa.*

Issues of democratization and human rights are increasingly dominating the world's interest in Africa, overcoming a legacy of indifference to the fate of democracy on the continent. This legacy has its roots in the colonial era, when political discourse excluded not only democracy but even the idea of good government, and politics was reduced to the clash of one exclusive claim to power against another.

This attitude persisted even after Africa gained political independence. By deciding to take over the colonial system instead of transforming it in accord with popular nationalist aspirations, most African leaders found themselves on a collision course with their people. Faced with this challenge to their newly won power, they opted for "development," using it largely as an ideological blind. Resisting pressures for structural transformation and redistribution, they claimed that the overriding priority for Africa must be to seek development—the cake had to be baked before it could be shared. To discourage opposition and perpetuate their power, they argued that the problems of development demanded complete unity of purpose, justifying on these grounds the criminalization of political dissent and the inexorable march to political monolithism.

The rest of the world heartily encouraged these political tendencies. Africa's former colonial masters, anxious for leverage with the new leaders, embraced the idea of partnership in development and gave these regimes their indulgent support. The great powers ignored human rights violations and sought clients wherever they could. All these factors helped crystallize a climate of opinion in the West hostile to democracy in Africa. From time to time (as during the Carter administration in the United States) human rights abuses in Africa became an issue, but never democracy. On the rare occasions when Western leaders did discuss democracy in Africa, it was mainly to raise doubts about its feasibility.

Why is the West now suddenly preoccupied with the prospect of democracy in Africa? The reforms in Eastern Europe have contributed to this change of heart by providing the West with a dramatic vindication of its own values and a sense of the historical inevitability of the triumph of democracy. The aggressive vacuity of the Cold War has been replaced by the mission of democratization, a mission which, it is widely believed, will firmly consolidate the hegemony of Western values all over the world. Thus the West has come to regard democracy as an important item on the African agenda. This change in attitude also reflects the fact that the long struggle for democracy in Africa is beginning to show results, results too impressive and too widespread to be ignored: the popular rejection of military rule in Nigeria; the demise of apartheid in South Africa; the downfall of Samuel Doe in Liberia and Kérékou in Benin; the gains for pluralism and multipartyism in Niger, Madagascar, Cameroon, Zambia, Algeria, Gabon, Côte d'Ivoire, Guinea, Zaire, Mozambique, Angola, the Congo, and São Tomé and Príncipe; and the growing pressures for democratization in Kenya, Somalia, Sudan, Togo, Ghana, Sierra Leone, Ethiopia, Cameroon, and Zimbabwe.

The West's changing attitude toward democracy in Africa draws additional impetus from Africa's economic marginalization. The world economy is now driven less by trade than by capital movements; there has been a massive shift from the production of goods to the provision of services, and from material-intensive to knowledge-intensive industries. At the same time, advances in science and technology have created an increasing number of synthetic products more flexible and more versatile than those that Africa has traditionally exported. These changes have made Africa's primary economies far less relevant to the current economic needs of the West. Now, with the winding down of the Cold War, Africa's strategic significance to the West has also greatly declined. As Europe draws closer to unification, even the former colonial powers—notably France—are finding it necessary to downgrade their special relationships with their former colonies, relations far less useful now than they have been in the past.

The marginalization of Africa has given the West more latitude to conduct its relations with Africa in a principled way. In the past, the West adopted a posture of indifference to issues of human rights and democracy in Africa in order to avoid jeopardizing its economic and strategic interests and to facilitate its obsessive search for allies against communism. Now that these concerns have diminished, the West finds itself free to bring its African policies into greater harmony with its democratic principles.

The Desirability of Democracy

It is a striking fact that democracy is now on the agenda in Africa. But should it be? To answer this question, we must examine the traditional arguments against establishing democracies in Africa.

Africa, it has been claimed, has its own unique history and traditions and the introduction of democracy, an alien concept, would violate the integrity of African culture. This argument, premised on the misconception that democracy is solely a Western creation, stems from a confusion between the principles of democracy and their institutional manifestations. The principles of democracy include widespread participation, consent of the governed, and public accountability of those in power. These principles may prevail in a wide variety of political arrangements and practices, which naturally vary according to historical conditions. Traditional African political systems were infused with democratic values. They were invariably patrimonial, and consciousness was communal; everything was everybody's business, engendering a strong emphasis on participation. Standards of accountability were even stricter than in Western societies. Chiefs were answerable not only for their own actions but for natural catastrophes such as famine, epidemics, floods, and drought. In the event of such disasters, chiefs could be required to go into exile or "asked to die."

Another argument against democracy in Africa revolves around the social pluralism of African societies, particularly ethnic differences. Some contend that because African societies are replete with ethnic conflict, they must be firmly governed; the liberties of democracy would inflame ethnic rivalries and pose the danger of political disintegration. This argument has acquired credibility because of the high incidence of ethnic conflicts in Africa, some of which have been markedly destructive, most notably in Uganda, Equatorial Guinea, Burundi, Nigeria, and Rwanda.

Nonetheless, the problem is not ethnicity but bad leadership. There is nothing inherently conflictual about ethnic differences. They lead to strife only when they are politicized, and it is the elites who politicize ethnicity in their quest for power and political support. Leaders also gain a second advantage from exploiting ethnicity. Having incited ethnic-based conflict, they then use the threat of such conflict to justify political authoritarianism.

Even now, after 30 years of self-government, some African leaders still enlist this spurious defense to rationalize one-party rule. President Daniel arap Moi of Kenya, under increasing pressure to democratize, has repeatedly made this claim. So has Zambian president Kenneth Kaunda, who warned that the adoption of a multiparty system would bring "chaos, bloodshed, and death." President Paul Biya of Cameroon has defended the power monopoly of his Cameroon People's Democratic Movement with similar language; he stresses the party's vanguard role in creating "a united Cameroon devoid of ethnic, linguistic, and religious cleavages." Somehow these leaders cannot see that repeating this argument after 30 years is precisely its refutation. A treatment applied for 30 years that continues to worsen the illness cannot be right.

A third argument ties the issue of democratization to economic development, asserting that the quest for democracy must be considered in the context of Africa's most pressing needs, especially emancipation from "ignorance, poverty, and disease." The pursuit of democracy will not, it is argued, feed the hungry or heal the sick. Nor will it give shelter to the homeless. People must be educated and fed before they can appreciate democracy, for there is no choice in ignorance and there are no possibilities for self-fulfillment in extreme poverty.

This claim is as seductive as it is misguided. Even if it were true that democracy is competitive with development, it does not follow that people must be more concerned with improving nutrition than casting votes, or more concerned with health than with political participation. The primary issue is not *whether* it is more important to eat well than to vote, but *who* is entitled to decide which is more important. Once this is understood, the argument that democracy must be sacrificed to development collapses into the arbitrary insistence that we ought to decide for the peasants of Botswana and Burkina Faso whether they should prefer better health or the right to vote.

In any case, Africa's failed development experience suggests that postponing democracy does not promote development; during the past decades of authoritarianism, Africa's standard of living has been falling steadily, and its share of world trade and industrial output has been declining. Poverty in both relative and absolute terms is worsening so rapidly that sub-Saharan Africa's share of the developing world's poor will have grown from 16 percent in 1985 to 30 percent by the end of the century. The average growth rate for the region between 1980 and 1989 was *minus* 2.2 percent.

Perhaps it is misleading to talk about the failure of development in Africa, for in a sense it has never really been tried. When African leaders chose to take over the colonial system instead of transforming it and thus became alienated from their own people, the genuine pursuit of development became all but impossible. Besieged by the hostile forces unleashed by their repression, they became totally absorbed in survival, and relegated everything else, including development, to a very low priority. What passed for development was usually a crudely fabricated plan that an embattled and distracted leadership put together for the sake of appearances, often with an eye to luring prospective donors.

Any chance that this externally driven development would contribute significantly to material progress was doomed by authoritarianism. Development strategies, reflecting both the scientific dogmatism of development experts and the isolation of African leaders, worked from the top down and were imbued with attitudes hostile to the poor majority. The common people were seen as a major obstacle to development: their expectations were too high, they consumed too much of their meager incomes, they lacked ambition and self-reliance, they were too lazy and too superstitious. In short, the common people were inherent enemies of progress, even their own progress. This became a justification for disregarding their interests and for brutalizing them in the name of development. As a result, most Africans tend to view the state and its development agents as hostile forces to be evaded, cheated, or thwarted as opportunities permit. They conform as they must and get on with their struggle for survival. They are simply not available to be mobilized for development.

Apparently the lesson has been learned. At the April 1990 Bretton Woods Committee meeting in Washington, World Bank president Barber Conable listed better governance as the primary requirement for economic recovery in Africa. The World Bank's new African blueprint, *Sub-Saharan Africa: From Crisis to Sustainable Growth*, highlights the need for accountability, participation, and consensus building in order to achieve successful development. The Bank's press clips on the report demonstrate that this view has won approval all over the world.

A conference of over 500 groups representing nongovernmental organizations, grassroots organizations, United Nations agencies, and governments, which convened in February 1990 in Arusha, Tanzania under the auspices of the United Nations Economic Commission for Africa, adopted an "African Charter for Popular Participation in Development and Transformation." Its major point is that the absence of democracy is the primary cause of the chronic crisis in Africa. A speech by U.N. secretary general Javier Pérez de Cuéllar at the Arusha meeting identified an inescapable link between economic recovery in Africa and popular participation. In addition, a declaration entitled "The Political and Socio-Economic Situation in Africa and the Fundamental Changes Taking Place in the World," adopted by the Organization of African Unity in Addis Ababa, 9-11 July 1990, acknowledges that a political environment guaranteeing human rights and the rule of law would be more conducive to governmental accountability and probity and that "popular-based political processes would ensure the involvement of all . . . in development efforts." But how do we proceed with democratization?

Some Misconceptions

Several disturbing misconceptions persist about the process of democratization in Africa. One is the tendency to see democratization as an offshoot of the survival strategies that the African crisis has engendered. Some Africanists emphasize that, although African states are tottering under a protracted fiscal crisis and national institutions are in danger of disintegrating under the stress of economic austerity, there is tremendous vitality at the grassroots. People are organizing themselves in order to limit their vulnerability to a predatory state, to improvise rudimentary social welfare networks through community efforts, and to improve their material well-being. We get a picture of a thriving associational life, of a turning away from the state, of ordinary people assuming greater control over their own destinies.

This is certainly happening. Its democratic potential is limited, however, as the case of Kenya illustrates. Kenya is one of the African countries in which rural grassroots organizations are the most advanced, and it has achieved immense success in grassroots economic development. For instance, grassroots self-help development projects ("Harambee" projects) account for about 70 percent of the 1,400 secondary schools in the country and for a substantial proportion of the rural water-supply facilities, clinics, cattle dips, and community centers. Yet Kenya is anything but democratic. These grassroots organizations do not appear to have brought about, as of now, any substantial decentralization of power, and they have not diminished the state's arbitrariness and coercion. Part of the problem is that they are isolated and are not usually aggregated at higher organizational levels where they could have some potential for influencing policy.

Except in a few countries, such as Senegal, grassroots organizations in Africa do not significantly contribute to democracy. In fact, in their political effects they are not markedly different from the local government systems that African regimes have been instituting in order to lower administrative costs and deflect participatory pressures. That is the kind of reform that President Rawlings is currently putting in place in Ghana under the pretext of democratization. People are given some local political space, not to integrate them into a democratic polity but to separate them from meaningful participation at the national level; the granting of local authority is not a liberty but a constraint. It underlines the confinement of local people and their disenfranchisement. Initiatives and directives flow from the central to the local government in a strictly one-way traffic.

Recently, yet another misconception about the process of democratization in Africa has begun to emerge—the view that democratization entails "destatization." This theory has been finding fertile ground in the West, particularly among international financial institutions (IFIs), because it meshes with the liberal commitment to the primacy of the market and the notion that democracy is associated with minimal government. Having agreed that authoritarianism presents a serious obstacle to development, the IFIs now recommend as a solution reducing the expenditures, powers, and controls of the state. It is critical, however, to distinguish between the size of the state and its strength. The public sector in many African countries has grown too bloated. Indeed, the bloated state has become a strategy for massive corruption, and it makes sense to try to trim the state by reducing the extent of state economic ownership and control. But it is a very different matter to claim that democracy can be promoted in Africa by *weakening* the state. The state in Africa needs to become both leaner *and* stronger in order to carry out successfully its essential development tasks.

The coercive monolithism of most African political systems readily gives the impression of strong states with immense penetrative capacity, states which are everywhere doing everything. Yet African states are actually very weak. In Nigeria, for instance, the state has little influence on the lives of the rural people. Much of the development that has taken place in rural communities has occurred not because of the state but in spite of it. To many rural dwellers, the state exists primarily as a nuisance to be avoided in their daily struggle for survival. In most other African countries, state influence is even weaker. In Zaire, President Mobutu does not effectively control more than 40 percent of the nation's territory. The state delivers so few services that it is all but irrelevant to its citizens except when they encounter it on the rampage.

Only the violent arbitrariness of states like Zaire makes them seem so powerful. By contrast, in Western countries like the United States, the state is very strong and penetrates far more deeply into the lives of its citizens. The West has created societies that are very homogeneous, interdependent, cohesive, and amenable to control. The refinement of bureaucratic organization backed by modern science and technology has given these states extraordinary powers of intervention, penetration, and control. But their citizens do not find these powerful states threatening. Instead, they perceive a benign aloofness, an impression fostered by the use of state power according to law and, more importantly, by the virtual automation of conformity and control. Democracy is not, and can never be, a matter of weakening the state.

The Role of the West

What role, if any, should the West play in the democratization of Africa? Like development, democratization is not something that one people does for another. People must do it for themselves or it does not happen. The question of the role of the West in the democratization of Africa has arisen only because Africans have become more committed to the quest for democracy and are struggling determinedly to attain it. But the extent to which they will succeed depends in part on the international environment, in which the West currently plays a decisive role.

In recent months, Western leaders have articulately proclaimed their support for democracy in Africa, and news about Africa in the Western media is now dominated by issues of democratization. But what can the West do beyond verbal exhortations to democratize? The answer to this question must focus on the leverage available to the West in its relations with Africa. This leverage can be exerted in two ways: through bilateral relations and through Western influence over the IFIs, especially the International Monetary Fund (IMF) and the World Bank.

In the realm of bilateral relations, the West has already agreed to use its leverage over development assistance, aid, and investment to encourage support for human rights and democracy. The U.S. Congress has indicated that its limited aid will be awarded to "newly forming democracies" and not be wasted on autocratic regimes. U.S. assistant secretary of state for African affairs Herman Cohen, speaking at the April 1990 Bretton Woods Committee meeting in Washington, announced that, in addition to previous requirements on economic policy reform and human rights, democratization would become a third condition for U.S. assistance. On 8 May 1990, the U.S. ambassador to Kenya stated that "there is a strong tide flowing in our Congress, which controls the purse strings, to concentrate our economic assistance on those of the world's nations that nourish democratic institutions, defend human rights, and practice multiparty politics." He went on to suggest that this would be a "fact of political life in other donor countries tomorrow." Speaking at a meeting of the Overseas Development Council on 6 June 1990, British foreign secretary Douglas Hurd said that Britain's assistance will favor "countries tending toward pluralism, public accountability, respect for the rule of law, human rights, and market principles." President François Mitterand, addressing a French-African conference at La Baule in June 1990, stated that in the future French aid would flow "more enthusiastically" to countries moving toward democracy.

The West has already started using economic pressures to induce political change, a concept now referred to as political conditionality. A debate is currently raging about whether political conditionality is necessary or desirable. It is an odd debate because political conditionality has always been present, not only in bilateral relations but even in the relations of multilateral agencies with the Third World. I say this not to justify political conditionality by the fact that it has always existed; it is as unnecessary to justify it as it is useless to dispute its legitimacy. The very nature of relations between nations demands that political conditionality underlie economic relations. What appears to have started this debate over the obvious is the explicitness of political conditionality and its extension beyond the issues of friendly relations and human rights to democratization.

Democracy cannot be obtained by trying to convert undemocratic regimes through bribery and coercion. Democracy is not simply bestowed

upon a nation from above. It may prevail with minimal conflict in those
rare instances in which the rulers, recognizing the inevitable, concede
gracefully. More often than not, it is won amidst considerable turmoil
against the determined opposition of those in power. There are no easy
paths to democracy, and offering incentives to autocrats is not the way
to democratize.

This is not to say that sanctions have no place in encouraging
democratization in Africa. On the contrary, sanctions can play an
important role. They can weaken an antidemocratic regime's capacity to
oppress and block democratic forces. In Benin, for instance, sanctions
weakened President Kérékou and emboldened the democratic forces,
creating considerable room for a democratic transition. In Liberia,
sanctions contributed to the overthrow of President Samuel Doe. They
could have the same effect in Kenya, Cameroon, Sierra Leone, Zambia,
Somalia, Malawi, Ghana, and other African nations.

The question is whether the West can muster the political will to
apply sanctions. While preaching the new line on political conditionality,
the West confines its actions to relatively harmless gestures. Aid
continues to flow to President arap Moi of Kenya despite his repulsive
efforts to crush members of the democracy movement "like rats," and
despite calls for sanctions by leaders of the democratic movement such
as human rights lawyer Gibson Kamau Kuria. In May 1990, a thousand
French troops intervened to protect Omar Bongo's 23-year-long rule in
Gabon. Britain's support of political conditionality has yet to go beyond
lectures on democracy, despite pressures from its media. An editorial in
the influential *Times* of London on 11 July 1990, entitled "An
Ignominious Silence," angrily reprimanded the government for neither
condemning nor taking action against President arap Moi: "The British
Government has had not one word to say about President Moi's
savagery. This is a disgrace."

Western rationalizations for not imposing sanctions echo the old
uncritical paternalism that has been such a comfort to Africa's autocrats
in the past. One concern repeatedly expressed is that there may be no
apparent alternative to the existing ruler. But this merely reflects the age-
old policy of tyrants—namely ensuring that they have no competitors. To
accept the absence of visible alternatives as an excuse for doing nothing
is to reward the techniques of tyranny. Another standard argument asserts
that withholding aid will hurt the economy and the people. But how can
aid given to violently repressive leaders—rather than channeled through
nongovernmental organizations—possibly help "the people," as opposed
to helping these leaders themselves to remain in power? The plea that
aid must continue in order not to impede national development overlooks
the fact that most African leaders have been "underdeveloping" the
continent for years in spite of aid—indeed, probably because of it.
Between 1980 and 1988, sub-Saharan Africa received a total aid flow of

$83 billion, yet during the same period the average annual growth rate was minus 2.2 percent. In Zaire, one of the largest aid recipients in Africa, the average annual income has fallen to a fraction of what it was when President Mobutu came to power 25 years ago.

Political conditionality can weaken antidemocratic forces, but any serious effort to promote democracy must go further and seek to identify and strengthen democratic forces. This will be a difficult, messy, and disagreeable task. It will entail working around the government and reaching into civil society to support those groups struggling for democracy. Dictatorial regimes will object to this approach, and if it is not abandoned, confrontations will ensue, raising awkward questions about circumventing another country's sovereignty. Faced with such difficulties, the will of Western governments to support democracy may well weaken.

The Politics of Structural Adjustment

The importance of the international financial institutions to the success of any policy of political conditionality is underscored by the fact that the World Bank alone controls $12 billion of the $15 billion in international aid to Africa. As for the IMF, its power far surpasses its lending capacity and the financial resources it directly controls, because Western governments take their cue from the IMF in their relations with Africa. Any African country that cannot obtain IMF certification of aid-worthiness will get no cooperation from the West. Professor Adebayo Adedeji, the executive secretary of the United Nations Economic Commission for Africa, may well be right in saying that the IMF and the World Bank are now more powerful in Africa than the former colonial masters. These agencies, notorious in the past for presenting development as apolitical, today acknowledge that political factors have been a major stumbling block to the development effort in Africa. They are now calling for participation, the rule of law, transparency, accountability, and consensus building.

Yet despite their new recognition that political factors constrain development efforts, the IFIs still appear to believe that they are not in the business of politics. They think that political variables can simply be treated as an engineering problem and "factored in" to improve the effectiveness of their structural adjustment programs, and thus that they can avoid changing their overall approach to development. They argue that this does not mean turning their backs on democratization, because the cause of democracy is best served by pressing on with adjustment programs that strengthen the market relative to the state. They point out that privatization will enhance pluralism and that a freer market will decentralize decision making, multiply the centers of power, and strengthen civil society. This view is widely held in Western government circles and among intellectuals. Writing in the *Washington Post* on 24 May 1990, Chester Crocker, former U.S. assistant secretary of state for African affairs, argued that structural adjustment programs "are vital to the liberation of market forces, which in turn, represent the building blocks of pluralist democracy."

This is a dangerous error. In African countries, structural adjustment entails draconian measures that are unpalatable and often disastrous. Unemployment and inflation rise steeply, yet at the same time subsidies are removed and wages frozen. The combined effect of these measures can cause real incomes to fall as much as 50 percent. Given that 40 percent of the people in these countries already live below absolute poverty levels, structural adjustment does not entail minor inconvenience. These programs cause deep despair, widespread malnutrition, and premature death; as UNICEF reports indicate, much of the burden falls upon children.

As should be expected, adjustment policies generate a great deal of political opposition even in countries like Gabon, which implemented a relatively moderate version. Adjustment in that country meant cutting government spending by 50 percent, removing subsidies, freezing wages, dismissing public employees, and selling government-owned enterprises. Yet that was only the first phase. When the government announced the second wave of austerity measures in January 1990, there were protests and strikes in every government agency, including the postal, bus, rail, air traffic, and telephone services; even the police and the army went on strike. In all cases, adjustment programs have been vigorously resisted by the public. To implement them, governments have been forced to resort to a large dose of coercion. For this reason, African regimes have become more, not less, authoritarian over the past decade.

The IFIs have collaborated enthusiastically in this political authoritarianism. In *Sub-Saharan Africa: From Crisis to Sustainable Growth*, the World Bank argued quite correctly that "programs of action can be sustained only if they arise out of consensus built on dialogue within each country." Yet not once has the Fund or the Bank encouraged discussion and consensus building before the introduction of structural adjustment programs. In every case, they were quite content to settle the issues with the president of the client country or his economics or finance minister. Having done so, they constantly urged the necessity of political will to carry out the program—a euphemism for its coercive imposition.

No Easy Road

The indications are that political conditionality will not be seriously pursued in Africa by Western governments or the IFIs. In the United States, although many key congressional leaders strongly support political conditionality, the Bush administration has been circumspect. It remains preoccupied with keeping its options open, causing no offense to friendly governments, and avoiding conflicts in the pursuit of seemingly intangible objectives. Thus, despite considerable public and congressional pressure, the administration moved very slowly and reluctantly to impose sanctions on South Africa, Zaire, and Liberia. More recently, Congressional calls for sanctions against President arap Moi of Kenya elicited a visit to that country from assistant secretary of state Herman Cohen, after which a delighted arap Moi declared that relations between Kenya and the United States were back to normal. In Britain and France, the governments have been more reluctant still.

It is now beginning to look as though the economic and strategic marginalization of Africa may not, as has been assumed, encourage political conditionality by leaving the West freer to act on its democratic principles. This marginalization may instead make the West too indifferent to Africa to care even about democratization. In any case, Africa's marginalization has translated into reduced economic relations, investment, and trade and development assistance. External bank loans and credits to sub-Saharan Africa fell from $4 billion in 1980 to $1 billion in 1986, and private investment dropped from $2.3 billion in 1982 to $500 million in 1986. Africa's trade with Western Europe dropped by more than 25 percent between 1980 and 1987. Export credits from France to sub-Saharan Africa have fallen dramatically—investment is running at only $50 million a year, down from $1 billion a year in the early 1980s. U.S. bilateral aid to sub-Saharan Africa, at $1 billion in 1990, is only half its 1985 level. Political conditionality presupposes economic leverage. If current economic trends continue, the question of political conditionality may become moot.

Even if economic leverage remains available, the IFIs are unlikely to support political conditionality in more than a nominal way. They have become so fixated on structural adjustment that they will accept and protect any regime that submits to it. Somalia is a case in point. It is virtually isolated because of President Siad Barre's brutal dictatorship; even Italy, traditionally considered Somalia's "mother" country, has severed its ties. After the July 9 massacres in Mogadishu, the Italian government announced that it was withdrawing its ambassador, its military advisers, and its professors at the National University of Somalia. Yet the World Bank is currently processing a new loan of $18.5 million to Somalia; it approved $26.1 million earlier this year and $70 million last year.

By such actions, the IFIs give African leaders the chance to substitute structural adjustment for democratization. That is the preferred alternative for both sides, and it ensures their peaceful coexistence. The IFIs fear anything that will bring them into conflict with most African regimes and prevent them from doing business. In order to keep relations cordial and funds flowing, they readily collude in circumventing the economic conditionality that they themselves impose. If they subvert their own economic rules to keep the peace, it is easy to imagine how they would deal with political conditionality.

Still, the IFIs may be contributing to democratization in spite of themselves. If one is a Leninist and believes that "the worse, the better," one may indeed welcome their tenacity in pursuit of adjustment, for the escalation of political repression associated with it has helped to spawn the democracy movement in Africa. However, seeking progress by the intensification of contradictions is both costly and risky. It will cause a great deal of suffering and may give rise to extremist ideologies and political forms that serve neither development nor democracy.

Africans who have been struggling to bring democracy to their societies are now finding themselves the beneficiaries of growing international sympathy and support. All too often, however, well-wishers of African democracy in the West have been led astray by insensitivity to local conditions and erroneous theories (like those underlying the imposition of structural adjustment programs). Misguided support, however sincere, is bound to prove counterproductive. The West must guard against this by recognizing that Africa's democrats know what they are doing, and that they should be helped to advance their own agenda.

7.
THE CULTURE OF LIBERTY

Mario Vargas Llosa

Peruvian novelist and essayist **Mario Vargas Llosa** *is the author of many renowned works of fiction, including* Conversation in the Cathedral, The War of the End of the World, Aunt Julia and the Scriptwriter, The Storyteller, *and most recently,* In Praise of the Stepmother. *In 1990 he was a candidate for the presidency of Peru, winning a plurality in the first round but then losing in the runoff to Alberto Fujimori. His article is based on a speech that he presented in Managua, Nicaragua, in March 1991 at a Democracy Commission conference organized by the Washington-based Puebla Institute.*

It is said that the fashionable curse during the Chinese Cultural Revolution was, "May you live in interesting times." Our times would doubtless qualify—we cannot complain on that score. Over the last few years almost every day has brought fresh surprises, leaving us to gape at each new breakthrough for freedom: the fall of the Berlin Wall and the subsequent reunification of Germany; the overthrow of Nicolae Ceauşescu in Romania; Václav Havel's stunning rise from the depths of prison to the presidency of Czechoslovakia; Violeta Chamorro's upset victory in the Nicaraguan elections; and the democratization of Haiti.

We are still rubbing our eyes at some of the things we see on our television screens. There is, for example, the sight of Red Square teeming with demonstrators calling for an end to Soviet repression in the Baltics and demanding free elections throughout the USSR. Everywhere, it seems, communist parties are expiring or seeking to survive (as in Italy) by changing their names and disowning such essential features of Marxism-Leninism as class struggle, centralized planning, and social ownership of the means of production. We are witnessing the abandonment of all the myths, stereotypes, arguments, and methods that gave birth to communism, made it grow, put a third of the human race under its yoke of servitude and terror, and finally led to its self-destruction.

Under the circumstances, great pronouncements are difficult to avoid. Are we not launching a new era in human history? The term "history" is one of many concepts that has been prostituted by ideology. Appeals to history have served as alibis for the grand intellectual deceptions of our times; history has been invoked in our century to justify genocide and the basest political crimes ever recorded.

Should we, then, join Francis Fukuyama in claiming that communism's last gasp marks the true "end of history" in the Hegelian sense? I think we should not. On the contrary, events in the Soviet Union and Eastern Europe have unexpectedly revitalized the very notion of "history." Humanity is now free of the blinders and fictions that Marxism—orthodox or heterodox—imposed upon it for so long. Humankind's taste for healthy risk-taking has been restored, as has its instinct for free improvisation undertaken in defiance of all reductionist conceptual schemes.

Today, we can confirm the position that Karl Popper, Friedrich Hayek, and Raymond Aron always held in opposition to thinkers like Machiavelli, Vico, Marx, Spengler, and Toynbee. The former insisted, rightly, that history is never "written" before it happens; it does not proceed according to some script determined by God, nature, reason, or the class struggle and the means of production. History is rather a continuous and variable creation that can move through the most unexpected turns, evolutions, involutions, and contradictions. Its complexity always threatens to sweep away those who attempt to predict and explain it.

We are right to be thrilled by current trends such as the resurgence of the individual vis-à-vis the state; of economic freedom versus central planning; of private property and enterprise versus collectivism and statism; of liberal democracy versus dictatorship and mercantilism. But let us not fool ourselves. None of this was "written." No hidden force, waiting in the catacombs of obscurantism and terror that impoverished and humiliated entire peoples, led to the fall of Ceauşescu, the triumph of Solidarity, or the demolition of the wall that divided Berlin. These victories—and all the others like them that have recently inspired totalitarianism's foes—were hard-won by the stubborn resistance of victims, sometimes aided by the desperation of communist oligarchs. These latter, brought face-to-face with the need for drastic change by communism's inability to solve pressing economic and social problems, found themselves haunted by the unmitigated national catastrophes that failure to reform would surely bring about.

The victory of freedom over totalitarianism has been overwhelming, but it is far from fully secured. Indeed, the toughest part of the struggle lies ahead. The dismantling of statism and the dispersal of the economic and political power expropriated by a despotic bureaucracy are exceedingly complex tasks. They are demanding enormous sacrifices from those peoples who still labor under the illusion that political democracy and economic liberty provide instant solutions to all problems. These peoples need to overcome the legacy of stupefaction and rigidity that collectivism has left behind. They must restore their sense of individual responsibility. They must put to rest the alienating assumption, fostered by communism, that all problems must be referred first to the state for solution, and only as a last resort to themselves. Bringing about such a profound and widespread change of ingrained attitudes is a far more daunting challenge than ousting petty tyrants ever was.

> "Freedom, which is always necessary for progress and justice, exacts a price that people must pay daily if they wish to remain free."

For countries like Poland, Hungary, Romania, Bulgaria, Czechoslovakia, and the Soviet Union, then, the true revolutionary task has barely begun. The job is nothing short of staggering: to build the foundations of a free society on the ruins of socialism. This will require citizens who know that without economic freedom there can be no political liberty, much less any progress. They must also learn that a market economy needs discipline, firm rules, risk-taking, initiative, and above all, plenty of hard work and sacrifice. The culture of success—that extraordinary wellspring of prosperity that sustains all advanced democratic societies—also demands that entrepreneurs and companies accept the risk of failure without expecting the state to cushion all their falls.

Accepting this new-found liberty, then, means standing ready to pay the piper for inefficiency or miscalculation. The competitive market generates the most efficiency and creates the most wealth of any economic system, but it is also cold and merciless toward inefficiency. It is best, I think, to take this sobering truth into account right now, at the threshold of the new era. Freedom, which is always necessary for progress and justice, exacts a price that people must pay daily if they wish to remain free. No country, neither the most prosperous nor the one with the longest democratic tradition, is exempt from this danger.

What is happening in Eastern Europe is also happening, though in a less obvious and much less spectacular way, in Latin America. Here it is a slow, indirect process, not always conscious, but still visible to the dispassionate observer. Except for Cuba, all our dictatorships have given way to civilian governments. Democratic regimes—although admittedly with varying degrees of legitimacy—govern our countries from the Rio Grande to the Straits of Magellan. The case of Nicaragua, our host country, is especially significant. No more so, however, than Paraguay, Chile, or Haiti. Violent revolutionary myths have also lost their power to sway more than a few young people, peasants, and workers. Some radical academics and intellectuals (along with other unassimilated and marginal sectors), while still capable of causing considerable harm, are day by day coming to be regarded as eccentrics with no real popular support.

The real change, however, is that welcome signs of pragmatism and modernization are starting to spring up all over Latin America in spite of (or perhaps because of) the great economic crisis we confront. With rare exceptions, few governments still dare to follow the Keynesian model that has wreaked so much havoc and continues to do so. A renewed liberalism—in the classical sense—is making headway in the region as a healthy alternative to the worn-out notions of "internal development" and "import substitution."

Some approach the task with enthusiasm, some with reluctance, while others do not know exactly why they are doing it, yet almost all the new governments are starting to take necessary, if sometimes small, steps to attack the root causes of poverty. It is a great achievement of our own era in comparison to previous ones that the evil of poverty has become curable, as long as the ailing country has the will to get better.

This means, in social and economic terms, the will to modernize, to clean up, and to cut the state down to the proper size for ensuring order, justice, and liberty. It means fostering the right to create wealth in an open system, based on merit, without bureaucratic privileges and interference. It also means that the state must assume responsibility for ensuring that each generation will enjoy that which, together with liberty, is the basis of all democratic societies—namely, equality of opportunity.

Little by little, Latin America is learning that a government "redistributes" more intelligently by offering outstanding public education than by smothering private enterprise with oppressive taxes, and by making sure that private property is accessible to the largest number rather than by harassing those who have property already.

Economic nationalism—which along with cultural nationalism is one of the most tenacious aberrations in our history—is beginning to show signs of receding at last. Nationalism has contributed substantially to the underdevelopment of Latin America. Yet slowly we are learning that health does not derive from fortifying our borders, but from opening them up wide and going out into the world to capture markets for our products, along with the technology and capital and ideas that the world can offer us to develop our resources and create the jobs that we so urgently need.

Given this new cultural climate, many would now admit that the much-touted regional integration of Latin America never worked because it was always hampered by the "nationalist spirit." It was promoted as a defense against the rest of the world and its notorious "imperialism," but came a cropper because each Latin American country tried to use regional unity for its own benefit, not for that of others.

Now that growing numbers of Latin Americans finally seem to be learning that highest of political virtues—common sense—integration is starting to be understood in its modern sense: as a joining together to speed Latin America's integration with the rest of humanity. Entering into today's world with an awareness of possibilities, of risks, and of markets is the best way for poor and backward countries like our own to start being modern—that is, prosperous. Without prosperity, there is little true freedom, for freedom in poverty is at best a precarious and limited sort of freedom.

> **"Let us be rid of nationalism, which has bloodied and divided us, and in whose name we have wasted enormous resources in order to arm ourselves against one another."**

Let us be rid of nationalism, which has bloodied and divided us, and in whose name we have wasted enormous resources in order to arm ourselves against one another. These resources would have been much better spent fighting the real enemies of any nation, which are not its neighbors but rather hunger, ignorance, and backwardness. It is essential that we not backslide into the sorts of methods that bad governments use to muzzle their critics. Let there be no more intimidating talk about alleged "threats from foreign enemies" or the supposed need for absolute "national unity." We need to work diligently to overcome reciprocal mistrust, solving problems peacefully as they arise. We must also keep struggling to ensure that barriers between our nations are lowered by the beneficent power of friendship, common interests, and the shared consciousness that only by working together can we exorcise those persistent demons that have kept us so far behind other, more prosperous regions of the world.

Fortunately, the number of Latin Americans who can distinguish clearly between nationalism and patriotism is growing all the time. While patriotism, as Dr. Johnson observed, may sometimes serve as the last refuge of scoundrels, it is more often a generous, unselfish sentiment of love for the land where one was born and one's ancestors died. It represents a moral and emotional commitment to the web of historical, geographical, and cultural references that frame the destiny of every individual. But even patriotism, with all its beautiful and noble qualities, cannot be made obligatory without degrading it, any more than would be the case for such private experiences as sex, friendship, faith, and love.

In these times of upheaval and wonder, even capitalism—that most odious of words, so greatly feared by Latin American politicians—is starting to wend its way ever so subtly and delicately into our public vocabulary. Shorn of frightening old connotations, it comes down objectively to this: it is the system that, despite its limitations and flaws, has made possible the greatest progress in collective welfare, social security, human rights, and individual liberty that history has ever seen.

Let me hasten to add that this does not necessarily mean that because of capitalism, human happiness has been measurably increased. Happiness is not something to be measured according to social coordinates, only individual ones. That is why, as Karl Popper says, happiness is not the duty of governments. Those who try to achieve it for everyone—"holistic" governments like those of Fidel Castro, the Shiite ayatollahs of Iran, or the superstitious antediluvians of the People's Republic of China—tend to turn their societies into a hell. Happiness, which is mysterious and variable, like poetry, concerns only oneself and one's intimates; there are no formulas to produce it and no explanations to decipher it.

It needs to be recognized that the quickest way out of poverty is a clear and resolute decision for the market, private enterprise, and individual initiative. As a necessary first step, we must reject statism, collectivism, and populist demagogy. To avoid serious confusion we must insist upon the sharp distinction that separates genuine capitalism—which, for clarity, we might call liberal and which we have never actually had—from those adulterated forms of rentier or mercantile capitalism that have always been present until now in Latin America.

Cozy agreements between political authorities and influential business groups aimed at giving the latter monopoly privileges and exemptions from competition—that is, from having to exert themselves to satisfy the demands of the consumer—have been inexhaustible sources of inefficiency and corruption in our economies. Corruption is inevitable when the success of an enterprise depends not on the market but on some bureaucrat signing a decree. Such a system warps both business and the businessman, who must focus his ingenuity and efforts not on serving the consumer, but on obtaining state privileges. Mercantilism has been one of the principal causes of our underdevelopment, and of the discrimination and injustices that our societies visit upon the poor. Mercantilism has made legality a privilege accessible only to those with "pull," and thus has condemned the poor to seeking opportunities for work and profit at the margins, in the so-called informal economy. Such an existence is admittedly precarious, but free. In some ways, the informals are the harbingers of an authentic popular capitalism for Latin America.

Ending mercantilism is a moral and political imperative fully as urgent as eradicating the social and economic "reforms" that in our societies have led to the nationalization of businesses, the collectivization of land, and the entrenchment of statism. Mercantilism, collectivism, and statism are all different expressions of the same phenomenon that strangles individual initiative, makes the bureaucrat instead of the businessman or the worker the protagonist of productive life, stimulates inefficiency and corruption, legitimates discrimination and privilege, and, sooner or later, brings about the erosion and disappearance of liberty.

Establishing a free economy that banishes monopolies and guarantees everyone access to markets governed by simple, clear, and equitable rules will not weaken Latin America's nation-states. On the contrary, it will strengthen them by giving them the authority and credibility they now lack. Despite their size, they are too weak and impotent to provide the basic services expected of them: health, security, justice, education, and a minimal infrastructure.

> *"...there must be efforts to promote the ownership of property among those who still have none. Private property is not theft, as Proudhon held, but rather the sign and sustenance of liberty."*

But denying the state the right to intervene as producer in order to allow it more efficiently to fulfill its role as arbitrator and promoter of economic life does not mean exempting it from its essential responsibilities. Among these, for example, is keeping the market free of interference and distortions that sap its efficiency and promote abuses. Another is continual improvement of the system of justice, since without a fair, strong, and universal judicial system that all citizens, especially the poor, can rely on to defend their rights, there can be no functioning market economy. Finally and most especially, there must be efforts to promote the ownership of property among those who still have none. Private property is not theft, as Proudhon held, but rather the sign and sustenance of liberty.

A liberal state is inconceivable without a policy of support for the disabled and the infirm, for the person who because of age, nature, or fate is not able to provide for himself and would be crushed if subjected to the strict laws of the market. Critics of the liberal state often charge that it is systematically inhumane. But when and where did Adam Smith or the other great classical liberal thinkers propose that the state be indifferent toward the weak? The truth is that liberal democracies have the best record in the world when it comes to protecting the aged and children, as well as insuring against unemployment, industrial accidents, and illness.

Above all, there is an order, the cultural order, in which the liberal state has the obligation to take initiatives, to invest resources, and to promote action and participation by everyone. Making cultural benefits accessible to all and stimulating curiosity, interest, and pleasure in what the human imagination and artistic spirit are capable of inventing to counteract life's shortcomings—these are the ways to ensure that people's sensibilities and critical faculties remain sharp, promoting that permanent dissatisfaction without which there can be no social renewal. Nothing keeps this kind of healthy discontent awake and stimulated like a rich cultural life.

It goes without saying that the state should not "direct," or even nudge, cultural activity one inch beyond what it needs to be free and autonomous. The state's function is to guarantee that culture is diverse, abundant, and open to every current and influence, because only thus exposed to challenges and competition can it remain close to experience and help people live, believe, and hope.

> *"The drug subculture... amounts to a rejection of that quality of enlightenment which forms the very backbone of the culture of liberty."*

Culture has no need for protection, since when it exists in an authentic sense, it protects itself much better than any government could. But states certainly have a duty to give everyone the means of acquiring and producing culture; that is, to provide the education and minimally adequate life circumstances that allow people to enjoy it.

An intense cultural activity, furthermore, is one of the ways in which the liberal state can exorcise a danger that seems to be a congenital affliction of capitalist society: a certain dehumanization of life, a materialism that isolates the individual, destroys the family, and fosters selfishness, loneliness, skepticism, snobbishness, cynicism, and other forms of spiritual emptiness. No modern industrial society has been capable of meeting this challenge effectively; in all of them, high standards of living and large-scale material progress have weakened the sense of social solidarity that, paradoxically, tends to be very strong in primitive communities. This weakening has in turn generated a proliferation of wildly irrational cults and rites that seem to derive their appeal from an unconscious need for a sense of the sacred that we have somehow lost but apparently cannot live without.

The drug subculture that has become perhaps the most formidable present-day backlash against reason amounts to a rejection of that quality of enlightenment which forms the very backbone of the culture of liberty. Drugs seem to provide one of the most extreme ways of expressing—particularly in highly advanced countries—that perennial hunger for transcendence and the absolute that previously was satisfied by magic, myth, and religion.

Those of us who are struggling to modernize our countries by means of the only system that brings prosperity without diminishing freedom should learn a lesson from all this. We must formulate a speedy and imaginative response to these dangers, by establishing a system of patronage for culture, for human creativity in all its myriad forms and bold expressions, for the artistic enterprise, critical thought, research, experimentation, and intellectual exercise. Also, whatever may be our personal religious convictions, we must inspire the development of a deeply spiritual life, since, for the great majority, religion seems to be the most effective vehicle in our tradition for curbing the death wish, expressing solidarity, advancing respect for ethical codes, promoting coexistence and order, and generally maintaining peace and taming the savage desires that all humans, even those seemingly most civilized, harbor within ourselves.

In my youth, as an avid reader of the French existentialists, I came to believe that man determines his own destiny by constantly choosing from among the various possibilities that his changing circumstances present to him. This belief helped me, I think, to become the writer that ever since childhood I had always dreamed of being. But today, after having passed through many perils, I tell myself somewhat sadly that individual destinies are perhaps influenced as much by circumstances and luck as by the freely choosing will.

Yet the "history" of an individual is not "written" in advance any more than is the "history" of a whole society. We must "write" our lines, day by day, without abdicating our right to choose, but knowing that our choices may occasionally do nothing more than confirm—openly and ethically, we hope—that which has already been chosen for us by circumstances and by others. This is cause neither for mourning nor celebration; this is life as we must live it, cherishing the whole experience of this terrible and inspiring adventure.

For Latin Americans today, the challenge could not be clearer, or more urgent. We must transform our countries into nations that are in step with their times, with no more hunger or violence, with freedom and with work, so that all may achieve a decent existence through their own efforts. It will be difficult, though assuredly not impossible, to realize the promises held by the culture of liberty that now seems to be radiating out in all directions around the globe. The expansive and lively ideas of this culture have been found workable elsewhere, and they remain capable of overcoming the barbarity of underdevelopment everywhere in the world.

II.
Problems of Democratic Institutionalization

8.
THREE PARADOXES
OF DEMOCRACY

Larry Diamond

Larry Diamond *is coeditor of the* Journal of Democracy *and senior research fellow at the Hoover Institution. He is coeditor, with Juan Linz and Seymour Martin Lipset, of the multivolume series* Democracy in Developing Countries *(1988-89) and author of* Class, Ethnicity, and Democracy in Nigeria *(1988). He has written widely on problems of democracy and democratic transitions in Nigeria and the Third World.*

The world in 1990 is in the grip of a democratic revolution. Throughout the developing world, peoples are resisting and rebelling against communist and authoritarian rule. The ferment has spread to the world's most isolated, unlikely, and forgotten places: Burma, Mongolia, Nepal, Zaire, even Albania. From the postcommunist world of Eastern Europe to the post-bureaucratic-authoritarian nations of Latin America, from the poverty-stricken heart of tropical Africa to newly rich and industrializing East Asia, nations are on the march toward democracy. Never in human history have so many independent countries been demanding or installing or practicing democratic governance. Never in history has awareness of popular struggles for democracy spread so rapidly and widely across national borders. Never have democrats worldwide seemed to have so much cause for rejoicing.

But committed democrats would do well to restrain their impulse to celebrate. Democracy is the most widely admired type of political system but also perhaps the most difficult to maintain. Alone among all forms of government, democracy rests on a minimum of coercion and a maximum of consent. Democratic polities inevitably find themselves saddled with certain "built-in" paradoxes or contradictions. The tensions these cause are not easy to reconcile, and every country that would be democratic must find its own way of doing so.

This essay explores three contradictions that will bear very heavily on the struggles now underway around the world to develop and institutionalize democracy. My analysis will draw on evidence gleaned from a comparative study of experiences with democracy in 26 developing countries.[1]

Many of the problems that democracy has experienced in the developing world spring from three tensions or paradoxes that inhere in democracy's very nature. First is the tension between *conflict* and *consensus*. Democracy is, by its nature, a system of institutionalized competition for power. Without competition and conflict, there is no democracy. But any society that sanctions political conflict runs the risk of its becoming too intense, producing a society so conflict-ridden that civil peace and political stability are jeopardized. Hence the paradox: Democracy requires conflict—but not too much; competition there must be, but only within carefully defined and universally accepted boundaries. Cleavage must be tempered by consensus.[2]

A second tension or contradiction sets *representativeness* against *governability*. Democracy implies an unwillingness to concentrate power in the hands of a few, and so subjects leaders and policies to mechanisms of popular representation and accountability. But to be stable, democracy (or any system of government) must have what Alexander Hamilton called "energy"—it must always be able to act, and at times must do so quickly and decisively. Government must not only respond to interest-group demands; it must be able to resist them and mediate among them as well. This requires a party system that can produce a government stable and cohesive enough to represent and respond to competing groups and interests in society without being paralyzed or captured by them. Representativeness requires that parties speak to and for these conflicting interests; governability requires that parties have sufficient autonomy to rise above them.

This leads to the third contradiction, between *consent* and *effectiveness*. Democracy means, literally, "rule by the people," or at least rule with the consent of the governed. This is the message of people all over the world who are fed up with the repression and corruption of authoritarian or totalitarian ruling elites. As the articles in this publication attest, people across the globe are making it clear that they want the right to turn their rulers out of office, to be governed only with their consent.

But founding a democracy and preserving it are two different things. To be stable, democracy must be deemed legitimate by the people; they must view it as the best, the most appropriate form of government for their society. Indeed, *because* it rests on the consent of the governed, democracy depends on popular legitimacy much more than any other form of government. This legitimacy requires a profound moral commitment and emotional allegiance, but these develop only over time, and partly as a result of effective performance. Democracy will not be valued by the people unless it deals effectively with social and economic problems and achieves a modicum of order and justice.

If democracy does not work, people may prefer *not* to be governed through their own consent—they may choose not to put up with the pain of political choice any longer. Herein lies the paradox: Democracy requires consent. Consent requires legitimacy. Legitimacy requires effective performance. But effectiveness may be sacrificed to consent. Elected leaders will always be reluctant to pursue unpopular policies, no matter how wise or necessary they may be.

These three paradoxes have important implications for the development of democracy in those underdeveloped polities of Eastern Europe and what is commonly called "the Third World" that are struggling now, after so much repression and frustration, to build lasting democracies. Let us consider the implications of each of these paradoxes, beginning with the last.

Consent versus Effectiveness

Democracies—and especially new democracies—suffer from a special problem with regard to government performance: Popular assessments of how the government has done tend to take the short view. Democratic governments everywhere—in the industrialized world every bit as much as the developing one—are thus constantly tempted to trim their policies with an eye on the next election. This may make good political sense in the short run, but it does not make for good *economic* policy. And when we are talking about performance, it is primarily economic performance that counts.

Authoritarian regimes like Pinochet's Chile are not dependent on popular consent, and can therefore afford politically to make their populations suffer through long periods of economic austerity and structural adjustment for the sake of long-term payoffs. Chile's economy is booming now—but at what price in human suffering, poverty, unemployment, and political repression over the past 15 years?

East European and many Latin American countries need urgently to implement sweeping structural reforms to generate productive and internationally competitive economies. But how long and how hard will new democratic or democratizing governments push economic reform if the short-term pain proves devastating, while the gains, however great, will not become apparent until well after the next election?

In such circumstances, the consolidation of democracy—so intimately linked to structural economic reform—requires the negotiation of some kind of agreement or "pact" among competing political parties and social forces on: 1) the broad direction and principles of structural economic reform, which all parties will support, no matter which one(s) come to power; 2) a renunciation of certain political appeals and strategies—in particular an irresponsible but tempting politics of outbidding; 3) sacrifices that all social forces will share, including demands they will

mutually postpone, during the critical and highly unstable period of
economic adjustment and democratic installation; and 4) a method of
ensuring that the burdens of adjustment are shared more or less fairly
and eased by relief measures for the hardest-hit groups, such as workers
rendered jobless by structural reforms.[3]

Such pacts may be as narrow as agreements on core principles of
long-term economic policy, or may be far-reaching enough to produce
broad coalitions capable of governing in the name of a firm policy
consensus. One possible model in this regard may be the political and
economic pacts negotiated by elites in Venezuela in 1958 that facilitated
the successful and enduring restoration of democracy there. In addition
to sharing power, these pacts set the broad outlines of the country's
major economic policies, thus removing potentially contentious issues
from partisan debate.[4]

The scale of the relief required to make economic reform politically
palatable may lie well beyond what the bankrupt and debt-ravaged
economies of Eastern Europe, Latin America, Africa, and other
developing countries (such as the Philippines) can finance on their own.
Successful adjustment through democracy would seem to require an
international compact as well. The industrialized democracies and the
international community could offer substantial new investment and aid
and genuine debt reduction in exchange for reforms designed to break
the economic stranglehold of statism and launch these countries into self-
sustaining growth.

What reforms and principles might serve as the basic tenets of a new
economic policy consensus for these troubled democracies?

The past four decades of Third World economic development have
furnished invaluable lessons for distinguishing the policies that work from
those that do not. Broadly speaking, market-oriented economies develop,
while state-socialist economies fall behind. Internationally open and
competitive economies work; closed (or at least rigidly and persistently
closed) economies do not. Economies grow when they foster savings,
investment, and innovation, and when they reward individual effort and
initiative. Economies stagnate and regress when bloated, mercantilist,
hyperinterventionist states build "a structure of inflexible favoritisms for
different groups, curtailing change, experimentation, competition,
innovation, and social mobility."[5]

Furthermore, economies that invest in the human capital of the poor
by meeting their basic human needs develop a continuing momentum of
growth. But those that effectively prevent half, two-thirds, or more of the
population from gaining the skills and opportunities needed to partake in
and benefit from development ultimately founder.

Democratic development, like democratic culture, requires a
considerable measure of balance, moderation, and respect for all interests.
Markets must be sufficiently open, flexible, and competitive to generate

increases in savings, investment, and rates of return. This requires getting or keeping the state off the backs of producers. But the state must be sufficiently involved to ensure that there is adequate investment in human and physical capital, and that development is responsible to environmental and other community interests. Taxes must be substantial enough (and sufficiently fairly and efficiently collected) to provide revenue for these essential purposes, but must also be limited and designed so that they operate "in ways most neutral to the incentives to save, invest, and efficiently allocate resources."[6]

Around these general principles lies much variation, and also much complexity. Countries develop with differing types and mixes of state involvement in fostering indigenous enterprise (and even temporarily protecting it). But countries fall behind when the state becomes the *dominant* producer and employer, or an enduring protector of inefficient economic actors, whether capital or labor.

Perhaps the most important lesson from our comparative study of 26 countries is very simple, but very commonly neglected. Whatever the exact shape of a country's policy, it can only work if it is pursued consistently and pragmatically. Drastic shifts between radical populist redistributive policies and radical neoliberal austerity policies are bound to invite economic miseries and crises of the sort that now threaten the future of democracy in Argentina, Brazil, and Peru.

This is not the inevitable fate of electoral regimes in the developing world. Botswana, Colombia, and (more problematically) India, with very different development levels and natural resource endowments, have all achieved steady economic growth through stable, prudent policies. Entrepreneurs at all levels in these countries can save, invest, profit, and reinvest with some confidence in a predictable future. Most notably perhaps, Colombia's eclectic, pragmatic economic policies have produced constant growth with low inflation in the three decades since its democratic transition. Although India is often believed to be an economic basket case, it has in fact achieved significant socioeconomic development in the past three decades—and would have done much better had its population not doubled to 800 million. Since independence, India has achieved self-sufficiency in agriculture, significant industrialization, and quite tangible improvements in literacy, life expectancy, and infant mortality. It has done all this, moreover, while holding inflation and foreign borrowing to some of the lowest levels in the developing world.

If India can develop, why cannot Africa? With a population more than half again as large as Africa's—and no greater bounty of natural resources, plus a level of poverty as great as Africa's at independence—why has India been able to perform so much better economically?

The answers are in part political, for they involve policies and institutions. India had the political institutions—not only the bureaucracy but also a stable and institutionalized political party system—to pursue a consistent and pragmatic long-run strategy for economic development. By and large it worked, although there is still enough inefficiency, corruption, and waste—deriving from a misplaced socialist idealism and a suffocating statism—to threaten the economic progress that India has made so far.

This comparative evidence holds two important lessons. The first is that democracies do not, inherently, perform worse economically than dictatorships. Very probably, they do not *inherently* perform better, either. The policies chosen—and the skill with which they are implemented—are far more important. The second is that, since consistency, prudence, and pragmatism in policy are so important to economic development, struggling young democracies must give serious thought to how they can form and maintain a broad consensus on economic policy. This will require creative institution-building, public education, and elite accommodation. Above all, it will require political leadership with courage, vision, and determination.

This brings us back, then, to our second paradox—how to balance representativeness and accountability with the need for governability?

Representativeness versus Governability

Governability requires sufficient concentration and autonomy of power to choose and implement policies with energy and dispatch. This generally conflicts with the need to hold power accountable to popular scrutiny, representation, and control. In some respects, however, vigorous public accountability may strengthen the capacity to govern and the effectiveness of government. This is most clearly seen with regard to political corruption.

Widespread government corruption is poisonous to democracy. It impedes economic growth by misdirecting the flow of capital and resources, and by distorting investment decisions and economic competition generally. Although some have argued that corruption may enhance political legitimacy by dispersing material benefits, these are typically concentrated rather than "spread around." A narrow class of government officials and their business cronies is enriched at the expense of the bulk of the population—and of the legitimacy of the entire democratic system.

Moreover, where the prospect of ill-gotten gain is an important motive for the pursuit of office, the democratic process becomes a mere power struggle rather than a contest over policies. The premium on political power becomes so great that competing forces will do anything to win. This threatens the very essence of the democratic process—free, fair, and peaceful elections.

Statism exacerbates corruption by giving public officials numerous opportunities to collect rents from the state's regulatory activities. But opportunities for corruption are perennial features of public life everywhere. The only remedy is accountability, which requires a free press willing and able to expose corruption; an organized citizenry ready to monitor the political process and the conduct of public officials; and an assertive, independent legal system equipped to prosecute and punish official misconduct.

These are at least some of the ways in which accountability serves governability. They involve limiting the power of the state, and especially the executive, in order to prevent abuses. But there are trade-offs, for if power is too limited or too diffused, government may be hamstrung.

Each country must find its own way of resolving this universal tension. Juan Linz has argued that parliamentary systems may be preferable in most developing countries because, *inter alia*, they make the executive branch more accountable before the legislature, avoid the rigidity and winner-take-all features of presidentialism, and at the same time serve governability by preventing the potential deadlock that can arise in a presidential system when the presidency is controlled by one party and the legislature by others.[7]

But here, too, there are no pat formulas, and some countries may be better served by the more decisive character of presidential systems, by the greater stability of presidential cabinets, and by the possibility that presidentialism provides to elect a single, overarching national leader in ways (and with rules) that induce the recruitment of broad constituencies.[8]

A vigorous civil society enhances not only the accountability, but also the representativeness and vitality of democracy. Voluntary associations represent a crucial institutional supplement to democratic political parties. The persistence of democracy in India and Costa Rica for four decades, and in Venezuela since 1958, owes much to these countries' dense networks of autonomous voluntary associations and mass media. These not only check and scrutinize state power; they also enhance the legitimacy of democracy by providing new means to express political interests; increasing the political awareness, efficacy, and confidence of citizens; and training and recruiting new political leaders.

At the same time, however, democratic governments and parties must have some autonomy from group demands in order to make and implement tough decisions. If political parties are too weak or too penetrated by other social groups; if the bureaucracy is a captive of such parties or interests; if the elected government cannot stand above, reconcile, and at times resist interest-group pressures; then that government may be unable to formulate workable policies. Such weakness could produce a regime-threatening crisis of confidence.

The relationship among party systems, electoral systems, and constitutional structure introduces another profound tension between representativeness and governability. In principle, the purest way to represent diverse social groups and interests, especially in deeply divided societies, is through proportional representation (PR). In fact, where social cleavages are multiple, deep, and politically mobilized, to obstruct their representation through the party system by abandoning PR would be to risk political alienation, turmoil, and violence that could threaten democratic stability.[8] The purer the form of PR, and the lower the minimum percentage of the vote required for a party to enter the parliament, the more significant parties there will tend to be and the more parliament will tend to mirror in its political composition the balance of social, cultural, and ideological interests in society.[10] This may make the system more representative—but less governable and even less accountable, for three reasons.

First, if none of the parliamentarians is elected from (manageably sized) territorial districts, none of them is individually accountable to any clearly identifiable portion of the electorate, other than the party bosses or electors who put them on the party list of candidates. Second, with the fragmentation of the party system, voters may keep getting virtually the same coalition governments, with minor shifts in cabinet portfolios, no matter how the vote may change among parties. Thus, it becomes difficult truly to change policy, and to "throw the rascals out." This may enhance stability of policy, even as it leads to frequent changes in government (as in Italy), but at the cost of denying voters clear electoral choice. Third, in a situation of evenly balanced large parties and numerous small parties, the latter derive vastly inordinate bargaining leverage or "blackmail" potential in negotiations to form a government. This leads either to an undemocratic concession of power and resources to these fringe groups or to a "national unity" coalition government so divided that it cannot act. This conundrum has increasingly crippled democratic politics in Israel, where electoral reform has become the rallying cry of an outraged Israeli population.

In such circumstances, a political system may be made *more* stably democratic by making it somewhat *less* representative. Thus West Germany, reflecting on the polarization and instability of the Weimar Republic, set an electoral threshold of five percent of the vote for a party to enter the Bundestag, and got a stable system comprising two dominant parties plus one or two minor ones. Reflecting on the political fragmentation and polarization that in 1980 brought its democracy down for the second time in as many decades, Turkey in 1982 adopted a ten-percent threshold and other changes that have also produced a much more consolidated party system. In the past year, a bipartisan electoral-reform commission in Israel has produced a wisely balanced proposal that, while retaining PR, would set the threshold at 3.5 percent and elect, as in West Germany, half the members of parliament from territorial districts and half from national party lists.[11]

There are, of course, more drastic mechanisms for streamlining the party system, such as the election of legislators from single-member districts by plurality vote and the presidential system. Either one will tend strongly to reduce the number of parties; the two together are a natural recipe for a two-party system. But we have already mentioned the problems with presidentialism, and in a situation with more than two parties enjoying significant electoral support—such as Britain in the last parliamentary election or India since independence—the plurality method of election by district can magnify a party's national electoral plurality into a staggering parliamentary majority. This may produce not governability so much as a decidedly undemocratic imbalance and arrogance of power. Part of the riddle of democracy is that its paradoxes are not often resolved through recourse to blunt and simple alternatives.

Conflict versus Consensus

Perhaps the most basic tension in democracy is between conflict and consensus. Democracy implies dissent and division, but on a basis of consent and cohesion. It requires that the citizens assert themselves, but also that they accept the government's authority. It demands that the citizens care about politics, but not too much. This is why Gabriel Almond and Sidney Verba, in their classic book *The Civic Culture*, called the democratic political culture "mixed." It balances the citizen's role as participant (as agent of political competition and conflict) with his or her role as subject (obeyer of state authority), and as "parochial" member of family, social, and community networks outside politics.[12] The subject role serves governability while the parochial role tempers political conflict by limiting the politicization of social life.

Other closely related elements of democratic political culture include tolerance of opposition and dissent; trust in fellow political actors; a willingness to cooperate, accommodate, and compromise; and hence a certain flexibility, moderation, civility, and restraint in one's partisanship. It is well understood that sturdy habits of moderation and conciliation make it possible for democracies to balance conflict and consensus.[13] To honor these virtues in deed as well as in speech is often one of the most important challenges facing nascent and troubled democracies.

How do such democratic habits develop? Certainly they are fostered by education, which, as Almond and Verba showed, increases a host of "democratic" tendencies in the individual. Socioeconomic development can also enhance democratic values and practices to the extent that it improves the income, education, skills, and life chances of citizens. Again we see why investment in human capital is so important for the preservation of democracy.

Yet is there not considerable historical evidence to suggest that democratic culture is as much the product as the cause of effectively functioning democracy? Elites may "back into" democracy for a variety of strategic reasons—including, for example, the historic lack or exhaustion of other means for resolving conflict,[14] or the unavailability in today's Eastern Europe or Latin America of any other legitimate alternative. Subsequently, however, the successful practice of democracy demonstrates the value of participation, tolerance, and compromise—indeed the efficacy and intrinsic desirability of democracy itself. Over time, citizens of a democracy become habituated to its norms and values, gradually internalizing them.[15] The trick, then, is for democracies to survive long enough—and function well enough—for this process to occur.

But this returns us to the paradox. To survive and function well, democracy must moderate conflict. But the cultural mechanisms for doing so do not develop overnight. In the meantime, how can conflicts be contained so that political cleavage and competition do not rip society apart?

Cleavages tend to run along lines of class, ethnicity (including religion and region), and party. The problem of class cleavage presents a paradox within a paradox. For democracy to be stable, class cleavage must be moderate. For class cleavage to be moderate, economic inequality must be moderate too. Severe inequality tends eventually to generate intense, violent political polarization, as Peru and the Philippines are discovering. To avoid this, to achieve a moderate degree of inequality, socioeconomic reforms must be undertaken. At a minimum, these include prudent investments in education, health care, housing, and other social services. In some cases, more thoroughgoing reforms, including land reform, may be necessary. But this may ignite the bitter resistance of entrenched elites, especially large landowners and employers of cheap labor. And therein lies the rub: to moderate class conflict in the long run, a political system may need to risk aggravating it in the short run.

There is no obvious way out of this conundrum. Democracy often gains a purchase in tense and conflict-ridden situations only when certain especially contentious issues are ruled off the agenda. But the nettle must eventually be grasped, for democracy cannot endure if massive inequality and exclusion go unchallenged. By its very nature, democracy permits only incremental reform rather than revolutionary change. Opposing interests must somehow be reconciled. Land may need to be redistributed—but only after its owners are fairly compensated and given opportunities to reinvest their assets in other productive enterprises. Wages may need to be increased, but only at a pace that will not threaten severe damage to corporate profits and economic growth. For only in a context of economic growth can inequality be reduced in a way that brings an enduring reduction in poverty.

Getting reform on the agenda requires that disadvantaged and excluded economic groups organize and mobilize politically. But if reform is to be adopted without provoking a crisis that might destroy democracy, the costs to privileged economic interests of overturning democracy must be kept greater than the costs of the reforms themselves. This requires realism and incrementalism on the part of those groups pressing for reform. It also requires sufficient overall effectiveness, stability, and guarantees for capital on the part of the democratic regime so that privileged economic actors will have a lot to lose by turning against it.

Ethnic and Party Cleavages

The social sciences may have discerned few true laws, but one that can be confidently stated concerns ethnicity: Ethnic cleavages do not die. They cannot be extinguished through repression or assimilation; however, they can be managed so that they do not threaten civil peace, and people of different groups are able to coexist tranquilly while maintaining their ethnic identities.

There are four principal mechanisms for managing ethnicity politically within a democratic framework: federalism, proportionality in the distribution of resources and power, minority rights (to cultural integrity and protection against discrimination), and sharing or rotation of power, in particular through coalition arrangements at the center.[16]

As the experiences of India and Nigeria demonstrate, and as Donald Horowitz has noted, federal systems are particularly effective in managing ethnic tension because they utilize a variety of mechanisms for reducing conflict. First, they *disperse conflict* by transferring much of it to state and local levels. They also generate *intraethnic conflict*, pitting different factions of ethnic groups against one another in the struggle for control of state and local governments. Third, they may induce *interethnic cooperation* as states find the need to coalesce with one another in shifting ways depending on the issue at the center. Fourth, they may generate *crosscutting cleavages* if some ethnic groups are split into different states, with different interests, advantages, and needs. Fifth, they can *reduce disparities* by enabling backward and minority peoples to rise within their own state bureaucracies and educational systems.[17]

More generally, federal systems give all major territorially based ethnic groups some control over their own affairs, and some chance to gain power and control resources at multiple levels. This points to another virtual law: the impossibility of stable democracy in a society where ethnic cleavages are deep and power is heavily centralized. There are compelling independent reasons why decentralization of power and strong local and state government promote the vitality of democracy, but these are especially striking imperatives in divided societies.

Finally, party cleavage can represent, independent of class and ethnicity, a quite sufficient basis for violent and destructive conflict. Even in the absence of deep differences over ideology and program, political parties represent competing organizations for the conquest of state power, and the greater and more pervasive the power of the state, the more will parties want to get it and keep it at any price. This is another reason why statism is so toxic to democracy: not only because it breeds corruption and economic inefficiency, but also because it raises the premium on political power to a degree approaching a zero-sum game. When so much is at stake in the electoral contest, trust, tolerance, civility, and obedience to the rules become formidably difficult to maintain. A balanced political culture—in which people care about politics, but not too much—is possible only in structural circumstances where people can *afford* not to care too much, where wealth, income, status, and opportunities for upward mobility are not mere functions of political power.

In Eastern Europe and much of the developing world, restraining the partisan battle requires deflating the state and invigorating the private economy. But it requires more as well. Where parties are only beginning to take shape, where open political life is only just emerging after decades of repression and fear, the culture of tolerance, trust, accommodation, and cooperation is yet to be born. Passions are intense, memories bitter. People lack the basis of mutual trust and respect on which they might combine political efforts or at least pursue their own political interests prudently and flexibly.

In such circumstances, elite actions, choices, and postures can have a formative impact in shaping the way their followers approach political discourse and conflict. Opposing party leaders must take the lead in crafting understandings and working relationships that bridge historic differences, restrain expectations, and establish longer, more realistic time horizons for their agendas. Pacts or formal arrangements for sharing power represent only one dimension of this general imperative. At a minimum, competing party elites must set an accommodating and civil tone for political life. Above all, they must manifest a faith in the democratic process and a commitment to its rules that supersedes the pursuit of power or other substantive goals.

Building among political competitors such a system of "mutual security," as Robert Dahl calls it, of transcendent respect for the rules of the game, may demand not only faith but a leap of faith from political leaders. They must believe that whatever results from the democratic process will, in the long run, serve their interests better than an intransigence that risks the breakdown of democracy. Among the manifold uncertainties that attend the founding of all new regimes, probably nothing is more important to democracy than the presence of party leaders with the courage and vision to join hands in taking this leap.

NOTES

1. Larry Diamond, Juan J. Linz, and Seymour Martin Lipset, eds., *Democracy in Developing Countries: Vol. 2, Africa; Vol. 3, Asia; Vol. 4, Latin America* (Boulder, Colorado: Lynne Rienner Publishers, 1988 and 1989).

2. Gabriel A. Almond and Sidney Verba, *The Civic Culture: Political Attitudes and Democracy in Five Nations* (Boston: Little, Brown and Co., 1965), 356-360.

3. O'Donnell and Schmitter define a pact as "an explicit, but not always publicly explicated or justified, agreement among a select set of actors which seeks to define (or better, to redefine) rules governing the exercise of power on the basis of mutual guarantees for the 'vital interests' of those entering into it." I enlarge slightly on their usage to denote an agreement on the basis of guarantees for the overall *national* interest. Guillermo O'Donnell and Philippe C. Schmitter, *Transitions from Authoritarian Rule: Tentative Conclusions about Uncertain Democracies* (Baltimore: Johns Hopkins University Press, 1986), 37-38.

4. Terry Lynn Karl, "Petroleum and Political Pacts: The Transition to Democracy in Venezuela," in *Transitions from Authoritarian Rule: Latin America*, eds. Guillermo O'Donnell, Philippe Schmitter and Laurence Whitehead (Baltimore: Johns Hopkins University Press, 1986), 210-215.

5. Nicolas Ardito-Barletta, "Democracy and Development," *The Washington Quarterly* 13 (Summer 1990): 161-171.

6. Ibid., 163.

7. "The Perils of Presidentialism," *Journal of Democracy* 1 (Winter 1990): 51-69.

8. Such possibilities for presidentialism in multiethnic societies are considered by Donald Horowitz, *Ethnic Groups in Conflict* (Berkeley: University of California Press, 1985), 636-639.

9. G. Bingham Powell, Jr., *Contemporary Democracies: Participation, Stability, and Violence* (Cambridge: Harvard University Press, 1982), 123-132.

10. Arend Lijphart, *Democracies: Patterns of Majoritarian and Consensus Government in Twenty-One Countries* (New Haven: Yale University Press, 1984), 150-168.

11. Israel-Diaspora Institute, "Electoral Reform in Israel—An Abstract," Tel-Aviv, Israel, February 1990.

12. Almond and Verba, op. cit., 339-360.

13. Robert Dahl, *Polyarchy: Participation and Opposition* (New Haven: Yale University Press, 1971), 150-162.

14. Michael G. Burton and John Higley, "Elite Settlements," *American Sociological Review* 52 (June 1987): 295-307.

15. Dankwart Rustow, "Transitions to Democracy: Toward a Dynamic Model," *Comparative Politics* 2 (April 1970): 358-361.

16. A more specific and far-reaching arrangement of these principles is embodied in "consociational democracy," which consists of a "grand coalition" cabinet in a parliamentary system; a mutual veto to protect minority interests; proportionality in political representation, civil service appointments, and revenue allocation; and considerable autonomy for each ethnic group in its own affairs. Arend Lijphart, *Democracy in Plural Societies: A Comparative Exploration* (New Haven: Yale University Press, 1977).

17. Horowitz, op. cit., 597-613.

9.
THE PERILS
OF PRESIDENTIALISM

Juan J. Linz

Juan J. Linz, Sterling Professor of Political and Social Science at Yale University, is widely known for his contributions to the study of authoritarianism and totalitarianism, political parties and elites, and democratic breakdowns and transitions to democracy. In 1987 he was awarded Spain's Principe de Asturias *prize in the social sciences. The following essay is based on a paper he presented in May 1989 at a conference in Washington, D.C. organized by the Latin American Studies Program of Georgetown University, with support from the Ford Foundation. An annotated, revised, and expanded version of this essay (including a discussion of semipresidential systems) will appear under the title "Presidentialism and Parliamentarism: Does It Make a Difference?" in a publication based on the conference being edited by the author and Professor Arturo Valenzuela of Georgetown University.*

As more of the world's nations turn to democracy, interest in alternative constitutional forms and arrangements has expanded well beyond academic circles. In countries as dissimilar as Chile, South Korea, Brazil, Turkey, and Argentina, policymakers and constitutional experts have vigorously debated the relative merits of different types of democratic regimes. Some countries, like Sri Lanka, have switched from parliamentary to presidential constitutions. On the other hand, Latin Americans in particular have found themselves greatly impressed by the successful transition from authoritarianism to democracy that occurred in the 1970s in Spain, a transition to which the parliamentary form of government chosen by that country greatly contributed.

Nor is the Spanish case the only one in which parliamentarism has given evidence of its worth. Indeed, the vast majority of the stable democracies in the world today are parliamentary regimes, where executive power is generated by legislative majorities and depends on such majorities for survival.

By contrast, the only presidential democracy with a long history of constitutional continuity is the United States. The constitutions of Finland and France are hybrids rather than true presidential systems, and in the case of the French Fifth Republic, the jury is still out. Aside from the United States, only Chile has managed a century and a half of relatively undisturbed constitutional continuity under presidential government—but Chilean democracy broke down in the 1970s.

Parliamentary regimes, of course, can also be unstable, especially under conditions of bitter ethnic conflict, as recent African history attests. Yet the experiences of India and of some English-speaking countries in the Caribbean show that even in greatly divided societies, periodic parliamentary crises need not turn into full-blown regime crises and that the ousting of a prime minister and cabinet need not spell the end of democracy itself.

The burden of this essay is that the superior historical performance of parliamentary democracies is no accident. A careful comparison of parliamentarism as such with presidentialism as such leads to the conclusion that, on balance, the former is more conducive to stable democracy than the latter. This conclusion applies especially to nations with deep political cleavages and numerous political parties; for such countries, parliamentarism generally offers a better hope of preserving democracy.

Parliamentary vs. Presidential Systems

A parliamentary regime in the strict sense is one in which the only democratically legitimate institution is parliament; in such a regime, the government's authority is completely dependent upon parliamentary confidence. Although the growing personalization of party leadership in some parliamentary regimes has made prime ministers seem more and more like presidents, it remains true that barring dissolution of parliament and a call for new elections, premiers cannot appeal directly to the people over the heads of their representatives. Parliamentary systems may include presidents who are elected by direct popular vote, but they usually lack the ability to compete seriously for power with the prime minister.

In presidential systems an executive with considerable constitutional powers—generally including full control of the composition of the cabinet and administration—is directly elected by the people for a fixed term and is independent of parliamentary votes of confidence. He is not only the holder of executive power but also the symbolic head of state and can be removed between elections only by the drastic step of impeachment. In practice, as the history of the United States shows, presidential systems may be more or less dependent on the cooperation of the legislature; the balance between executive and legislative power in such systems can thus vary considerably.

Two things about presidential government stand out. The first is the president's strong claim to democratic, even plebiscitarian, legitimacy; the second is his fixed term in office. Both of these statements stand in need of qualification. Some presidents gain office with a smaller proportion of the popular vote than many premiers who head minority cabinets, although voters may see the latter as more weakly legitimated. To mention just one example, Salvador Allende's election as president of Chile in 1970—he had a 36.2-percent plurality obtained by a heterogeneous coalition—certainly put him in a position very different from that in which Adolfo Suárez of Spain found himself in 1979 when he became prime minister after receiving 35.1 percent of the vote. As we will see, Allende received a six-year mandate for controlling the government even with much less than a majority of the popular vote, while Suárez, with a plurality of roughly the same size, found it necessary to work with other parties to sustain a minority government. Following British political thinker Walter Bagehot, we might say that a presidential system endows the incumbent with both the "ceremonial" functions of a head of state and the "effective" functions of a chief executive, thus creating an aura, a self-image, and a set of popular expectations which are all quite different from those associated with a prime minister, no matter how popular he may be.

But what is most striking is that in a presidential system, the legislators, especially when they represent cohesive, disciplined parties that offer clear ideological and political alternatives, can also claim democratic legitimacy. This claim is thrown into high relief when a majority of the legislature represents a political option opposed to the one the president represents. Under such circumstances, who has the stronger claim to speak on behalf of the people: the president or the legislative majority that opposes his policies? Since both derive their power from the votes of the people in a free competition among well-defined alternatives, a conflict is always possible and at times may erupt dramatically. There is no democratic principle on the basis of which it can be resolved, and the mechanisms the constitution might provide are likely to prove too complicated and aridly legalistic to be of much force in the eyes of the electorate. It is therefore no accident that in some such situations in the past, the armed forces were often tempted to intervene as a mediating power. One might argue that the United States has successfully rendered such conflicts "normal" and thus defused them. To explain how American political institutions and practices have achieved this result would exceed the scope of this essay, but it is worth noting that the uniquely diffuse character of American political parties—which, ironically, exasperates many American political scientists and leads them to call for responsible, ideologically disciplined parties—has something to do with it. Unfortunately, the American case seems to be an exception; the development of modern political parties, particularly in socially and ideologically polarized countries, generally exacerbates, rather than moderates, conflicts between the legislative and the executive.

The second outstanding feature of presidential systems—the president's relatively fixed term in office—is also not without drawbacks. It breaks the political process into discontinuous, rigidly demarcated periods, leaving no room for the continuous readjustments that events may demand. The duration of the president's mandate becomes a crucial factor in the calculations of all political actors, a fact which (as we shall see) is fraught with important consequences. Consider, for instance, the provisions for succession in case of the president's death or incapacity: in some cases, the automatic successor may have been elected separately and may represent a political orientation different from the president's; in other cases, he may have been imposed by the president as his running mate without any consideration of his ability to exercise executive power or maintain popular support. Brazilian history provides us with examples of the first situation, while Maria Estela Martínez de Perón's succession of her husband in Argentina illustrates the second. It is a paradox of presidential government that while it leads to the personalization of power, its legal mechanisms may also lead, in the event of a sudden midterm succession, to the rise of someone whom the ordinary electoral process would never have made the chief of state.

Paradoxes of Presidentialism

Presidential constitutions paradoxically incorporate contradictory principles and assumptions. On the one hand, such systems set out to create a strong, stable executive with enough plebiscitarian legitimation to stand fast against the array of particular interests represented in the legislature. In the Rousseauian conception of democracy implied by the idea of "the people," for whom the president is supposed to speak, these interests lack legitimacy; so does the Anglo-American notion that democracy naturally involves a jostle—or even sometimes a melee—of interests. Interest group conflict then bids fair to manifest itself in areas other than the strictly political. On the other hand, presidential constitutions also reflect profound suspicion of the personalization of power: memories and fears of kings and caudillos do not dissipate easily. Foremost among the constitutional bulwarks against potentially arbitrary power is the prohibition on reelection. Other provisions like legislative advice-and-consent powers over presidential appointments, impeachment mechanisms, judicial independence, and institutions such as the Contraloría of Chile also reflect this suspicion. Indeed, political intervention by the armed forces acting as a *poder moderador* may even be seen in certain political cultures as a useful check on overweening executives. One could explore in depth the contradictions between the constitutional texts and political practices of Latin American presidential regimes; any student of the region's history could cite many examples.

It would be useful to explore the way in which the fundamental contradiction between the desire for a strong and stable executive and the latent suspicion of that same presidential power affects political decision making, the style of leadership, the political practices, and the rhetoric of both presidents and their opponents in presidential systems. It introduces a dimension of conflict that cannot be explained wholly by socioeconomic, political, or ideological circumstances. Even if one were to accept the debatable notion that Hispanic societies are inherently prone to *personalismo*, there can be little doubt that in some cases this tendency receives reinforcement from institutional arrangements.

Perhaps the best way to summarize the basic differences between presidential and parliamentary systems is to say that while parliamentarism imparts flexibility to the political process, presidentialism makes it rather rigid. Proponents of presidentialism might reply that this rigidity is an advantage, for it guards against the uncertainty and instability so characteristic of parliamentary politics. Under parliamentary government, after all, myriad actors—parties, their leaders, even rank-and-file legislators—may at any time between elections adopt basic changes, cause realignments, and, above all, make or break prime ministers. But while the need for authority and predictability would seem to favor presidentialism, there are unexpected developments—ranging from the death of the incumbent to serious errors in judgment committed under the pressure of unruly circumstances—that make presidential rule less predictable and often weaker than that of a prime minister. The latter can always seek to shore up his legitimacy and authority, either through a vote of confidence or the dissolution of parliament and the ensuing new elections. Moreover, a prime minister can be changed without necessarily creating a regime crisis.

Considerations of this sort loom especially large during periods of regime transition and consolidation, when the rigidities of a presidential constitution must seem inauspicious indeed compared to the prospect of adaptability that parliamentarism offers.

Zero-sum Elections

The preceding discussion has focused principally on the institutional dimensions of the problem; the consideration of constitutional provisions—some written, some unwritten—has dominated the analysis. In addition, however, one must attend to the ways in which political competition is structured in systems of direct presidential elections; the styles of leadership in such systems; the relations between the president, the political elites, and society at large; and the ways in which power is exercised and conflicts are resolved. It is a fair assumption that institutional arrangements both directly and indirectly shape the entire political process, or "way of ruling." Once we have described the differences between parliamentary and presidential forms of government that result from their differing institutional arrangements, we shall be ready to ask which of the two forms offers the best prospect for creating, consolidating, and maintaining democracy.

Presidentialism is ineluctably problematic because it operates according to the rule of "winner-take-all"—an arrangement that tends to make democratic politics a zero-sum game, with all the potential for conflict such games portend. Although parliamentary elections can produce an absolute majority for a single party, they more often give representation to a number of parties. Power-sharing and coalition-forming are fairly common, and incumbents are accordingly attentive to the demands and interests of even the smaller parties. These parties in turn retain expectations of sharing in power and, therefore, of having a stake in the system as a whole. By contrast, the conviction that he possesses independent authority and a popular mandate is likely to imbue a president with a sense of power and mission, even if the plurality that elected him is a slender one. Given such assumptions about his standing and role, he will find the inevitable opposition to his policies far more irksome and demoralizing than would a prime minister, who knows himself to be but the spokesman for a temporary governing coalition rather than the voice of the nation or the tribune of the people.

Absent the support of an absolute and cohesive majority, a parliamentary system inevitably includes elements that become institutionalized in what has been called "consociational democracy." Presidential regimes may incorporate consociational elements as well, perhaps as part of the unwritten constitution. When democracy was reestablished under adverse circumstances in Venezuela and Colombia, for example, the written constitutions may have called for presidential government, but the leaders of the major parties quickly turned to consociational agreements to soften the harsh, winner-take-all implications of presidential elections.

The danger that zero-sum presidential elections pose is compounded by the rigidity of the president's fixed term in office. Winners and losers are sharply defined for the entire period of the presidential mandate. There is no hope for shifts in alliances, expansion of the government's base of support through national-unity or emergency grand coalitions, new elections in response to major new events, and so on. Instead, the losers must wait at least four or five years without any access to executive power and patronage. The zero-sum game in presidential regimes raises the stakes of presidential elections and inevitably exacerbates their attendant tension and polarization.

On the other hand, presidential elections do offer the indisputable advantage of allowing the people to choose their chief executive openly, directly, and for a predictable span rather than leaving that decision to the backstage maneuvering of the politicians. But this advantage can only be present if a clear mandate results. If there is no required minimum plurality and several candidates compete in a single round, the margin between the victor and the runner-up may be too thin to support any claim that a decisive plebiscite has taken place. To preclude this, electoral laws sometimes place a lower limit on the size of the winning plurality or create some mechanism for choosing among the candidates if none attains the minimum number of votes needed to win; such procedures need not necessarily award the office to the candidate with the most votes. More common are run-off provisions that set up a confrontation between the two major candidates, with possibilities for polarization that have already been mentioned. One of the possible consequences of two-candidate races in multiparty systems is that broad coalitions are likely to be formed (whether in run-offs or in preelection maneuvering) in which extremist parties gain undue influence. If significant numbers of voters identify strongly with such parties, one or more of them can plausibly claim to represent the decisive electoral bloc in a close contest and may make demands accordingly. Unless a strong candidate of the center rallies widespread support against the extremes, a presidential election can fragment and polarize the electorate.

"In a polarized society with a volatile electorate, no serious candidate in a single-round election can afford to ignore parties with which he would otherwise never collaborate."

In countries where the preponderance of voters is centrist, agrees on the exclusion of extremists, and expects both rightist and leftist candidates to differ only within a larger, moderate consensus, the divisiveness latent in presidential competition is not a serious problem. With an overwhelmingly moderate electorate, anyone who makes alliances or takes positions that seem to incline him to the extremes is unlikely to win, as both Barry Goldwater and George McGovern discovered to their chagrin. But societies beset by grave social and economic problems, divided about recent authoritarian regimes that once enjoyed significant popular support, and in which well-disciplined extremist parties have considerable electoral appeal, do not fit the model presented by the United States. In a polarized society with a volatile electorate, no serious candidate in a single-round election can afford to ignore parties with which he would otherwise never collaborate.

A two-round election can avoid some of these problems, for the preliminary round shows the extremist parties the limits of their strength and allows the two major candidates to reckon just which alliances they must make to win. This reduces the degree of uncertainty and promotes more rational decisions on the part of both voters and candidates. In effect, the presidential system may thus reproduce something like the negotiations that "form a government" in parliamentary regimes. But the potential for polarization remains, as does the difficulty of isolating extremist factions that a significant portion of the voters and elites intensely dislike.

The Spanish Example

For illustration of the foregoing analysis, consider the case of Spain in 1977, the year of the first free election after the death of Francisco Franco. The parliamentary elections held that year allowed transitional prime minister Adolfo Suárez to remain in office. His moderate Union del Centro Democratico (UCD) emerged as the leading party with 34.9 percent of the vote and 167 seats in the 350-seat legislature. The Socialist Party (PSOE), led by Felipe González, obtained 29.4 percent and 118 seats, followed by the Communist Party (PCE) with 9.3 percent and 20 seats, and the rightist Alianza Popular (AP), led by Manuel Fraga, with 8.4 percent and 16 seats.

These results clearly show that if instead of parliamentary elections, a *presidential* contest had been held, no party would have had more than a plurality. Candidates would have been forced to form coalitions to have a chance of winning in a first or second round. Prior to the election, however, there was no real record of the distribution of the electorate's preferences. In this uncertain atmosphere, forming coalitions would have proven difficult. Certainly the front-runners would have found themselves forced to build unnecessarily large winning coalitions.

Assuming that the democratic opposition to Franco would have united behind a single candidate like Felipe González (something that was far from certain at the time), and given both the expectations about the strength of the Communists and the ten percent of the electorate they actually represented, he would never have been able to run as independently as he did in his campaign for a seat in parliament. A popular-front mentality would have dominated the campaign and probably submerged the distinct identities that the different parties, from the extremists on the left to the Christian Democrats and the moderate regional parties in the center, were able to maintain in most districts. The problem would have been even more acute for the center-rightists who had supported reforms, especially the *reforma pactada* that effectively put an end to the authoritarian regime. It is by no means certain that Adolfo Suárez, despite the great popularity he gained during the transition process, could or would have united all those to the right of the Socialist Party. At that juncture many Christian Democrats, including those who would later run on the UCD ticket in 1979, would not have been willing to abandon the political allies they had made during the years of opposition to Franco; on the other hand, it would have been difficult for Suárez to appear with the support of the rightist AP, since it appeared to represent the "continuist" (i.e., Francoist) alternative. For its part, the AP would probably not have supported a candidate like Suárez who favored legalization of the Communist Party.

Excluding the possibility that the candidate of the right would have been Fraga (who later became the accepted leader of the opposition), Suárez would still have been hard-pressed to maintain throughout the campaign his distinctive position as an alternative to any thought of continuity with the Franco regime. Indeed, the UCD directed its 1977 campaign as much against the AP on the right as against the Socialists on the left. Moreover, given the uncertainty about the AP's strength and the fear and loathing it provoked on the left, much leftist campaigning also targeted Fraga. This had the effect of reducing polarization, especially between longtime democrats, on the one hand, and newcomers to democratic politics (who comprised important segments of both the UCD's leadership and its rank and file), on the other. Inevitably, the candidate of the right and center-right would have focused his attacks on the left-democratic candidate's "dangerous" supporters, especially the Communists and the parties representing Basque and Catalan nationalism. In replying to these attacks the candidate of the left and center-left would certainly have pointed to the continuity between his opponent's policies and those of Franco, the putative presence of unreconstructed Francoists in the rightist camp, and the scarcity of centrist democrats in the right-wing coalition.

> *"There can be no doubt that in the Spain of 1977, a presidential election would have been far more divisive than the parliamentary elections..."*

There can be no doubt that in the Spain of 1977, a presidential election would have been far more divisive than the parliamentary elections that actually occurred. Had Suárez rejected an understanding with Fraga and his AP or had Fraga—misled by his own inflated expectations about the AP's chances of becoming the majority party in a two-party system—rejected any alliance with the Suaristas, the outcome most likely would have been a plurality for a candidate to the left of both Suárez and Fraga. A president with popular backing, even without a legislative majority on his side, would have felt himself justified in seeking both to draft a constitution and to push through political and social changes far more radical than those the Socialist Prime Minister Felipe González pursued after his victory in 1982. It is important to recall that González undertook his initiatives when Spain had already experienced five years of successful democratic rule, and only after both a party congress that saw the defeat of the PSOE's utopian left wing and a campaign aimed at winning over the centrist majority of Spanish voters. Spanish politics since Franco has clearly felt the moderating influence of parliamentarism; without it, the transition to popular government and the consolidation of democratic rule would probably have taken a far different—and much rougher—course.

Let me now add a moderating note of my own. I am *not* suggesting that the polarization which often springs from presidential elections is an inevitable concomitant of presidential government. If the public consensus hovers reliably around the middle of the political spectrum and if the limited weight of the fringe parties is in evidence, no candidate will have any incentive to coalesce with the extremists. They may run for office, but they will do so in isolation and largely as a rhetorical exercise. Under these conditions of moderation and preexisting consensus, presidential campaigns are unlikely to prove dangerously divisive. The problem is that in countries caught up in the arduous experience of establishing and consolidating democracy, such happy circumstances are seldom present. They certainly do not exist when there is a polarized multiparty system including extremist parties.

The Style of Presidential Politics

Since we have thus far focused mostly on the implications of presidentialism for the electoral process, one might reasonably observe that while the election is one thing, the victor's term in office is another: once he has won, can he not set himself to healing the wounds inflicted during the campaign and restoring the unity of the nation? Can he not offer to his defeated opponents—but not to the extremist elements of his own coalition—a role in his administration and thus make himself president of all the people? Such policies are of course possible, but must depend on the personality and political style of the new president and, to a lesser extent, his major antagonists. Before the election no one can be sure that the new incumbent will make conciliatory moves; certainly the process of political mobilization in a plebiscitarian campaign is not conducive to such a turn of events. The new president must consider whether gestures designed to conciliate his recent opponents might weaken him unduly, especially if he risks provoking his more extreme allies into abandoning him completely. There is also the possibility that the opposition could refuse to reciprocate his magnanimity, thus causing the whole strategy to backfire. The public rejection of an olive branch publicly proffered could harden positions on both sides and lead to more, rather than less, antagonism and polarization.

Some of presidentialism's most notable effects on the style of politics result from the characteristics of the presidential office itself. Among these characteristics are not only the great powers associated with the presidency but also the limits imposed on it—particularly those requiring cooperation with the legislative branch, a requirement that becomes especially salient when that branch is dominated by opponents of the president's party. Above all, however, there are the time constraints that a fixed term or number of possible terms imposes on the incumbent. The office of president is by nature two-dimensional and, in a sense, ambiguous: on the one hand, the president is the head of state and the representative of the entire nation; on the other hand, he stands for a clearly partisan political option. If he stands at the head of a multiparty coalition, he may even represent an option within an option as he deals with other members of the winning electoral alliance.

The president may find it difficult to combine his role as the head of what Bagehot called the "deferential" or symbolic aspect of the polity (a role that Bagehot thought the British monarch played perfectly and which, in republican parliamentary constitutions, has been successfully filled by presidents such as Sandro Pertini of Italy and Theodor Heuss of West Germany) with his role as an effective chief executive and partisan leader fighting to promote his party and its program. It is not always easy to be simultaneously the president, say, of all Chileans and of the workers; it is hard to be both the elegant and courtly master of La Moneda (the Chilean president's official residence) and the demagogic orator of the mass rallies at the soccer stadium. Many voters and key elites are likely to think that playing the second role means betraying the first—for should not the president as head of state stand at least somewhat above party in order to be a symbol of the nation and the stability of its government? A presidential system, as opposed to a constitutional monarchy or a republic with both a premier and a head of state, does not allow such a neat differentiation of roles.

Perhaps the most important consequences of the direct relationship that exists between a president and the electorate are the sense the president may have of being the only elected representative of the whole people and the accompanying risk that he will tend to conflate his supporters with "the people" as a whole. The plebiscitarian component implicit in the president's authority is likely to make the obstacles and opposition he encounters seem particularly annoying. In his frustration he may be tempted to define his policies as reflections of the popular will and those of his opponents as the selfish designs of narrow interests. This identification of leader with people fosters a certain populism that may be a source of strength. It may also, however, bring on a refusal to acknowledge the limits of the mandate that even a majority—to say nothing of a mere plurality—can claim as democratic justification for the enactment of its agenda. The doleful potential for displays of cold indifference, disrespect, or even downright hostility toward the opposition is not to be scanted.

Unlike the rather Olympian president, the prime minister is normally a member of parliament who, even as he sits on the government bench, remains part of the larger body. He must at some point meet his fellow legislators upon terms of rough equality, as the British prime minister regularly does during the traditional question time in the House of Commons. If he heads a coalition or minority government or if his party commands only a slim majority of seats, then he can afford precious little in the way of detachment from parliamentary opinion. A president, by contrast, heads an independent branch of government and meets with members of the legislature on his own terms. Especially uncertain in presidential regimes is the place of opposition leaders, who may not even hold public office and in any case have nothing like the quasi-official status that the leaders of the opposition enjoy in Britain, for example.

The absence in presidential regimes of a monarch or a "president of the republic" who can act symbolically as a moderating power deprives the system of flexibility and of a means of restraining power. A generally neutral figure can provide moral ballast in a crisis or act as a moderator between the premier and his opponents—who may include not only his parliamentary foes but military leaders as well. A parliamentary regime has a speaker or presiding member of parliament who can exert some restraining influence over the parliamentary antagonists, including the prime minister himself, who is after all a member of the chamber over which the speaker presides.

The Problem of Dual Legitimacy

Given his unavoidable institutional situation, a president bids fair to become the focus for whatever exaggerated expectations his supporters may harbor. They are prone to think that he has more power than he really has or should have and may sometimes be politically mobilized against any adversaries who bar his way. The interaction between a popular president and the crowd acclaiming him can generate fear among his opponents and a tense political climate. Something similar might be said about a president with a military background or close military ties—which are facilitated by the absence of the prominent defense minister one usually finds under cabinet government.

Ministers in parliamentary systems are situated quite differently from cabinet officers in presidential regimes. Especially in cases of coalition or minority governments, prime ministers are much closer to being on an equal footing with their fellow ministers than presidents will ever be with their cabinet appointees. (One must note, however, that there are certain trends which may lead to institutions like that of *Kanzlerdemokratie* in Germany, under which the premier is free to choose his cabinet without parliamentary approval of the individual ministers. Parliamentary systems with tightly disciplined parties and a prime minister who enjoys an absolute majority of legislative seats will tend to grow quite similar to presidential regimes. The tendency to personalize power in modern politics, thanks especially to the influence of television, has attenuated not only the independence of ministers but the degree of collegiality and collective responsibility in cabinet governments as well.)

A presidential cabinet is less likely than its parliamentary counterpart to contain strong and independent-minded members. The officers of a president's cabinet hold their posts purely at the sufferance of their chief; if dismissed, they are out of public life altogether. A premier's ministers, by contrast, are not his creatures but normally his parliamentary colleagues; they may go from the cabinet back to their seats in parliament and question the prime minister in party caucuses or during the ordinary course of parliamentary business just as freely as other members can. A president, moreover, can shield his cabinet members from criticism much more effectively than can a prime minister, whose cabinet members are regularly hauled before parliament to answer queries or even, in extreme cases, to face censure.

One need not delve into all the complexities of the relations between the executive and the legislature in various presidential regimes to see that all such systems are based on dual democratic legitimacy: no democratic principle exists to resolve disputes between the executive and the legislature about which of the two actually represents the will of the people. In practice, particularly in those developing countries where there are great regional inequalities in modernization, it is likely that the political and social outlook of the legislature will differ from that held by the president and his supporters. The territorial principle of representation, often reinforced by malapportionment or federal institutions like a nonproportional upper legislative chamber, tends to give greater legislative weight to small towns and rural areas. Circumstances like these can give the president grounds to question the democratic credentials of his legislative opponents. He may even charge that they represent nothing but local oligarchies and narrow, selfish clienteles. This may or may not be true, and it may or may not be worse to cast one's ballot under the tutelage of local notables, tribal chieftains, landowners, priests, or even bosses than under that of trade unions, neighborhood associations, or party machines. Whatever the case may be, modern urban elites will remain inclined to skepticism about the democratic bona fides of legislators from rural or provincial districts. In such a context, a president frustrated by legislative recalcitrance will be tempted to mobilize the people against the putative oligarchs and special interests, to claim for himself alone true democratic legitimacy as the tribune of the people, and to urge on his supporters in mass demonstrations against the opposition. It is also conceivable that in some countries the president might represent the more traditional or provincial electorates and could use their support against the more urban and modern sectors of society.

Even more ominously, in the absence of any principled method of distinguishing the true bearer of democratic legitimacy, the president may use ideological formulations to discredit his foes; institutional rivalry may thus assume the character of potentially explosive social and political strife. Institutional tensions that in some societies can be peacefully settled through negotiation or legal means may in other, less happy lands seek their resolution in the streets.

The Issue of Stability

Among the oft-cited advantages of presidentialism is its provision for the stability of the executive. This feature is said to furnish a welcome contrast to the tenuousness of many parliamentary governments, with their frequent cabinet crises and changes of prime minister, especially in the multiparty democracies of Western Europe. Certainly the spectacle of political instability presented by the Third and Fourth French Republics and, more recently, by Italy and Portugal has contributed to the low esteem in which many scholars—especially in Latin America—hold parliamentarism and their consequent preference for presidential government. But such invidious comparisons overlook the large degree of stability that actually characterizes parliamentary governments. The superficial volatility they sometimes exhibit obscures the continuity of parties in power, the enduring character of coalitions, and the way that party leaders and key ministers have of weathering cabinet crises without relinquishing their posts. In addition, the instability of presidential cabinets has been ignored by students of governmental stability. It is also insufficiently noted that parliamentary systems, precisely by virtue of their surface instability, often avoid deeper crises. A prime minister who becomes embroiled in scandal or loses the allegiance of his party or majority coalition and whose continuance in office might provoke grave turmoil can be much more easily removed than a corrupt or highly unpopular president. Unless partisan alignments make the formation of a democratically legitimate cabinet impossible, parliament should eventually be able to select a new prime minister who can form a new government. In some more serious cases, new elections may be called, although they often do not resolve the problem and can even, as in the case of Weimar Germany in the 1930s, compound it.

The government crises and ministerial changes of parliamentary regimes are of course excluded by the fixed term a president enjoys, but this great stability is bought at the price of similarly great rigidity. Flexibility in the face of constantly changing situations is not presidentialism's strong suit. Replacing a president who has lost the confidence of his party or the people is an extremely difficult proposition. Even when polarization has intensified to the point of violence and illegality, a stubborn incumbent may remain in office. By the time the cumbersome mechanisms provided to dislodge him in favor of a more able and conciliatory successor have done their work, it may be too late. Impeachment is a very uncertain and time-consuming process, especially compared with the simple parliamentary vote of no confidence. An embattled president can use his powers in such a way that his opponents might not be willing to wait until the end of his term to oust him, but there are no constitutional ways—save impeachment or resignation under pressure—to replace him. There are, moreover, risks attached even to these entirely legal methods; the incumbent's supporters may feel cheated by them and rally behind him, thus exacerbating the crisis. It is hard to imagine how the issue could be resolved purely by the political leaders, with no recourse or threat of recourse to the people or to nondemocratic institutions like the courts or—in the worst case—the military. The intense antagonisms underlying such crises cannot remain even partially concealed in the corridors and cloakrooms of the legislature. What in a parliamentary system would be a government crisis can become a full-blown regime crisis in a presidential system.

The same rigidity is apparent when an incumbent dies or suffers incapacitation while in office. In the latter case, there is a temptation to conceal the president's infirmity until the end of his term. In event of the president's death, resignation, impeachment, or incapacity, the presidential constitution very often assures an automatic and immediate succession with no interregnum or power vacuum. But the institution of vice-presidential succession, which has worked so well in the United States, may not function so smoothly elsewhere. Particularly at risk are countries whose constitutions, like the United States Constitution before the passage of the Twelfth Amendment in 1804, allow presidential tickets to be split so that the winning presidential candidate and the winning vice-presidential candidate may come from different parties. If the deceased or outgoing president and his legal successor are from different parties, those who supported the former incumbent might object that the successor does not represent their choice and lacks democratic legitimacy.

Today, of course, few constitutions would allow something like the United States' Jefferson-Burr election of 1800 to occur. Instead they require that presidential and vice-presidential candidates be nominated together, and forbid ticket-splitting in presidential balloting. But these formal measures can do nothing to control the criteria for nomination. There are undoubtedly cases where the vice-president has been nominated mainly to balance the ticket and therefore represents a discontinuity with the president. Instances where a weak vice-presidential candidate is deliberately picked by an incumbent jealous of his own power, or even where the incumbent chooses his own wife, are not unknown. Nothing about the presidential system guarantees that the country's voters or political leaders would have selected the vice-president to wield the powers they were willing to give to the former president. The continuity that the institution of automatic vice-presidential succession seems to ensure thus might prove more apparent than real. There remains the obvious possibility of a caretaker government that can fill in until new elections take place, preferably as soon as possible. Yet it hardly seems likely that the severe crisis which might have required the succession would also provide an auspicious moment for a new presidential election.

The Time Factor

Democracy is by definition a government pro tempore, a regime in which the electorate at regular intervals can hold its governors accountable and impose a change. The limited time that is allowed to elapse between elections is probably the greatest guarantee against overweening power and the last hope for those in the minority. Its drawback, however, is that it constrains a government's ability to make good on the promises it made in order to get elected. If these promises were far-reaching, including major programs of social change, the majority may feel cheated of their realization by the limited term in office imposed on their chosen leader. On the other hand, the power of a president is at once so concentrated and so extensive that it seems unsafe not to check it by limiting the number of times any one president can be reelected. Such provisions can be frustrating, especially if the incumbent is highly ambitious; attempts to change the rule in the name of continuity have often appeared attractive.

Even if a president entertains no inordinate ambitions, his awareness of the time limits facing him and the program to which his name is tied cannot help but affect his political style. Anxiety about policy discontinuities and the character of possible successors encourages what Albert Hirschman has called "the wish of *vouloir conclure.*" This exaggerated sense of urgency on the part of the president may lead to ill-conceived policy initiatives, overly hasty stabs at implementation, unwarranted anger at the lawful opposition, and a host of other evils. A president who is desperate to build his Brasilia or implement his program of nationalization or land reform before he becomes ineligible for reelection is likely to spend money unwisely or risk polarizing the country for the sake of seeing his agenda become reality. A prime minister who can expect his party or governing coalition to win the next round of elections is relatively free from such pressures. Prime ministers have stayed in office over the course of several legislatures without rousing any fears of nascent dictatorship, for the possibility of changing the government without recourse to unconstitutional means always remained open.

The fixed term in office and the limit on reelection are institutions of unquestionable value in presidential constitutions, but they mean that the political system must produce a capable and popular leader every four years or so, and also that whatever "political capital" the outgoing president may have accumulated cannot endure beyond the end of his term.

All political leaders must worry about the ambitions of second-rank leaders, sometimes because of their jockeying for position in the order of succession and sometimes because of their intrigues. The fixed and definite date of succession that a presidential constitution sets can only exacerbate the incumbent's concerns on this score. Add to this the desire for continuity, and it requires no leap of logic to predict that the president will choose as his lieutenant and successor-apparent someone who is more likely to prove a yes-man than a leader in his own right.

The inevitable succession also creates a distinctive kind of tension between the ex-president and his successor. The new man may feel driven to assert his independence and distinguish himself from his predecessor, even though both might belong to the same party. The old president, for his part, having known the unique honor and sense of power that come with the office, will always find it hard to reconcile himself to being out of power for good, with no prospect of returning even if the new incumbent fails miserably. Parties and coalitions may publicly split because of such antagonisms and frustrations. They can also lead to intrigues, as when a still-prominent former president works behind the scenes to influence the next succession or to undercut the incumbent's policies or leadership of the party.

Of course similar problems can also emerge in parliamentary systems when a prominent leader finds himself out of office but eager to return. But parliamentary regimes can more easily mitigate such difficulties for a number of reasons. The acute need to preserve party unity, the deference accorded prominent party figures, and the new premier's keen awareness that he needs the help of his predecessor even if the latter does not sit on the government bench or the same side of the house—all these contribute to the maintenance of concord. Leaders of the same party may alternate as premiers; each knows that the other may be called upon to replace him at any time and that confrontations can be costly to both, so they share power. A similar logic applies to relations between leaders of competing parties or parliamentary coalitions.

The time constraints associated with presidentialism, combined with the zero-sum character of presidential elections, are likely to render such contests more dramatic and divisive than parliamentary elections. The political realignments that in a parliamentary system may take place between elections and within the halls of the legislature must occur publicly during election campaigns in presidential systems, where they are a necessary part of the process of building a winning coalition. Under presidentialism, time becomes an intensely important dimension of politics. The pace of politics is very different under a presidential, as opposed to a parliamentary, constitution. When presidential balloting is at hand, deals must be made not only publicly but decisively—for the winning side to renege on them before the next campaign would seem like a betrayal of the voters' trust. Compromises, however necessary, that might appear unprincipled, opportunistic, or ideologically unsound are much harder to make when they are to be scrutinized by the voters in an upcoming election. A presidential regime leaves much less room for tacit consensus-building, coalition-shifting, and the making of compromises which, though prudent, are hard to defend in public.

Consociational methods of compromise, negotiation, and power-sharing under presidential constitutions have played major roles in the return of democratic government to Colombia, Venezuela, and, more recently, Brazil. But these methods appeared as necessary antinomies—deviations from the rules of the system undertaken in order to limit the voters' choices to what has been termed, rather loosely and pejoratively, *democradura*. The restoration of democracy will no doubt continue to require consociational strategies such as the formation of grand coalitions and the making of many pacts; the drawback of presidentialism is that it rigidifies and formalizes them. They become binding for a fixed period, during which there is scant opportunity for revision or renegotiation. Moreover, as the Colombian case shows, such arrangements rob the electorate of some of its freedom of choice; parliamentary systems, like that of Spain with its *consenso*, make it much more likely that consociational agreements will be made only *after* the people have spoken.

Parliamentarism and Political Stability

This analysis of presidentialism's unpromising implications for democracy is not meant to imply that no presidential democracy can be stable; on the contrary, the world's most stable democracy—the United States of America—has a presidential constitution. Nevertheless, one cannot help tentatively concluding that in many other societies the odds that presidentialism will help preserve democracy are far less favorable.

While it is true that parliamentarism provides a more flexible and adaptable institutional context for the establishment and consolidation of democracy, it does not follow that just any sort of parliamentary regime will do. Indeed, to complete the analysis one would need to reflect upon the best type of parliamentary constitution and its specific institutional features. Among these would be a prime-ministerial office combining power with responsibility, which would in turn require strong, well-disciplined political parties. Such features—there are of course many others we lack the space to discuss—would help foster responsible decision making and stable governments and would encourage genuine party competition without causing undue political fragmentation. In addition, every country has unique aspects that one must take into account—traditions of federalism, ethnic or cultural heterogeneity, and so on. Finally, it almost goes without saying that our analysis establishes only probabilities and tendencies, not determinisms. No one can guarantee that parliamentary systems will never experience grave crisis or even breakdown.

In the final analysis, all regimes, however wisely designed, must depend for their preservation upon the support of society at large—its major forces, groups, and institutions. They rely, therefore, on a public consensus which recognizes as legitimate authority only that power which is acquired through lawful and democratic means. They depend also on the ability of their leaders to govern, to inspire trust, to respect the limits of their power, and to reach an adequate degree of consensus. Although these qualities are most needed in a presidential system, it is precisely there that they are most difficult to achieve. Heavy reliance on the personal qualities of a political leader—on the virtue of a statesman, if you will—is a risky course, for one never knows if such a man can be found to fill the presidential office. But while no presidential constitution can guarantee a Washington, a Juárez, or a Lincoln, no parliamentary regime can guarantee an Adenauer or a Churchill either. Given such unavoidable uncertainty, the aim of this essay has been merely to help recover a debate on the role of alternative democratic institutions in building stable democratic polities.

10.
COMPARING DEMOCRATIC SYSTEMS

Donald L. Horowitz

Donald L. Horowitz, *Charles S Murphy Professor of Law and Professor of Political Science at Duke University, has done extensive studies of divided societies and of institutional design for democratizing countries. He is author of* Ethnic Groups in Conflict *(1985); his book,* A Democratic South Africa? Constitutional Engineering in a Divided Society, *was published in 1991 by the University of California Press.*

In "The Perils of Presidentialism" [Journal of Democracy 1 (Winter 1990): 51-69], Professor Juan Linz makes the claim that parliamentary systems are "more conducive to stable democracy" than are presidential systems. "This conclusion," he continues, "applies especially to nations with deep political cleavages and numerous political parties." This theme forms a *leitmotiv* in Professor Linz's recent works, has been picked up by other scholars, and runs the risk of becoming conventional wisdom before it receives searching scrutiny.

Linz argues that the presidential office introduces an undesirable element of winner-take-all politics into societies that need mechanisms of conciliation instead. A presidential candidate is either elected or not, whereas in parliamentary systems many shades of outcome are possible. Moreover, a directly elected president may think he has a popular "mandate," even if he has been elected with only a small plurality of the vote, perhaps even less than 40 percent. The potential for conflict is accordingly enhanced.

Conflict is promoted, in Linz's view, by the separation of powers that divides the legislature from the president. The fixed term of a separately elected president makes for rigidity between elections. By contrast, parliamentary systems are able to resolve crises at any time simply by changing leaders or governments. Separate presidential election also produces weak cabinets and fosters electoral contests in which extremists either have too much influence or the whole society becomes polarized.

This is a powerful indictment, supported by an abiding concern for the stability of precarious democratizing regimes. Linz's claims, however, are not sustainable. First, they are based on a regionally skewed and highly selective sample of comparative experience, principally from Latin America. Second, they rest on a mechanistic, even caricatured, view of the presidency. Third, they assume a particular system of electing the president, which is not necessarily the best system. Finally, by ignoring the functions that a separately elected president can perform for a divided society, they defeat Linz's own admirable purposes.

Presidentialism and Political Instability

As frequent references to Brazil, Colombia, Venezuela, and Chile attest, Linz believes that presidentialism has contributed to instability in Latin America. If, however, his focus had been on instability in postcolonial Asia and Africa, the institutional villain would surely have been parliamentary systems. Indeed, Sir Arthur Lewis argued 25 years ago in his lectures on *Politics in West Africa* that the inherited Westminster system of parliamentary democracy was responsible for much of the authoritarianism then emerging in English-speaking Africa. What Lewis emphasized was the winner-take-all features of the Westminster model, in which anyone with a parliamentary majority was able to seize the state.

Lewis's understanding conforms to that of many Africans seeking to restore democratic rule. The most impressive efforts at redemocratization, those of Nigeria in 1978-79 and again at the present time, involve adoption of a presidential system to mitigate societal divisions. Under the parliamentary system inherited at independence, a cluster of ethnic groups from the north had managed to secure a majority of seats and shut all other groups out of power. This game of total inclusion and exclusion characterized Nigerian politics after 1960, precipitating the military coups of 1966 and the war of Biafran secession from 1967 to 1970. By choosing a separation of powers, the Nigerians aimed to prevent any group from controlling the country by controlling parliament.

Now it is possible that parliamentary systems helped stifle democracy in Africa while presidential systems helped stifle it in Latin America, but there are grounds for doubt. Linz refers to the emergence of conciliatory practices in the presidential systems of Colombia, Venezuela, and Brazil, but he dismisses them as "deviations." Chile under Salvador Allende, on the other hand, is regarded as closer to the norm, with presidentialism exacerbating social conflict. Yet at least some research by Arturo Valenzuela suggests that, before Allende, many Chilean presidents actually bolstered centrist, moderating tendencies. The experience of the presidency in the United States, where the presidency was invented, is also explained away as "an exception." Consequently, Chile's exacerbated conflict is traced to its presidency, while the moderated conflict of the

United States is said to have other roots. Political success has, so to speak, many parents; political failure, only one: the presidency.

In a variety of ways, Linz characterizes the presidency as a rigid institution, conducive to zero-sum politics. But that is the straw presidency he has conjured, rather than the presidency in fact. He says, for example, that parliamentary systems, unlike presidential systems, do not dichotomize winners and losers. In parliamentary regimes, coalition governments may form; and government and opposition may cooperate in the legislative process.

These outcomes, however, are equally possible in presidential systems. The Nigerian Second Republic had both a president and a coalition in the legislature. In presidential systems, moreover, government and opposition frequently cooperate in the legislative process. The United States Congress is notorious for such cooperation. Linz ascribes this cooperation to the "uniquely diffuse" party system of the United States. That party system has its roots in federalism, which also underpins the way the president is elected. Does that not argue against condemnation of a single institution like the presidency without examining the total configuration of institutions proposed for a given country?

It is difficult to see how a presidential system could produce more absolute win or lose outcomes than a parliamentary system does. One of Linz's objections to presidentialism is that it sets up a needless conflict between the executive and the legislature, especially if the two are controlled by different parties. But if the two are controlled by different parties, the system has not produced a winner-take-all result. It is difficult to complain about interbranch checks and balances and winner-take-all politics at the same time.

The presidency, says Linz, is an office that encourages its occupant to think that he has more power than he actually does. Where several candidates have contested, a president elected with, say, one-third of the vote gains the full power of the office. (The example of Allende, elected with a 36.2-percent plurality, is cited.) The new president can make appointments, propose and veto legislation, and, given his fixed term of office, even survive fluctuations in the strength of party support. A crisis in government during a fixed presidential term becomes, according to Linz, a constitutional crisis, since there is generally no lawful way to bring down a failed president in the middle of his term. By contrast, a parliamentary government that has lost its majority in the legislature will fall, whether or not elections are due. So conflict is routinized and need not ripen into a crisis.

Before responding to these claims, it is necessary to underscore a central assumption of the Linz analysis: that the president will be elected under a plurality (first-past-the-post) system or a majority system, with a runoff election if necessary. From this assumption follow most of Linz's complaints. Consequently, it needs to be said clearly that presidents do not need to be elected on a plurality or majority-runoff basis. In divided societies, as I shall explain shortly, presidents should be elected by a different system, one that ensures broadly distributed support for the president. This greatly alleviates the problem of the narrowly elected president who labors under the illusion that he has a broader mandate. Winner-take-all is a function of electoral systems, not of institutions in the abstract.

Modes of Presidential Election

Electoral assumptions color all of Linz's analysis. He suggests that presidential candidates in plurality systems habitually cultivate the political extremes to facilitate election, thus giving the extremes influence denied them in a parliamentary system. But the supposed need to make concessions to extremists for the sake of building a plurality dissolves if presidents are not elected in this manner. By the same token, the influence of extremists in parliamentary systems is variable. One thing governing it, as the Israeli system shows, is the mode of election.

Electing the president by a majority attained in a runoff between the top two candidates poses a different problem, according to Linz. The runoff may facilitate alliances among moderates, but it also promotes a "confrontation" between the top two candidates, with a possibility that the society as a whole might become polarized.

Now, in fact, election of the president by straight plurality or majority vote is not a principle in favor with all those who have adopted presidential constitutions lately. Even the Electoral College system by which presidents of the United States are chosen is far more complex than a straight majority or runoff system. Presidential candidates in the United States are induced by the way electoral votes are distributed among the states to make discerning judgments about which interests are powerful in which states. The process cannot be captured in terms of extremism or polarization. But since Linz is especially keen to discourage presidentialism in societies with deep cleavages, it is preferable to focus on examples of presidential electoral systems in two such severely divided societies: Nigeria and Sri Lanka.

In the Nigerian Second Republic, which began in 1979, a presidential system was created. (The same presidency and electoral system will be used in the Third Republic, scheduled to begin in 1992.) To be elected, a president needed a plurality plus distribution. The successful candidate was required to have at least 25 percent of the vote in no fewer than two-thirds of the then-19 states. This double requirement was meant to ensure that the president had support from many ethnic groups. To put the point in Linz's terms, the aim was to shut out ethnic extremists and elect a moderate, centrist president. That is precisely the sort of president the Nigerians elected under the new system. The extremists, in fact, were elected to parliament, not the presidency. Nor was there any of the polarization that Linz associates with majority runoffs. Carefully devised presidential-election arrangements can bolster the center and knit together the rent fabric of a divided society. In choosing a presidential electoral system with incentives for widely distributed support, the Nigerians were rejecting winner-take-all politics. They aimed instead for a president bent on conciliation rather than on conflict. They succeeded.

In 1978, Sri Lanka also moved to a presidential system. Its principal purpose was to create a political executive with a fixed term that would permit the incumbent to make unpopular decisions, particularly those concerning the reduction of ethnic conflict. A majority requirement was instituted. Since most candidates were unlikely to gain a majority in Sri Lanka's multiparty system, a method of alternative voting was adopted. Each voter could vote for several candidates, ranking them in order of preference. If no candidate attained a majority of first preferences, the top two candidates would be put into what amounted to an instant runoff. The second preferences of voters for all other candidates would then be counted (and likewise for third preferences) until one of the top two gained a majority. It was expected that presidential candidates would build their majority on the second and third choices of voters whose preferred candidate was not among the top two. This would put ethnic minorities (especially the Sri Lankan Tamils) in a position to require compromise as the price for their second preferences. So, again, the presidential system would rule out extremists, provide incentives to moderation, and encourage compromise in a fragmented society.

The majority requirement originated in a fear that Linz shares. Like him, the Sri Lankans were concerned that a plurality election could result in the choice of a president who enjoyed the support of only 30 or 35 percent of the voters and perhaps had won election by a very narrow margin. Lest such a chief executive think himself in possession of a "mandate," the Sri Lankans insisted on aggregating second and subsequent preferences in order to produce the requisite majority. The ease of devising such a system entirely vitiates the objection.

Indeed, had the Sri Lankans and Nigerians adopted their presidential electoral systems earlier, there is every reason to think that their conflicts would have been moderated by those systems. Instead, their conflicts worsened because of the winner-take-all rules that governed their parliamentary systems and excluded minorities from power.

Insubstantial Differences

The remaining elements of the indictment—the rigidity of the fixed term, the weak cabinet, and the prospects for abuse of presidential power—are all said to be inherent drawbacks of presidentialism. All are insubstantial in practice.

It is true, of course, that presidents serve during a fixed term of years and cannot be removed on a vote of no confidence. Nevertheless, the fixed term of a directly elected president is not more likely than the more flexible term of a parliamentary government to cause a governmental crisis. When parliamentary regimes begin with secure majorities, they tend to serve their full terms. The exception occurs when a government calls an early election to take advantage of its transient popularity. In theory, it is easier to remove a parliamentary government in the middle of its term than it is to remove a president. In practice, however, the need seldom arises unless the government consists of an unstable coalition because the society is fragmented. In that event, there is a good case for shifting to a presidential system, supported by a mode of election that fosters conciliation and consensus building. That, in fact, would be a sound interpretation of what the French did when they created the presidency of the Fifth Republic in 1958.

In presidential systems, as Linz observes, cabinets are typically weaker than they are in parliamentary systems. The weakness of cabinet ministers in presidential systems is due in part to the separation of powers. Since cabinet ministers are not elected legislators, they owe their offices to the president. If the president is conciliatory, they too will be conciliatory—which is more important for the polities about which Linz is properly concerned than whether cabinet ministers are weak or strong.

In any case, the difference is exaggerated. Linz argues that the weakness of the cabinet is a function of the undue strength of the president. But there is another reason. In the United States, for example, cabinets are composed as they are because they represent special interests: agriculture, commerce, labor, and so on. What this means is that the president does *not* have a completely free hand in selecting them. Furthermore, strong prime ministers like Margaret Thatcher or Indira Gandhi have been able to dominate and reshuffle their parliamentary cabinets with impunity. This distinction between the two systems is breaking down.

Finally, abuse of power is hardly a presidential monopoly. Parliamentary regimes in Asia and Africa have produced more than their share of abuses of power. In Latin America and southern Europe, as well as Asia and Africa, abuse of power is made possible principally by the military coup or the growth of single-party hegemony. On this score, there is nothing to choose between presidential and parliamentary systems. Both have succumbed.

Choosing Among Democratic Institutions

Although the sharp distinction between presidential and parliamentary systems is unwarranted, Linz's disquiet is not. He has genuine cause for concern about the institutions adopted by democratizing states, particularly those with deep cleavages and numerous parties. He is right to worry about winner-take-all outcomes and their exclusionary consequences in such societies. Nevertheless, it is Westminster, the Mother of Parliaments, that produces such outcomes as often as any presidential system does.

As this suggests, Linz's quarrel is not with the presidency, but with two features that epitomize the Westminster version of democracy: first, plurality elections that produce a majority of seats by shutting out third-party competitors; and second, adversary democracy, with its sharp divide between winners and losers, government and opposition. Because these are Linz's underlying objections, it is not difficult to turn his arguments around against parliamentary systems, at least where they produce coherent majorities and minorities. Where no majority emerges and coalitions are necessary, sometimes—but only sometimes—more conciliatory processes and outcomes emerge. As a result, Linz's thesis boils down to an argument not against the presidency but against plurality election, not in favor of parliamentary *systems* but in favor of parliamentary *coalitions*.

These are indeed important arguments, because democratizing societies need to think, and think hard, about electoral systems that foster conciliation and governmental systems that include rather than exclude. Prominent among innovations they might consider are presidents chosen by an electoral formula that maximizes the accommodation of contending political forces. Democratic innovators can only be aided by Linz's emphasis on institutional design. But they can only be distracted by his construction of an unfounded dichotomy between two systems, divorced from the electoral and other governmental institutions in which they operate.

11.
THE CENTRALITY
OF POLITICAL CULTURE

Seymour Martin Lipset

Seymour Martin Lipset *is the Hazel Professor of Public Policy at George Mason University and a senior fellow of the Hoover Institution at Stanford University. His many books include* Political Man, The First New Nation, Revolution and Counterrevolution, *and* Consensus and Conflict. *His most recent book is* Continental Divide: The Values and Institutions of the United States and Canada *(1990).*

Juan Linz and Donald Horowitz are to be commended for reviving the discussion of the relationship between constitutional systems—presidential or parliamentary—and the conditions that make for stable democracy. Linz, basing himself largely on the Latin American experience, notes that most presidential systems have repeatedly broken down. Horowitz, a student of Asia and Africa, emphasizes that most parliamentary systems, particularly those attempted in almost all African countries and some of the new nations of postwar Asia, have also failed. He could also have pointed to the interwar collapse of democratic parliamentarism in Spain, Portugal, Greece, Italy, Austria, Germany, and most of Eastern Europe. Conversely, in addition to the successful parliamentary regimes of northern Europe and the industrialized parts of the British Commonwealth, countries such as France under the Fifth Republic, pre-Allende Chile, Costa Rica, and Uruguay (for most of this century) offer examples of stable and democratic presidentialism.

Clearly, it is not obvious that constitutional variations in type of executive are closely linked to democratic or authoritarian outcomes. As Linz emphasizes, parliamentary government (especially where there are several parties but none with a clear majority) gives different constituencies more access to the decision-making process than they would enjoy in presidential systems, and presumably helps bind these constituencies to the polity. Under presidential government, those opposed to the president's party may regard themselves as marginalized, and thus may seek to undermine presidential legitimacy. Because presidential government entrusts authority and ultimate responsibility to a single person, some scholars regard it as inherently unstable; failures can lead to a rejection of the symbol of authority. Power seems more diversified in parliamentary regimes.

The reality is more complicated. Given the division of authority between presidents and legislatures, prime ministers and their cabinets are more powerful and may pay less attention to the importunings of specific groups. A prime minister with a majority of parliament behind him has much more authority than an American president. Basically, such parliaments vote to support the budgets, bills, and policies that the government presents. Government members must vote this way, or the cabinet falls and an election is called. Unlike members of a legislative branch, opposition parliamentarians, though free to debate, criticize, or vote against the policies set by the executive, rarely can affect them.

The situation is quite different in a presidential system. The terms of the president and cabinet are not affected by votes in the legislature. As a result, party discipline is much weaker in, say, the U.S. Congress than it is in the British Parliament. In the United States and other presidential systems, the representation of diverse interests and value groups in different parties leads to cross-party alliances on various issues. Local interests are better represented in Congress, since a representative will look for constituency support to get reelected and can vote against his president or party. An MP, however, must go with his prime minister and his party, even if doing so means alienating constituency support.

The fact that presidencies make for weak parties and weak executives, while parliaments tend to have the reverse effect, certainly affects the nature of and possibly the conditions for democracy. But much of the literature wrongly assumes the opposite: that a president is inherently stronger than a prime minister, and that power is more concentrated in the former. I should emphasize that a condition for a strong cabinet government is the need to call a new election when a cabinet loses a parliamentary vote. Where parliament continues and a new cabinet is formed from a coalition of parties, no one of which has a majority, parliamentary cabinets may be weak, as in the Weimar Republic, the Third and Fourth French Republics, or contemporary Israel and India.

In my recent book *Continental Divide*, which compares the institutions and values of the United States and Canada, I note that the difference between presidential and parliamentary systems in comparable continent-spanning, federal polities results in two weak parties in the United States and multiple strong ones in Canada. The U.S. system appears to be the more stable of the two; since 1921, Canada has seen the rise and fall of over half a dozen important "third parties." The U.S. system's emphasis on electing one person president or governor forces the "various groups . . . [to] identify with one or another of the two major electoral alliances on whatever basis of division is most salient to them. Each major alliance or coalition party contains different interest groups which fight it out in primaries."

I conclude with respect to Canada that its "electoral changes have clearly been the result not of great instability or tension," but rather of the political system. In effect, the need for disciplined parliamentary parties "encourages the transformation of political protest, of social movements, of discontent with the dominant party in one's region or other aspects of life, into third, fourth, or fifth parties." The loose parties inherent in the presidential system of the U.S. absorb protest more easily within traditional mechanisms than do the parliamentary parties of Canada.

The Cultural Factor

The question remains, why have most Latin American polities not functioned like the U.S. political system? The answer lies in economic and cultural factors. If we look at the comparative record, it still suggests, as I noted in 1960 in *Political Man*, that long-enduring democracies are disproportionately to be found among the wealthier and more Protestant nations. The "Fourth" or very undeveloped world apart, Catholic and poorer countries have been less stably democratic. The situation has of course changed somewhat in recent times. Non-Protestant southern European countries like Greece, Italy, Portugal, and Spain have created parliamentary democracies, while most Catholic Latin American countries have competitive electoral systems with presidential regimes.

I will not reiterate my past discussions of the diverse social conditions for democracy, other than to note that the correlations of democracy with Protestantism and a past British connection point up the importance of cultural factors. In this connection, it may be noted that in Canada the "Latin" (French-speaking and Catholic) province of Quebec seemingly lacked the conditions for a pluralistic party system and democratic rights until the 1960s, while the anglophone and Protestant part of the country has had a stable multiparty system with democratic guarantees for close to a century. In seeking to explain in 1958 why "French Canadians have not really believed in democracy for themselves," and did not have a functioning competitive party system, political scientist Pierre Trudeau, who would later serve as prime minister of Canada for 16 years, wrote, "French Canadians are Catholics; and Catholic nations have not always been ardent supporters of democracy. They are authoritarian in spiritual matters; and . . . they are often disinclined to seek solutions in temporal matters through the mere counting of heads."[1]

Trudeau mentioned other factors, of course, particularly those inherent in the minority and economically depressed situation of his linguistic compatriots, but basically, as he noted, Canada had two very different cultures and political systems within the same set of governmental and constitutional arrangements. Quebec, like most of South America, may be described as Latin and American, and its pre-1960 politics resembled that of other Latin societies more than it did any in the anglophone world, whether presidential or parliamentary. Quebec, of course, has changed greatly since the early 1960s, and now has a stable two-party system. But these political developments have occurred in tandem with major adjustments in the orientation and behavior of the Catholic Church, in the content of the educational system, and in economic development and mobility, particularly among the francophones. What has not changed is the formal political system.

Islamic countries may also be considered as a group. Almost all have been authoritarian, with monarchical or presidential systems of government. It would be hard to credit the weakness of democracy among them to their political institutions. Some writers claim that Islamic faith makes political democracy in a Western sense extremely difficult, since it recognizes no separation of the secular and religious realms. Such claims should not be categorical, since, as with Christianity, doctrines and practices can evolve over time.

This emphasis on culture is reinforced by Myron Wiener's observation that almost all of the postwar "new nations" that have become enduring democracies are former British colonies, as are various others, such as Nigeria and Pakistan, which maintained competitive electoral institutions for briefer periods. Almost none of the former Belgian, Dutch, French, Portuguese, or Spanish colonies have comparable records. In the comparative statistical analyses that I have been conducting of the factors associated with democracy among the Third World countries, past experience with British rule emerges as one of the most powerful correlates of democracy.

Cultural factors deriving from varying histories are extraordinarily difficult to manipulate. Political institutions—including electoral systems and constitutional arrangements—are more easily changed. Hence, those concerned with enhancing the possibilities for stable democratic government focus on them. Except for the case of the Fifth French Republic, and the barriers placed on small-party representation in West Germany, there is little evidence, however, that such efforts have had much effect, and the latter case is debatable.

NOTES

1. Pierre Elliot Trudeau, *Federalism and the French Canadians* (New York: St. Martin's Press, 1968), 108.

12.
THE VIRTUES OF
PARLIAMENTARISM

Juan J. Linz

Juan J. Linz *is Sterling Professor of Political and Social Science at Yale University. His English-language publications include* Crisis, Breakdown and Reequilibrium—*volume one of the four-volume work,* The Breakdown of Democratic Regimes, *which he edited with Alfred Stepan. His article "The Perils of Presidentialism" appeared in the Winter 1990 issue of the* Journal of Democracy.

The critical comments that Professor Horowitz and Professor Lipset have offered on my essay provide stimulating contributions to the debate over the respective merits of various forms of democratic politics. This debate is most timely, as controversy seems to be subsiding about the merits of democracy versus other types of government. My essay, itself an abbreviated version of a much longer paper still in progress, was meant as a spur to further study of the problem.[1] By raising more questions than can be answered given the current state of our knowledge about how democracy works, Horowitz and Lipset confirm the need for more research and reflection.

To avoid any misunderstanding, I must stress that I did not argue that *any* parliamentary system is *ipso facto* more likely to ensure democratic stability than *any* presidential system. Nor was I suggesting that any parliamentary regime will make better policy decisions than any presidential government, which would be an even harder case to make. There are undoubtedly bad forms of both these types of government. My essay did not discuss possible new forms of presidentialism, confining itself instead to the existing democratic presidential systems and excluding detailed consideration of the United States, which I consider quite exceptional.[2] I do not think that I have constructed a "straw-man" version of presidentialism; my analysis is based on careful study of many prominent presidential systems, though I did not include the Nigerian and Sri Lankan versions of presidentialism that Professor Horowitz so skillfully discusses. Yet my article (like Horowitz's comments) also omits consideration of the many possible varieties of parliamentarism, and of the complex issues surrounding semipresidential or semiparliamentary systems with dual executives. These deserve separate analysis.

I agree with Professor Horowitz that the study of democratic regimes cannot be separated from the study of electoral systems, and acknowledge that my analysis does not cover all possible methods of presidential election. The Nigerian system represents a unique method of presidential election that might be applicable in federal states, particularly multiethnic ones, but I doubt very much that one could justify it in more homogeneous societies, even in the federal states of Latin America. My analysis concentrates on the two most common methods of election: the simple majority or plurality system, and the two-candidate runoff. The case where an electoral college may make a decision irrespective of the popular vote is left out, as is the very special case of Bolivia. The Bolivian Congress chooses among presidential candidates without regard to their popular vote totals, a practice that has certainly not contributed to either political stability or accountability in that country. I also refrained from mentioning the practice of directly electing a plural executive or a president and vice-president to represent two different constituencies (of Greek and Turkish Cypriots, for example). My argument concerns the *likelihood* of certain patterns of politics in the most common types of presidential systems, and does not attempt an exhaustive analysis of all types of directly elected executives. The patterns in question are likely to contribute to instability or difficulties in the performance of presidential executives. I use the word "likelihood" to stress that those consequences need not be present in each and every presidential system, or lead to the breakdown of democracy itself. On the contrary, recent experience shows that even rather inept democratic regimes stand a good chance of surviving simply because all relevant actors find the nondemocratic alternatives to be even less satisfactory.

Horowitz stresses that the majoritarian implications of presidentialism—the "winner-take-all" features that I have emphasized—may also be present in parliamentary systems with plurality elections in single-member districts, especially under the two-party systems that so often go together with Westminster-style parliamentary government. In societies that are polarized, or fragmented by multiple cleavages, a multiparty system with proportional representation may allow the formation of alternative coalitions (as in Belgium, for example), and thus forestall dangerous zero-sum outcomes.

As for parliamentary systems with plurality elections, Mrs. Thatcher is certainly a first above unequals, like a president, and probably has more power than an American chief executive. Certainly, parliamentary democracies in which a single disciplined party obtains the absolute majority of all seats find themselves in what is close to a "winner-take-all" situation. But this is not the most frequent pattern in parliamentary systems, particularly when there is proportional representation. Indeed, Horowitz implies that I should probably extend some of my concerns about the style of politics in presidentialism to take in the case of such majoritarian prime ministers, and that I might have a slight bias in favor of stable coalition government. I must once again note that I am dealing with ideal types that cannot subsume all of the possible varieties of political systems; indeed, I deal only with the more frequent tendencies in those ideal types. Nevertheless, while the actual situation of a powerful prime minister like Mrs. Thatcher might be comparable to that of a president with a legislative majority, the de jure difference is still significant. If Mrs. Thatcher were to falter or otherwise make herself a liability, for instance, the Conservative majority in the House of Commons could unseat her without creating a constitutional crisis. There would be no need to let her linger ineffectually in office like former presidents Raúl Alfonsín of Argentina or Alan García of Peru. Parliamentary elections may be called not only to benefit from popularity, but also when governing becomes difficult because of a lack of cohesion among the parliamentary majority. That was what happened in Spain in 1982, when Prime Minister Leopoldo Calvo Sotelo's dissolution of the Cortes allowed Felipe González to assume power at the head of a Socialist majority. Moreover, in cases where the parliamentary majority remains intact but the prime minister becomes discredited or exhausted (like Spanish premier Adolfo Suárez in 1981), he can resign without having to wait for the end of his term or a coup to remove him from office.

The "winner-take-all" character of the presidential election and the "unipersonal" executive (to use Arend Lijphart's term) does not rule out either weak presidents in particular or a weak presidency in general, Horowitz's suggestion to the contrary notwithstanding. The "all" that the winner takes may not include much effective power, especially if congressional support is not forthcoming. This is doubly so if popular support ebbs as the next election approaches. Presidents, especially those who come to power after a plebiscitarian or populist campaign, often find that the power they possess is hopelessly insufficient to meet the expectations they have generated. Constant presidential efforts to obtain new powers or invoke emergency authority are reflections of this fact.

Horowitz fails to address the basic problem of the competing claims to legitimacy of presidents and congresses, and the resulting potential for conflict between the two branches. Presidents occasionally win such conflicts, no doubt, but my argument is about institutions, not about how particular persons will fare in this or that set of circumstances. Horowitz might respond that conflicts between the legislature and the executive are not inevitable in a presidential democracy. That may be, but they are certainly likely. Although they have not caused democracy to break down in the United States, it should be recalled that for most of U.S. history, the party that controlled the presidency also controlled both houses of Congress. More recently, divided control has led to a politics of stalemate and mutual recrimination. Moreover, as a deeply institutionalized democracy, the United States is much better able to survive these difficulties of presidentialism than are many new or weak democracies in the developing world.

Horowitz tends to overstate my position by ignoring the necessarily qualified nature of my analysis. I was merely trying to evaluate the existing evidence and offer an estimate of probabilities; I would never place myself in the absurd position of claiming certitude about matters that remain only partly understood.

Varieties of Presidentialism

Horowitz further claims that my sample is skewed and highly selective, drawing as it does mostly on Latin American cases. I did not do a quantitative analysis, but the presidential systems of Latin America, together with those of the Philippines and South Korea (which I also had in mind), comprise almost all of the world's pure presidential regimes; the only exceptions are the systems of the United States, Nigeria, and Sri Lanka. Horowitz bases much of his argument on these last two countries.[3] I did not limit my generalizations to Latin America, since I think them largely valid for South Korea and the Philippines as well. The South Korean presidential election of 1987, for instance, saw Roh Tae Woo of the Democratic Justice Party (DJP) win office with 36.6 percent of the vote—almost the same percentage of the vote (34.7) as Adolfo Suárez's UCD garnered in Spain in 1977. Roh's victory frustrated opposition leaders Kim Young Sam and Kim Dae Jung, who had insisted on a direct presidential election and then split 55 percent of the vote between them.

As for Africa, close attention to the postcolonial history of that continent does not sustain Horowitz's claim that "the institutional villain would surely have been parliamentary systems." It was not simply parliamentarism, but rather democratic institutions as a whole—alien and weakly rooted as they were—that failed in Africa. The British Westminster model has winner-take-all features, to be sure, but these were even more prominent in presidential systems. Indeed, the emergence of authoritarian regimes in countries like Ghana, Uganda, and Senegal coincided with and was consolidated by "constitutional change from a parliamentary to a presidential system, with extreme concentration of power in the presidency and marked diminution of legislative authority."[4]

Horowitz criticizes me for holding a mechanistic and even caricatured view of the presidency. Certainly my main effort was to analyze the mechanics of presidential systems, but I think that my remarks on the style of politics in presidential countries, the responses of voters to presidential elections, the patterns of interaction among political leaders in presidential systems, and so on, raised my essay far above the level of the merely mechanical. I might be guilty of caricature, but many observers of the Latin American scene find my characterizations to be fairly accurate descriptions of events in those countries.

Horowitz's third claim—that I did not deal with each and every possible system for electing a president—is accurate enough, though I did cover the predominant ones (with the exceptions he presents). As for his fourth point, concerning the functions that a separately elected president can perform in a divided society, I concede that under certain very special circumstances (like those of Nigeria and perhaps Sri Lanka), a president *might* be able to help build political consensus. Still, there are counterexamples like Cyprus and Lebanon (to mention two other presidential systems) which show that presidentialism cannot overcome certain types of cleavages. Moreover, in view of the failure of Nigeria's Second Republic and the transition from military rule to a presidential Third Republic that is now underway, the jury is still out on the Nigerian presidency. The same might be said about Sri Lanka, where ethnic violence continues to rage and the deterioration of democratic institutions and liberties has yet to be reversed. The political problems of multiethnic societies under whatever system of rule (democratic or authoritarian, for that matter) present complexities that I could not address within the confines of a short essay.

Horowitz insists that a presidential electoral system with incentives for seeking widely distributed support (as in Nigeria) can obviate the winner-take-all politics that prevail in most presidential systems, particularly those with a weak separation of powers, no true federalism, and no strong judiciary. I have no doubt that requiring each candidate to gain, say, at least 25 percent of the vote in no fewer than two-thirds of the states will tend to produce a president with broad support across ethnic-cum-territorial divisions, thereby reducing ethnic polarization. But in any event, none of this did much to mitigate the winner-take-all aspect of Nigeria's presidential system. That system twice gave a minority party the exclusive right to constitute the executive branch, and helped to undermine democracy by spurring the massive rigging of the 1983 presidential election. Such a system can also backfire by leading to the election of a weak compromise candidate. Perhaps I overgeneralized from the cases included in my analysis, but to make contrary generalizations on the basis of highly unusual arrangements seems to me even less satisfactory. I still wonder how easy it is for Sri Lanka's president to make the sorts of unpopular decisions of which he is supposed to be capable (thanks to a method of election that aggregates second and subsequent preferences) in the face of a hostile legislative majority.

Much more research is needed concerning the composition and stability of cabinets in presidential systems. The president's secure tenure in office for the whole of a fixed term does not mean that his cabinet is immune to remodeling. In parliamentary systems, even those with unstable governments, cabinet members tend to accumulate considerable experience. The premiers generally have served in government before, and the system benefits from the accumulated political and administrative experience of the executive ministers. In most presidential systems, that experience is likely to be lost with a change of presidents, since each chief executive is likely to select those persons in whom he has personal confidence. In addition, since the president and his cabinet do not absolutely require the confidence of congress or the parties represented there, he can choose advisors and ministers from outside the political class and, as Brazilian presidents seem to have done, from parties besides his own—even from those that opposed his election. This might seem admirable and occasionally might work well, but it weakens parties by encouraging factionalism and clientelism. Just as a president who cannot be reelected is hard to hold accountable for his performance, a president who forms a cabinet without systematically involving the parties that back him makes it difficult for the voters to hold parties accountable in the next election. My analysis focuses on multiparty rather than two-party systems, but even in a two-party system it is not clear whom the voters will blame: the president's party, or the party with the majority in congress that obstructed his otherwise presumably successful performance.

The Problem of Divided Government

Giovanni Sartori has used the U.S. experience to argue that once the pattern of undivided consonant majorities (the coincidence of presidential and legislative majorities) and consociational practices (especially bipartisan concurrence in foreign affairs) is broken, there emerges an antagonistically divided government whose two main elements perceive that their respective electoral interests are best served by the failure of the other institution. For a Democrat-controlled Congress to cooperate with a Republican administration is to aid the election of future Republican presidents. Conversely, a president whose party is the minority in Congress will seek to restore undivided government by running against Congress. In short, he will play the "blame game." Thus the answer to the question of whether presidentialism provides for effective government is, with reference to its most acclaimed incarnation, a resounding no. The American system works or has worked in spite of, rather than because of, the presidential constitution of the United States. To the extent that it can still perform, it needs three things that tend to unblock it: flexibility or lack of ideological rigidity; weak, undisciplined parties; and pork-barrel and locality-oriented politics.[5]

These considerations weigh against the notion that since the United

States is both a successful democracy and a presidential regime, other presidential systems should also stand a good chance of being similarly successful. I cannot go into greater detail here, but recommend Fred Riggs's excellent study of the uniqueness of the U.S. political system, a system of which the presidency forms but a single part.[6]

At stake here are two separate issues: the stability of the democratic system, and the quality of its performance. Not all presidential regimes are unstable, nor are all of them weak in spite of their apparent strength. Many, however, have proven unstable and quite weak, though I would never exclude the possibility of a stable and strong presidential system if the president has the support of both an electoral and a legislative majority. Yet such a combination is rare in actual presidential systems, and might not be a good thing anyway: a popular president with a disciplined party behind him might defeat the constitutional scheme of checks and balances, thus obviating a key advantage of presidentialism. Even so, as Michael Coppedge's excellent study of the Venezuelan presidential system shows, a ban on presidential reelection hurts the president's ability to govern in the latter part of his term.[7]

I am grateful to Professor Horowitz for his comments, especially regarding the unusual systems of Nigeria and Sri Lanka. As I said at the outset, we need more systematic comparisons and more research on particular examples of presidential government (a largely neglected subject) before we can reach final conclusions. None of the existing research challenges my basic claim, which is that certain structural problems inherent in presidentialism make it likely that many presidential systems will run into serious difficulties of a sort that some parliamentary systems have successfully overcome. After all necessary qualifications have been made, my conclusion might be reformulated as follows: certain parliamentary systems are more likely than most of their presidential counterparts to solve certain knotty problems of multiparty politics. Even as I make qualifications, however, I am anxious that we avoid the error of forsaking comparative analysis for mere assessment of particular political systems, considered in isolation. Comparative analysis has to settle for probabilities rather than certainties, and therefore will always be open to question. The need for such analysis, however, is beyond question.

The Importance of Institutions

Professor Lipset's comments rightly stress the effect of economic, social, historical, and cultural factors on the fate of democracy in many countries past, present, and future. These factors operate more or less independently of political institutions. Culture, as Lipset notes, is difficult if not impossible to change. Historical legacies do not fully disappear, and socioeconomic transformation cannot be achieved by fiat, so we are left with the search for those political institutions that will best suit the circumstances in this or that particular country. This is a modest quest, but a worthy one. Presidentialism, parliamentarism, or some hybrid of the two; centralism or federalism; one-round or two-round elections—in every case the question is the same: what mix of laws and institutions will direct the contending interests of a given society into peaceful and democratic channels? Here is where I seek to make a contribution.

Lipset's able comparison between the United States and Canada confirms that even when societies are relatively similar, the type of democratic government each one has does make a difference. His observation that prime ministers who command a solid majority (not necessarily from one party) may have more power than presidents indirectly contributes to my argument. Also intriguing are Lipset's assertions about the greater weight of interest groups and local interests in presidential systems; if proven, they would be grist for the mill of those who complain about the invidious clientelism that pervades presidential countries like the Philippines and Brazil. He notes too the weakness both of parties and of presidents who depend on them for support. Will more research confirm my hypothesis that presidentialism helps to make parties weaker and less responsible? Would parliamentarism oblige parties to behave differently?

NOTES

1. See Oscar Godoy Arcaya, ed., *Hacia una democracia moderna: La opción parlamentaria* (Santiago: Ediciones Universidad Catolica de Chile, 1990), for a Spanish version of my extended paper, as well as those by Arend Lijphart and Arturo Valenzuela. I expect to publish it as an introductory essay in a book I will edit jointly with Arturo Valenzuela which will include country studies by many authors and theoretical contributions by Lijphart and Giovanni Sartori that in part support my argument, but also disagree with some of the points I make.

2. Fred W. Riggs, "The Survival of Presidentialism in America: Para-Constitutional Practices," *International Political Science Review* 9 (October 1988): 247-78.

3. Horowitz also refers to Colombia as a more successful case of presidentialism, but that country's transition to and early maintenance of presidential democracy was made possible only by the *Concordancia* of 1958, an arrangement under which the two major parties agreed to suspend their electoral competition for the presidency and accept alternating terms in power instead. While this helped to stabilize the country after a period of civil war and dictatorship, it can hardly be considered a model of democratic politics, or a method for making government accountable to the voters. To call it a deviation may be too mild.

4. Larry Diamond, "Introduction: Roots of Failure, Seeds of Hope," in *Democracy in Developing Countries*, vol. 2, *Africa*, eds. Larry Diamond, Juan J. Linz, and Seymour Martin Lipset (Boulder, Colo.: Lynne Rienner, 1988), 3.

5. Giovanni Sartori, "Neither Presidentialism nor Parliamentarism," (unpublished paper given at Georgetown University, May 1989).

6. Riggs, op. cit.

7. Michael Coppedge, "Venezuela: Democratic Despite Presidentialism," (unpublished paper given at Georgetown University, May 1989).

13.
CONSTITUTIONAL CHOICES
FOR NEW DEMOCRACIES

Arend Lijphart

Arend Lijphart, *professor of political science at the University of California at San Diego, is a specialist in comparative politics whose current research involves the comparative study of democratic regimes and electoral systems. His most recent books are* Democracies: Patterns of Majoritarian and Consensus Government in Twenty-One Countries *(1984),* Power-Sharing in South Africa *(1985), and, coedited with Bernard Grofman,* Choosing an Electoral System: Issues and Alternatives *(1984) and* Electoral Laws and Their Political Consequences *(1986). This essay is a revised version of a paper first presented to the Philippine Council for Foreign Relations.*

Two fundamental choices that confront architects of new democratic constitutions are those between plurality elections and proportional representation (PR) and between parliamentary and presidential forms of government. The merits of presidentialism and parliamentarism were extensively debated by Juan J. Linz, Seymour Martin Lipset, and Donald L. Horowitz in the Fall 1990 issue of the *Journal of Democracy*.[1] I strongly concur with Horowitz's contention that the electoral system is an equally vital element in democratic constitutional design, and therefore that it is of crucial importance to evaluate these two sets of choices in relation with each other. Such an analysis, as I will try to show, indicates that the combination of parliamentarism with proportional representation should be an especially attractive one to newly democratic and democratizing countries.

The comparative study of democracies has shown that the type of electoral system is significantly related to the development of a country's party system, its type of executive (one-party vs. coalition cabinets), and the relationship between its executive and legislature. Countries that use the plurality method of election (almost always applied, at the national level, in single-member districts) are likely to have two-party systems, one-party governments, and executives that are dominant in relation to their legislatures. These are the main characteristics of the Westminster or *majoritarian* model of democracy, in which power is concentrated in the hands of the majority party. Conversely, PR is likely to be associated with multiparty systems, coalition governments (including, in many cases, broad and inclusive coalitions), and more equal executive-legislative power relations. These latter characteristics typify the *consensus* model of democracy, which, instead of relying on pure and concentrated majority rule, tries to limit, divide, separate, and share power in a variety of ways.[2]

Three further points should be made about these two sets of related traits. First, the relationships are mutual. For instance, plurality elections favor the maintenance of a two-party system; but an existing two-party system also favors the maintenance of plurality, which gives the two principal parties great advantages that they are unlikely to abandon. Second, if democratic political engineers desire to promote either the majoritarian cluster of characteristics (plurality, a two-party system, and a dominant, one-party cabinet) or the consensus cluster (PR, multipartism, coalition government, and a stronger legislature), the most practical way to do so is by choosing the appropriate electoral system. Giovanni Sartori has aptly called electoral systems "the most specific manipulative instrument of politics."[3] Third, important variations exist among PR systems. Without going into all the technical details, a useful distinction can be made between *extreme* PR, which poses few barriers to small parties, and *moderate* PR. The latter limits the influence of minor parties through such means as applying PR in small districts instead of large districts or nationwide balloting, and requiring parties to receive a minimum percentage of the vote in order to gain representation, such as the 5-percent threshold in Germany. The Dutch, Israeli, and Italian systems exemplify extreme PR and the German and Swedish systems, moderate PR.

The second basic constitutional choice, between parliamentary and presidential forms of government, also affects the majoritarian or consensus character of the political system. Presidentialism yields majoritarian effects on the party system and on the type of executive, but a consensus effect on executive-legislative relations. By formally separating the executive and legislative powers, presidential systems generally promote a rough executive-legislative balance of power. On the other hand, presidentialism tends to foster a two-party system, as the presidency is the biggest political prize to be won, and only the largest parties have a chance to win it. This advantage for the big parties often carries over into legislative elections as well (especially if presidential and legislative elections are held simultaneously), even if the legislative elections are conducted under PR rules. Presidentialism usually produces cabinets composed solely of members of the governing party. In fact, presidential systems concentrate executive power to an even greater degree than does a one-party parliamentary cabinet—not just in a single *party* but in a single *person*.

Explaining Past Choices

My aim is not simply to describe alternative democratic systems and their majoritarian or consensus characteristics, but also to make some practical recommendations for democratic constitutional engineers. What are the main advantages and disadvantages of plurality and PR and of presidentialism and parliamentarism? One way to approach this question is to investigate why contemporary democracies made the constitutional choices they did.

Figure 1 illustrates the four combinations of basic characteristics and the countries and regions where they prevail. The purest examples of the combination of presidentialism and plurality are the United States and democracies heavily influenced by the United States, such as the Philippines and Puerto Rico. Latin American countries have overwhelmingly opted for presidential-PR systems. Parliamentary-plurality systems exist in the United Kingdom and many former British colonies, including India, Malaysia, Jamaica, and the countries of the so-called Old Commonwealth (Canada, Australia, and New Zealand). Finally, parliamentary-PR systems are concentrated in Western Europe. Clearly, the overall pattern is to a large extent determined by geographic, cultural, and colonial factors—a point to which I shall return shortly.

Figure 1 — Four Basic Types of Democracy

	Presidential	Parliamentary
Plurality Elections	United States Philippines	United Kingdom Old Commonwealth India Malaysia Jamaica
Proportional Representation	Latin America	Western Europe

Very few contemporary democracies cannot be accommodated by this classification. The major exceptions are democracies that fall in between the pure presidential and pure parliamentary types (France and Switzerland), and those that use electoral methods other than pure PR or plurality (Ireland, Japan, and, again, France).[4]

Two important factors influenced the adoption of PR in continental Europe. One was the problem of ethnic and religious minorities; PR was designed to provide minority representation and thereby to counteract potential threats to national unity and political stability. "It was no accident," Stein Rokkan writes, "that the earliest moves toward proportional representation (PR) came in the ethnically most heterogeneous countries." The second factor was the dynamic of the democratization process. PR was adopted "through a convergence of pressures from below and from above. The rising working class wanted to lower the thresholds of representation in order to gain access to the legislatures, and the most threatened of the old-established parties demanded PR to protect their position against the new waves of mobilized voters created by universal suffrage."[5] Both factors are relevant for contemporary constitution making, especially for the many countries where there are deep ethnic cleavages or where new democratic forces need to be reconciled with the old antidemocratic groups.

The process of democratization also originally determined whether parliamentary or presidential institutions were adopted. As Douglas V. Verney has pointed out, there were two basic ways in which monarchical power could be democratized: by taking away most of the monarch's personal political prerogatives and making his cabinet responsible to the popularly elected legislature, thus creating a parliamentary system; or by removing the hereditary monarch and substituting a new, democratically elected "monarch," thus creating a presidential system.[6]

Other historical causes have been voluntary imitations of successful democracies and the dominant influence of colonial powers. As Figure 1 shows very clearly, Britain's influence as an imperial power has been enormously important. The U.S. presidential model was widely imitated in Latin America in the nineteenth century. And early in the twentieth century, PR spread quickly in continental Europe and Latin America, not only for reasons of partisan accommodation and minority protection, but also because it was widely perceived to be the most democratic method of election and hence the "wave of the democratic future."

This sentiment in favor of PR raises the controversial question of the *quality* of democracy achieved in the four alternative systems. The term "quality" refers to the degree to which a system meets such democratic norms as representativeness, accountability, equality, and participation. The claims and counterclaims are too well-known to require lengthy treatment here, but it is worth emphasizing that the differences between the opposing camps are not as great as is often supposed. First of all,

PR and plurality advocates disagree not so much about the respective effects of the two electoral methods as about the weight to be attached to these effects. Both sides agree that PR yields greater proportionality and minority representation and that plurality promotes two-party systems and one-party executives. Partisans disagree on which of these results is preferable, with the plurality side claiming that only in two-party systems can clear accountability for government policy be achieved.

In addition, both sides argue about the *effectiveness* of the two systems. Proportionalists value minority representation not just for its democratic quality but also for its ability to maintain unity and peace in divided societies. Similarly, proponents of plurality favor one-party cabinets not just because of their democratic accountability but also because of the firm leadership and effective policy making that they allegedly provide. There also appears to be a slight difference in the relative emphasis that the two sides place on quality and effectiveness. Proportionalists tend to attach greater importance to the *representativeness* of government, while plurality advocates view the *capacity to govern* as the more vital consideration.

Finally, while the debate between presidentialists and parliamentarists has not been as fierce, it clearly parallels the debate over electoral systems. Once again, the claims and counterclaims revolve around both quality and effectiveness. Presidentialists regard the direct popular election of the chief executive as a democratic asset, while parliamentarists think of the concentration of executive power in the hands of a single official as less than optimally democratic. But here the question of effectiveness has been the more seriously debated issue, with the president's strong and effective leadership role being emphasized by one side and the danger of executive-legislative conflict and stalemate by the other.

Evaluating Democratic Performance

How can the actual performance of the different types of democracies be evaluated? It is extremely difficult to find quantifiable measures of democratic performance, and therefore political scientists have rarely attempted a systematic assessment. The major exception is G. Bingham Powell's pioneering study evaluating the capacity of various democracies to maintain public order (as measured by the incidence of riots and deaths from political violence) and their levels of citizen participation (as measured by electoral turnout).[7] Following Powell's example, I will examine these and other aspects of democratic performance, including democratic representation and responsiveness, economic equality, and macroeconomic management.

Due to the difficulty of finding reliable data outside the OECD countries to measure such aspects of performance, I have limited the analysis to the advanced industrial democracies. In any event, the Latin American democracies, given their lower levels of economic development, cannot be considered comparable cases. This means that one of the four basic alternatives—the presidential-PR form of democracy prevalent only in Latin America—must be omitted from our analysis.

Although this limitation is unfortunate, few observers would seriously argue that a strong case can be made for this particular type of democracy. With the clear exception of Costa Rica and the partial exceptions of Venezuela and Colombia, the political stability and economic performance of Latin American democracies have been far from satisfactory. As Juan Linz has argued, Latin American presidential systems have been particularly prone to executive-legislative deadlock and ineffective leadership.[8] Moreover, Scott Mainwaring has shown persuasively that this problem becomes especially serious when presidents do not have majority support in their legislatures.[9] Thus the Latin American model of presidentialism combined with PR legislative elections remains a particularly unattractive option.

The other three alternatives—presidential-plurality, parliamentary-plurality, and parliamentary-PR systems—are all represented among the firmly established Western democracies. I focus on the 14 cases that unambiguously fit these three categories. The United States is the one example of presidentialism combined with plurality. There are four cases of parliamentarism-plurality (Australia, Canada, New Zealand, and the United Kingdom), and nine democracies of the parliamentary-PR type (Austria, Belgium, Denmark, Finland, Germany, Italy, the Netherlands, Norway, and Sweden). Seven long-term, stable democracies are excluded from the analysis either because they do not fit comfortably into any one of the three categories (France, Ireland, Japan, and Switzerland), or because they are too vulnerable to external factors (Israel, Iceland, and Luxembourg).

Since a major purpose of PR is to facilitate minority representation, one would expect the PR systems to outperform plurality systems in this respect. There is little doubt that this is indeed the case. For instance, where ethnic minorities have formed ethnic political parties, as in Belgium and Finland, PR has enabled them to gain virtually perfect proportional representation. Because there are so many different kinds of ethnic and religious minorities in the democracies under analysis, it is difficult to measure systematically the *degree* to which PR succeeds in providing more representatives for minorities than does plurality. It is possible, however, to compare the representation of women—a minority in political rather than strictly numerical terms—systematically across countries. The first column of Table 1 shows the percentages of female members in the lower (or only) houses of the national legislatures in these 14 democracies during the early 1980s. The 16.4-percent average for the parliamentary-PR systems is about four times higher than the 4.1

Table 1 — Women's Legislative Representation, Innovative Family Policy, Voting Turnout, Income Inequality, and the Dahl Rating of Democratic Quality

	Women's Repr. 1980-82	Family Policy 1976-80	Voting Turnout 1971-80	Income Top 20% 1985	Dahl Rating 1969
Pres.-Plurality (N=1)	4.1	3.00	54.2%	39.9%	3.0
Parl.-Plurality (N=4)	4.0	2.50	75.3	42.9	4.8
Parl.-PR (N=9)	16.4	7.89	84.5	39.0	2.2

Note: The one presidential-plurality democracy is the United States; the four parliamentary-plurality democracies are Australia, Canada, New Zealand, and the United Kingdom; and the nine parliamentary-PR democracies are Austria, Belgium, Denmark, Finland, Germany, Italy, the Netherlands, Norway, and Sweden.

Sources: Based on Wilma Rule, "Electoral Systems, Contextual Factors and Women's Opportunity for Election to Parliament in Twenty-Three Democracies," *Western Political Quarterly* 40 (September 1987): 483; Harold L. Wilensky, "Common Problems, Divergent Policies: An 18-Nation Study of Family Policy," *Public Affairs Report* 31 (May 1990): 2; personal communication by Harold L. Wilensky to the author, dated 18 October 1990; Robert W. Jackman, "Political Institutions and Voter Turnout in the Industrial Democracies," *American Political Science Review* 81 (June 1987): 420; World Bank, *World Development Report 1989* (New York: Oxford University Press, 1989), 223; Robert A. Dahl, *Polyarchy: Participation and Opposition* (New Haven: Yale University Press, 1971), 232.

percent for the United States or the 4.0-percent average for the parliamentary-plurality countries. To be sure, the higher social standing of women in the four Nordic countries accounts for part of the difference, but the average of 9.4 percent in the five other parliamentary-PR countries remains more than twice as high as in the plurality countries.

Does higher representation of women result in the advancement of their interests? Harold L. Wilensky's careful rating of democracies with regard to the innovativeness and expansiveness of their family policies—a matter of special concern to women—indicates that it does.[10] On a 13-point scale (from a maximum of 12 to a minimum of 0), the scores of these countries range from 11 to 1. The differences among the three groups (as shown in the second column of Table 1) are striking: the PR countries have an average score of 7.89, whereas the parliamentary-plurality countries have an average of just 2.50, and the U.S. only a slightly higher score of 3.00. Here again, the Nordic countries have the highest scores, but the 6.80 average of the non-Nordic PR countries is still well above that of the plurality countries.

The last three columns of Table 1 show indicators of democratic quality. The third column lists the most reliable figures on electoral participation (in the 1970s); countries with compulsory voting (Australia,

Belgium, and Italy) are not included in the averages. Compared with the extremely low voter turnout of 54.2 percent in the United States, the parliamentary-plurality systems perform a great deal better (about 75 percent). But the average in the parliamentary-PR systems is still higher, at slightly above 84 percent. Since the maximum turnout that is realistically attainable is around 90 percent (as indicated by the turnouts in countries with compulsory voting), the difference between 75 and 84 percent is particularly striking.

Another democratic goal is political equality, which is more likely to prevail in the absence of great economic inequalities. The fourth column of Table 1 presents the World Bank's percentages of total income earned by the top 20 percent of households in the mid-1980s.[11] They show a slightly less unequal distribution of income in the parliamentary-PR than in the parliamentary-plurality systems, with the United States in an intermediate position.

Finally, the fifth column reports Robert A. Dahl's ranking of democracies according to ten indicators of democratic quality, such as freedom of the press, freedom of association, competitive party systems, strong parties and interest groups, and effective legislatures.[12] The stable democracies range from a highest rating of 1 to a low of 6. There is a slight pro-PR bias in Dahl's ranking (he includes a number-of-parties variable that rates multiparty systems somewhat higher than two-party systems), but even when we discount this bias we find striking differences between the parliamentary-PR and parliamentary-plurality countries: six of the former are given the highest score, whereas most of the latter receive the next to lowest score of 5.

No such clear differences are apparent when we examine the effect of the type of democracy on the maintenance of public order and peace. Parliamentary-plurality systems had the lowest incidence of riots during the period 1948-77, but the highest incidence of political deaths; the latter figure, however, derives almost entirely from the high number of political deaths in the United Kingdom, principally as a result of the Northern Ireland problem. A more elaborate statistical analysis shows that societal division is a much more important factor than type of democracy in explaining variation in the incidence of political riots and deaths in the 13 parliamentary countries.[13]

A major argument in favor of plurality systems has been that they favor "strong" one-party governments that can pursue "effective" public policies. One key area of government activity in which this pattern should manifest itself is the management of the economy. Thus advocates of plurality systems received a rude shock in 1987 when the average per capita GDP in Italy (a PR and multiparty democracy with notoriously uncohesive and unstable governments) surpassed that of the United Kingdom, typically regarded as the very model of strong and effective government. If Italy had discovered large amounts of oil in the

Mediterranean, we would undoubtedly explain its superior economic performance in terms of this fortuitous factor. But it was not Italy but Britain that discovered the oil!

Economic success is obviously not solely determined by government policy. When we examine economic performance over a long period of time, however, the effects of external influences are minimized, especially if we focus on countries with similar levels of economic development. Table 2 presents OECD figures from the 1960s through the 1980s for the three most important aspects of macroeconomic performance—average annual economic growth, inflation, and unemployment rates.

Table 2 — Economic Growth, Inflation, and Unemployment (in percent)

	Economic Growth 1961-88	Inflation 1961-88	Unemployment 1965-88
Pres.-Plurality (N=1)	3.3	5.1	6.1
Parl.-Plurality (N=4)	3.4	7.5	6.1
Parl.-PR (N=9)	3.5	6.3	4.4

Sources: *OECD Economic Outlook*, No. 26 (December 1979), 131; No. 30 (December 1981), 131, 140, 142; No. 46 (December 1989), 166, 176, 182.

Although Italy's economic growth has indeed been better than that of Britain, the parliamentary-plurality and parliamentary-PR countries as groups do not differ much from each other or from the United States. The slightly higher growth rates in the parliamentary-PR systems cannot be considered significant. With regard to inflation, the United States has the best record, followed by the parliamentary-PR systems. The most sizable differences appear in unemployment levels; here the parliamentary-PR countries perform significantly better than the plurality countries.[14] Comparing the parliamentary-plurality and parliamentary-PR countries on all three indicators, we find that the performance of the latter is uniformly better.

Lessons for Developing Countries

Political scientists tend to think that plurality systems such as the United Kingdom and the United States are superior with regard to democratic quality and governmental effectiveness—a tendency best explained by the fact that political science has always been an Anglo-American-oriented discipline. This prevailing opinion is largely contradicted, however, by the empirical evidence presented above. Wherever significant differences appear, the parliamentary-PR systems almost invariably post the best records, particularly with respect to representation, protection of minority interests, voter participation, and control of unemployment.

This finding contains an important lesson for democratic constitutional engineers: the parliamentary-PR option is one that should be given serious consideration. Yet a word of caution is also in order, since parliamentary-PR democracies differ greatly among themselves. Moderate PR and moderate multipartism, as in Germany and Sweden, offer more attractive models than the extreme PR and multiparty systems of Italy and the Netherlands. As previously noted, though, even Italy has a respectable record of democratic performance.

But are these conclusions relevant to newly democratic and democratizing countries in Asia, Africa, Latin America, and Eastern Europe, which are trying to make democracy work in the face of economic underdevelopment and ethnic divisions? Do not these difficult conditions require strong executive leadership in the form of a powerful president or a Westminster-style, dominant one-party cabinet?

With regard to the problem of deep ethnic cleavages, these doubts can be easily laid to rest. Divided societies, both in the West and elsewhere, need peaceful coexistence among the contending ethnic groups. This requires conciliation and compromise, goals that in turn require the greatest possible inclusion of representatives of these groups in the decision-making process. Such power sharing can be arranged much more easily in parliamentary and PR systems than in presidential and plurality systems. A president almost inevitably belongs to one ethnic group, and hence presidential systems are particularly inimical to ethnic power sharing. And while Westminster-style parliamentary systems feature collegial cabinets, these tend not to be ethnically inclusive, particularly when there is a majority ethnic group. It is significant that the British government, in spite of its strong majoritarian traditions, recognized the need for consensus and power sharing in religiously and ethnically divided Northern Ireland. Since 1973, British policy has been to try to solve the Northern Ireland problem by means of PR elections and an inclusive coalition government.

As Horowitz has pointed out, it may be possible to alleviate the problems of presidentialism by requiring that a president be elected with a stated minimum of support from different groups, as in Nigeria.[15] But this is a palliative that cannot compare with the advantages of a truly collective and inclusive executive. Similarly, the example of Malaysia shows that a parliamentary system can have a broad multiparty and multiethnic coalition cabinet in spite of plurality elections, but this requires elaborate preelection pacts among the parties. These exceptions prove the rule: the ethnic power sharing that has been attainable in Nigeria and Malaysia only on a limited basis and through very special arrangements is a natural and straightforward result of parliamentary-PR forms of democracy.

PR and Economic Policy Making

The question of which form of democracy is most conducive to economic development is more difficult to answer. We simply do not have enough cases of durable Third World democracies representing the different systems (not to mention the lack of reliable economic data) to make an unequivocal evaluation. However, the conventional wisdom that economic development requires the unified and decisive leadership of a strong president or a Westminster-style dominant cabinet is highly suspect. First of all, if an inclusive executive that must do more bargaining and conciliation were less effective at economic policy making than a dominant and exclusive executive, then presumably an authoritarian government free of legislative interference or internal dissent would be optimal. This reasoning—a frequent excuse for the overthrow of democratic governments in the Third World in the 1960s and 1970s—has now been thoroughly discredited. To be sure, we do have a few examples of economic miracles wrought by authoritarian regimes, such as those in South Korea or Taiwan, but these are more than counterbalanced by the sorry economic records of just about all the nondemocratic governments in Africa, Latin America, and Eastern Europe.

Second, many British scholars, notably the eminent political scientist S.E. Finer, have come to the conclusion that economic development requires not so much a *strong* hand as a *steady* one. Reflecting on the poor economic performance of post-World War II Britain, they have argued that each of the governing parties indeed provided reasonably strong leadership in economic policy making but that alternations in governments were too "absolute and abrupt," occurring "between two sharply polarized parties each eager to repeal a large amount of its predecessor's legislation." What is needed, they argue, is "greater stability and continuity" and "greater moderation in policy," which could be provided by a shift to PR and to coalition governments much more likely to be centrist in orientation.[16] This argument would appear to be equally applicable both to developed and developing countries.

Third, the case for strong presidential or Westminster-style governments is most compelling where rapid decision making is essential. This means that in foreign and defense policy parliamentary-PR systems may be at a disadvantage. But in economic policy making speed is not particularly important—quick decisions are not necessarily wise ones.

Why then do we persist in distrusting the economic effectiveness of democratic systems that engage in broad consultation and bargaining aimed at a high degree of consensus? One reason is that multiparty and coalition governments *seem* to be messy, quarrelsome, and inefficient in contrast to the clear authority of strong presidents and strong one-party cabinets. But we should not let ourselves be deceived by these superficial appearances. A closer look at presidential systems reveals that the most successful cases—such as the United States, Costa Rica, and pre-1970 Chile—are at least equally quarrelsome and, in fact, are prone to paralysis and deadlock rather than steady and effective economic policy making. In any case, the argument should not be about governmental aesthetics but about actual performance. The undeniable elegance of the Westminster model is not a valid reason for adopting it.

The widespread skepticism about the economic capability of parliamentary-PR systems stems from confusing governmental strength with effectiveness. In the short run, one-party cabinets or presidents may well be able to formulate economic policy with greater ease and speed. In the long run, however, policies supported by a broad consensus are more likely to be successfully carried out and to remain on course than policies imposed by a "strong" government against the wishes of important interest groups.

To sum up, the parliamentary-PR form of democracy is clearly better than the major alternatives in accommodating ethnic differences, and it has a slight edge in economic policy making as well. The argument that considerations of governmental effectiveness mandate the rejection of parliamentary-PR democracy for developing countries is simply not tenable. Constitution makers in new democracies would do themselves and their countries a great disservice by ignoring this attractive democratic model.

NOTES

I gratefully acknowledge the assistance and advice of Robert W. Jackman, G. Bingham Powell, Jr., Harold L. Wilensky, and Kaare Strom, the research assistance of Markus Crepaz, and the financial support of the Committee on Research of the Academic Senate of the University of California at San Diego.

1. Donald L. Horowitz, "Comparing Democratic Systems," Seymour Martin Lipset, "The Centrality of Political Culture," and Juan J. Linz, "The Virtues of Parliamentarism," *Journal of Democracy* 1 (Fall 1990): 73-91. A third set of important decisions concerns institutional arrangements that are related to the difference between federal and unitary forms of government: the degree of government centralization, unicameralism or bicameralism, rules for constitutional amendment, and judicial review. Empirical analysis shows that these factors tend to be related; federal countries are more likely to be decentralized, to have significant bicameralism, and to have "rigid" constitutions that are difficult to amend and protected by judicial review.

2. For a fuller discussion of the differences between majoritarian and consensus government, see Arend Lijphart, *Democracies: Patterns of Majoritarian and Consensus Government in Twenty-One Countries* (New Haven: Yale University Press, 1984).

3. Giovanni Sartori, "Political Development and Political Engineering," in *Public Policy*, vol. 17, eds. John D. Montgomery and Alfred O. Hirschman (Cambridge: Harvard University Press, 1968), 273.

4. The first scholar to emphasize the close connection between culture and these constitutional arrangements was G. Bingham Powell, Jr. in his *Contemporary Democracies: Participation, Stability, and Violence* (Cambridge: Harvard University Press, 1982), 67. In my previous writings, I have sometimes classified Finland as a presidential or semipresidential system, but I now agree with Powell (pp. 56-57) that, although the directly elected Finnish president has special authority in foreign policy, Finland operates like a parliamentary system in most other respects. Among the exceptions, Ireland is a doubtful case; I regard its system of the single transferable vote as mainly a PR method, but other authors have classified it as a plurality system. And I include Australia in the parliamentary-plurality group, because its alternative-vote system, while not identical with plurality, operates in a similar fashion.

5. Stein Rokkan, *Citizens, Elections, Parties: Approaches to the Comparative Study of the Processes of Development* (Oslo: Universitetsforlaget, 1970), 157.

6. Douglas V. Verney, *The Analysis of Political Systems* (London: Routledge and Kegan Paul, 1959), 18-23, 42-43.

7. Powell, op. cit., esp. 12-29 and 111-74.

8. Juan J. Linz, "The Perils of Presidentialism," *Journal of Democracy* 1 (Winter 1990): 51-69.

9. Scott Mainwaring, "Presidentialism in Latin America," *Latin American Research Review* 25 (1990): 167-70.

10. Wilensky's ratings are based on a five-point scale (from 4 to 0) "for each of three policy clusters: existence and length of maternity and parental leave, paid and unpaid; availability and accessibility of public daycare programs and government effort to expand daycare; and flexibility of retirement systems. They measure government action to assure care of children and maximize choices in balancing work and family demands for everyone." See Harold L. Wilensky, "Common Problems, Divergent Policies: An 18-Nation Study of Family Policy," *Public Affairs Report* 31 (May 1990): 2.

11. Because of missing data, Austria is not included in the parliamentary-PR average.

12. Robert A. Dahl, *Polyarchy: Participation and Opposition* (New Haven: Yale University Press, 1971), 231-45.

13. This multiple-correlation analysis shows that societal division, as measured by the degree of organizational exclusiveness of ethnic and religious groups, explains 33 percent of the variance in riots and 25 percent of the variance in political deaths. The additional explanation by type of democracy is only 2 percent for riots (with plurality countries slightly more orderly) and 13 percent for deaths (with the PR countries slightly more peaceful).

14. Comparable unemployment data for Austria, Denmark, and New Zealand are not available, and these countries are therefore not included in the unemployment figures in Table 2.

15. Horowitz, op. cit., 76-77.

16. S.E. Finer, "Adversary Politics and Electoral Reform," in *Adversary Politics and Electoral Reform*, ed. S.E. Finer (London: Anthony Wigram, 1975), 30-31.

14.
THE PROBLEM WITH PR

Guy Lardeyret

Guy Lardeyret is president of the Paris-based Fondation pour la Démocratie, a nongovernmental organization that is currently providing advice and support to heads of state, government officials, or party leaders in about 20 countries in Asia, Africa, the Middle East, Eastern Europe, and South America.

Arend Lijphart's article on "Constitutional Choices for New Democracies" [*Journal of Democracy* 2 (Winter 1991): 72-84] attempts to provide scientific evidence for the superiority of proportional representation (PR) to the system of plurality elections. The author presents a comparative analysis designed to show that regimes based on plurality elections do not measure up to parliamentary-PR regimes in terms of "democratic performance."

Lijphart considers the effects of electoral systems on eight variables, which we will consider successively. The first correlation suggests that PR favors the representation of "minorities" and pressure groups. As clearly shown by the statistics, women legislators are more numerous in Nordic countries, which also tend to spend more money on family policies. Although tradition plays a role, the phenomenon is made possible by PR: candidate slates are chosen by party leaders, who are more easily influenced by strong women's movements.

The relationship between PR and voter participation is not as clear. If it were calculated on the European basis (as a proportion of registered voters), U.S. voter turnout would be similar to that of Western Europe. Moreover, Lijphart's figures would look quite different if he had not made some questionable decisions in categorizing countries. France, for instance, might be counted as a presidential-plurality democracy alongside the United States. Germany (whose mixed electoral system has majoritarian effects) belongs among the parliamentary-plurality regimes, while Spain and Portugal (which Lijphart ignores) should be included among the third group, the parliamentary-PR democracies.

Lijphart's next set of figures indicates that northern European countries have a more equal distribution of income, which is not surprising. If there is a link between the electoral system and the greater degree of economic equality in these countries, it may not have much to do with democracy. When conservatives win elections in such countries as Sweden, Denmark, Norway, and Finland, they must form coalitions with other parties, which makes it hard for them to pursue their democratically mandated program of reducing the welfare state.

Lijphart's use of Robert Dahl's system for rating "democratic quality" raises the question of what criteria best measure democratic performance. If the index includes variables such as turnout (as measured in the U.S.), the number of parties, and the strength of interest groups, it introduces a strong bias in favor of PR with this sample of countries.

Finally, the correlations with inflation, economic growth, and unemployment (underestimated in Nordic countries because of highly protected jobs) are difficult to exploit. These indicators are much more powerfully influenced by many other important factors.

Consequences of Electoral Systems

Lijphart accepts from the beginning a fundamental hypothesis—namely, that the electoral system largely determines the party system and through it the structure of the government. Thus, countries where PR is the rule end up with multipartism and coalition governments, while plurality elections favor the two-party system and single-party governments. But as Lijphart notes, opinions diverge on how the party system affects the exercise of democratic governance. It is precisely on this point that it would have been fruitful for Lijphart to test the hypothesis against empirical data.

Such an analysis would have clearly shown that bipartism favors governmental stability and decision-making capacity as well as periodic alternations in power. Multipartism, on the other hand, is positively correlated with ephemeral governments, periods when the chief executive office goes unfilled, repeated elections, and long tenures in office for fixed groups of key politicians. The more parties a country has, moreover, the greater is the incidence of these phenomena.

When the government rests on a homogeneous majority, it remains in power for the duration of its mandated term (stability); can apply its program (efficiency); and is likely, should it falter, to lose power to a strong and united opposition (alternation). By contrast, the coalition governments so common in PR systems often cannot survive serious disagreement over particular measures (instability); need inordinate amounts of time to build new coalitions (executive vacancy); and when they fall, call new elections that generally return the same people (nonalternation).

The contention that PR favors the representation of "minorities" is true, in a sense: PR gives any well-organized pressure group—be it a union, a religion, an ethnic group, a profession, or an ideological faction—a chance to win seats. A party that polarizes one important issue of common interest like environmental protection will attract votes.

Dividing the electorate in this way tends to exacerbate the conflicts in a society. For example, the introduction of PR in local and European elections in France during the 1980s made possible the growing prominence of Jean-Marie Le Pen's National Front (FN), a far-right party that condemns immigration. The Front's rise has in turn sparked the formation of a number of left-wing "antiracist" groups that are no less intolerant than the FN itself. This unhealthy situation can be attributed largely to PR.

It can also be shown that PR is dangerous for countries faced with ethnic or cultural divisions. In Belgium, for instance, linguistic parties sprang up after PR was introduced early in this century. Belgian politics became little more than a feud between the Flemings and the French-speaking Walloons. Without the monarchy to cement its national unity, Belgium could have fallen apart.

The risks of coalition governments should also be recalled. Such governments are often reluctant to make unpopular decisions because of the resistance of some coalition partner. The Palestinian problem in Israel will probably never be solved unless Israel's electoral law is changed or extraordinary foreign pressure is exerted.

Proportional representation tends to give small parties disproportionate power because such parties control the "swing" seats needed to make up a majority coalition. Germany's Free Democratic Party, for instance, has been able to participate in all governments since World War II. Sometimes coalitions can be political absurdities: in Greece recently, the right forged an alliance with the communists in order to keep the socialists out of the government. The political annals of the Scandinavian countries offer numerous examples of cases where the only party to have made significant gains in a given election was unable to find partners and had to remain in opposition.

Even more problematic is PR's tendency to give extremist parties a chance to participate in government. Such a party may eliminate its coalition partners by an internal coup, as Mussolini's Fascists did in Italy in the 1920s. Without PR, the Communists and the Nazis would probably not have been able to storm onto the German political scene as they did in the 1930s.

An election is not a poll aimed at giving the most accurate representation of all the various opinions or interests at play in a given society. Were that the case—there being no fixed limit to the possible divisions in a society—the most democratic assembly would be one where each member represented a sharply defined interest or particular

ideological nuance. Such an assembly would present an absurd caricature
of democratic government.

An electoral system is intended to give citizens the power to decide
who shall rule and according to what policy. It should produce an
efficient government, supported by the bulk of the citizens. Plurality
elections force the parties to coalesce before the balloting occurs. They
must synthesize the divergent interests and opinions of as many voters
as possible, offer the electors a coherent program for governing, and
prove their ability to gather a majority. Parties in plurality systems tend
to be moderate because most votes are to be gained among the
undecided voters of the center.

Proportional representation places the responsibility of choosing both
the personnel and the policy of the new government on party leaders,
deliberating out of public view and after all the votes have been cast.
What distinguishes one system from the other thus has less to do with
"consensus" than with differences in their methods of forging political
compromises. The method of plurality elections is more democratic as
well as more efficient, because the decisions are taken by the citizens
themselves. The choice is clear, and the contract is limited in time.

Rediscovering the Westminster Model

Once a homogeneous majority exists in parliament, there is no need,
strictly speaking, for the direct election of a separate chief executive. The
head of the majority party in parliament can do the job, and this avoids
the risk of conflict between the two sources of democratic legitimacy.
The parliamentary majority provides competent ministers who remain in
touch with the legislature. The executive has the initiative in proposing
legislation; the legislators' main role is to improve bills through
amendments, and not to obstruct policies that have received the support
of the electorate.

We thus rediscover the Westminster model, which has been working
smoothly for the past 300 years in England while France has changed
regimes 20 times in two centuries and is still experimenting with various
possible combinations of electoral systems with parliamentary and
presidential regimes. France's greatest single institutional advance came
in 1958, when the faltering parliamentary-PR Fourth Republic gave way
to the presidential-de-facto-plurality Fifth Republic under Charles de
Gaulle. Yet serious conflicts of competence emerged between the
president and the prime minister during the "cohabitation" period of
1986-88, when for the first time in the history of the Fifth Republic, a
president from one party (Socialist François Mitterand) was teamed with
a premier from another (Gaullist Jacques Chirac). This situation, which
could soon recur, creates pressure for a move toward the parliamentary-
plurality model.

There is now massive evidence that, among the four possible combinations of institutions (presidential or parliamentary) and electoral systems (PR or plurality), the order of rank according to standards of both efficiency and democracy is the following: the Westminster model, presidential-plurality, parliamentary-PR, and presidential-PR. Among the PR systems, the worst is pure PR (Italy, Israel), and the least bad is PR with majoritarian devices (Germany, Greece).

It is almost impossible to get rid of PR, because doing so requires asking independent parties to cooperate in their own liquidation. The coalition of threatened parties will almost always be strong enough to thwart electoral reform, which must then await a major national crisis. The shift from presidentialism to parliamentarism is fairly easy in semi-presidential regimes. Portugal has recently made this move, and Finland has done practically the same thing, which may soon be confirmed by a constitutional change (not that one is indispensable: parties can agree not to nominate their leaders as presidential candidates).

This helps to explain the institutional problems which, as Lijphart acknowledges, can be observed in Latin America. Electoral divisions in parliament tend to reinforce the power of the president. Political competition then focuses on the presidency to a degree that can encourage military coups. One way to avoid that risk is the establishment of a presidential party that entrenches itself in both the state apparatus and many sectors of society. The classic case is Paraguay, where President Alfredo Stroessner stayed in office for 35 years at the head of his Colorado Party machine. To prohibit the reelection of the president simply shifts the power to the ruling party, as Mexicans have learned under the longstanding rule of the PRI.

Building a Democracy

Although the electoral system is a major determinant of a political regime—albeit one curiously omitted in most constitutions—it would be a mistake for new democracies to assume that good democratic performance can be ensured by choosing the right electoral system, or that democracy can be simply defined as a political system where the rulers are freely elected (although that is certainly a necessary condition). Although Boris Yeltsin was freely elected president of the Russian Republic, the RSFSR is still not a democracy.

To become a democracy, a regime must meet two fundamental conditions. Because sovereignty resides with the citizens, who delegate power only to solve problems of common concern, a democracy must above all respect the distinction between the private and public spheres.[1] The transition to democracy in most of the countries of Eastern Europe will depend primarily on their capacity to disengage the state from economic and social life. It is much more difficult to restore the springs of individual initiative, which have been destroyed by years of stifling bureaucracy and irresponsibility, than to ratify a formal constitution. On the other hand, countries such as Korea, Taiwan, or Singapore, where an authoritarian regime has allowed the growth of an effervescent private and economic life, can easily become democratic as soon as free and fair elections are organized.

The second great principle to follow in building a democracy is to diffuse power by dividing control over the public sphere among various levels and centers of authority. The rule here is that decisions should be taken at the level closest to the citizen. Switzerland presents a splendid example of this principle in action. Decentralization can also be spread by competence, with decisions delegated to people concerned with the subject. To set the executive and legislative branches directly against one another, whether at the local or the national level, is more likely to cause inefficiency than political equilibrium. When a country contains populations from widely differing cultures, each intent upon its autonomy, federalism (usually involving a second legislative chamber) is the best institutional solution. A good constitution will find ways to establish these prerequisites of democracy, along with an independent judiciary to guarantee the rule of law.

Ethnic divisions present especially thorny difficulties in Africa. Despite the existence of interesting local democratic traditions in many parts of the continent, national elections there tend to degenerate into ethnic contests over legislative seats and public offices. The best way to counteract these propensities is to oblige members of each group to run against one another on (transethnic) political and ideological grounds in single-member districts. The worst way is to adopt PR, which tends to reproduce ethnic cleavages in the legislature.

In this regard, the unique case of South Africa becomes especially intriguing. The "white tribe" has installed a political regime that basically respects the first two conditions of democracy. As the country moves toward fuller democracy, it remains to be seen whether South Africa's new citizens will array themselves along cleavages of ideology or ethnicity. South Africa's prospects will be grim if it cannot build big and moderate multiethnic parties. There can be no question that a system of plurality elections offers the best conditions for the growth of such parties.

Lijphart's article proves at least that political scientists still have a long way to go even to reach a consensus, much less to discover the definitive truth—if it exists—on this fundamental issue.

NOTES

1. For a thorough analysis of the concept of democracy, see Jean Baechler, *Démocraties* (Paris: Calmann-Levy, 1985). An English translation is forthcoming from New York University Press.

15.
PR AND DEMOCRATIC STATECRAFT

Quentin L. Quade

Quentin L. Quade is professor of political science at Marquette University in Milwaukee, Wisconsin, where he has also served as dean of the graduate school and executive vice-president. His writings include over 60 essays in journals such as the Review of Politics, Freedom at Issue, First Things, Thought, *and* Parliamentary Affairs.

In "Constitutional Choices for New Democracies," Arend Lijphart sets out to describe and evaluate some of the primary institutional alternatives available to new democracies. Lijphart knows that the choice of electoral system is especially important, since it will likely determine whether many or few parties will compete, and whether coalition or single-party governments will result. He also knows that once chosen, the electoral system will be hard to change. Lijphart favors proportional representation (PR), welcomes proliferated parties, and esteems coalitions. I have publicly defended the opposite view. I urge plurality voting in single-member districts, hope and expect that this will encourage a two-party system, and applaud the single-party government that would result.[1]

How is it that two democrats with similar starting points like Lijphart and myself could come up with such starkly contrasting practical advice for newly emerging democracies? As in real estate, the key is to inspect the premises. Even a brief and selective inspection, as this one must be, will show why our recommendations differ so sharply, and why I think Lijphart's position rests on questionable, even utopian, foundations.

Advocates of proportional representation typically describe it as more "fair" and more "just." Lijphart's article says PR produces "consensus" politics, promotes "conciliation and compromise," and is more "representative" than plurality voting. In fact, each of these good words applied to PR begs a question and calls for a rarely given philosophical argument to establish a meaning for "fair," "just," "representative," and so on. No such arguments are presented or even summarized by Lijphart. The only thing certain about PR is that it will tend to re-create society's divisions and locate them in the legislature. That is its purpose, logic, and result.[2]

Whether a system that encourages party proliferation is any of the good things its proponents call it—fairer, more just, more representative—depends on a theory of statecraft and democratic form. What is the purpose of the state? Does the adoption of democracy eliminate or even lessen the traditional requirements of state action? In particular, does democratic statecraft have a diminished responsibility to synthesize society's parts, unify and defend its people, or identify and pursue the common good—meaning those values that no particular part of society will ever seek as its own but on which all particular parts depend? Or does democratic politics exist to do all the things states exist for, but to do them in a new way, a responsible and accountable way? If it does, then the first test of fairness, justice, and representation that democratic politics must pass will be the test of excellence in state action. The second and no less important test will be that of accountability. But for Lijphart and his fellow PR advocates, the first question appears to be: how well are society's natural divisions re-created and relocated in the legislature? Where he equates the number of women in legislatures with representation of women's interests, for example, Lijphart uses the term "representation" as identical to re-creation. In his uncritical implicit reliance on the "picture theory" of legislative representation, Lijphart writes as if Edmund Burke had never lived.

To prove that PR's tendency to re-create divisions and proliferate parties is indeed a good thing, an extended argument is required. It must explain how a political system will be "fair" if it succumbs to the centrifugal pull of interests, how it can advance the general welfare if it "represents" only minute and particular aspects of society, and how a government cobbled together out of postelection splinters by a secretive process of interparty bartering can be considered responsible and accountable. Only by doing this can PR advocates escape the charge of question-begging.

Easy Cases and Unfounded Speculations

I have suggested that PR advocates generally, and Lijphart in particular, tend to make their work easy by eliding from PR's tendency to re-create societal divisions to an unexamined designation of such re-creation as good. Another labor-saving approach, greatly evident in Lijphart's article, is to build the argument for PR on easy cases developed in unusually auspicious circumstances.

It is axiomatic that the difficulty of the tests a political system faces will be commensurate with the severity of the prepolitical conditions it must confront. I refer to such obvious variables as economic health or sickness, ethnic tension or harmony, religious cleavages or unity, geopolitical peril or security. It is also obvious that a relatively weak political structure may work under "fair-weather" prepolitical conditions, while a stronger system may founder if it must endure unusually foul prepolitical weather. Thus, if one could know for sure that nation X would never confront any but the most peaceful circumstances, the strength of its political structure would be of little concern. Such an idyllic environment would leave ample room for error; even if the government were prone to stumble, the natural buoyancy of society would save the state from falling.

> *"...the Weimar Republic, where coalition was endemic and weakness perpetual, might be the best of all test cases for PR."*

Much of my difference with Lijphart derives from his inclination to test PR in too-easy cases. Most of his "successful" examples of PR are drawn from very small societies. Some, like the Scandinavian countries, are nearly homogeneous, with low levels of racial, ethnic, or religious turbulence. Nor have they experienced any severe economic stress during the period of Lijphart's observations. Moreover, all the positive examples from the era he studies have lived under the umbrella of American military protection, an artificial and temporary condition that has spared them most of the stresses of balance-of-power machinations. Many also were beneficiaries of the Marshall Plan, which spurred an era of unprecedented economic recovery and growth in Western Europe.

Lijphart's list of examples contains mostly fair-weather cases; the favorable conditions they enjoyed bear scant resemblance to the arduous circumstances that now confront struggling new democracies. Nor does his list include any of the obvious and dramatic cases in which PR clearly contributed to governmental weakness and systemic collapse. Pre-Mussolini Italy, with its splintered parties and political gridlock, would be a worthy example. France's Fourth Republic (1945-1958), chronically crippled and finally made suicidal by its inability to deal with colonial and domestic problems, would be another. Finally, the Weimar Republic, where coalition was endemic and weakness perpetual, might be the best of all test cases for PR. F.A. Hermens definitively established PR's direct contribution to the regime's inability to develop moderate strength and to rid itself of its extremist elements.[3] As Herman Finer once observed, PR's version of "justice"—lodging social splinters in the legislature—kept both Nazism and Communism alive so that together they could murder the Weimar Republic.[4] "Conciliation and compromise" were conspicuous by their absence.

It seems strange to me that a list of PR examples contains only the beneficiaries of sunny prepolitical conditions. It seems stranger still that it makes no reference to illustrations of PR's most calamitous effects.

In addition to its unwarranted ascription of "good" words to PR and its reliance on easy cases, Lijphart's effort suffers from a third difficulty. To put the case broadly, Lijphart presumes to know things that the evidence simply does not indicate. He imagines, for instance, that Italy's relative economic success over the last few decades, Germany's evident success during the same period, and Britain's relative weakness can all be appreciably attributed to the shape of the central political institutions in each country. If that were true, then one could infer that splintered parties and weak, unstable coalitions (as in Italy) are as good as or better than majority-forming parties that produce strong single-party governments (as in Britain).

Though Lijphart says that the "empirical evidence" suggests all this, it actually suggests nothing of the sort. Instead, the empirical evidence should remind us of the numerous and sometimes mysterious variables that one must take into account when considering such complex social and economic realities. As previously noted, all we know *for certain* about electoral systems is that PR tends to proliferate parties, while plurality voting encourages two-party arrangements. All we know *for certain* about coalitions is that they are subject to stress and dissolution more than a single-party majority would be (witness Italy in the spring of 1991 as it deposed its forty-ninth postwar government); and that to govern they must form postelection groupings outside of public view (no member of Italy's electorate voted for its fiftieth government). Abstract logic—plus experience with cases like Weimar Germany and the Fourth French Republic—suggests that coalitions will be a less secure basis for governance than would be a single-party majority. Such majorities are clearly able to act, even while constantly debating and maneuvering against an opposition striving to become the next government.

But what of Italy's economic good fortune, Germany's robustness, Britain's pale comparison? One could attribute these conditions to their respective political institutions only by arguing *post hoc, ergo propter hoc*. Such an argument simply ignores the array of other variables that any objective analysis should bring to mind. I have mentioned already the artificiality of the foreign-affairs responsibilities that have confronted Italy and Germany in the age of the Marshall Plan and the NATO alliance, as well as the jump-start that the former gave to their economies. I would also note that policies which encourage economic growth can be adopted by weak governments, while strong governments are not assured of making all the right decisions. It is not unreasonable to suggest, for example, that Germany's economic strength since the Marshall Plan derives in great part from the horrible economic lessons learned during the PR-induced paralysis of the Weimar period. Certainly the deep-seated German fear of inflation is derived from those experiences. It would be a mistake to attribute Germany's cautious monetary policy to the country's contemporary system of modified PR when in fact this penchant for caution is a negative lesson from Germany's ruinous pre-Hitler PR experience.

By the same token, attempts to attribute Britain's relatively pallid economic record to its majority-forming system are entirely unconvincing. Britain has performed poorly by comparison to some other countries—a weak showing that is traceable in part to poor decisions and not just difficult circumstances. But wise decisions are not guaranteed by *any* political system, and the impact of unpromising circumstances should not be underestimated. Britain, after all, went into World War II in substantial decline, and emerged from it greatly weakened. It did not receive the same massive help from the Marshall Plan that others did. It had to endure the rapid dissolution of a massive overseas empire that was tightly interwoven with the fabric of its economy. Decolonization has required not merely economic adaptation, but a seismic social-psychological adjustment as well. On top of all this is the extraordinarily thorny prepolitical problem posed by the Irish question.

The point of this litany is this: while Britain's economic performance in the postwar era can hardly be called a triumph of the Westminster model, neither can it be explained simply as one of that model's failures. The array of influences on those countries that have done better, the degree to which an economy operates independently of day-to-day political influence, and the large number of debilitating conditions Britain has confronted all make it simply unrealistic to cite the British political system as the main debilitator of the British economy. It is wise, as a rule, never to speculate when you can ascertain. Among this rule's many corollaries is this one: never fail to speculate when you cannot ascertain, but never imagine you have ascertained when in fact you are only speculating. The causal relationships that Lijphart claims his "empirical evidence" has established turn out, upon closer inspection, to be purely speculative.

The Virtues of Plurality Systems

Lijphart's dedication to PR rests on his assumption that we can get all of PR's alleged virtues (re-creationist representation, all voices heard, consensus, compromise, etc.) without any of its alleged vices (invitation to extremism, governmental weakness and instability, political unrealism, unaccountability to the electorate, etc.). But both analysis and history strongly suggest that you cannot buy it that way. Even if fair-weather conditions make PR tolerable over some period of time, it is unlikely that modern mass nation-states will forever or even for long have such happy circumstances before them. The natural centrifugal stresses and strains in human existence that call the state into being argue for majority-based systems to ensure its capacity for action. And if popular control is to be genuine, the people need to be able to see who is doing what and what each side has to offer, and to make serious judgments between them.

Plurality voting encourages the competing parties to adopt a majority-forming attitude. The parties incline to be moderate, to seek conciliation, to round off their rough edges—in short, to do *before* the election, in the public view, the very tasks that Lijphart applauds PR systems for doing *after* the election. Majorities formed in plurality systems are more likely to be strong enough to sustain effective government without becoming unresponsive and rigid, for majorities thus formed are innately fickle, always falling apart, always needing rebuilding.

Moreover, well-chosen policies, including respect for subsidiarity, can foster vibrant local governments and civil societies, thus encouraging the very multiplicity for which PR strives without incurring the deleterious effects of governmental weakness and unaccountability. In contrast to Lijphart, I maintain that PR's true virtues (accommodation of differences, a hundred flowers blooming, etc.) can be had without any of its debilitating vices under a majority-forming plurality system. That being the case, why run the well-known risks of PR? Emerging democracies, facing very difficult prepolitical circumstances, need the best political structures they can get. The best combine great capacity for action with clear accountability and thus provide power-made-responsible. This happy combination is most likely to occur in majority-forming electoral systems operating within parliamentary structures. Of course, even the best arrangements cannot guarantee success in this imperfect world, any more than inferior systems make wise policy impossible. But the best systems will ensure both that the paralysis of government itself does not become the chief problem before the nation, and that it will be the voters who truly elect and depose governments.

NOTES

1. Compare my essay "Democracies-to-Be: Getting It Right the First Time," in *Freedom at Issue* 113 (March-April 1990), 4-8.

2. Since societal divisions are potentially innumerable, one sometimes finds PR advocates like Lijphart introducing distinctions between "extreme" and "moderate" forms of PR. In the latter, PR's natural tendencies are frustrated by devices that give government a better chance to form and function—a repudiation, however unacknowledged, of the logic of PR.

3. F.A. Hermens, *Democracy or Anarchy? A Study of Proportional Representation* (Notre Dame, Indiana: University of Notre Dame Press, 1941).

4. Herman Finer, *Governments of Greater European Powers* (New York: Henry Holt, 1956), 623.

16.
DOUBLE-CHECKING
THE EVIDENCE

Arend Lijphart

Arend Lijphart, *professor of political science at the University of California at San Diego, is the coeditor of* Electoral Laws and Their Political Consequences *(1986) and the author of numerous other books. His article "Constitutional Choices for New Democracies" appeared in the Winter 1991 issue of the* Journal of Democracy.

In my article "Constitutional Choices for New Democracies," I presented systematic empirical evidence concerning the relative performance of various types of democratic systems in an effort to transcend the usual vague and untestable claims and counterclaims that surround this topic. I compared four parliamentary-plurality democracies (the United Kingdom, Canada, Australia, and New Zealand) with nine parliamentary-proportional representation (PR) democracies (Germany, Italy, Austria, the Netherlands, Belgium, and four Nordic countries—Sweden, Denmark, Norway, Finland) with regard to their performance records on minority representation and protection, democratic quality, the maintenance of public order and peace, and the management of the economy. I found that, where differences between the two groups of democracies appeared, the parliamentary-PR systems showed the better performance. There were sizable differences with regard to minority representation (as measured by the representation of women in national parliaments), the protection of minority interests (measured by innovative family policy), democratic quality (measured by voter turnout), and control of unemployment; smaller differences on income inequality and control of inflation; and little or no difference with regard to the maintenance of public order (as measured by riots and deaths from political violence) and economic growth. Since, according to the conventional—but also rather old-fashioned—wisdom, PR may be superior to plurality as far as minority representation is concerned but leads to less effective decision making, even my finding of minor or no differences on some of the performance indicators must be counted in favor of the parliamentary-PR type.

Guy Lardeyret and Quentin L. Quade, both eloquent exponents of this conventional wisdom, raise a series of objections to my analysis and conclusions—very welcome challenges because they present an opportunity to double-check the validity of my evidence. Lardeyret and Quade argue that 1) the differences in governmental performance may be explained by other factors than the type of democracy, and hence that they do not prove any parliamentary-PR superiority; 2) that, when other important effects of the different types of democracy are considered, plurality systems are superior; 3) that some of my findings are the result of incorrect measurement; and 4) that my findings are biased by my choice and classification of the countries included in the analysis. I shall demonstrate, however, that whenever their objections can be tested against the facts, they turn out to be invalid.

Alternative Explanations

I agree with Lardeyret's and Quade's argument that economic success is not solely determined by government policy; I said as much in my original article. There are obviously many external and fortuitous factors that influence a country's economic performance. Neither do I disagree with Quade's argument that several special circumstances have had a negative effect on Britain. On the other hand, some of the PR countries suffered similar setbacks: the Netherlands and Belgium also lost sizable colonial empires, the "seismic social-psychological" shock of decolonization suffered by Britain was no greater than the shock of defeat and division suffered by Germany, and ethnic strife has plagued Belgium as well as the Celtic periphery of the United Kingdom. But my comparison was not just between Britain and one or more PR countries; I compared the four parliamentary-plurality democracies as a group with the group of nine parliamentary-PR countries. I assumed that when the economic performance of groups of democracies is examined over a long period of time, and when all of the countries studied have similar levels of economic development, external and fortuitous influences tend to even out. In the absence of any plausible suggestion that, as a group, the parliamentary-PR countries enjoyed unusual economic advantages from the 1960s through the 1980s—and neither Lardeyret nor Quade offers any such suggestion—my assumption and hence my findings concerning differences in economic performance remain valid.

Lardeyret and Quade do mention a few things that might provide a basis for alternative explanations: the special characteristics of the Nordic countries, the advantage of having a constitutional monarchy, the difference between moderate and extreme PR, and the advantage of U.S. military protection. All of these can be tested empirically. Lardeyret claims that unemployment in the Nordic countries is underestimated because of "highly protected jobs" and that income inequality is relatively modest because of unusual handicaps that conservative parties must contend with in these countries. Whether these factors change my findings can be checked easily by excluding the Nordic countries and comparing the non-Nordic parliamentary-PR countries with the parliamentary-plurality countries. Average unemployment in the Nordic countries was indeed lower than in the non-Nordic countries—2.7 percent compared with 5.7 percent—but the latter percentage is still slightly better than the 6.1 percent for the parliamentary-plurality countries. As far as income inequality is concerned, there is virtually no difference between the Nordic and non-Nordic parliamentary-PR countries—39.0 and 38.9 percent respectively—both of which score lower than the 42.9 percent in the parliamentary-plurality democracies.

When we compare monarchies with republics, the first point to be made is that, if a constitutional monarchy is an advantage, all of the parliamentary-plurality countries enjoy this advantage, whereas only about half of the parliamentary-PR democracies do. Second, when we compare the monarchical countries (Belgium, the Netherlands, Sweden, Norway, and Denmark) with the republican PR countries (Germany, Italy, Austria, and Finland), their growth rates are virtually identical and their inflation rates exactly the same. Only their unemployment rates differ somewhat: the monarchies have a 4.0 percent average unemployment rate compared with 4.9 percent in the nonmonarchical countries; again, the latter percentage is still better than the 6.1-percent average of the parliamentary-plurality countries. On all of the indicators of minority representation and protection and of democratic quality, there are slight differences between the monarchical and non-monarchical groups, but both still clearly outperform the parliamentary-plurality countries.

Is PR's Achilles' heel revealed when we focus on the countries that have extreme PR (Italy, the Netherlands, Denmark, and Finland) and contrast these with the more moderate PR systems (Germany, Sweden, Norway, Belgium, and Austria)? The empirical evidence disproves this. The inflation and unemployment rates in the extreme PR group are indeed higher (7.4 and 5.5 versus 5.4 and 3.6 percent) but still at least a bit lower than the 7.5 and 6.1 percent in the parliamentary-plurality systems; their growth rates are virtually identical. On the four indicators of representation and democratic quality, the differences are slight, and both groups of PR countries remain way ahead of the parliamentary-plurality countries. My own firm preference remains for moderate PR, but the dangers of extreme PR must not be exaggerated.

As Quade correctly states, the parliamentary-PR countries have had the advantage of living under "the umbrella of American military protection"—but so have all four of the parliamentary-plurality countries. In fact, the only slight exceptions are in the PR group: Sweden's neutral but strongly armed posture entailed heavy military expenditures, and Finland lived in precarious dependence on Soviet restraint. On the whole, however, American military protection benefited all 13 parliamentary democracies more or less equally, and therefore cannot explain any differences in their performance records.

Alternative Standards and Classifications

Partly in addition to and partly instead of the measures that I used to evaluate the performance of different types of democracy, Lardeyret and Quade state that democracies should be judged in terms of factors like accountability, government stability, decision-making capacity, and the ability to avoid "repeated elections." There are several problems with these suggestions. First of all, while accountability is certainly an important aspect of democratic government, it cannot be measured objectively. Second, it is not at all clear that coalition governments are less responsible and accountable than one-party governments. Quade's description of coalition cabinets as governments "cobbled together out of postelection splinters by a secretive process of interparty bartering" may apply to a few exceptional cases like Israel (which combines extreme PR with an evenly split and polarized electorate), but for most PR countries it is a grossly overdrawn caricature. In fact, once they are formed, coalition cabinets tend to be a good deal *less* secretive and more open than one-party cabinets.

Third, government stability can be measured in terms of average cabinet duration. On the basis of previously collected figures, my calculation shows that the average cabinet life in the parliamentary-plurality countries is about twice that in the parliamentary-PR systems.[1] Longer cabinet duration, Lardeyret assumes, means greater decision-making strength because of greater continuity in government personnel. But when coalition cabinets change they usually do not change as much as the radically alternating cabinets in the parliamentary-plurality countries. Lardeyret admits this when he complains about the "long tenures in office for fixed groups of key politicians" in the PR countries. Fourth, if Lardeyret is right about the superior decision-making capacity of parliamentary-plurality governments, the only convincing proof is that their decisions result in more effective policies. This brings us back to the evaluation of government performance in terms of successful macroeconomic policy making and the successful maintenance of public order. As we have already seen, this hard evidence does not show any parliamentary-plurality superiority.

Lardeyret's complaint about unnecessarily frequent elections in the parliamentary-PR systems suggests an additional useful measure of democratic performance—and one that, happily, can be measured and tested easily. In the 29-year period from 1960 to 1988—the same period for which two of the three OECD economic indicators were collected—the parliamentary-plurality countries conducted an average of

10.0 national legislative elections, compared with an average of 8.8 in the parliamentary-PR countries.[2] The frequency of elections is actually *smaller* in the PR systems, contrary to Lardeyret's assertion, although the difference is slight. However, Lardeyret's hypothesis is clearly disproved by this simple test.

Lardeyret and Quade have only a few disagreements with my measurements. One question that Lardeyret does raise is the measurement of voter turnout: the U.S. voter-turnout figure would be considerably higher if counted as a proportion of registered voters. He is quite right on this point, but all of my turnout figures are percentages of eligible voters—which means that all countries are treated equally. Moreover, if turnout figures are used as a measure of democratic quality, the low figure for the United States accurately reflects not only an unusually high degree of political apathy but also the fact that voting is deliberately discouraged by the government by means of onerous registration procedures.

Quade questions my equation of "the number of women in legislatures with representation of women's interests." But I did not equate the two at all: I used a separate measure (the innovativeness and expansiveness of family policy, which is of special concern to women) to test whether women's interests were actually better taken care of in the PR countries—and I found that this was indeed the case.

Finally, Lardeyret questions my use of Robert Dahl's ratings of democratic quality because of their alleged pro-PR bias. I already admitted a slight bias of this kind in my original article, but I decided to use the Dahl ratings anyway since they are the most careful overall ratings that are available. However, since they are obviously less objective than my other indicators, I shall not insist on their being used as evidence.

Quade criticizes my favorable judgment of the parliamentary-PR combination by pointing out some examples in which PR did not work well, especially the two cases that are often regarded as spectacular failures of democracy: the Weimar Republic and the French Fourth Republic. Nobody can disagree with the assessment that the Weimar Republic was a failure, but it is less clear that PR was the decisive factor or that plurality would have been able to save Weimar democracy. Moreover, Weimar was a semi-presidential rather than a parliamentary system. In France, the Fourth Republic indeed did not work well, but a reasonable argument can be made that relatively small reforms within the parliamentary-PR framework might have cured the problems and that the radical shift to semi-presidentialism and away from PR was not absolutely necessary. And examples of PR failures can be matched by examples of the failure of plurality systems, such as the failed democracies of West Africa. Sir Arthur Lewis, who served as an economic advisor to these governments, became convinced that "the surest way to kill the idea of democracy" in these divided societies "is to adopt the Anglo-American electoral system of first-past-the-post [plurality]."[3]

Lardeyret does not question my focus on stable contemporary democracies, but argues instead that some of these countries should have been classified differently. Although France is neither fully presidential nor fully plurality, I accept his suggestion that it is close enough on both counts to be classified alongside the United States. I agree that Spain and Portugal belong in the parliamentary-PR category, but comparable data are lacking since the two countries were not yet democratic during the full period covered by the empirical evidence. I disagree that Germany lacks PR and should be classified as a plurality system; it is almost entirely PR in terms of how Bundestag seats are allocated to the parties, though its 5-percent threshold makes it a moderate PR system.

But let us concede Germany to the plurality category; my analysis still stands. Lardeyret's counter-hypothesis is that in "the order of rank according to standards of both efficiency and democracy," the two plurality systems (parliamentary and presidential) are ahead of the parliamentary-PR systems. This can be tested by comparing the seven plurality systems (the parliamentary-plurality countries plus the United States, France, and, arguably, Germany) with eight PR systems (all of the parliamentary-PR systems except Germany). Thus reclassified, the PR countries still have the better record with regard to control of unemployment (4.6 percent versus 5.5 percent average unemployment) and do not differ much with regard to growth (3.5 versus 3.4 percent) and inflation (6.6 versus 6.5 percent). On the indicators of minority representation and protection and of democratic quality, the PR countries are still far ahead of the plurality systems: 17.5 versus 4.5 percent women in parliament; a score of 8.0 versus 4.4 on family policy; 84.5 versus 73.5 percent on voter turnout; and 38.9 versus 41.9 percent of total income earned by the top 20 percent of households. The evidence clearly disproves Lardeyret's counter-hypothesis.

Choices and Changes

The demonstrable advantages of parliamentarism and PR appear to be appreciated by the citizens and politicians of democratic countries. In many, if not most, presidential countries, there is widespread dissatisfaction with the operation of presidentialism and sizable support for a shift to a parliamentary form of government; the contrary sentiment can be found in hardly any parliamentary democracy. Similarly, there is great unhappiness about how plurality elections work and strong sentiment for a shift to PR in most democracies that use plurality, but few calls for plurality in PR countries. One important reason for this pattern is that the divisive, winner-take-all nature of plurality and presidentialism is widely understood. From the turn of the century on, democracies with ethnic or other deep cleavages have repeatedly turned to PR in order to accommodate such differences. Lardeyret's recommendation of plurality elections for South Africa and other deeply divided countries is therefore particularly dangerous.

Another important reason for PR's popularity is the feeling that disproportional election results are inherently unfair and undemocratic. None of postwar Britain's governing parties was put in power by a majority of the voters; all of these parties gained power in spite of the fact that most of the voters voted against them. Lardeyret's and Quade's opinion that electoral disproportionality is unimportant is simply not shared by most democrats. As a recent editorial in the London *Economist* puts it, "since the perception of fairness is the acid test for a democracy—the very basis of its legitimacy the unfairness argument overrules all others."[4]

Fundamental constitutional changes are difficult to effect and therefore rare, but the prevailing pattern of democratic sentiment makes shifts from plurality to PR more likely than the other way around. The reason for this is not, as Lardeyret suggests, that "it is almost impossible to get rid of PR, because doing so requires asking independent parties to cooperate in their own liquidation." On the contrary, this is the main reason why the big parties that benefit from the plurality rule will try to keep it. In PR systems, the large parties usually have enough votes to shift to a system that would greatly benefit them, especially because, as Lardeyret correctly observes, the electoral system is "curiously omitted in most [written] constitutions." That they rarely try to do so cannot be explained in terms of narrow partisan self-interest; the feeling that scrapping PR is undemocratic and dangerous plays a major role. Both the empirical evidence and the weight of opinion in existing democracies make a strong case for the proposition that PR and parliamentarism are also the wisest options for new democracies.

NOTES

1. Arend Lijphart, *Democracies: Patterns of Majoritarian and Consensus Government in Twenty-One Countries* (New Haven: Yale University Press, 1984), 83. A cabinet is defined as the same cabinet if its party composition does not change; on the basis of this definition and for the 1945-80 period, average cabinet life in the four parliamentary-plurality countries was 88 months and in the parliamentary-PR countries, 44 months.

2. The dates of parliamentary elections for the 13 countries can be found in the respective country chapters of Thomas T. Mackie and Richard Rose, *The International Almanac of Electoral History*, 3rd ed. (London: Macmillan, 1991).

3. W. Arthur Lewis, *Politics in West Africa* (London: Allen and Unwin, 1965), 71.

4. *The Economist*, 11 May 1991, 13.

17.
POLLWATCHING
AND PEACEMAKING

Jennifer McCoy, Larry Garber, & Robert Pastor

Jennifer McCoy *is associate professor of political science at Georgia State University and senior research associate at the Carter Center of Emory University.* **Larry Garber** *is senior consultant with the National Democratic Institute for International Affairs.* **Robert Pastor** *is professor of political science at Emory University and Director of the Latin American and Caribbean Program of Emory's Carter Center. Among them they have observed elections in more than 20 countries.*

Even before the Gulf War rekindled hopes that the United Nations could enforce the elusive principle of collective security, sovereign states had begun to request another form of security assistance from the international community—help in resolving internal conflicts and guaranteeing processes of democratization. International organizations like the UN and the Organization of American States (OAS) were designed primarily to keep the peace among states, not to resolve civil wars, even those involving external intervention. Similarly, such domestic affairs as designing the rules of the political game and conducting elections have been considered to lie outside the purview of international organizations.

The Nicaraguan elections of February 1990, however, challenged traditional concepts of sovereignty and introduced an unprecedented role for international actors in the internal affairs of that troubled country. Since then, the model developed in Nicaragua has been used in Haiti; modified for use in Suriname, Guyana, and El Salvador; and proposed as a means for resolving civil conflicts in Africa and Asia.

The model consists of an old formula, free elections, applied in a radically new manner. In Nicaragua, groups of international observers helped both to negotiate the rules of the electoral "game" and to implement a collectively guaranteed democratization process arising from a regional peace plan. The outcome was the world's first peaceful transfer of power from a revolutionary government to its opposition, and the first election in Nicaraguan history in which all major parties competed and accepted the results. The principal actors both inside and outside Nicaragua were satisfied that the process had worked. The defeated Sandinistas, while obviously unhappy with the results, recognized that their long-term interests and those of Nicaragua were better served by respecting the vote than by defiantly holding onto power. The Nicaraguan experience, as well as other recent cases where international election monitors have been present, suggests the usefulness of this model in resolving the world's most intractable conflicts.

Historically, most Latin American governments have advocated respect for the principle of "nonintervention"—a principle that obviously favors incumbent governments. No principle has been more frustrating to an expansive power and more sacred to a weak nation. Latin America enshrined the principle in Article 15 of the OAS Charter: "No State or group of States has the right to intervene, directly or indirectly, for any reason whatever, in the internal or external affairs of any other State. The foregoing principle prohibits not only armed force but also any other form of interference." Yet as Venezuelan president Carlos Andrés Pérez told the OAS on 27 April 1990, the nonintervention solution had become part of the problem by "allowing the protection of dictatorships like those of Somoza, Stroessner, Duvalier, and Trujillo. . . . Nonintervention became a passive intervention against democracy."

Frustrated by the protracted internal wars that were ravaging their region, the five Central American presidents devised a way through this problem at Esquipulas, Guatemala, in 1987. There they approved a plan to end the conflict in the region by undertaking a collectively guaranteed process of national reconciliation and democratization. That plan represented a conceptual breakthrough in international relations, slicing through the cord connecting internal strife and external intervention by dealing with both dimensions of the conflict at the same time. It laid the basis for the ultimate resolution of the Nicaraguan conflict.

The 1990 Nicaraguan elections illustrate how outside actors—the other Central American governments and the international election observers— can serve as collective guarantors helping to promote national reconciliation and democratization. In this case, a massive observer presence by two intergovernmental organizations—the UN and the OAS—combined with the active participation of the Council of Freely Elected Heads of Government (the Council), a distinguished group of current and former Western Hemispheric leaders chaired by former president Jimmy Carter, contributed significantly to the success of the voting.

The worldwide upsurge of democracy and the reduction of tension between the superpowers offer an unprecedented opportunity for outside actors to help domestic groups negotiate and accept new political rules of the game that, in turn, could permit peaceful change and the resolution of longstanding conflicts. The UN Security Council plan for resolving the Cambodian conflict through UN-administered elections and the agreement of the UN and OAS to mediate the civil conflict and monitor the March 1991 elections in El Salvador indicate the breadth of the potential role that could be played by international organizations. Likewise, the U.S.-Soviet agreements to cooperate in joint efforts to resolve the Angolan and Afghan civil wars through internationally monitored elections indicate the potential role of such elections for resolving other long-term internal conflicts tied to foreign intervention.

In some cases, however, foreign governments cannot effectively negotiate internal matters, and intergovernmental organizations are often unable or unwilling to do so. In such cases, the best method of resolution may be private mediation rather than state-led diplomacy. Whether they are private individuals or intergovernmental organizations, outside mediators can often successfully bring the antagonists to the table, help devise the rules of the game, and guarantee a modicum of fairness in the election process.

Defining the Problem

Elections held in different types of situations pose distinct problems and opportunities. The most visible and significant role for international actors is during "first elections," when countries are making a democratic transition and opposition groups are genuinely competing for the first time. In cases where civil violence is likely, there may be a need for special measures to guarantee not only the election's fairness, but also the security of the participants. In July 1990, for example, Haitian president Ertha Pascal-Trouillot asked the UN for security advisors. The request initiated a debate that lasted until the General Assembly and the Security Council agreed in October to provide such advisors, together with civilian observers. The May 1991 Angolan accord, signed by government and UNITA leaders and mediated by Portugal, calls for a joint political and military commission—to be made up of representatives from the Angolan government and UNITA, plus Portugal, the U.S., and the Soviet Union—to prepare for elections in 1992.

Besides physical peril, lack of confidence in the election machinery and the government personnel supervising the elections is the greatest obstacle to a successful outcome. The danger lies in the deep distrust among contending parties and the possibility that a party might boycott the election because of perceived inequities or bias in the process. In countries where mutual distrust runs deep, observers thus play a dual role: They serve the government by helping to keep the opposition in the race, a prerequisite for a legitimate process, and they serve the opposition by ensuring that the election will either be fair or else be denounced as fraudulent.

Depending on the outcome of the elections, observers do one of three things. They can legitimize a ruling-party victory where such a victory would not otherwise be credible. This was the case in the elections in Korea in 1987, in Bulgaria in 1990, and in the Dominican Republic in 1990. Observers can also confirm an opposition victory and persuade the surprised incumbents to accept defeat, as happened in Nicaragua and Chile. Finally, observers can cry fraud if a government refuses to acknowledge the true outcome of an election, as in Panama and the Philippines, with significant costs for the incumbent.

In countries with limited democratic experience or where incumbent leaders or parties are accustomed to or accused of using the electoral machinery to maintain power, governments may actually benefit from international observers. Confident incumbents have been known to invite international observers, who can certify elections no matter who wins. This was the case with the Sandinistas, and may have been the reasoning of Guyanese president Hugh Desmond Hoyte, who has invited both the Commonwealth and, with the encouragement of the opposition, Carter and the Council of Freely Elected Heads of Government to observe elections to be held in the fall of 1991. This same reasoning may convince other governments historically hostile to observers, such as Mexico, to permit their presence as a means of making a ruling-party victory credible in the eyes of a skeptical opposition and international community.

Even in countries that have previously held free elections, international observers can play an important role in reducing tensions and ensuring that the rules of the game are respected by all sides. In the recent elections in the Dominican Republic, for example, the observer delegation led by Jimmy Carter defused a potentially explosive situation by proposing procedures to review disputed election results. In the end, opposition leader Juan Bosch found it awkward to reject the observers' conclusion that he had lost to incumbent president Joaquín Balaguer, for Bosch had himself been the principal force behind the invitation to Carter's group. In Suriname, a country with a history of free elections tarnished by military intervention, the OAS was invited not only to observe the May 1991 elections, but more importantly, to stay until the inauguration of the new civilian government.

In some circumstances, an intergovernmental organization may actually have to administer or supervise an election process in order to establish the legitimacy of the result. Such was the case with the 1989 Namibian elections, which the South African government administered under UN supervision. Similarly, the current plan for resolving the Cambodian conflict calls for UN control over the entire election process. More commonly, domestic authorities administer elections in accord with their country's constitution, while the presence of observers is invited or permitted as a means of reassuring parties and voters alike.

In Nicaragua and Haiti in 1990, the governments invited

intergovernmental and private groups to observe the elections. In other cases, the government may be unwilling to give intergovernmental organizations a formal role, though private groups may be permitted to observe. This happened in Chile, Pakistan, Romania, Bulgaria, Hungary and Czechoslovakia, as well as in the failed cases of Panama in 1989, Haiti in 1987, and the Philippines in 1986.

Election observing, in its simplest form, has a long history.[1] Since World War II, the UN has observed elections, referenda, and plebiscites—most often in situations involving transitions from colonial to independent status. The November 1989 elections in Namibia were a harbinger of the expanding role of international observers as conflict mediators. The peaceful conduct of those elections helped to resolve a 30-year-old war between South Africa and the South West African Peoples Organization (SWAPO), and set the stage for Namibian independence.

Because of Namibia's unique legal status, the UN assumed a formal role in supervising the elections there. While South Africa maintained administrative control during the transition period, UN police and election monitors were in the country for the eight months preceding the elections. During this period, UN representatives, often acting at the urging of private observer groups, negotiated critical changes in the election law that South Africa had originally proposed. Outside observers joined most Namibians in crediting the UN team, whose members were at every polling site, with ensuring the success of the five-day voting process.

In the Western Hemisphere, the OAS sent observers to more than 15 countries between 1962 and 1989. Usually, however, OAS teams stayed for a very short time around election day. The purpose was less to monitor the electoral process per se than to show moral support for democratic elections.

During the past decade, the phenomenon of private groups observing elections has become commonplace all over the world, although their role in the election process generally has been limited. Until recently the history of election observing has been mostly one of passive onlooking rather than active mediation.

Before the Nicaraguan case, the UN had never accepted an invitation to observe elections in a member country, and never before had the OAS agreed to furnish a massive observer presence for the duration of an electoral campaign and voting process. Each organization signed a formal protocol with the government of Nicaragua, reflecting the unprecedented nature of the effort. Each organization stressed the uniqueness of this case—especially its relation to the regional peace process—and warned that it was not setting a precedent for similar efforts in other countries.

Nonetheless, other sovereign countries and opposition groups within them are now requesting or discussing the possibility of similar efforts.

The model of international election monitoring developed in Nicaragua and other recent cases therefore needs to be carefully evaluated.[2]

The Functions of International Observers

The need for international observers derives from several sources. International observers provide psychological support to participants in the election process. In many cases, the observers' mere presence reassures a skeptical population regarding the secrecy of the ballot, the efficacy of the process, and the safety of the voters.

The presence of more than 2,500 observers in Nicaragua, along with an education campaign by the Catholic Church, served to reassure voters that the ballot would be secret. When asked how they voted, many voters responded with the words of the educational campaign—"El voto es secreto." The visible presence of high-level observers in Panama in May 1989 seemed to encourage a large voter turnout, despite widespread skepticism about Noriega's intentions. The reassurance furnished to skittish Haitian voters by large numbers of international observers was crucial in 1990, especially in light of the election-day massacre that had occurred in 1987.

A more classic rationale for the presence of election-day observers is that they can deter fraud in the balloting and counting processes. To serve this purpose, however, the observer delegation's presence must be well publicized, the delegation must have enough members to visit a significant number of polling sites, and it must obtain adequate information regarding the counting of the results. The latter is particularly important since serious manipulation is most likely to occur during the counting phase. Election-day fraud was a major concern of the Nicaraguan opposition from the outset. By fielding large delegations and deploying them systematically around the country, the OAS and UN were well-positioned to deter any significant attempt at manipulation. Together, the two organizations visited more than 80 percent of the country's polling sites on election day.

A third function of observers is to report to the international community on the overall fairness of an election process. Such an evaluation generally requires a sustained observation effort that considers the quality of the election laws, voter registration, the election campaign, the balloting and counting processes, and the degree to which the results are respected. This purpose has gained significance as countries like the United States have made a government's commitment to periodic and genuine elections a factor in bilateral relationships.

Finally, the presence of observers may provide a vehicle for resolving longstanding disputes. Observers may act as mediators and facilitators, promoting confidence in the process and easing the mutual distrust that might otherwise flare into full-blown conflict. This is obviously the most complicated role that observers can play, requiring a considerable commitment of resources and skill.

The UN, OAS, and Council delegations to Nicaragua together fulfilled the four functions described above. Their presence during the registration phase, the campaign period, and on election day boosted public confidence in the credibility and efficacy of the election process, and allayed some of the fear that inevitably exists in a society with a limited democratic tradition. At least as important, the observers helped to transform the antagonists' attitudes, contributing to an easing of hostility on both sides. The significance of this change in attitudes became clear on the day after the election, when all sides committed themselves to a smooth transition and began negotiations to achieve it.

Lessons from International Observing

The first lesson is that where distrust is deep, the major parties must be motivated to participate in elections and to accept the presence of observers. The government needs to view international observers as a vehicle for ensuring that the world will recognize its victory, or for proving that it is indeed committed to free elections. The opposition needs to believe that it can win free elections or at least do well enough to magnify its influence, and then it needs to find third parties who can guarantee that any election tampering will be exposed. An invitation from both sides provides the international observers with real leverage to insist on fair elections since neither side will want to be accused of manipulation or an insincere commitment to free elections.

In Nicaragua, for example, the successful conduct of free and fair elections in which all parties accepted the outcome depended on several factors: 1) strong motivation on the part of the ruling Sandinistas and the opposition to participate in elections; 2) the willingness of the Nicaraguan government to invite international organizations to observe and judge the overall conduct of the election process; and 3) the long-term presence of credible international observers who gained the trust of both sides.

The Sandinistas clearly stood to gain from holding elections deemed honest by world—and U.S.—opinion. Nicaraguan history is replete with examples of the opposition withdrawing from or boycotting elections conducted by a distrusted government. Most recently in 1984, major opposition groups, encouraged by the U.S. government, withdrew from the race due to harassment and their fear that the Sandinistas would rig the election. Although the elections were judged reasonably fair by a few international groups, they were marred by the boycott of these parties. The Sandinistas thus sought to avoid another boycott in 1990.

The Sandinistas also nourished a strong, unwavering belief that they would win a fair contest. Their calculation was that an observer-certified

Sandinista victory might end U.S. support for the contras and the trade embargo, open the way for renewed international aid and loans, and eventually lead to peace and economic recovery.

The opposition was wary of participating in elections administered by a government it did not trust. Yet even those sectors that had boycotted the previous elections decided to participate in the 1990 elections, for several reasons. First, most realized that the 1984 boycott and the contra war had failed to unseat the Sandinistas; elections offered the opposition its best chance of gaining power. Second, the Central American peace accords helped reassure them and reinforced the process. Third, the opposition thought that it could win free elections, and that the international observers could ensure a fair process. Finally, the U.S. government shifted its policy to support a peaceful resolution of the Nicaraguan conflict and thus encouraged opposition parties to unite and participate in the elections.

Even where there are serious flaws in the electoral process, the opposition can gain from participating, provided that there are observers who can effectively monitor the vote and denounce the government if it tries to rig the result. The elections in the Philippines and Panama were cases where the opposition decided to participate even though they were skeptical that the incumbents would permit or accept the results of a fair election. Opposition groups used their campaigns to mobilize supporters, and also drew enough international attention to raise the pressure on the incumbents to open the political process somewhat.

Both Marcos and Noriega severely underestimated how much discontent could be tapped by opposition forces competing even under inequitable conditions. When the extent of their miscalculation was revealed and the opposition won overwhelming victories, the incumbents resorted to blatant fraud. In the Philippines, denunciation of the elections by international observers brought strained relations with several foreign governments, and soon thereafter, a popular revolt that toppled Marcos. In Panama, Noriega's attempt at massive fraud during the vote count was exposed by Jimmy Carter, acting as an observer, thus leaving Noriega domestically and internationally isolated.

The second lesson is the importance of a sustained and active observer presence. In most cases, credible domestic groups can provide such a presence. If no domestic group is viewed as neutral and fair, however, then intergovernmental or international nongovernmental organizations might have to step in.

The Philippine National Movement for Free Elections (NAMFREL) has provided a model for domestic monitoring organizations. Relying on a nationwide network of volunteers, NAMFREL played a critical role in the 1986 presidential election between Ferdinand Marcos and Corazon Aquino. NAMFREL first lobbied for changes in the election law, many of which were included in a 1985 revision of the Philippine election code. Then, overcoming impediments from pro-Marcos forces, NAMFREL sent volunteers to polling sites throughout the country on election day. Finally, NAMFREL's "quick count," which relied on reports by its volunteers, supported Aquino's claim that she had won, a conclusion accepted by the Filipino people and the international community.

The NAMFREL model has been followed, with some modifications, by civic activists in other countries. In Chile, the Committee for Free Elections and the National Citizens Crusade played important roles in encouraging voter registration for the 1988 plebiscite and in monitoring the balloting and counting processes on plebiscite day. In Panama, a lay Catholic group organized a quick count of the 1989 election results, demonstrating that the opposition had won an overwhelming victory over the Noriega camp. More recently, the Bulgarian Association for Fair Elections recruited, in less than two months, more than 10,000 volunteers who monitored polling sites throughout the country and carried out a parallel vote tabulation that showed a ruling-party victory, thus negating the opposition's charges of fraud.

In the above cases, international observers concluded that, despite contrary claims by the government or opposition, volunteers from these domestic groups conducted themselves in a nonpartisan manner on election day. In other instances, however, international observers have been more wary about relying on information from ostensibly nonpartisan organizations. In the 1987 Korean elections, for example, international observers considered an organization operating under the auspices of the Korean Council of Churches as too openly partisan and thus discounted much of the information it supplied.

After a decade of extreme political polarization in Nicaragua, there was no domestic group perceived as politically neutral. Under these circumstances, the UN and OAS shouldered the burden of mounting a sustained and continuous presence. Both organizations established permanent missions in August 1989, well in advance of the October voter registration period. The Council began a series of monthly visits in September and established an office and permanent representative in October. Other private groups sent one or more delegations to observe the campaign and elections, and the Washington-based Center for Democracy established a permanent office as well.

The continued presence of the observers and repeated visits by the leaders of the missions allowed the three main observer groups to become well acquainted with the participants, build trust in the process, help mediate disputes, and reassure the public. By election day, the ties established between political leaders and observers helped the latter to persuade all parties to accept the results.

The observers' presence also minimized campaign violence and encouraged voter participation. Periodic reports by the main observer groups helped to correct specific shortcomings or irregularities in the process. Equally important, the high profile of the observers and the local and international media attention they received ensured that their statements carried domestic and international weight, thus giving all parties, but particularly the government, an incentive to behave in ways that minimized criticism.

In contrast, in the Panamanian and the 1987 Haitian elections, the observers, despite several preelection visits, were unable to build up the trust that might have prevented a breakdown of the electoral process. The Romanian elections in May 1990, meanwhile, illustrate the limits of a short-term observer mission. The official U.S. delegation, with a brief stay and limited focus, issued a positive statement regarding the election-day events. Their statement was subsequently disavowed, however, by the U.S. State Department, which relied on statements by other international observer groups who evaluated the overall context of the elections and were more critical in their assessment of the process.

Despite their comparative advantage in underwriting large-scale, long-term observer missions, intergovernmental organizations also have certain limitations. First, they are generally barred from intervening in the internal affairs of their members. Second, because states are their constituencies, they have different relationships with governments than with opposition parties. This bias was recognized in Nicaragua, but the opposition decided that it was offset by the benefits accorded to their electoral prospects by the presence of large numbers of observers. Finally, observer missions as large and sophisticated as the ones sent to Nicaragua impose heavy burdens on the budget and personnel of the sponsoring institutions.

Private Groups and Parallel Counts

A third lesson is the important role that private groups can play by organizing periodic high-level visits during various phases of the electoral process. Such visits can both provide opportunities to focus on particular issues that threaten the credibility of the process, and help to reinforce the work of domestic and intergovernmental observer groups. As the Council delegation demonstrated in Nicaragua, private groups have a flexibility to facilitate the resolution of problems that intergovernmental organizations lack; this is particularly true where the group is led by prominent figures who have the confidence of all parties.[3]

In Guyana, the Council's direct mediation has achieved important electoral reforms that address fundamental opposition concerns and allegations of past electoral fraud. Most significantly, President Hoyte agreed during Carter's October 1990 visit to changes that will make it easier for opposition-party pollwatchers to check the vote count. Hoyte also agreed to discard Guyana's old, discredited voter lists and undertake a new house-by-house registration. A subsequent Council visit in April 1991 ended with both sides agreeing on a complete restructuring of the Election Commission.

There is a wide range of private election-monitoring groups with distinct roles and comparative advantages. The National Democratic and National Republican Institutes for International Affairs (NDI and NRI, respectively) have individually and jointly fielded large bipartisan and multinational delegations that have provided respected judgments on the quality of elections in several countries. After the October 1990 elections in Pakistan, for instance, the NDI delegation was able to determine that irregularities were not serious enough to have significantly altered the overall outcome. This served to defuse former prime minister Benazir Bhutto's charges that the elections had been stolen, and alleviated some of the tension that was building in the country. In Bulgaria, NDI pre-election missions encouraged changes in election procedures and contributed to a more equitable campaign.

The International Human Rights Law Group (IHRLG) has observed some 25 elections since 1983, and has developed guidelines that are used by other groups. IHRLG has a comparative advantage in analyzing electoral laws and procedures, and directs particular attention to the question of how the electoral process may affect overall human rights situations.

In some cases, even a single observer can have an effect on the international community's evaluation of an election. A notable example occurred following the 1979 elections in Rhodesia. A report prepared by Lord Pratap Chitnis and presented at a U.S. congressional hearing countered the accepted wisdom that the elections had been free and fair.

Governments seeking legitimacy are often more responsive to the suggestions made by outside observers and by private groups than those of other governments or domestic groups. By focusing on specific issues, even a relatively small delegation can help to calm tensions within a country, particularly on election night or the day after, and can present an objective report to the international community. Finally, the level of international attention directed toward an election by the media and policy makers is related to the prestige and effectiveness of the observer group.

The fourth lesson is that parallel vote counts can greatly boost confidence in the electoral process and provide verification of official results. Parallel counts are tabulations of actual results gathered at the polling site, not "exit polls" or opinion surveys. Political parties generally perform such tabulations to provide strategic information for their leaders on election night; however, in cases where the parties do not trust either the election administrators or one another, local or international groups may be needed to do a parallel tabulation.

In Nicaragua, the Supreme Electoral Council gave the OAS and UN permission to do parallel vote counts, and furnished each organization with copies of the vote tallies from each voting site. Based on a sample of these tallies, the organizations computed a "quick count" that provided crucial information early on election night indicating that the Sandinistas were losing by a significant margin. This information was used by Carter's Council, the OAS, and the UN in their discussions with President Ortega and later with President-elect Chamorro to help defuse a tense and potentially violent situation.

In the Philippines and Panama, the parallel vote tabulations provided the basis upon which international observers were able to conclude that the opposition candidates won the elections, despite the fact that official results showed a different outcome. In Chile, as in Nicaragua, the parallel vote tabulations provided the leverage needed to convince surprised government leaders that the opposition victory should be accepted. In the June 1990 Bulgarian elections, the parallel vote tabulation served to legitimize a ruling-party victory despite claims of election-day irregularities and delays in releasing the official results.

In the December 1990 Haitian elections, the OAS-UN joint parallel tabulation was vital given the extreme volatility of the political situation and the formidable administrative problem of conducting an election in a country with poor communications, a high illiteracy rate, and no history of free elections. The official count took more than a week to complete, so it was the "quick count" that allowed election officials to make an early announcement of Father Jean-Baptiste Aristide's victory, thus forestalling possible violence.

Where a parallel vote tabulation is not possible, other forms of analysis may prove useful. In Pakistan's 1988 elections, for example, the National Democratic Institute used statistical analysis to counter Benazir Bhutto's claim that she was unfairly denied an absolute majority in parliament. Similarly in 1990, an analysis comparing 1988 and 1990 voter turnout and results failed to support allegations of massive fraud.

An Expanded Role

In 1980, Maurice Bishop, the Prime Minister of Grenada, mocked elections as a "five-second exercise every five years," and many agreed with him. Today, Bishop's comment is rightly seen as a self-serving justification for his attempt to hold on to unquestioned power. The point of an election is not the five-second exercise, but rather the right of citizens to replace their leaders. Using those five seconds five years later, the people hold their leaders and the system accountable for what has happened in the interim.

Elections, however, are not the culmination of democracy; they are rather the first, crucial step toward building it. In many Central American countries, for example, newly elected civilian presidents do not have the kind of authority over the armed forces that democracy requires. It will take time for these countries to consolidate their democratic institutions.

An expanded role for international observers in settling conflicts and promoting democratization has not been easily achieved. Governments, jealous of their prerogatives as the guardians of state sovereignty, remain wary of officially recognizing the presence of election observers, whether representing intergovernmental or private groups. Yet over time the usefulness of international observers and mediators has been recognized and institutionalized, particularly in "first elections" or in countries torn by civil violence or longstanding distrust among political parties.

Even in Europe, where dramatic changes occurred during the past year with limited civil violence, the role of election observers has been explicitly recognized. A June 1990 document adopted by the 35 countries participating in the Conference on Security and Cooperation in Europe declares: "The participating states consider that the presence of observers, both foreign and domestic, can enhance the electoral process for states in which elections are taking place."

Elections are a means for allocating power peacefully. When they fail, international as well as domestic peace is often put at risk. The international community therefore has both a need and a duty to reinforce and assure the legitimacy of democratic elections. Observers and mediators have already helped; they could do still more, if only more nations would support their efforts.

NOTES

1. See Larry Garber, *Guidelines for International Election Observing* (Washington, D.C.: International Human Rights Law Group, 1984).

2. For more information on election observing in specific cases, see the following reports: The Council of Freely-Elected Heads of Government, Observing Nicaragua's Elections, 1989-90, Special Report #1 (Atlanta, Georgia: Carter Center of Emory University, 1990); The Council of Freely-Elected Heads of Government and National Democratic Institute, *The 1990 General Elections in Haiti* (Washington, D.C., 1991) and *The 1990 Dominican Republic Election* (Washington, D.C., 1990); National Democratic Institute and National Republican Institute, *The June 1990 Election in Bulgaria* (Washington, D.C., 1990), *The May 1990 Elections in Romania* (Washington, D.C., 1991), and *The May 7, 1989 Panamanian Elections* (Washington, D.C., 1989); National Democratic Institute, *Nation-Building: The UN and Namibia* (Washington, D.C., 1990), *The October 1990 Elections in Pakistan* (Washington, D.C., 1991), *The Pakistan Elections: Foundation for Democracy* (Washington, D.C., 1989), *Chile's Transition to Democracy: The October 5, 1988 Plebiscite* (Washington, D.C., 1991), and *Reforming the Philippine Electoral Process: Developments, 1986-1988* (Washington, D.C., 1991); and the International Human Rights Law Group, *The 1987 Korean Presidential Election* (Washington, D.C., 1988).

3. For a more detailed account of the role played by the Council and other international observers in Nicaragua, see Robert A. Pastor, "The Making of a Free Election," *Journal of Democracy* 1 (Summer 1990): 13-25.

III.
Political Corruption
and Democracy

18.
HISTORICAL CONFLICT
AND THE RISE OF STANDARDS

Michael Johnston

Michael Johnston *is professor and chair of the department of political science at Colgate University in Hamilton, New York. He has written extensively on political corruption, and is the coeditor (with Arnold J. Heidenheimer and Victor T. LeVine) of* Political Corruption: A Handbook *(1989). He also serves as coeditor of the journal* Corruption and Reform.

Sooner or later, citizens and scholars concerned about the prospects for sustainable democracy must come to terms with the problem of corruption. The two concepts are closely intertwined, posing fundamental questions about the accountability and limits of government, as well as about the legitimacy and limits of private influence over public policy. Sometimes corruption appears as an adaptive force, "humanizing" government and enabling citizens to influence policy. More often, corruption allows those with disproportionate money and access to protect and enhance their advantages. Regimes parlay "planned corruption" from above into short-term political advantage, sometimes at the expense of long-term public interests.[1] In developing nations, the powerful may misappropriate vast sums, exporting capital to safe havens for personal use. At other times, corruption props up institutions and regimes that might otherwise be ready for needed changes.

Studying corruption is a tricky business: Definitions are controversial, and solid evidence is often elusive. Descriptive accounts may be clouded by self-serving equivocations. Equally subtle is the question of the significance of a corrupt act—not only its consequences, but also its meaning as perceived by citizens and officials alike. The frequency with which corruption sparks scandals and coups shows that this issue is often far from settled.

Make the analysis comparative, and things get even cloudier. Definitions suited to one place and time fit poorly in others. Legal and social norms, state and nation, are broadly congruent in some places and fundamentally at odds elsewhere. Even behavior widely regarded as corrupt can vary in significance: nepotism, for example, may be viewed quite differently in societies with more or less extensive kinship obligations. The level of socioeconomic development may also affect the types and amount of corrupt behavior by shaping the balance between political and economic opportunities, the sources and depth of governmental legitimacy, and the pace of social change. Corrupt behavior can in turn influence development by helping or hindering the growth of parties or the assimilation of new groups, and by affecting the pace, direction, and distribution of economic growth.

Among the gravest problems confronting the comparative study of corruption is the question of *whose standards to apply*. Legal standards are relatively precise, but most reflect distinctly "modern" or "Western" values that may well be at odds with the realities of other societies. If we use cultural norms to identify corruption, we can claim legitimacy for our standards, but lose much precision and comparability. Furthermore, if we make popular approval (or tolerance) of a particular practice our test of corruption, do we then lose sight of more enduring questions of political morality?

Perhaps it would be better to use both legal and cultural standards, making an explicit issue of the differences between them. This perspective views corruption in the context of what Rogow and Lasswell call a society's "system of public order." That system includes both the dominant values of the society and its basic institutions—both the "realities" of behavior and the "formalities" of political structure.[2] Systems of public order are not inevitable "end points" of development; they may include many "traditional" elements, and disruptive change can topple them.[3]

Corruption, then, may be defined as behavior seen as abusing—according to a society's legal or social standards—a public role or resource for private benefit. Seen in this way, corruption is a politically contested concept that gains its meaning in the course of basic developmental conflicts. These conflicts over the limits of official power and the legitimacy of private interests are also integral to the emergence of democratic politics, and continue in one form or another in advanced as well as developing societies. Understanding these conflicts not only lets us grasp the standards of political propriety at work in various nations; it also shows us how outwardly similar corrupt practices can differ in significance from nation to nation, and how scandals and revelations of corruption in developing nations might actually contain the seeds of new and more legitimate systems of public order.

The Origins of Public Order

Where does a system of public order come from? As a point of departure, consider an absolute autocrat. Such a person cannot commit a corrupt act in any meaningful sense: What limits exist upon his power? To whom or what is he accountable? Clearly, several important changes must take place before the notion of corruption can apply. Let us consider two:

• the emergence of *a degree of political pluralism*—that is, the existence of "intermediary groups" beyond the sovereign's personal or patrimonial control that can make politically significant demands.

• the definition of *bounded political roles* with impersonal powers and obligations.

The conflicts through which such changes generally take place hardly encompass the whole of political development, nor do they follow the same course in every nation. But they are elements of political development essential to the idea of corruption, as well as to the emergence of limited, accountable government. The following discussion may appear "Eurocentric" to some, but it was in Europe and places where European institutions took root that many formal standards of corruption first emerged (China is a major exception). In many places these "Western" laws coexist uneasily with cultures of much longer standing—a conflict made worse by the fact that those nations have often adopted, or been left with, the most demanding "modern" standards. By treating formal legal standards as parts of a larger system of public order, and regarding conflicts among standards as a problem of development, one may avoid major problems of cultural bias.

Debates over political propriety once began and ended with what Carl J. Friedrich calls "the ancient rule that 'the King can do no wrong.'"[4] Under these circumstances, the state (both its territory and offices) is regarded as personal property. Not every state began precisely this way, but if an absolute autocrat cannot be corrupt until some limitations are placed upon his power, then any real notion of corruption will depend upon the existence of countervailing or intermediary groups that can check the ruler's power. Such groups can make powerholders take interests beyond their own into account. An extensive array of countervailing groups might eventually make the ruler "responsible" in several senses of that term.

This is not to suggest that early counterelites were tribunes of the people, moral innovators, or even advocates of any interests beyond their own. Intermediary groups began to limit the sovereign in order to protect themselves. Even as some limits became institutionalized, they were often based on stalemate rather than principle. During the era of medieval "government with estates," "Laws were few and legislation rare, and medieval constitutionalism could thus concentrate its attention on the problem of the regulation of the abuse of the monarch's executive power."[5]

Eventually, however, the role of opposition changed the opposition itself: "The Parliaments of the Middle Ages, which were primarily courts, found themselves confronted with the fact that the law had increasingly to be *made* rather than discovered and declared."[6] With the making of law came the task of devising explicit standards. But it is worth noting that officials and intermediary groups contend over the limits of power in advanced as well as developing societies, as social and economic changes bring into play new interests and new views on the proprieties of politics.

Politics and Development

Modern definitions of corruption are based upon the idea of explicitly public roles bounded by impersonal obligations and endowed with limited powers. In an age of widespread constitutionalism and bureaucratization, it is easy to take such ideas for granted. Nevertheless, they too grow out of developmental conflicts.

At one time, having "a role in politics" meant being a relative, retainer, or crony of some powerful person, and thus having a share of loot or favor. Public-private distinctions and notions of service or merit were nonexistent; indeed, there were few obligations to anyone other than one's patrons. "Politics" was the exercise and defense of power, aimed at little more than personal or dynastic aggrandizement. But as societies grew larger, and as more numerous and powerful intermediary groups emerged, political roles began to change. Ruling elites grew beyond the bounds of extended households and became increasingly differentiated and factionalized. Sovereigns increasingly needed money, along with the effective support of minions whom they could not easily oversee.

Expansion of these "protogovernments" made expedient such practices as tax- and customs-"farming," whereby revenue functions were franchised out to well-connected entrepreneurs who recouped their investments by keeping a share of the revenues. A related practice was the outright sale of offices, as in Stuart England. No notions of merit were involved (though merit selection might well have recruited many of the same people), and the "public" was still more to be exploited than served. But these "freehold offices" were defended by Montesquieu and Bentham on grounds of efficiency, and by Burke as a legitimate property right. Tax- and customs-farming raised money in a manner that was rather orderly compared to previous smash-and-grab methods of revenue collection. To argue that an office could be purchased was to acknowledge that it was distinct from its buyer and could entail certain duties. In France, Spain, England, and to a degree in China, networks of "freehold bureaucrats" supplied their patrons with revenue, political support, and an intelligence network.

From the sovereign's point of view, however, there were drawbacks as well. Once sold, an office was generally sold for good; to supplant a freeholder by creating a rival office might well mean a fight. In time, civil servants would become an intermediary group in their own right, jealous of their independence. Eventually would-be elites became too numerous to be co-opted through patronage. In Elizabethan England, for example, university graduates had long been accustomed to obtaining church or state offices via personal preferment. But when Oxford and Cambridge began to turn out graduates in unprecedented numbers, many were left out; these took the lead in objecting to what had been the accepted mode of recruitment.

In time, extended personal networks became insufficient for the expanding scope of government. Administration became a full-time task vested in groups of functionaries that more closely resembled modern-day bureaus than branches of some grandee's household.[7] To compensate these officials, various systems of benefices—shares of grain, for example, or entitlement to the produce for a tract of land—were developed. These, however, were mere halfway measures. The rise of a money economy made regular taxation possible, while the growth of government made it necessary. Taxation did more than just enhance revenues; it allowed regular salaries for officials, thus weakening the notion of service to patrons as the primary obligation of office. Taxation also created incentives to effective administration and record keeping, and paved the way for a permanent civil service that could enforce its own codes of behavior.

New political ideas also promoted change. Rousseau contended that all are obligated to participate directly in society's business, and to do so in a manner that transcends personal appetites.[8] Friedrich points to "secularized versions of natural law" and the Christian notion of "the transcendental importance of each man's soul" as fostering notions of accountability.[9] Thomas Jefferson saw officials as specialized parts of governmental mechanisms much larger than themselves.[10] The rise of political parties and the expansion of electorates similarly transformed elected positions, with representation and service taking a place alongside the goal of winning power. It is still a long way from Rousseau and Jefferson to the contemporary state, but as James Scott notes:

> [I]n the nineteenth century, when the more democratic form of government limited the aristocracy, and the modern idea of the State came into existence, the conception of public office as private property disappeared. The State became considered as a moral entity and the exercising of public authority as a duty.[11]

Official roles continue to change: in many nations, the personal finances and campaign funds of government officials are extensively scrutinized under rules that did not exist a generation ago. The private lives of public figures are now more open to public scrutiny than ever before. Modern public roles reflect political developments and conflicts that are still in progress.

Comparative Corruption: Britain and the U.S.

Examples of corruption abound in both British and American history, as do conflicts over the proprieties of political behavior. Development and change do not stop with modernity; both societies continue to debate new standards while everyday politics tests the older ones.

Britain today is generally regarded as having low levels of corruption, particularly when we consider transgressions for the sake of money or power (most recent political scandals have revolved around sex). Corruption is more common in American politics, particularly at the state and local levels; the U.S. would rank closer to the middle of a global corruption scale. The differences between standards of political propriety are more subtle than striking, particularly when judged against other international comparisons.[12]

A basic contrast, however, has to do with sources of legitimacy. Britain is the classic case of democratic politics built through the gradual limitation of sovereign powers. While the Glorious Revolution of 1688-89 placed the monarchy on a constitutional footing, in the eighteenth century the balance of power between Crown and Parliament was a matter of frequent dispute, and the Reform Bills of the nineteenth century brought the populace into politics on terms and at a pace largely determined from above. The legitimacy of elected and appointed offices likewise borrows from tradition and the symbolic power of the monarchy. Britain's oft-noted lack of a written constitution means that official positions are not defined by "contracts" enumerating or limiting their powers; ethical standards in politics are maintained more through custom and personal honor than written codes of ethics. There is a legitimate elite "political class" that contrasts with the American ideal of "citizen-politicians." Institutions scrupulously maintain traditional forms, but political conflict and the evolving national agenda can lead to substantial changes over time in how they really operate.

American institutions, by contrast, draw their legitimacy from a revolution against a monarchy, and from an explicit written agreement among private citizens. Traditions of republican government, in which power flows from the people and is ceded to officials only in temporary trust, have fostered elaborate limitations upon official power; these, however, furnish no obvious solution to citizens' apprehensions about one another. Madison, in his analysis of the "mischiefs of faction" in *Federalist* 10, recognized that since depriving citizens of their liberty would be folly, the remedy lay in dividing and limiting the power of government while also encouraging private interests to contend among themselves. American politics has thus been caught in a prolonged struggle between republican moralism and individual entrepreneurialism; Americans hold officials to strict ethical expectations while giving private interests a comparatively free rein. When corruption appears, the American response has typically been legalistic—to change the rules of politics, particularly if the competition among private interests seems out of balance, and to hand down extensive codes of ethics for those entrusted with public power.

"When corruption appears, the American response has typically been legalistic—to change the rules of politics...and hand down extensive codes of ethics for those entrusted with public power."

Looked at in this way, corruption in British and American politics reflects different dynamics. In Britain, as Alan Doig suggests, corruption has often been used from above, "by and for governments," to control forces from below rather than to achieve direct personal benefit.[13] In the American case, by contrast, corruption is more often a tactic in the contention among private interests (with some officials taking the initiative, through extortion, to cash in on their powers in the political market). Either way, the American corruption problem is one of "privatizing politics." This is not to say that British private interests do not bribe, or that American corruption does not serve official interests. Yet contrasts in political development can give outwardly similar practices different meanings, and common ethical dilemmas may be resolved in different ways.

Let us briefly consider two examples. The bribery of voters reveals differing relationships among elites (the "pluralism" factor), while dealings between legislators and private interests illustrate contrasts in the powers and obligations of official roles.

Bribery of voters peaked in British elections during the eighteenth and early nineteenth centuries, and roughly a century later in the United States.[14] While the electorates differed greatly in size and composition, the practices were similar: food and drink, money, or other tangible goods were given to electors in exchange for their votes. In Britain, exceedingly small prereform electorates often meant that just a few "bought" voters would be sufficient to win. In the United States, precinct captains canvassed their neighborhoods both during and between elections, buying rounds of drinks or handing out cash, buckets of coal, and the now legendary Christmas turkeys.

In both nations, the aim of this petty bribery was to control public participation and election results; we should neither exaggerate the size of the gifts nor romanticize the motives behind them. But however similar, these practices—like the subsequent drives for reform they inspired—rested upon contrasting patterns of elite conflict and competition. In Britain, bribery was often carried out from above—by members of the government, local notables, or their agents—and the purpose was to keep such voting as had to be allowed under control. In many American cities, however, old political alignments had already been overwhelmed by immigration and urban growth, and vote-buying was done by party or ethnic entrepreneurs trying to pick up the "scattered fragments of power."[15] The purpose was to "privatize" local government, exploiting rapid change in order to enrich oneself and one's backers, and not to protect an established political class from change. Once they had firmly entrenched themselves, many machine bosses in the United States preferred monopoly-party discipline to vote-buying as a more profitable way to maintain power.[16]

Contrasting patterns of pluralism are also manifest in the reform efforts that ensued. In Britain, "new men," often Nonconformist in background, played a major role in pushing reform and thereby challenged the old ruling class. Many reformers represented developing industrial and mercantile interests, but they also spoke for places that had been left out of electoral politics, and so were a force for political development as well. They were not the only advocates of reform: a few aristocrats objected to voters' profiting from the franchise, and some MPs disliked bribery too, if only on grounds of expense. But these new intermediary groups, seeking an entree into politics as well as opposing corruption, led the fight first for reformed election practices, and then for a fundamental broadening of political participation through the Reform Bills of 1832 and 1867.

Reform in the United States, by contrast, occurred under much more fluid conditions. Immigration and rapid urban growth had already swept aside the old political order in many cities; by bribing voters, ambitious politicians with even small followings could aspire to fill the resulting power vacuums. Reform attracted the support of a loose coalition of interests, including nonimmigrant (and anti-immigrant) groups displaced from power by the new urban bosses. The reform ranks also included advocates of "modern" urban planning and institutions; the Anti-Saloon League; social reformers (whose settlement houses the machine politicians viewed as competitors for the loyalty of the poor); and business leaders, especially heads of smaller firms who had grown tired of political extortion.

This reform coalition reflected the fragmentation characteristic of a time of rapid social change, and of American politics in general. Once the main battles were won, the coalition partners soon went their separate ways as businesses grew beyond single-city scale and social reformers and would-be planners found themselves fighting even reformed city halls. American reformers did much to change the institutions of many cities and states, but the temporary reform coalition was not a coherent intermediary group.

The rapid expansion of American electorates encouraged voter bribery by providing an ample field for interfactional competition. By contrast, the extensions of the franchise brought about by the Reform Bills in Great Britain helped to reduce bribery by turning the old practices into expensive exercises in futility, bringing new countervailing interests into politics, and rendering the emergent parties more useful as instruments for organizing mass participation.

Honor Codes or Ethics Laws?

A degree of legislative independence is a virtue in any system of representation, yet democratic politics inevitably keeps legislators and private interests in close contact. Striking a balance between legislators' independence and their responsiveness to such interests is one of the continuing dilemmas of any representative democracy.

British and American responses to such conflict-of-interest problems reveal differing conceptions of the powers and limits of the representative's role. It is not unusual for a member of the House of Commons to be a paid consultant and spokesperson for a political interest group or business association. "All-party groups" of MPs working on a particular policy issue are often staffed, provided with data, and wined and dined by representatives of interested parties. Relatively few explicit rules govern the relationship between such dealings and legislative duties. Still, instances of bribery are rare, and many Britons regard their MPs as less vulnerable to such abuses than U.S. congressmen.

Conflict-of-interest situations in Britain, Atkinson and Mancuso point out, are regulated primarily through "etiquette":

> Honour is the foundation of the etiquette solution. In an etiquette system legislators are encouraged to believe that they belong to a privileged elite, one whose behaviour is governed by a standard not intended for others. The critical moral dictum is the requirement that legislators place the public interest before their own private advantage. The concept of honour permits representatives to use their discretion in the application of this principle to concrete situations of conflict of interest. No explicit instructions are needed.[17]

Members of Parliament have long been forbidden from taking bribes or selling confidential information. Their private contractual dealings and investments have been scrutinized and (for ministers) restricted, and it is considered a breach "to advocate a cause in Parliament solely for a fee or retainer" (but not to speak on an issue in which the MP has a financial interest, so long as that interest is disclosed). These rules, however, have always been largely matters of unwritten custom and tradition. Indeed, when more formal procedures for declaring personal interests were enacted in the mid-1970s, a number of MPs failed to comply, "refus[ing] to accept that a 'requirement of honour' could be turned into 'a mere formality of registration.'"[18]

In the United States, by contrast, members of the Senate and House are subject to written codes of ethics, and to most provisions of laws like the Ethics in Government Act of 1978. Senators and representatives must make regular financial disclosures. The campaign contributions they receive are subject to extensive disclosure requirements, and their ability to collect honoraria has recently been strictly limited. A legislator who has a financial interest in an issue is generally expected to withdraw from roll calls and debates. The American approach is an example of regulation by "edicts":

> The foundation of this edifice is a written set of public rules. . . . In addition, the edict approach implies an institutionalized system of compliance, investigation and sanction. Unlike the etiquette system, the response to a conflict situation is predetermined, not ad hoc.[19]

Despite these extensive codes, conflicts of interest remain a serious problem in American legislative politics. Jim Wright's links to Texas businessmen, which forced him to resign as Speaker of the House in 1989, were but one example; the Abscam scandal of the early 1980s also showed that all too many legislators were willing to put their influence up for sale. Americans hold Congress as a whole in low esteem; many recall Will Rogers's quip that the nation has "the best congressmen money can buy."

It is tempting to write off these contrasts as products of culture or political habit, but they reflect important differences in the conceptions and limits of representative roles. Some are matters of practical politics: American legislators are free agents in a decentralized, weak party system; they decide on their own votes, fund their own (increasingly expensive) campaigns, and must deal by themselves with organized interests in their states or districts. British MPs, by contrast, conduct inexpensive campaigns in comparatively small constituencies, and vote as the party directs; they have considerably less need for money, and little of value to sell.

There are other important contrasts in the meaning of representation. As we might expect in a diverse republic, "In the United States representation has always been of persons; the representation of interests has been viewed as an inevitable evil, to be tamed by a well-constructed government."[20] Demands are to be made (and excesses checked) through political competition; too close a link between legislators and interests confers unfair advantage.

The House of Commons, by contrast, claimed legitimacy by checking the Crown and practicing "virtual representation," in which it spoke for the people as an estate but not necessarily for all individuals in all places. Today's MPs are members of a national legislative body—not a collection of local advocates—in which strong parties represent interests as segments of the nation as a whole. The individual representative is much less critical in this scheme of things; indeed, for centuries membership in the House of Commons was part-time, unpaid service, and even today, traditions of "amateurism" (in its positive sense, closely linked to personal honor) remain important. Interests are aggregated and policies are made at a much higher level in the British system, with individual MPs playing a minor role: there, lobbying is done by groups with regular access to the permanent civil service. "That access has been promoted by successive governments as part of the corporatist faith in representation, cooperation, and conciliation." So collegial are public-private relationships at that level that "consensual decisionmaking and the regular movements of officials to posts with such [lobbying] organizations" have become widely accepted.[21]

Thus, a common dilemma—how to resolve the tension between legislative independence and the liberty to advocate private interests—has been resolved in differing ways in Britain and the United States. Critics of the British system suggest that it lacks "teeth" and rests upon an unduly optimistic view of human nature, while the American approach is accused of putting too much emphasis on the letter—and hence perhaps the loopholes—of the law, and not enough on its substance and spirit. More to the point, though, is the fact that these contrasting approaches developed out of the conflicts through which representatives were empowered and their legitimacy defined. In that sense, the basic issue is not which system is better in the absract, but rather how each one fits its own nation's conception of official roles.

The Continuing Significance of Corruption

I have sought to portray corruption as a politically contested concept that is best understood in the context of a nation's political development and system of public order. It embodies neither legal not cultural values alone, but both—and can incorporate contradictions, gray areas, and controversy. The developmental conflicts that help fix the meaning of corruption—among them, the checking of rulers' powers by emerging private interests, and the definition of the powers and limits of official roles—are also part of the origins of democratic politics. They can take many paths, with the result that corruption varies in meaning and significance. As we have seen, even in nations that are as much alike as Britain and the United States similar types of corruption reflect different political dynamics, and similar ethical problems are often resolved in different ways.

Indeed, even in the most stable nations with the most settled systems of public order, developmental conflict continues. The issues include the proper boundaries between the public and private spheres of life; the extent and mechanisms of elite accountability; the extent and control of mass political participation; and the proper balance among market, bureaucratic, and personalistic processes of distribution. Corruption can provide useful clues about such conflicts: Thatcherism has led to more vigorous lobbying by businesses, for example, with new conflict-of-interest and business-ethics issues as a result.[22] The U.S. savings and loan scandal can be traced to similar policy shifts, and has spawned the Keating Five case as its own corruption connection. The significance of that scandal may lie less in the dollars contributed to political campaign funds, or in the political influence obtained, than in what it says about a particular stress point in the changing public-private balance.

Episodes such as Watergate, Britain's Poulson scandal, and the dealings of multinational business interests in many nations have demolished the notion that corruption is a problem that advanced nations have somehow "solved." But if we consider corruption as a politically contested concept, and recall the origins of our own standards, scandals in developing nations may take on a new appearance. These nations, after all, are trying to accomplish in a few decades what the industrialized democracies took centuries to do, namely, construct systems of public order that embody a durable balance between social values and legal institutions. Scandals and conflicts over corruption are an integral part of that process, and may indeed be steps toward new and lasting settlements between social values and legal institutions. This is not to minimize the problems of corruption in the developing world, or to suggest that such convergence is inevitable. But perhaps it takes a good political fight to hammer out standards that command respect; likewise, conflicts over the abuses of rulers and the limits of public roles may prove a force for more democratic politics. In that sense, accounts of corruption in developing nations may portray not only the scope of a problem, but also the origins of new political settlements.

NOTES

1. John Waterbury, "Endemic and Planned Corruption in a Monarchical Regime," *World Politics* 25 (July 1973): 534.

2. Arnold A. Rogow and Harold D. Lasswell, *Power, Corruption, and Rectitude* (Englewood Cliffs, N.J.: Prentice-Hall, 1990), 67-68.

3. Michael Johnston, "The Political Consequences of Corruption: A Reassessment," *Comparative Politics* 18 (July 1986): 471-77.

4. Carl J. Friedrich, *Limited Government: A Comparison* (Englewood Cliffs, N.J.: Prentice-Hall, 1974), 102.

5. Ibid., 27.

6. Ibid., 32.

7. Robin Theobald, *Corruption, Development, and Underdevelopment* (Durham, N.C.: Duke University Press, 1990), 24-25.

8. Jean-Jacques Rousseau, *Of the Social Contract,* ed. and tr. Charles Sherover (New York: Harper and Row, 1984), Book 1, Sec. VIII, "Of the Civil State," 18-19. Friedrich gives similar credit to Rousseau in *The Pathology of Politics* (New York: Harper and Row, 1972), 131-33.

9. Friedrich, *Limited Government*, 13-14.

10. Garry Wills, *Inventing America: Jefferson's Declaration of Independence* (New York: Random House/Vintage, 1978), ch. 7.

11. James Scott, *Comparative Political Corruption* (Englewood Cliffs, N.J.: Prentice Hall, 1972), 96.

12. Michael Johnston, "Right and Wrong in American Politics," *Polity* 18 (Spring 1986): 367-91; "Right and Wrong in British Politics: 'Fits of Morality' in Comparative Perspective," *Polity* 23 (Fall 1991), forthcoming.

13. Alan Doig, *Corruption and Misconduct in Contemporary British Politics* (Harmondsworth: Penguin, 1984), 347.

14. See, for general accounts, Doig, *Corruption and Misconduct in Contemporary British Politics*, chs. 2 and 3; Cornelius O'Leary, *The Elimination of Corrupt Practices in British Elections, 1968-1911* (Oxford: Clarendon Press, 1962); Michael Pinto-Duschinsky, *British Political Finance, 1830-1980* (Washington, D.C.: American Enterprise Institute, 1981). See, for examples Harold F. Gosnell, *Machine Politics: Chicago Model*, 2nd ed. (Chicago: University of Chicago Press, 1968); William L. Riordon, *Plunkitt of Tammany Hall* (New York: Dutton, 1963); Bruce M. Stave, ed., *Urban Bosses, Machines and Progressive Reformers* (Lexington, Mass.: Heath, 1972); and J. Lincoln Steffens, *The Shame of the Cities* (New York: Hill and Wang, 1969 [orig. publ. 1902]).

15. Robert K. Merton, *Social Theory and Social Structure* (New York: Free Press, 1957), 73-74.

16. Martin Shefter, "The Emergence of the Political Machine: An Alternative View," in Willis D. Hawley et al., *Theoretical Perspectives on Urban Politics* (Englewood Cliffs, N.J.: Prentice-Hall, 1976), 41.

17. Michael M. Atkinson and Maureen Mancuso, "Edicts and Etiquette: Managing Legislative Conflict of Interest in the United States and Britain" (International Political Science Association, Research Committee on Political Finance and Corruption, 1988), 10.

18. Doig, "An Apparent Abuse in the Use of Dining Rooms: The British Parliament and Lobbying," *Corruption and Reform* 6 (Fall 1990): 190-93.

19. Atkinson and Mancuso, "Edicts and Etiquette," 19.

20. Ibid., 6.

21. Doig, "An Apparent Abuse," 195.

22. Ibid., 194-98.

19.
THAILAND'S SEARCH FOR
ACCOUNTABILITY

Catharin E. Dalpino

Catharin E. Dalpino *is a resident associate at the Carnegie Endowment for International Peace in Washington, D.C., where she specializes in issues related to democratization in Asia. Now on leave from The Asia Foundation, she served from 1988 to 1990 as the Foundation's representative for Thailand. The views expressed in this article are not necessarily those of The Asia Foundation.*

The 1991 military takeover that deposed the elected government of Prime Minister Chatichai Choonhaven was commonly, and correctly, viewed as one more chapter in Thailand's apparently interminable civil-military power struggle. On a deeper level, however, the coup revealed the acute lack of political accountability that plagues Thailand's version of parliamentary democracy.

Certainly this military takeover, the seventeenth coup or attempted coup in 60 years, demonstrated that a democratic consensus has not yet taken hold throughout Thailand. Democracy made gains under Chatichai, but they were not effectively reconciled with the military and bureaucratic power structure. In the eyes of this traditional oligarchy, democratization is a zero-sum game. As democratic institutions grew stronger the military began charging that the elected government had created a "parliamentary dictatorship," a term that most Thais found confusing, if not outright contradictory.

Although a political role for the military has never been institutionalized, the armed forces have served as unofficial power brokers throughout Thailand's history as a constitutional monarchy. A succession of constitutions, most of them drafted by the military itself, reshaped the Westminster model to suit military prerogatives. The 1978 constitution, which stood until it was suspended by this year's coup, provided for an elected lower house, but did not require (though it did not forbid) the prime minister and cabinet members to be MPs.

This gaping loophole enabled military officers or their hand-picked surrogates to become cabinet ministers, and was seen by some as a standing invitation to military intervention. Beyond that, it severed the organic link between the executive branch and the legislature that forms the basis of a parliamentary system. Under the 1978 constitution, the executive branch was only partially accountable to the legislature; parliament could pass a no-confidence vote against the government, but could not necessarily form a new administration. In reality, the executive branch was much more accountable to the armed forces. The Chatichai administration consisted mainly of elected MPs, bringing the system closer to a standard parliamentary model. But although accountability of the executive to the legislature might be promised, it was not required.

Apart from civil-military relations and the structure of the political system, the coup also called into question the ethics of elected politicians and the very nature of Thailand's political parties. Although the coup leaders (headed by armed forces supreme commander General Sunthorn Konsomphong and army commander-in-chief General Suchinda Kraprayoon) presented an extensive list of grievances against the Chatichai government, including charges of attempting to exert undue control over the military and to decimate the bureaucracy, they focused on the corruption of elected politicians. Of all the junta's charges, this one resonated most deeply with public opinion.

The perception of unabashed and mounting corruption in high government circles, inflamed by an export boom that gave Thailand the fastest-growing economy in the world, was a growing source of public discontent as the Chatichai administration entered the second half of its term. Recognition of the problem had spread to the government itself, and leading politicians, Chatichai included, grew increasingly worried about the weaknesses in the party system. Just days before the coup Chatichai publicly vowed that unless sufficient measures were taken to prevent widescale vote-buying in the next general election, he would not run for a second term. Although no one could claim that corruption in Thailand had originated with elected government, parliament and the parties were widely criticized for failing to address the problem. Indeed, the best evidence of the government's lack of credibility was less the coup itself than the public's acquiescence in the generals' actions.

In order to understand the problems of establishing political accountability in Thai democracy and to propose appropriate remedies, it is necessary to consider the roots of civil-military tensions, the development of political parties, and the character of popular participation in modern Thailand.

Thailand's "Iron Triangle"

Unlike the armed forces of Indonesia and Burma whose original mandate to govern stemmed from their role in anticolonialist struggles, the Thai military had no independence movement upon which to base its claim to be a legitimate ruling power. It had instead the 1932 coup, which overthrew the absolute monarchy and made possible Thailand's first constitution. The junior officers and bureaucrats who led the coup saw themselves as bringing democracy to Thailand. In their understanding, however, democracy simply meant taking power away from the Crown. More significantly, the 1932 revolutionary group spawned a military-bureaucratic partnership and division of labor that would endure (with only brief interruptions) for almost 60 years. Bureaucrats ran the daily affairs of state, while the military remained ready to step in if a change in leadership seemed necessary. Heads of government were often generals, a circumstance that served to encourage factionalism and politicking within the military. Indeed, most of the coups in Thai history have simply been instances of one military faction displacing another.

Parliament, when it was permitted to convene, was relegated to a largely symbolic role. Although the House of Representatives was usually elected, it was composed primarily of bureaucrats. The first political parties were founded at the time of the 1932 coup, but they were poorly organized and fragmented from the beginning. The Senate consisted of appointees, most of them from elite military and bureaucratic circles. After each new takeover, the coup leaders abrogated the constitution and altered the system as they wished.[1] Reforms, constitutional or otherwise, were usually aimed at enabling the military to retain control in the face of changes in Thai society.

Until the 1970s, civil-military relations in Thailand meant bureaucratic-military relations. That other elements of society might also be given voice did not occur to the political elite. The general population, still overwhelmingly rural in character, had learned reticence during centuries of monarchical rule and did not challenge its exclusion from politics.

A third partner in this alliance, but one that was expected to serve silently, was the private business sector. In the earlier decades of the constitutional monarchy, the military's control over the business class was largely a function of ethnic relations. Thai capitalism has been dominated since the nineteenth century by Chinese immigrants. Sino-Thai entrepreneurs, many of whom worked under royal patronage before 1932, became clients of the military in the modern state. Vulnerable to nativist campaigns, they maintained a low public profile and were doggedly apolitical. Additional self-protection came in the form of an underground system (*jao poh*) of Chinese merchants who acted as rural warlords. The *jao poh* found it easiest to establish itself in provincial areas where patron-client networks were already fixtures of local life. In order to avoid conflicts at a higher level, however, the *jao poh* also cultivated the military in a symbiotic relationship that lasted into the early 1970s.

To strengthen Thailand's commercial structure, the top rungs of Sino-Thai society were assimilated through intermarriage with military and bureaucratic elites. It is for this reason that Thai and Chinese cultures are blended in Thailand to a degree unusual for Southeast Asia. Relations with overseas Chinese in Thailand lack the sharp edges found in Indonesia, where Chinese have been subjected to oppressive measures, or in Malaysia, where the government has tried to propel ethnic Malays above Malaysian-Chinese for several years with its New Economic (or "Sons of the Soil") Policy.

While intermarriage offered the Chinese an entree to other sectors of Thai society, and even Thai names, it also turned the military into a class of "commercial soldiers." From 1947 to 1973, military cliques often set up their own companies or gained control over state enterprises. This solidification of the economic marriage became especially important to the Sino-Thai community when communism appeared in Southeast Asia in the late 1940s and early 1950s. Full-fledged membership in the "iron triangle" of business, army, and bureaucracy shielded the ethnic Chinese from suspicions of subversive intent.

When communist insurgency was at its height in Thailand in the 1970s, the Sino-military alliance played a distinct role in the counterinsurgency campaign. As the military launched a program to promote capitalism, the Chinese-Thai community was pulled closer to the center stage of national decision making. Sino-Thai business leaders were encouraged to become more involved in government, if not in politics, and were invited to serve on public-private consultative committees. With capitalism enjoying official support, and its purveyors a more prominent public voice, a new bourgeoisie emerged. To the military, this class would increasingly come to seem like a Frankenstein's monster.

The Rise of Political Parties

Anxious to protect its own interests, but unwilling to rely on the traditional military-bureaucratic power centers, the new middle class put its trust in the political parties. In contrast to the more common Asian model of a dominant-party system, a multiplicity of parties emerged in Thailand.[2] Its fluid, diffuse, and personalistic party system lent itself easily to the aspirations of new actors eager to get involved in politics, especially those with enough capital to bankroll financially hard-pressed factions. Moreover, in contrast to Malaysia, where political affiliation is largely determined by ethnic group, parties in Thailand do not form along racial lines. The parties thus offered the new Sino-Thai commercial elites a way of entering the political arena without bringing their ethnic identity to the fore.

Parties proliferated in the 1970s thanks to the new political activism of the private sector and the democracy movement, which culminated in three years of elected rule (1973-76). By the end of the decade, however, the weaknesses of the party system were apparent. The large number of parties contesting for power produced unruly coalition governments and great instability within the legislature. The consequences were the frequent threat of parliamentary dissolution, leadership discontinuity, and severe disruption of the policy process. Moreover, the tendency of parties to coalesce around individuals made it difficult to inject issues into electoral politics, and often impeded parliament from facing policy issues in a reasoned and methodical manner. Finally, most of the contesting political parties were Bangkok-based. With their parties lacking grassroots penetration, MPs found it hard to form solid constituent relationships; parliament's agenda was often hard to distinguish from the desires of the Bangkok commercial class.

In the 1980s, initial efforts were made to address these problems. The 1980-88 administration of Prime Minister Prem Tinsulanond (a former armed forces supreme commander) made cautious use of party leaders in the policy process, but relied mainly upon highly placed technocrats in ministries important to Thailand's economic development. Prem's strength lay in his political "neutrality"; the technocratic leadership followed his lead. This practice set the stage for the country's economic boom at the end of the decade. The 1978 Constitution, with its appointed prime minister and elected parliament, had created a stable "semi-democracy"[3] that encouraged foreign investment.

The reform of party politics was also the aim of the Political Party Law of 1981, which attempted to reduce the number of parties and thus make parliament more coherent. The law sought to exclude parties that lacked sufficient strength to contend seriously for parliamentary power. To be "legal" a party had to contest at least half the seats apportioned to each of the country's four regions. Smaller parties, it was reasoned, would not be able to field such extensive slates and would be forced to withdraw from competition.

But the government had not foreseen that monied interests could easily outmaneuver the 1981 law. Parties had become heavily subsidized political arms of the private sector. Mandatory quotas of party members—and even candidates themselves—could be bought to fill out slates. Moreover, the price of persuasion, particularly in the rural areas, was usually low enough to ensure that even the poorest and smallest parties could stand for election.

The greatest abuse in party finance, however, was not in bringing parties up to minimal strength on paper. Rather, it was in the conduct of campaigns themselves. Parties tried to compensate for all of their institutional weaknesses through vote-buying. Lacking both issue-centered platforms and broad-based infrastructures, they conducted widescale vote-buying through local cliques. Party canvassers were usually local politicians, often village headmen and subdistrict councilmen with lifetime tenure. The *jao poh* pulled away from its more traditional patrons and found a new growth industry "managing" local politics. Like the Sino-Thai elite, the *jao poh* were violating a centuries-old agreement with the traditional power structure. By the 1988 general election, vote-buying had become so common that economists estimated that the amount of money changing hands was enough to raise that year's GDP by half a percentage point.[4] Vote-buying spiralled upward, and some MPs entered the legislature less as lawmakers than as investors intent on recouping their campaign costs through the regular business of parliament.

Although parliamentary politics were severely factionalized and, some charged, venal in the Chatichai era, the House of Representatives as an institution gained power. The lower house became more active in the appropriations process, challenging top bureaucrats over budgets that had traditionally been sacrosanct. Even the Defense Ministry budget—including the "secret fund" originally established by the military during the counterinsurgency campaign of the 1970s—came into question. A 1990 constitutional amendment designated the speaker of the house as president of parliament, reversing the custom of granting that top role to the president of the senate, which was still largely the preserve of military and bureaucratic figures. Cabinet ministers, now elected MPs rather than technocrats, made decisions that bureaucrats saw as preemptive and overly political. Agencies like the Central Bank became the objects of power struggles between ministers and top bureaucrats. To maintain calm (if not direction) in the policy-making process, Chatichai reshuffled the cabinet several times.

Strategies for Enhancing Accountability

But in this new era of parliamentary prominence, the House made few attempts to regulate either itself or the excesses of the political parties. While the parties were eager to carry democracy's banner, they were neither aware of, nor willing to submit to, the demands of democratic accountability. Yet the move to elected leadership meant that worries about corruption that had traditionally been focused on the bureaucracy had shifted to the world of elected officialdom.

Without mechanisms like legislative codes of ethics and ethics committees to make parliament police its own members, the governmental apparatus could do little to help curb political corruption. The Office of the Counter-Corruption Commission (OCCC), which is based in the Office of the Prime Minister, is the official government instrument charged with identifying and investigating corruption, leaving actual prosecution to the courts. With the elected cabinet and the bureaucracy in a state of almost continual conflict, however, the OCCC's ability to go after corruption in high places was severely constrained.

After the 1991 coup, the military junta established a special committee, under military oversight, to investigate politicians in the Chatichai government who were suspected of being "unusually" wealthy. Ad hoc measures such as these, however, whether or not they ferret out and punish some abuses, do nothing to enable the system to deal with corruption on a regular basis.

Nevertheless, some developments in the later days of the Chatichai government suggest that its concern for accountability was growing. Constitutional changes were discussed that would have made voting compulsory and thus, it was reasoned, driven the cost of buying an election out of reach. Another proposed amendment would have established a parliamentary ombudsman to monitor the conduct of MPs and investigate complaints of political corruption.

Two more long-range measures to enhance electoral politics were also under consideration at about the same time. One was a plan to strengthen the parliamentary committee system by organizing legislative affairs around public policy issues and giving politicians training in these issues. Committees would have been empowered to launch investigative studies independent of proposed legislation. Subcommittees to address specific issues of importance to the population were proposed as a means of narrowing the focus of parliamentary groups. Open hearings were also advocated, and some committees actually did travel outside of Bangkok to conduct hearings.

Progress along this avenue was bound to be slow, however, as these initiatives depended on beefed-up committee staffs and extra funds for salaries and staff training. Moreover, some politicians themselves claimed that stronger committees were contrary to the parliamentary model and would give undue prominence and power to backbenchers and minority-party MPs. In rebuttal, others argued that the plan was an interim strategy that would help to buffer the House against turbulent coalition politics and would ultimately improve party discipline. By providing a forum for MPs to iron out differences at an early stage, issues could be debated and accommodations reached before proposals came up for floor votes. Most compellingly, it was argued that encouraging committees to focus on issues and on public outreach would help to curb vote-buying by raising public awareness of a legislator's duty to his constituents. When citizens realized that parliament could make changes that would affect them, they might become less ready to sell their only assured leverage on the system.

A second strategy, even more ambitious than the first, was to expand and strengthen elected government at the local level. Local elected rule in Thailand is uneven in both scope and mandate. Provincial councils are elected, but they have little lawmaking power and even less budget authority. Their executive counterparts, the provincial governors, are appointed by the Ministry of Interior, the most powerful ministry in the

Thai bureaucracy. In fact, until the 1950s local government in all its forms came under the Ministry of Interior. While municipal councils in the larger cities are elected and have some budgetary control, most local revenue goes to the central government, and only a small percentage is available to the councils for development. Being elected for life, subdistrict councilmen and village headmen are not known for their accountability. Lacking budget authority, they rely on the Ministry of Interior to fund local development projects and other substantial outlays.

In the late 1980s, public pressure began to mount for greater government decentralization. Previous efforts along these lines had proved disheartening: Bangkok kept sending to the provinces bureaucrats who asked for little local input into their decisions. Yet with the help of increasingly powerful provincial business groups, the wealthier regions kept pressing their demands for greater autonomy. Bangkok itself became the first (and so far the only) "province" to boast an elected governor. Other major provinces, particularly those like Chiang Mai and Phuket that earn considerable tourist revenue, have continued to campaign for elected governors. Public opinion thus gradually coalesced against Thailand's strongly unitary system, though the Ministry of Interior, part of a bureaucracy that was feeling increasingly besieged by parliament at the national level, remained reluctant to loosen its grip on the provinces.

Nevertheless, democratic thinkers argued that democratization at the grass roots would improve the political party system in four ways. First, by making local officials more accountable to the electorate, it would decrease their role as middlemen in vote-buying. Second, democratization would encourage party development at the local level, giving MPs natural counterparts and, eventually, a party structure that was both top-down and bottom-up. Third, it would help train future MPs, for successful local elected officials would be likely to end up in the National Assembly. As MPs, they would have a better grasp of the issues that concerned their constituencies, as well as more first-hand knowledge of their constituents. Last, but hardly least, fully elected local government would foster popular participation at the grassroots level, giving the people easier access to elected leaders and encouraging citizen activism.

Finding the Voice of the People

Horace's observation that "laws without mores are in vain" aptly expresses the dilemma of accountability in Thailand, and indeed in all societies: morality within the political culture, like morality in general, cannot be a matter of legislation only. In a democratic society, accountability requires a vigilant electorate. To a certain extent, the instruments of popular participation that go beyond free and open elections (a free press, citizens' groups, and advocacy organizations) were at work in Thailand prior to the most recent coup. The strongest of these was, and is, the press. Yet in a political tradition where input from the general population is neither expected nor encouraged, such institutions are relatively new and fragile.

The rise of the democratic spirit in the Thailand of the early 1970s encouraged the formation of nongovernmental organizations ranging from student groups to farmers' associations. These were logical complements to the popular demand for elected rule that fueled the student revolution of 1973. But to the leaders of the 1976 military coup, voluntary organizations of any kind were at best stalking horses for political parties, and at worst potential channels of communist subversion.[5] Popular participation, the generals reasoned, must therefore be controlled. The armed forces even went so far as to make the promotion of orchestrated civic participation part of their counterinsurgency campaign. Joining forces with the bureaucracy, the military formed mass-based organizations and set up "democracy pavilions" to serve as centers of political and administrative activity in the villages. By co-opting popular participation in form, the government of the late 1970s was in effect attempting to extinguish it in spirit.

In the more conciliatory climate of the 1980s, however, voluntary organizations began to reemerge. By the end of the decade, there were nearly 3,000 active nongovernmental organizations in Thailand, of which approximately 400 were concerned with social issues. The newest of these were advocacy groups that sought to draw attention to social, economic, or environmental problems. Among them were the Population Development Association, which helped to revolutionize family planning in Thailand; the Thailand Environmental and Community Development Organization, which acted as the spearhead of the growing environmental movement; and the Duang Prateep Foundation, which publicized the plight of the urban poor. Although these new groups crystallized around public policy issues, some of which parliament was also attempting to address, they tended to avoid the legislature. Rather, they concentrated on raising public awareness and, when government action was required, approached the bureaucracy.

Several things may explain this missed connection. First, as discussed above, representative institutions in Thailand are not yet equipped to solicit the views and concerns of the public on a regular basis. Conversely, and more seriously, citizens have few means to determine whether their representatives have fulfilled promises or acted in the best interests of their constituents: parliamentary votes are not even recorded, much less published for public consumption. Second, with military intervention more the norm than the exception, Thailand has never had a transition from one democratically elected government to another. Citizens have not yet been allowed a full exercise in political accountability through elections. Until the Thai electorate is allowed to eject a corrupt or inefficient government with ballots, the military and the political parties will stay locked in their vicious circle, excluding the public. Finally, education in democratic processes is not widespread in Thailand, and many citizens' groups remain largely ignorant of the principles and techniques of participatory government. Until these obstacles are overcome, the Thai public will be unable to express their needs and wishes effectively to their elected representatives, much less act as guardians of honest government.

A Constitutional Conundrum

Whether progress can be made in promoting accountability—and therefore in restraining political corruption—will depend in part upon the shape of the next constitution. The leaders of the 1991 coup have abrogated the 1978 Constitution and charged their appointed National Assembly with ratifying a new one before general elections for a new parliament can be called. Although a draft charter will not be released until late 1991, the military has made public its own preferences regarding the new political order.

At the center of the military's plan is a separation of powers that would bar MPs from serving in the cabinet unless they first resign from the legislature. The junta leaders argue that this measure would curb vote-buying, since MPs would not be able to recover campaign costs by securing ministerial posts and exploiting them for private enrichment. Some Thais, however, point to a similar reform that was imposed in 1968, only to be quickly abandoned when some MPs began demanding that the executive branch pay them to approve legislation.

More fundamental reservations have been raised about the military's plan. The first, and most obvious, regards the selection of a prime minister and cabinet. A parliamentary system requires the majority party or coalition to form, or at the very least to choose, the government. Some pundits have speculated that the military's plan is meant to pave the way for a shift toward presidentialism by instituting direct election of the prime minister. Although the junta itself has not thus far espoused this idea, its silence on the question has been ominous. Also unsettling is the lack of any talk about boosting the legislature's power under the new system in order to check the executive branch. Rather, the military seems to favor a decrease in legislative power, and has said outright that the parliamentary committees must be brought to heel. The main question in Thailand's own debate about parliamentarism versus presidentialism, however, is whether the military is advocating a working system in either sense. Whether the above questions can be aired and resolved before the next constitution is put into place will affect the progress of democracy in Thailand for years to come.

Several lessons in accountability can be learned from Thailand's most recent disrupted experiment with democracy. These may be useful not only to Thailand, but to other countries that find themselves hovering at the midpoint of democratization. First, although capitalism can spur the growth of democracy, measures are also needed to guard against its detrimental effects. Thus an emphasis on political accountability should be a ground-floor strategy in assisting democratic institutions and promoting the development of a democratic political culture. Too often, concern for accountability is an afterthought, to be applied only when democracy has foundered or is seriously at risk.

Second, a sudden surge in the power and status of representative institutions, unaccompanied by accommodation with the traditional holders of power, can seriously hinder the development of democracy, regardless of how encouraging such a surge may initially appear to be. The fine line between accommodation and capitulation can vary dramatically from one society to the next, and attention must be paid to the cultural context from which a democratic movement has arisen.

Finally, successful democratization requires education in democratic principles and processes across the entire spectrum of society. That the military in Thailand will need this education if democracy is to succeed is self-evident. Less obvious, but equally important, is the need for greater education of the electorate and the political parties themselves. A continued tug-of-war between the military-bureaucratic alliance and the political parties is probably in Thailand's immediate future. Proving their accountability to the armed forces will be difficult for the parties in any event, since the military will probably keep changing the standard rather than give up power. Proving their accountability to the people, a more complicated and long-range task, will in the end have a far more profound effect on the course of democracy in Thailand.

NOTES

1. Sukhumbhand Paribatra and Chai-Anan Samudavanija, "Liberalization Without Democracy: Growth, Development and Political Change in Thailand" (Paper delivered at a workshop on "Economic Growth and Change in the Asia-Pacific Region," sponsored by the East Asian Institute of Columbia University, 20-22 June 1988), 12-13.

2. For an explanation of the dominant-party model in Asia, see Samuel P. Huntington, "Democracy's Third Wave," *Journal of Democracy* 2 (Spring 1991): 26-27. Huntington theorizes that economic progress and Asian culture combine to form a distinctly East Asian one-party system. Thailand's exception to this rule may be explained by the fact that the military-bureaucratic alliance has functioned as a dominant political party, albeit unelected, for most of the country's parliamentary history.

3. This label was given to the political structure by Chai-Anan Samudavanija in his article, "Democracy in Thailand: A Case of a Semi-Democratic Regime," in Larry Diamond, Juan Linz, and Seymour Martin Lipset, eds., *Democracy in Developing Countries, vol. III, Asia* (Boulder, Colo.: Lynne Rienner, 1989), 198.

4. "Perennial Prem Again," *Far Eastern Economic Review*, 4 August 1988, 16-17.

5. Suchit Bunbongkarn, Chai-Anan Samudavanija, and Kusuma Snitwongse, *From Armed Suppression to Political Offensive: Attitudinal Transformation of Thai Military Officers* (Bangkok: Institute of Security and International Studies, 1990), 106.

20.
NIGERIA'S
PERENNIAL STRUGGLE

Larry Diamond

Larry Diamond is coeditor of the Journal of Democracy *and a senior research fellow at the Hoover Institution. He is the author of* Class, Ethnicity and Democracy in Nigeria *and is coediting a new study of democratic transition and structural adjustment in Nigeria. His article on "Nigeria's Search for a New Political Order" appeared in the Spring 1991 issue of the* Journal of Democracy.

As Nigeria wends its way toward its third attempt at democracy in as many decades, it confronts daunting challenges: persistent ethnic and regional tensions, growing religious conflict, shallow political institutions, an assertive military and secret police establishment, a deeply depressed economy, and a cynical and increasingly despairing populace. No problem, however, is more intractable and more threatening to the future of Nigerian democracy than political corruption.

Few students of modern Nigeria would gainsay Chinua Achebe's claim that political corruption has grown more "bold and ravenous" with each succeeding regime.[1] During the last decade of colonial rule, as the scope of the state expanded and an indigenous political elite achieved power, bribery, nepotism, embezzlement, and extortion became rampant. In these final preindependence years, and under the First Republic (1960-66), state contracts and loan programs were systematically milked to enrich elected officials and their cronies at both the regional and federal levels. Although the First Republic fell mostly because of ethnic and regional conflict, growing public disgust with corruption—and with politicians as a class—also played a role.

In the late 1960s, the onset of the Biafran civil war and major oil production coincided with a marked increase in the scale of corruption. Under the administration of General Yakubu Gowon (1966-75), military governors, federal ministers, and others closely associated with the regime flaunted scandalous wealth. The oil boom of 1973-74 more than tripled government revenue virtually overnight, giving dramatic boosts to corruption, ostentatious display, and sheer waste. A commission of inquiry, appointed by General Murtala Muhammed after he assumed power in an August 1975 coup, convicted ten of the country's twelve military governors of diverting funds totaling over $20 million.

The popular Murtala, a vigorous reformist, was assassinated on 13 February 1976. His successor, General Olusegun Obasanjo, hewed faithfully to Murtala's timetable for a return to civilian, democratic government. The Second Republic began with many important institutional innovations, including a 19-state federal system, a ban on ethnic parties, and provisions requiring the government to "reflect the federal character of Nigeria" in major appointments and the distribution of resources. The National Party of Nigeria (NPN), which took power in October 1979, reflected the spirit of the new republic. The NPN was a broad, multiethnic (albeit northern-dominated) party, devoid of ideology and preoccupied with the business of distributing Nigeria's resources.

Distribute resources the NPN did: to its ministers, party officials, supporters, contributors, and business allies, in a staggering outpouring of public wealth that peaked with the second oil boom in 1979-80. The boom rapidly doubled government revenue to $24 billion, but corruption and a plunge in oil prices bankrupted the country within three years. Of course, the NPN was not the only offender, even though it was the most brazen. The other four parties, each of which controlled at least two state governments, were also implicated in extensive wrongdoing. Corruption had become truly systemic, the standard practice of the politicians from every political party and ethnic group, crippling the functioning of almost every state.

Directly and indirectly, this systemic corruption generated enough popular disaffection to undermine the legitimacy of the Second Republic. In addition to the demoralizing and seemingly endless trail of scandals and exposés, there was the sheer economic drain caused by so much fraud and mismanagement. State governments became unable to pay teachers and civil servants or to purchase drugs for hospitals, and many services (including schools) were shut down by strikes. The growing disparity between the opulence of the elite and the misery of the average household compounded the problem, as did the widespread violence associated with party politics. As the 1983 elections approached, political thuggery reached frightening proportions, leaving some cities virtual ghost towns on the first day of voting. Massive electoral rigging by the ruling party triggered riots that left more than 100 people dead and over $100 million worth of property destroyed. Although the Second Republic briefly staggered on, its fate had been sealed. On the last night of 1983, the military struck to popular rejoicing.

Generals Muhammadu Buhari and Tunde Idiagbon took power at the start of 1984 with a strong popular mandate to attack political corruption. Attack they did—with an authoritarian vengeance. Hundreds of senior political figures were detained. Huge sums of cash were seized from many of their homes, and their accounts were frozen. Military tribunals meted out long prison terms (none less than 21 years) to many of the worst offenders.

While the accountability drive was initially popular, public opinion soon soured as the regime's blatant disregard of due process discredited its campaign. In setting up the military tribunals, Decree Number 3 placed the "onus of proving" innocence on the accused, prohibited appeals, and closed the proceedings to the public. These provisions led the Nigerian Bar Association to boycott the proceedings. The entire process was ad hoc and arbitrary. Some of the most powerful suspects were never arrested, convictions seemed to spare northern Muslim politicians disproportionately, and a great many politicians lingered endlessly in detention without trial.

Moreover, the Buhari regime made it clear that, like all previous regimes, it had no intention of letting itself be held accountable. Although it launched a "War Against Indiscipline," it laid down no procedures for the policing of its own conduct, preferring instead to jail critics, ban independent interest groups, and persecute the press. These abuses made a travesty of the principle of accountability.

Thus when Major General Ibrahim Babangida seized power in August 1985, the country was ready for his easier ways. It welcomed his professed commitments to human rights and free expression and his release of dozens of detained politicians who had not been charged or tried. In response to the recommendations of two judicial tribunals that he appointed, Babangida reduced the sentences of more than 50 convicted former officials and acquitted 12 completely. Later in 1986, he banned 49 politicians from public office for life and cleared 100 others. Some 800 were ordered to be tried for corruption, but those trials never took place.

Under President Babangida, the pursuit of accountability has ground to a halt, although the rhetoric has continued and new institutions have been created. Running beneath the regime's promising political and economic initiatives, the democratic transition and the World Bank-inspired Structural Adjustment Program (SAP), has been a third, profoundly contradictory development: the resurgence of corruption.

The Resurgence of Corruption

It is difficult to establish the facts about corruption in any type of government, and especially a military one. Nigeria has buzzed for years with rumors about the fabulous ill-gotten wealth of senior military and civilian officials in the Babangida government. Many officers, both serving and recently retired, have flaunted their new-found riches. As one prominent newsweekly reported last year: "The rumor mill is agog with tales of the 'Arabian mansions' being put up by some serving military officers. Criticisms abound of how military governors have continued to allocate land to themselves and their relations."[2]

Despite the risks involved, the press has tried to expose the problem. Last year it reported detailed charges of corruption against the military governors of four states. Public complaints have occasionally forced Babangida to cashier some of the worst military governors, and he created an internal panel in March 1990 to monitor their performance. But the very frequency with which military governors and ministers have shuffled in and out of office has sharpened public cynicism, for the spectacle of officers lobbying and pulling strings to be made governors or ministers itself suggests dubious motives.

Corruption today seems rife in every area of government and public service. The 1988 report of the federal auditor general listed numerous cases of unrepaid loans, payments without vouchers, purchases and reimbursements without receipts, and "huge losses in stock and cash plus gross abuse of official property."

Abuses of this sort are old news in Nigeria, but there are some novel and ominous aspects to this latest upsurge of corruption. International drug enforcement authorities, including the U.S. Drug Enforcement Administration, believe that Nigeria has become a leading shipper of narcotics, especially cocaine and heroin. Both international authorities and Nigerian observers believe that the drug trade could not proceed so brazenly without the connivance of highly placed Nigerian officials. In March of this year, a well-connected Lagos society woman was arrested for attempting to bribe her friend, the chairman of Nigeria's National Drug Law Enforcement Agency (NDLEA), to win the release of arrested drug traffickers. In the ensuing scandal, the chairman was removed on suspicion of corruption, a magazine charged that the NDLEA press officer had bribed judicial correspondents to slant coverage of the story, two TV news anchors were fired for not immediately using the vice-president's statement on the controversy, and police closed the *Lagos Evening News* and arrested 15 of its staffers after it headlined that the woman had used the names of the president and first lady in the effort to bribe the NDLEA boss.[3]

Another new aspect involves widespread stories of corrupt conduct by the president himself. Never before in Nigeria has the head of state been so widely suspected of extensive personal involvement in corruption. Tales have been circulating for years of Babangida's large cash gifts to military officers, cabinet ministers, traditional rulers, and potentially contentious opponents; of Mercedes Benz cars given to major newspaper editors and directors of state broadcasting corporations; of the president's secret personal investments in banks and companies; of off-the-books oil being lifted offshore by private tankers. While none of these stories has been publicly documented, they have been conveyed by diverse and well-placed sources with enough consistency to lend them an air of plausibility. If they are mainly true, they would confirm many Nigerians' suspicions that Babangida is indeed—as the U.S. magazine *Ebony* was falsely rumored to have alleged two years ago, in a hoax that triggered furious and deadly rioting—one of the richest rulers in Africa.[4]

Concern over top-level corruption exploded anew recently when Britain's *Financial Times* reported that at least $3 billion of the estimated $5 billion oil windfall that Nigeria reaped from the Persian Gulf crisis was unaccounted for in Central Bank reports.[5] Among the drains on revenue, the paper noted the start on construction of a billion-dollar aluminum smelter (contracted to a German firm); military spending hikes associated with Nigeria's intervention in Liberia; and the recent hosting of the OAU summit in the new capital of Abuja. The report was explosive in part because it implied massive waste and excess, which are typically associated with corruption. Capital costs of the aluminum plant were said by diplomatic sources to be "60-100 percent higher than similar plants elsewhere in the world." The OAU meeting "is believed to have cost more than $150 million," much of it in rush construction projects. Just "the cost of the Mercedes stretch limousines bought to transport the heads of state exceeded the level of contributions made to the OAU by member countries last year." The government called the estimates inflated and promptly expelled the *Times* correspondent.

The tragedy of the Babangida administration is that its lack of concern for accountability—its persecution of press critics, and its refusal to publish the assets declarations of its officials—intensifies suspicions about high-level corruption and thus fuels the already considerable public cynicism about much-needed political and economic reforms. Policy specialists increasingly regard corruption as a major reason why the economy has not responded more positively to SAP. Corruption continues to drain the country's revenue and developmental potential. Moreover, it is undermining the willingness of ordinary Nigerians to endure the pain of economic adjustment when "the gentlemen in power" indulge in an "unrestrained, provocative, and enraging display of wealth of unsubstantiated means."[6] Finally, the persistence of corruption has negated whatever potential may have existed to effect changes in the political culture, especially as regards the ethics of and motives for public service. This is likely to have grave consequences for the Third Republic.

The Scramble for Enrichment

The resumption of electoral politics in Nigeria shows depressingly little change from the Second Republic. The 1987 voter registration exercise, for example, handed out 72 million certificates, even though Nigeria has no more than 55 million eligible voters. The National

Electoral Commission (NEC) concluded that, as in the past, "there had
been multiple registration, the registration of children and of nonexistent
people," and other instances of fraud instigated by powerful persons and
condoned by registration officials.[7] Former NEC chairman Eme Awa
also revealed threats against electoral officials (most prominently
himself), rigging, and attempts to sabotage the December 1987 local
government elections.

Once again, politics is drowning in money. During 1989, more than
a dozen associations competed to be recognized as one of the two
political parties to be allowed in the new system. Staggering sums were
invested in these efforts by wealthy businessmen and political patrons
(including many former politicians). *Newswatch* estimated the total cost
of mounting a thorough drive for party registration at N250 million.[8]
Probably each of the top four parties in NEC's final rankings spent
something like this amount—though all for naught, as it turned out,
because Babangida rejected all their bids and decided to create the two
new parties by fiat.

Money continued to flow profusely as the politicians regrouped into
the new parties and wrangled their way through a series of caucuses and
conventions. At the two national conventions in July 1990, votes were
bought and sold; candidates and state-delegation leaders were routinely
bribed—all in the presence of high officials in the military regime. The
state conventions and local caucuses were also riddled by controversy,
and election tribunals have been flooded with petitions claiming
irregularities in the December 1990 local government elections. Even
more ominously, political violence has increased markedly this year,
claiming a number of lives, as various factions have wrestled in the
states for gubernatorial nominations and control of the party branches.

After 30 years, the central question of Nigerian politics remains: Why
do politicians—and since 1966, soldiers—want political power so badly
that they will do virtually anything to get it? Why does politics become
"warfare, a matter of life and death"?[9]

Plainly, the stakes of politics are too high. The welfare of too many
communities and the fortunes of too many families and groups depend
almost entirely on control of the state. Officeholding in Nigeria has
come to mean the opportunity for phenomenal illicit gain. Since the
flood of oil wealth that began in 1973-74 washed away virtually all
pretense of discretion and restraint, the scramble for irregular personal
and group enrichment has become the bane of every Nigerian
government, civilian and military alike. Yet the scale of the dishonesty
seems to increase with each successive regime.

For many years now, Nigerians in general have recognized corruption
as a central threat to the economic and political future of their country.
Regime after regime has inveighed against it. In January of this year, the
newly elected local government officials took office amidst a hail of

public warnings from the press, the military, the public, the judiciary, and themselves "to shun the urge to amass wealth through impious, dubious, and unpatriotic means," and "to comport [yourselves] in such a way as to retain effectiveness and popular support."[10] Nigerian history is littered with the wreckage of governments that uttered and then flagrantly violated such injunctions.

Words versus Deeds

Since the 1950s, Nigeria has suffered from an increasingly profound disjunction between word and deed. It is not that politicians and public servants are unable to grasp the requirements of a democratic political culture. On the contrary, they know full well the norms of democracy, and incant them like a mantra with every new government. But these norms have not sunk deep roots, so the psychic costs of violating them are negligible. In the years just after independence, it was plausible to attribute this divergence to colonialism's bifurcation of the public realm. On one side was the "primordial public" of village and ethnic community with their strong traditional strictures against corruption; on the other lay the new "civic public"—the modern administrative state—an alien and exploitative sphere in which customary norms did not apply.[11] Yet with power now passing to a third postindependence generation, this explanation hardly suffices.

At work is a crude process of class formation. For 40 years, Nigerian officials of every rank have systematically misappropriated public wealth. For 40 years, the gulf has widened between an impoverished general populace and the dominant class. Riven by ethnic, regional, and religious cleavages, by shifting partisan and factional divisions, and by continual civil-military tensions, Nigeria's dominant groups nevertheless constitute a class bound together by a shared taste for extravagant consumption and acquisition financed by access to state power. Indeed, they are best designated a "political class" precisely because their wealth flows from control over "relations of power, not production."[12]

Ordinary Nigerians know that they have been betrayed from above, yet like Americans, they keep reelecting their own local representatives. For political corruption is driven not only by the ambitions of the higher-ups, but also by the aspirations of a much larger number of clients below who besiege their relations, friends, bosses, and ethnic kin for jobs, contracts, licenses, favors, money, or other illicit largess.[13] As one former military governor reflected, officeholders who fail to comply are viewed as selfish rather than honorable. "Those who refuse to be corrupted and are poor are called fools. . . . So what use is it to be righteous?"[14]

The dense network of vertical ties joining political patrons to clients largely sustains the system, but with great instability. Both the elite and the masses have schizophrenic mentalities: The politicians want to make democracy work and to get rich doing so, even though their corrupt enrichment will quite likely bring democracy down. The masses, meanwhile, retain their profound cynicism regarding politics, but remain ready to join in the scramble for whatever morsels can be had. Such schizophrenia produces all of the intensity and passion of mass politics, but with none of the loyalty to democracy that would deter a military coup.

The resulting fragility of democracy will be accentuated by changes within the Nigerian military. Junior officers have come to view a lucrative tour of duty in government as their right; young people now join the armed forces (or marry into military families) toward this end. They are not about to be shut out permanently from political power and its huge rewards merely because the president keeps asking them to show "unalloyed loyalty to the constitution and subordination to democratically elected government."[15] Heightening the danger is the considerable loss of esprit de corps and internal cohesion the Nigerian military has suffered from two decades of intervening in politics.

The "new breed" in Nigeria—both civilian and military—is a hungry breed. No appeal to values or principles is likely to deter them, any more than it deterred the "new breed" politicians of the Second Republic, or the new generation of military politicians that succeeded them.

The Root of the Problem

Despite this continuing decay, Nigeria is not condemned to relive the past. It is wise to avoid excessive cynicism, which can in itself become a self-fulfilling prophecy, and there are hopeful signs. The Second Republic made considerable progress in evolving institutions to ameliorate ethnic conflict. These institutions have been retained in the Third Republic, and important innovations added. As Richard Sklar has argued, "Democracy comes to every country in fragments or parts; each fragment becomes an incentive for the addition of another."[16] Nigeria either has or is developing many of these parts: robust associational life; a pluralistic and inquisitive press; a cultural commitment to freedom; a competent bench and bar; federalism; a competitive party system. Virtually all of these have suffered damage from the repression and corruption attending military rule, but still retain considerable vitality and promise. The absence of other key parts—free and fair elections, political tolerance, accountability, effective government, democratic legitimacy—is linked to the central problem of political corruption. If that can be addressed, democracy *can* develop in Nigeria.

The fundamental mistake to date has been the assumption that the root of the problem lies in political culture. There *is* an entrenched culture of corruption in Nigeria, but it is not the cause of the problem. Corruption has flourished in Nigeria because of perverse incentives that only structural change can remedy.

The incentive structure in Nigeria offers a low-risk path to easy riches through political corruption, while opportunities to accumulate wealth through real entrepreneurship are limited and chancy. Ethical revolutions and social mobilizations will not change these underlying realities of lawlessness and political economy. They will change—and eventually so will the culture—if opportunities for corrupt gain shrink while its risk rises, and legitimate methods for accumulating wealth expand.

The latter may be happening under SAP, but it is a slow process, retarded by a nasty dilemma: pervasive corruption and the resulting political instability make for a very poor investment climate, but without growing investment in legitimate enterprise, corruption will retain its appeal. Effective implementation of SAP may yet generate a dynamic capitalist sector outside the state, but Nigerians are unlikely to reinvest at home the $30 billion or so they have sent abroad unless other, easier avenues of gain are restricted.

The SAP also aims to reduce rent-seeking in state office by cutting back on the state's role in the economy. Some of this has already been achieved. In the modern state, however, there are limits to such adjustment, especially in countries that rely heavily on oil revenues controlled by the state. For the indefinite future, opportunities for Nigerians to enrich themselves in public office will be extensive.

Nigeria is thus left looking mainly to the third avenue of change—increasing the risks and costs of corrupt conduct. The venal character of politics cannot be altered unless corrupt public officials are exposed and punished in large numbers. Punishment must involve both substantial prison terms and massive seizure of ill-gotten assets, if it is to have the kind of serious impact that was missing from the halfhearted sentences and truncated prison stays meted out to Second Republic politicians from 1984 to 1986.

The Second Republic's 1979 Constitution contained a strict Code of Conduct that required public officers to declare all their assets at regular intervals to a Code of Conduct Bureau, which was empowered to monitor compliance and refer charges to the Code of Conduct Tribunal. The latter, a quasi-judicial body, had the authority to impose serious penalties including dismissal, seizure of assets, and disqualification from office for ten years. But neither of these bodies ever worked as intended, because the National Assembly buried their enabling legislation and the president appointed a Conduct Bureau chairman who did not take the job seriously, and was never meant to do so.

The Code of Conduct apparatus still holds the key to combating political corruption in Nigeria. The 1989 Constitution contains a strengthened version of the 1979 Code, which was thorough and explicit in its provisions. But unless these are enforced by an ably led and properly staffed Bureau and Tribunal, they will have no more impact in the Third Republic than they did in the Second. The Achilles' heel of these bodies is their subservience to partisan politicians. The military administration has partially ameliorated this weakness by accepting the recommendation of its civilian Political Bureau to get these two bodies up and running before the civilians return to power. (The Political Bureau was appointed by President Babangida in January 1986 to propose a new political "blueprint" for the country.) Still, both the Conduct Bureau and the Tribunal have been given very limited resources and politically weak, superannuated leaders who will retire after 1992. After the transition, the new civilian president will name the members of these and other crucial bodies. Furthermore, important aspects of the Bureau's operations (including public access to the assets declarations) will again be subject to the jurisdiction of the National Assembly.

Significantly, the Babangida administration rejected Political Bureau recommendations designed to make the Code of Conduct a more effective instrument of accountability. The first was that the assets declarations should "be published for general public assessment, claims and counterclaims." The second would have entrusted the appointment of Bureau and Tribunal members to the Council of State rather than the president.[17] These important recommendations point to some of the contradictions that vex the current transition. Even with the offices it now has in every state, the Conduct Bureau alone cannot thoroughly enforce the Code of Conduct. Credible enforcement requires the assistance of a vigilant press and public with access to the declarations of assets. Yet as one prominent politician recently confided, that would pose an insoluble dilemma: If the politicians were to lie about their assets, a great many would be discovered, discredited, and removed from office; but if they were to declare them honestly, "the public's shock at discovering the real extent of their wealth would cause a revolution in this country."[18]

The problem of oversight cannot be solved by giving the Council of State the power of appointment. Under the current Constitution, as under its predecessor, that body is chaired by the president and includes numerous serving politicians, including all 21 state governors. What is needed is a smaller, more active, and independent body composed mostly of citizens who are not involved in partisan politics. General Obasanjo has proposed that the incumbent president be the only politician on the council (and not its chairman), while all other members be required to relinquish any party memberships or affiliations.[19]

As Obasanjo and other Nigerians have suggested, such a nonpartisan Council of State should have responsibility not only for the Conduct Bureau and Tribunal, but for other bodies that have been rife with partisan pressures in the past and that must operate with rigorous integrity if democracy is to work. This applies especially to the National

Electoral Commission and the Judicial Service Commissions (both of the federation and of the several states). These various bodies would then answer only to the Council of State, which would appoint, supervise, and dismiss their members, and even perhaps determine their funding. To restore judicial integrity, some have proposed shifting the powers to appoint, pay, and dismiss judges from the president and governors to independent commissions.

Helpful as such constitutional innovations would be in the struggle against corruption, they would not in themselves be sufficient. If the Conduct Bureau is to be an effective monitor of Nigeria's thousands of elected and unelected federal, state, and local officials, it will need a considerably larger staff both at its headquarters in Abuja and in each of the state offices. Justice Patrick C. Akpamgbo, the current chairman of the Conduct Tribunal, has estimated that a comprehensive enforcement effort would require the Bureau to provide each state office and its headquarters with "nothing less than one hundred professional staff"—meaning university graduates trained in fields like criminology, accounting, and law, and rigorously screened for moral integrity.[20] The Bureau also needs more money, computer technology, and most crucially, enhanced legal authority. Under current law, the Bureau lacks the authority to investigate the affairs of public officers and evaluate the veracity of their declarations of assets.[21] Although it began operating in May 1988, and has begun to send the Tribunal (launched in January 1989) scores of officials who have failed to file assets declarations, the conduct apparatus has yet to punish a single public official for actual corruption. The problem promises to grow even worse in the Third Republic, when the Bureau will have to depend on a partisan attorney general's office to investigate cases of possible misconduct.

The Need for Realism

If the Third Republic is to witness a significant drop in corruption, the struggle against it must begin in earnest, and the institutional arsenal must be augmented, during the transition. This means establishing a legacy of accountability *now*, by trying and punishing new civilian officials who breach the Code of Conduct. As Nigeria's prominent weekly *African Concord* observed in a 1990 article listing "ten ways to end corruption": "Government should seize property of corrupt public officers, jail them, and let them complete their [prison] terms."[22] Other items on the list point to the long-term and multipronged effort that is needed: "Government should separate the running of the economy from the state." The "revolution in values" must continue, through leadership by example as well as through education. Government institutions at all levels (especially the Code of Conduct bodies) need fiercely honest and vigorous leaders who will brook no abuses on their watch. Forceful and exemplary leadership is especially needed in the office of president, which will set the moral tone for the new administration and the entire country.

In addition, realism is needed in restoring official pay and benefits to respectable levels. Greed aside, many Nigerian officials are drawn to corruption merely in pursuit of economic security. With the drastic devaluation of the naira under the SAP, retirement benefits and official salaries have become absurd: a junior bank executive may now make more on paper than the president of the country. To help deter corruption, salaries of public officials (particularly senior ones) must increase at least several hundred percent. This could prove politically dangerous for the government at a time when it is trying to hold down wages for fear of inflation and debilitating new deficits. If the people see corruption being vigorously rooted out, however, they may be more inclined to understand the need for higher public pay. Giving the power to determine official salaries to an independent commission might also increase the palatability of large pay hikes.

Realism is needed not only in the struggle against corruption, but in the larger effort to foster viable democracy in Nigeria. No matter what happens, electoral politics in Nigeria will continue to be turbulent, raucous, and corrupt for many years to come. Democracies do not simply spring into being pure and whole like Athena from the brow of Zeus; they must develop over time. In the world's two oldest democracies, Britain and the United States, the struggle for reform unfolded through more than a century of legal, political, and social ferment. In important respects, that effort continues. No country in the world has a perfect democracy. Reform in Nigeria may not take a century, yet it will surely take a good while. During that time, civil society must mobilize aggressively, outside of party politics, to make politicians accountable and elections honest. It must be ready to sustain these efforts for many years. The only hope for building democracy in Nigeria lies in a long, contentious, and incremental process of political reform and civic education—not in another "mass mobilization," burst of rioting, or military coup.

NOTES

1. Chinua Achebe, *The Trouble with Nigeria* (Enugu, Nigeria: Fourth Dimension Publishers, 1983), 42.

2. *This Week*, 2 April 1990, 12.

3. *Newswatch*, 4 March 1991, 8-16; 25 March 1991, 15-19; and 1 April 1991, 25-29.

4. For more on these May 1989 anti-SAP riots, which claimed more than 50 lives, see Larry Diamond, "Nigeria's Third Quest for Democracy," *Current History* 90 (May 1991): 203.

5. *Financial Times* (London), 25 and 27 June 1991.

6. "The Unequal Sacrifice," *The Democrat*, 15 October 1988.

7. Eme O. Awa, "Elections and Electoral Administration in the Transition" (Paper delivered at a conference on "Democratic Transition and Structural Adjustment in Nigeria," Hoover Institution, Stanford, California, 26-29 August 1990), 16-17.

8. *Newswatch*, 17 July 1989, 16. The naira, worth more than one dollar in the early 1980s, is now equal to about 10 cents U.S.

9. This oft-quoted phrase is drawn from the 1981 presidential address of Claude Ake to the Nigerian Political Science Association, *West Africa*, 25 May 1981, 1162-63.

10. Sola Akinsiku, "Local Government Autonomy: A Right Step," *Sunday Punch*, 20 January 1991; the newly elected chairman of the Ogbomosho local government council, in a swearing-in speech quoted in *Sunday Punch*, 20 January 1991.

11. Peter Ekeh, "Colonialism and the Two Publics—A Theoretical Statement," *Comparative Studies in Society and History* 17 (January 1975): 91-112.

12. Richard L. Sklar, "Contradictions in the Nigerian Political System," *Journal of Modern African Studies* 3 (1965): 201-213, and "The Nature of Class Domination in Africa," *Journal of Modern African Studies* 17 (1979): 531-52. The quote is from the latter article, 537. Use of the term "political class" is further elaborated in Larry Diamond *Class, Ethnicity, and Democracy in Nigeria* (London: Macmillan; Syracuse: Syracuse University Press, 1988), 31-41.

13. Richard A. Joseph, *Democracy and Prebendal Politics in Nigeria: The Rise and Fall of the Second Republic* (Cambridge: Cambridge University Press, 1987).

14. *African Concord*, 26 March 1990, 29.

15. Address of President Babangida to the Chief of Army Staff Annual Conference, quoted in *Daily Times*, 22 January 1991, 1.

16. Richard L. Sklar, "Developmental Democracy," *Comparative Studies in Society and History* 29 (October 1987): 714.

17. *Report of the Political Bureau*, 216 and 219; *Government's Views and Comments on the Findings of the Political Bureau*, 76-77. Neither does the 1989 Constitution fully honor the Political Bureau's concern (expressed at 216) "that the Code of Conduct Bureau must, as much as possible, be insulated from undue influences and pressures from the National Assembly."

18. Private interview with a politician currently active in party politics, January 1991.

19. Olusegun Obasanjo, *Constitution for National Integration* (Lagos: Friends Foundation Publishers, 1989), 90-91. Other Nigerians have pondered whether it might be possible to have additional members of the Council nominated from recognized and respected organizations like the Nigerian Bar Association, the Nigerian Medical Association, the Nigeria Labour Congress, the National Association of Nigerian Students, and the National Council of Women's Societies.

20. Interview with Justice Patrick Akpamgbo, 18 January 1991. At that time, the Bureau had at its Abuja headquarters only 17 staff positions (4 of which were vacant) in the key division that monitors official conduct, Research and Statistics. Only 4 of those 17 employees actually examine the declarations of assets (the rest are support staff). Staffing of state offices is even more skeletal. (Interview with the chairman of the Code of Conduct Bureau, Reverend Canon Mohammed, 17 January 1991).

21. The Bureau is only empowered to "examine" the assets declarations, which is construed to mean a rather cursory review to determine that all the questions are fully answered. Justice Akpamgbo has urged that the Bureau be given explicitly authority to "investigate."

22. *African Concord*, 26 March 1990, 34.

21.
STRATEGIES FOR REFORM

Robert Klitgaard

Robert Klitgaard *is an American who is currently visiting professor of economics at the University of Natal, Pietermaritzburg, South Africa. Formerly a professor at Harvard University's John F. Kennedy School of Government, he is the author of six books, including* Elitism and Meritocracy in Developing Countries *(1986),* Controlling Corruption *(1988), and* Tropical Gangsters *(1990). He has worked in 22 developing countries. Material in this article is drawn from his new book* Adjusting to Reality: Beyond State versus Market in Economic Development *(ICS Press and International Center for Economic Growth, 1991).*

Corruption is an embarrassing subject. Many citizens in developing countries are simply exhausted by it. They have watched their leaders posture and moralize and make half-hearted efforts against corruption, all to no avail. When Tanzanians debated a campaign against corruption in February 1990, for example, public reactions recorded in the government-run newspaper were overwhelmingly skeptical. "We have the Anti-Corruption Squad under the president's office, the Permanent Commission of Inquiry, the Leadership Code, the Control and Discipline Commission of the Party, and courts of law," noted an intellectual affiliated with the ruling party. "What else do we need?"[1] Despite all, corruption still reigned.

At about the same time, a Guatemalan journalist gave voice to another widespread view. "When . . . the shameless triumph; when the abuser is admired; when principles end and only opportunism prevails; when the insolent rule and the people tolerate it," she lamented, then "perhaps it is time to hide oneself; time to suspend the battle; time to stop being a Quixote."[2]

Such defeatism and despair are responses to ever deeper corruption in much of the developing world. Robert Wade's remarkable study of corruption in India describes systematic government predation. "The essential business of a state minister," he concludes, "is not to make policy. It is to modify the application of rules and regulations on a particularistic basis, in return for money and/or loyalty."[3] Jean-François Bayart's monumental study of African politics is subtitled *la politique du ventre*—"the politics of the belly." Corruption, he says, is now the abiding reality of the African state.[4] A recent United Nations meeting concluded:

> Corruption in government is pervasive at all levels of public management, including, in some countries, the deliberate mismanagement of national economies for personal gain. . . . Corruption is pervasive and is apparently expanding. . . . [I]t has become systematic and a way of life in many countries.[5]

Around the globe, corruption is increasingly a central issue in election campaigns, popular uprisings, and military coups.

If the current worldwide trend toward democracy and the free market continues, it will eventually help reduce corruption. Competition and accountability—both noteworthy features of democracy and free markets—are the enemies of corruption. Yet while democracy, the separation of powers, a free press, and freer markets are surely to be welcomed, it remains true that actions to control corruption must go beyond broad-gauged reforms at the top. More than one country has discovered that free elections and economic reform do not immediately reduce corruption. Whatever size and type of state a country chooses, the threat of bribery, extortion, influence peddling, kickbacks, fraud, and other illicit activities remains—in the private sector as well as the public.

Even though almost every new Third World government—elected or not—places the fight against corruption at the top of its agenda, the scholarly literature on development offers little guidance. Indeed, a tradition in Western social science has excused corruption as a market-like response when markets malfunction, or as an analogue to democratic logrolling when democracy is absent.

There are exceptions. Some new theoretical work does show how rent seeking and "directly unproductive profit-seeking activities" can cause harm by distorting incentives.[6] And new empirical research shows—no surprise to people living in poor countries—that corruption in fact causes harm.[7]

But many students of development have been reluctant to investigate corruption. Scarce data and uncooperative countries are partly to blame. There is another factor as well: First World scholars do not want to be seen as calling Third World people corrupt. Over 20 years ago, the Nobel Prize-winning Swedish economist Gunnar Myrdal decried the Western condescension that led to such a "taboo on research."[8] Some social scientists have argued that bribes cannot be distinguished from transactions, that to try to do so is to import Western or one's own normative assumptions. A bribe, a fee for service, a gift—analytically, it is said, they are the same.

As many poor countries have slid into deeper economic distress, however, the sheer fact that corruption is so widespread and so economically and socially devastating has become impossible to deny. Professor Ledivina Cariño of the University of the Philippines, in a paper written before the overthrow of Ferdinand Marcos, complained that the "careful balancing of good and bad effects seems to be a recognition that everyone knows corruption is not really beneficial but positive effects must be discovered so that one does not condemn a country completely. Compare the outrage of American scholars against Nixon's indiscretions and their near-approval of more blatantly corrupt regimes in countries where they have worked."[9]

And so corruption has not received the attention it deserves. Amid all the moralisms and excuses, policy analysis has languished.

The Institutional Dimension

It would be tempting to write off corruption as a product of perennial human weakness, selfishness, and dishonesty, and let the matter rest there. Yet this approach is insufficient. Political corruption may be perpetrated by individuals, but it always takes place in an institutional context. As Thomas C. Schelling reminds us:

> An organization, business or other, is a system of information, rules for decision, and incentives; its performance is different from the individual performances of the people in it. An organization can be negligent without any individual's being negligent. To expect an organization to reflect the qualities of the individuals who work for it or to impute to the individuals the qualities one sees in the organization is to commit what logicians call the 'fallacy of composition.'[10]

Schelling's insight should caution us against assuming that institutions are corrupt simply because of immoral people and that nothing can be done about corruption short of generations of moral education. Is it not possible that organizations can alter their "system of information, rules for decision, and incentives" in order to reduce corruption? How? The approach that I recommend begins by distinguishing the various types of corruption, and then highlights structural failures of information and incentives (rather than moral failures of individuals). Such a model might help to stimulate policy makers and managers to address creatively their own unique circumstances. Finally, case studies show that reform is possible—and is at least partially intelligible through the framework developed.

In my experience, many leaders *do* want to reduce corruption—not only heads of state, but ministers, police chiefs, jurists, controllers general, mayors, and minor officials. Yet even with the best will in the world, corruption cannot be eradicated overnight; trying to do so may simply backfire. One must grasp the situation as it is, not as one wishes it might be. Scholars who advise presidents or other top officials must analyze the types of corruption and their extent; discern who loses and who gains from corruption; identify its causes; and propose long-range strategies for reducing it. Beyond greater democracy and freer markets, these strategies often contain common features—for example, "frying a big fish" to show that the rules have changed; taking a preventive approach that focuses first on anticorruption efforts with the most favorable cost-benefit ratio; involving the bureaucracy in improving incentives; involving the public in reporting good and bad public behavior; and improving information and incentives all around. We will explore these components below; for now the point is that the president and his team need to recognize that the problems are not hopeless, that one can analyze corruption as a problem of policy and management. In my experience, this process of collaborative strategy formulation is possible, if always sensitive and difficult.

But suppose that such willingness and such access are not present. What then?

Particularly in today's Africa, international donors and lenders can exert remarkable leverage for change. In the past decade, more than 30 African countries have undertaken some form of structural adjustment—usually at the behest of the World Bank and the International Monetary Fund. Structural adjustment means increasing the scope and autonomy of the private sector; providing better incentives through prices and wages related to market valuations; and fostering competition, decentralization, and privatization. Many of these changes reduce the scope of government, and hence the scope of official (though not necessarily unofficial) corruption.

If the 1980s were the decade of structural adjustment in the private sector, perhaps the 1990s are the time for the structural adjustment of the public sector. The fundamental ideas would be similar: greater autonomy (for example, more authority to accountable public agencies and officials, debureaucratization); improved incentives for officials; more competition (among bureaucracies, local governments, and with the private sector); more decentralization; and new public-private hybrid agencies. These changes have much to recommend them besides their potential for reducing corruption, and would probably prove acceptable as part of conditionality in aid packages; even rent-seeking presidents would enact them rather than lose foreign assistance.

Many developed countries now allocate part of their foreign aid budgets to programs that assist the design and administration of democratic elections, while many democratizing countries encourage international observers to witness their voting. These are welcome steps; they provide information and appropriate incentives that help reduce corruption. But there are many other dangers. To mention just one example: the links between campaign financing and lobbying pose especially serious dangers to incipient democracies, where institutions are more fragile, power less dispersed, informational media less developed, and court systems more subject to influence. Thus it is essential to reduce the scope for rent seeking through such means as government-financed campaigns coupled with frugal spending limits.

Let us suppose, then, that a desire to reduce corruption exists or can be made to exist. How might a policy analysis proceed?

Types of Corruption

Corruption is the misuse of office for private ends. Examples range from the monumental to the trivial. Corruption can involve the misuse of important policy instruments—tariffs and credit, irrigation systems and housing policies, the enforcement of laws and rules regarding public safety, the observance of contracts, and the repayment of loans—or of simple procedures. Corruption may become systematic—for example, when it infects the daily business of government activities like collecting taxes, passing items through customs, distributing public building or supply contracts, or carrying out police work. Politicians or parties may dedicate their energies to raising funds—a legal if "directly unproductive" activity—or may cross the legal and moral line of influence peddling, bribery, even extortion.

On occasion a corrupt act may be socially harmless, even helpful. It may allow the circumvention of a needless rule, for example, or it may effect a kind of politically stabilizing redistribution. But as most citizens will attest, and as careful studies of several countries have repeatedly shown, most corruption is socially pernicious. Widespread corruption stunts economic growth, undermines political legitimacy, and demoralizes public officials and ordinary citizens.

Sound policy analysis begins by differentiating the various types of behavior, and then carefully assesses their extent, social costs, and particular beneficiaries. Corruption can encompass promises, threats, or both; can be initiated by the public servant or the interested client; can entail acts of omission or commission; can include illicit or licit services; and can occur inside or outside institutional channels. The borders of corruption are hard to define and depend on local laws and customs.

Consider the problems encountered by Justice Efren Plana when he took over the Philippines' Bureau of Internal Revenue (BIR) in 1975. Positions within the Bureau were being bought and sold. One job that paid $10,000 a year was going for $75,000 because of its lucrative opportunities for corruption. Justice Plana also learned of embezzlement, fraud, counterfeiting, extortion of taxpayers, and payoffs to speed up paperwork or reduce tax liabilities. The Bureau's internal investigation and enforcement division was not of much help, for it too was corrupt.

Confronted with such a teeming garden of illicit activities in an environment as corrupt as the Philippines, most officials would have concluded that nothing could be done. Plana, however, refused to admit defeat and instead launched a reform that succeeded in reducing corruption. How he did so is instructive.

First Justice Plana had to consider the causes of corruption. This is a topic on which much has been written from many viewpoints. Some ancient authors attributed official corruption to greed. The fourteenth-century Islamic scholar Ibn Khaldun blamed it on "the passion for luxurious living within the ruling group"—true enough, no doubt, but not particularly helpful. Others have ascribed corruption to particular cultures (be they dictatorial, personalistic, gift-giving) or peoples.[11] Still others have pointed out that corruption tends to be most prevalent when social norms are in flux or breakdown, and during booms and busts. Corruption has been blamed both on too much capitalism and competition and on too little; on colonialism and on the withdrawal of the colonial powers; on traditional regimes and on the breakdown of traditions.[12]

And then there are the thoroughgoing cynics, who do not understand why corruption needs to be explained since corruption is everywhere, including (as recent events underscore) the most "advanced" countries. This idea leads naturally to regarding anticorruption efforts as necessarily futile, as if one were to mount a campaign against the sun's daily setting.

When rhetoric deflates, however, several points seem important. First, corruption is a matter of degree and extent. It does and has varied over space and time. Second, experience shows that corruption can be reduced, if never eliminated. Third, most corrupt acts are not crimes of passion but crimes of calculation. Officials are not corrupt all the time, at every opportunity; and so it is reasonable to posit that an official undertakes a corrupt action when, in his judgment, its likely benefits outweigh its likely costs. The benefits and costs vary according to many factors—some of which may be influenced by public policy.

The Usefulness of Economic Metaphors

In the Philippines, Judge Plana asked why so much corruption existed inside the Bureau of Internal Revenue. He looked at the motives and opportunities facing agents within the BIR. We can appreciate this approach, I think, by using economic metaphors to analyze corruption.

First, imagine a public *agent*—such as a judge, civil servant, or politician—trading off the personal benefits from undertaking a corrupt act against the personal costs of doing so. (A similar analysis can be made of the person—or "client"—offering the bribe.) Second, imagine a noncorrupt *principal* like Justice Plana facing another tradeoff: between the social benefits of reducing the agent's corrupt activity and the social costs of effecting that reduction. The combination of these two metaphors is a *principal-agent-client model*.

The public official is an "agent" pledged to act on behalf of the principal to produce public services. But the agent can use her position to reap private benefits in transactions with the client. These transactions may create public bads. The agent engages in them depending on their costs and benefits to her. The principal's problem is to induce the agent to create the optimal amounts of public goods and bads.

Suppose a client offers the agent a bribe. The economic metaphor says that the agent faced with a bribe makes a calculation. She trades off the potential benefits to her of accepting the bribe and undertaking a corrupt act against the potential costs to her of doing so. (A similar analysis can be made of the person offering the bribe.)

If she refuses the bribe, she receives her usual pay and she enjoys what we might call the moral satisfaction of resisting a bribe.

If she is corrupt, she of course receives the bribe. But she also suffers what we can conceptualize as the "moral cost" of being corrupt. Like the moral satisfaction of refusing the bribe, the moral cost of accepting it may be high or low depending on the person, the situation, the organization, and the culture.

By accepting the bribe the official also runs a risk: there is some chance she will be caught and punished. She has to weigh this prospect when making her decision. The penalty could include the loss of her pay and her job, a fine or jail sentence, disgrace, and so forth.

She will accept the bribe if: the bribe minus the moral cost minus [(the probability of being caught and punished) times (the penalty for being corrupt)] is greater than her pay plus the satisfaction derived from not being corrupt.

Since public policy and management can affect all the variables in this calculation, it follows that they can influence the prevalence of corruption.

Much recent economic theory concerns itself with the principal-agent problem and its extensions, including the problems of implementing a "unified governance structure," which includes incentives, information systems, decision rules, hierarchical structures, and the control of "influence activities."[13] The complexity of the concrete problems faced by a real principal like Plana soon outstrips available models, but one can usefully continue with economic metaphors. For heuristic purposes, I have found it useful to put into five categories the principal's tools for controlling corruption: 1) the selection and training of agents; 2) the incentives facing agents and clients; 3) information gathering on the agents' and clients' efforts and results; 4) the restructuring of agent-client relationships (for example, by reducing monopoly powers, clarifying rules and procedures to circumscribe agents' discretion, changing decision making, or redefining the mission of the organization); and 5) raising the moral costs of corruption (for example, with ethical codes and changes in the organizational culture).

The principal needs to know how big a reduction in corruption he is likely to get for a given policy change, and must then decide whether this reduction is worth the direct and indirect costs of the reforms themselves.

Such decisions are, of course, complex and highly contingent; they exceed our current ability to model and estimate. The principal, moreover, must be concerned not only about corruption but also about the primary business of his agents (collecting taxes, convicting criminals, or whatever). The principal may also be involved with other agents in other "games" that may affect his efforts to reduce corruption; he must remain attentive to these externalities.

A Framework for Policy

The wise principal's first step is to analyze his organization in order to assess where and how much corruption occurs. Experience as well as theory indicates that an organization is most vulnerable to corruption at points where agents enjoy greater monopoly power over clients, have greater discretion over the provision of a licit or illicit service, and take actions that are more difficult to monitor. Reducing monopoly power is crucial to the fight against rent seeking.

Second, the principal evaluates the various costs (and possible benefits) that different kinds of corrupt activities entail, and to whom.

Third, he assesses the various policies through which he can affect the calculations of potentially corrupt officials and citizens. He imagines enacting these policies and asks, "As I turn the dial and spend more resources on them, how do various kinds of corruption respond and how much does turning the dial cost?" To allocate his resources efficiently, he must choose the appropriate types of corruption to attack and the appropriate types and levels and sequences of anticorruption policies to employ. In the first instance he should look for a type of corruption that is important but relatively cheap to address. For political purposes, it is often important to begin a campaign against corruption with actions that can make an impact in six months—even if not against the most serious form of corruption.

An anticorruption campaign should not be pushed so far that its costs outweigh the benefits in reduced corruption. Reducing corruption is only one of the principal's goals, and it is a costly one. Because preventing, discovering, and prosecuting corruption are costly, the optimal amount of corruption is not zero. The optimal campaign against corruption must

---

Table 1 - Controlling Corruption: A Framework for Policy Makers

A. Select agents
    1) Screen out the dishonest (past records, tests, predictors of honesty)
    2) Exploit outside "guarantees" of honesty (networks for finding dependable agents and making sure they stay that way)

B. Set agents' rewards and penalties
    1) Change rewards
        a. Raise salaries to reduce the need for corrupt income
        b. Reward specific actions and agents that reduce corruption
        c. Use contingent contracts to reward agents on the basis of eventual success (e.g., forfeitable nonvested pensions, performance bonds)
        d. Link nonmonetary rewards to performance (training, transfers, perks, travel, publicity, praise)
    2) Penalize corrupt behavior
        a. Raise the severity of formal penalties
        b. Increase the principal's authority to punish
        c. Calibrate penalties in terms of deterrent effects and breaking the culture of corruption
        d. Use nonformal penalties (training, transfers, perks, travel, publicity, loss of professional standing, blackballing)

C. Obtain information about efforts and results
    1) Improve auditing system and management information systems
        a. Gather evidence about possible corruption (red flags, statistical analysis, random samples of work, inspections)
        b. Carry out "vulnerability assessments"
    2) Strengthen information agents
        a. Beef up specialized staff (auditors, computer specialists, investigators, surveillance, internal security)

---

balance reducing corruption against such considerations as cost, morale, red tape, and reducing official discretion.

The analysis sketched above has proved useful to policy makers in developing countries. Table 1 is a heuristic framework designed to help policy makers think more creatively about ways to control corruption.

Justice Plana used each of the methods listed in this framework. (The other successful cases of reducing corruption that I have studied can also be usefully assimilated to this framework.) Plana's strategy had three parts.

First, he established a new performance evaluation system with the help of BIR employees, and he linked incentives (such as prizes and free travel) to it. Then he collected information about corrupt activities. Third, he fried some big fish, inflicting swift and well-publicized punishment on high-level violators. This latter step signaled to the BIR and the public that the rules of the game had changed.

b. Create a climate where agents will report improper activities (e.g., whistle-blowers)

c. Create new units (ombudsmen, special investigatory committees, anticorruption agencies, inquiry commissions)

3) Collect information from third parties (media, banks)

4) Collect information from clients and the public (including professional associations)

5) Change the burden of proof, so that the potentially corrupt have to demonstrate their innocence (e.g., public servants with great wealth)

D. Restructure the principal-agent-client relationship to leaven monopoly power, circumscribe discretion, and enhance accountability

1) Induce competition in the provision of the good or service (privatize, public-private competition, competition among public agents)

2) Limit agents' discretion

a. Define objectives, rules, and procedures more clearly and publicize them

b. Have agents work in teams and subject them to hierarchical review

c. Divide large decisions into separable tasks

d. Limit agents' influence (change decision rules, change decision makers, alter incentives)

3) Rotate agents functionally and geographically

4) Change the organization's mission, product, or technology to render them less susceptible to corruption

5) Organize client groups to render them less susceptible to some forms of corruption, to promote information flows, and to create an anticorruption lobby

E. Raise the "moral costs" of corruption

1) Use training, educational programs, and personal example

2) Promulgate a code of ethics (for civil service, profession, agency)

3) Change the corporate culture

Within three years, Plana had knocked out the internal market for jobs and extortion, and greatly reduced the incidence of various corrupt practices. Tax revenues were up, and even those opposed to the Marcos regime lauded Plana's sensational success.[14]

Information

In fighting corruption we should focus, as Justice Plana did, on *information* and *incentives*. Information about corruption is, of course, difficult to obtain. Legal activity can be a misleading indicator, for while one society may make almost no legal efforts against rampant corruption, another may define corruption so broadly that it seems ubiquitous when in fact it is relatively scarce. Nor will the information sought include survey data, economic indicators, and the like. More ingenious, indirect means must be devised.

For example, in Plana's case (and in the other successful anticorruption efforts that I have studied) policy makers used a variety of information-gathering devices:

• Finding "heroes" (people known to be clean) within the organization and having them work with outside auditors to examine a sample of cases, decisions, or offices for evidence of corruption or inefficiency.

• Convening inquiry commissions, as proved so successful in 1989 in Zimbabwe.

• Using undercover agents.

• Devising new, often indirect measures of corrupt behavior (for example, the wealth or spending habits of top officials; the prevalence of illegal activities that would be abetted by official corruption).

• Involving the public through devices ranging from hot lines to citizens' committees to random samples of clients.

In addition, "participatory diagnosis" proves surprisingly useful—that is, working with officials from corrupt institutions in the analysis of corrupt activities. In my experience, as long as one is not looking for particular individuals who are corrupt, it is surprising how much information about corruption can be obtained from officials within a supposedly corrupt organization. They are able and willing to identify places vulnerable to corruption, and even to design workable changes.

The greatest enemy of corruption is the people. This is why almost every new government—elected or not—justifies itself by promising to combat the corruption of the previous regime. Even though individual citizens participate in corruption, the people as a whole despise it and understand the warping of incentives that it entails.

Successful campaigns against corruption involve the public. For example, take Hong Kong's Independent Commission Against Corruption (ICAC).[15] When started in 1974, the ICAC had three major components. The Operations Department investigated, arrested, and helped prosecute the corrupt. The Corruption Prevention Department stressed prevention and worked with government agencies to determine which organizations were most vulnerable to corruption. The ICAC had the power to "secure" changes in working procedures in government agencies in order to reduce the opportunities for corruption. Many of its activities can be analyzed with the framework of Table 1.

The third component was the Community Relations Department. It gathered information and support from the people. The ICAC installed hot lines and complaint boxes so citizens could easily report corruption and inefficiency. A radio call-in show became a popular forum for citizens to air their complaints. The ICAC visited schools and work places; it set up offices in the neighborhoods, where ICAC employees, members of the neighborhood council or local government, and citizens (often from civic associations) could work side by side.

Six citizen-oversight bodies acted like boards of directors for various

ICAC activities. The civic associations brought both competence and credibility to their task. Members of auditors' and accountants' associations, for example, knew a lot about detecting corruption, and had a reputation for honesty and independence.

In societies where irresponsibility and inefficiency have been widespread, credibility is of central importance. The citizenry may have arrived at the sad point of simply not believing or trusting the government. Here the involvement of the people is crucial, for several reasons.

First, the people can be an invaluable source of information about where corruption and inefficiency occur. This does not mean, of course, that every anonymous accusation of corruption is to be believed. In fact, most are false. But a trustworthy body with technical competence to investigate corruption can sift through the reports it receives from the people, looking for patterns and serious cases. This is what the ICAC did in Hong Kong—with the people's involvement.

We have just mentioned the second and third reasons why the involvement of the people is important: *trustworthiness* and *competence*. Government may have too little of either, at least in the short run, to make much of a difference without the people taking part.

A final reason is political stability. Corruption is frequently a major issue in election campaigns. Polls in many developing countries support what many experienced politicians say: there are few things that disgust ordinary citizens more than corruption. Indeed, cynics may exaggerate corruption's prevalence and importance; all of government may be lumped together as bribe-takers and self-servers. In any case, it is now routine for the perpetrators of coups to justify themselves by pointing to the corruption of the previous regime.

At the same time, it is difficult to form a political constituency for an anticorruption effort. Unlike lobbies for, say, soya production or education, no well-organized citizens' group has a clear stake in fighting corruption. Moreover, civil servants often find anticorruption campaigns threatening. Honest officials may fear being tarred with a reckless accusation; dishonest ones will raise obstacles against efforts to expose and punish their illicit activities. It is possible to launch an anticorruption campaign during a wave of public resentment, but institutionalizing public concern is difficult.

Incentives

Successful campaigns against corruption begin with the positive. After an agency's employees have participated in defining objectives, performance measures, and so forth, and after their incentives for good performance have been improved, then the attack on corruption can begin. "You cannot just rush into an office," Justice Plana told me, "as if you were a knight in shining armor and assume everyone is a crook. Then, you don't get cooperation."

When performance measures become more available, incentives should be linked to them. As Justice Plana explained to me, reforming incentives was his first priority:

> We needed a system to reward efficiency. Before, inefficient people could get promotions through gifts. So I installed a new system for evaluating performance. I got the people involved in designing the system, those who did the actual tax assessment and collection and some supervising examiners. [Incentives were] based upon the amount of assessments an examiner had made, how many of his assessments were upheld, the amounts actually collected—all depending on the extent and type of the examiner's jurisdiction. In no time, the examiners were asking for more assignments and were more conscious of their work.

Incentive reform faces many obstacles, even in the private sector. In the public sector, difficulties of measurement, civil-service rules, budget problems, and politics add further complexities. Yet recent years have produced examples of incentive reforms that enhance productivity and discourage corruption.[16] In many cases team-based or even organization-wide incentives may be more feasible than individual incentives. This may be so for cultural and ideological as well as technical reasons.

In addition to rewards, penalties also have a vital role to play. Surprisingly, in many countries the only punishment for those found guilty of corruption is loss of employment. But leaders and administrators can do more and make punishment both fairer and more effective. Just as positive incentives include money but go much further, penalties can include restrictions, transfers, loss of discretion or autonomy, peer disapproval, and loss of professional status. Publicity can be used to spotlight wrongdoers, a form of "punishment" that is sometimes the most feared.

In the Philippines, for example, Judge Plana knew it would take two years to convict corrupt officials. He went ahead with that legal process, but he also let the press have lots of information about the transgressors and their offenses. The resulting torrent of investigative reporting led to shame (and three heart attacks), which both deterred corruption and helped to change the popular belief that the big boys are exempt.

The choice of penalties (and of those to be penalized) should be made with an eye to smashing what might be called the culture of corruption. When corruption is systematic, cynicism and alienation spread widely. Experience with successful anticorruption campaigns suggests that imposing a severe penalty on a "big fish" is one way to begin to subvert that culture. The big fish must be a clearly important miscreant, one who has or can be given public prominence and one whose prosecution cannot easily be interpreted as a political vendetta. For this last reason, it is best that the first big fish should come from the political party that is in power.

A Fresh Approach

In this article I have suggested that we suspend the usual terms of discourse about corruption—for example, that it is an ethical or legal problem, or one that requires a total overhaul of the social system and a change of mentality. Such considerations are valid, but a fresh approach may lead to useful, practical ideas. We have experimented with economic metaphors, with questions about the incentives that face government officials and the things that can be done to reshape those incentives in ways that will render corruption less attractive. The metaphors imply that all of us are corruptible, that our focus should go beyond individuals to corrupt institutions—corrupt systems of incentives, information, and power. Solutions must go beyond "throw the rascals out." Our approach suggests policy changes involving recruitment, rewards and penalties, information, the restructuring of government, and what might be called the moral costs of corruption.

Anticorruption efforts have to recognize that a culture of corruption and rent seeking is part of the problem. Campaigns against corruption must go beyond words and beyond party politics. Big fish must be fried, prevention must be stressed, and both bureaucrats and ordinary citizens must participate.

The political climate for anticorruption efforts varies. In some countries, the mere suggestion that corruption is a problem is likely to cause trouble; in others, as in Haiti today, the fight against corruption and abuse is a defining feature of a new regime. I think that cases like Haiti will become more common, for as democratic reforms proceed, new governments will be seeking ways to reduce the illicit activities of the past. Those who care about democracy and reform should take heart. Instead of paralyzing ourselves with the worry that no government will ever want to halt corruption, we should ask, "Suppose they do. Suppose they ask for help. What would we be able to offer them?" The answers should not be moralisms or despair, but useful analytical frameworks, lessons from success and failure elsewhere, and conditional aid.

NOTES

1. Jane Perlez, "As Tanzania Debates Corruption, Officials Say It Makes Ends Meet," *New York Times*, 4 March 1990, A8.

2. Marta Altolaguirre, "Cuando sucede . . ." *La Prensa* (Guatemala City), 22 February 1990 (my translation).

3. Robert Wade, "The Market for Public Office: Why the Indian State Is Not Better at Development," *World Development* 13 (1985): 480.

4. Jean-François Bayart, *L'état en Afrique: la politique du ventre* (Paris: Fayard, 1989), especially 87-138. See also Mark Gallagher, *Rent-Seeking and Economic Growth in Africa* (Boulder, Colo.: Westview, forthcoming).

5. United Nations Department of Technical Cooperation for Development, *Corruption in Government*, TCD/SEM. 90/2 INT-89-R56 (New York, 1990), 4, 6, 12.

6. Susan Rose-Ackerman, *Corruption: A Study in Political Economy* (New York: Academic Press, 1978); T.N. Srinavasan, "Neoclassical Political Economy, the State, and Economic Development," *Asian Development Review* 3 (1985): 38-58; Robert P. Inman, "Markets, Government, and the 'New' Political Economy," in Alan J. Auerbach and Martin Feldstein, eds., *Handbook of Public Economics*, 2nd ed. (Amsterdam: North-Holland, 1987); and Gerald M. Meier, ed., *Politics and Policy Making in Developing Countries: Perspectives on the New Political Economy* (San Francisco: ICS Press and International Center for Economic Growth, 1991).

7. For example, David J. Gould, *Bureaucratic Corruption and Underdevelopment in the Third World: The Case of Zaire* (New York: Pergamon Press, 1980); Marcela Márquez, Carmen Antony, José Antonio Pérez, and Aida S. de Palacios, *La corrupción administrativa en Panamá* (Panama City: University of Panama, 1984); Ledivina V. Cariño, ed., *Bureaucratic Corruption in Asia: Causes, Consequences, and Controls* (Quezon City: JMC Press, 1986); Robert Klitgaard, *Controlling Corruption* (Berkeley and Los Angeles: University of California Press, 1988); Gustavo Coronel, *Venezuela: la agonía del subdesarrollo* (Caracas: Litografía Melvin, 1990), 130-55; and Philip Heymann and Robert Klitgaard, eds., *Dealing with Corruption and Intimidation in Criminal Justice Systems* (Cambridge: Harvard Law School, 1991).

8. Gunnar Myrdal, "Corruption as a Hindrance to Modernization in South Asia," in Arnold J. Heidenheimer, Michael Johnston, and Victor T. LeVine, eds., *Political Corruption: A Handbook* (New Brunswick, N.J.: Transaction Publishers, 1989), 406-7 (this is an excerpt from Myrdal's *Asian Drama* [New York: Twentieth Century Fund, 1968]).

9. Ledivina V. Cariño, "Tonic or Toxic: The Effects of Graft and Corruption," in Cariño, ed., *Bureaucratic Corruption in Asia*, 168.

10. Thomas C. Schelling, "Command and Control," in James W. McKie, ed., *Social Responsibility and the Business Predicament* (Washington, D.C.: Brookings Institution, 1974), 83-84.

11. Samuel P. Huntington, *Political Order in Changing Societies* (New Haven: Yale University Press, 1968), 65. Max Weber was reluctant to attribute causation but was "inclined to think the importance of biological heredity was very great." Max Weber, *The Protestant Ethic and the Spirit of Capitalism* (New York: Charles Scribner's Sons, 1958 [orig. publ. 1904-5]), 31.

12. See Klitgaard, *Controlling Corruption*, 7-9, 62-67.

13. Useful references include Oliver Williamson, *The Economic Institutions of Capitalism* (New York: Free Press, 1985); Oliver Hart and Bengt Holmstrom, "The Theory of Contracts," in Truman Bewley, ed., *Advances in Economic Theory—Fifth World Congress* (Cambridge: Cambridge University Press, 1987); Paul Milgrom and John Roberts, "Economic Theories of the Firm: Past, Present, and Future," *Canadian Journal of Economics* 21 (1989): 444-58; and Bengt Holmstrom and Jean Tirole, "The Theory of the Firm," in R. Schmalensee and R. Willig, eds., *Handbook of Industrial Organization* (Amsterdam: North Holland, 1989).

14. For more details see Klitgaard, *Controlling Corruption*, ch. 3.

15. Ibid., ch. 4.

16. Robert Klitgaard, "Incentive Myopia," *World Development* 17 (1989): 447-59.

IV.
The Global Democratic Prospect

22.
THE NEW WORLD DISORDER

Ken Jowitt

Ken Jowitt *is professor of political science at the University of California at Berkeley. This article was adapted from two papers that were published in* The Crisis of Leninism and the Decline of the Left: The Revolutions of 1989, *edited by Daniel Chirot (University of Washington Press, 1991); and* Global Transformations and the Third World, *edited by Robert O. Slater, Barry Schutz, and Steven R. Dorr (Lynne Rienner, 1992).*

For nearly half a century, international and national boundaries and identities have been shaped by the existence of a world of Leninist regimes led in varying ways and to different degrees by the Soviet Union. For half a century we have thought in terms of East and West; now, with the mass extinction of Leninist regimes, the East as such has vanished, taking the primary axis of international politics along with it. Thermonuclear Russia still exists, but the imperial construct called the Soviet bloc is gone, and the Soviet Union proper (itself an empire) may soon follow. The "Leninist extinction" has radically altered the geopolitical frame of reference that countries throughout the world have long used to bound and define themselves.

The Third World, for instance, has bounded and defined itself since its beginning at the Bandung Conference of 1955 by distinguishing itself from the West on the one hand and the Leninist world on the other. Whatever shared political identity the "nonaligned" states of Africa, Asia, and the Middle East have had has been largely negative: they were neither liberal nor Leninist. The Third World's ideological identity, its geographical borders, and its capacity to secure development assistance have all hinged upon the conflict between the other two worlds, one led by the United States, the other by the Soviet Union. Yet now the bipolar alignment with reference to which the nonaligned states of the Third World defined themselves has disappeared.

Boundaries are an essential component of a recognizable and coherent identity. Whether the borders in question are territorial, ideological, religious, economic, social, cultural, or amalgams thereof, their erosion or dissolution is likely to be traumatic. This is all the more so when boundaries have been organized and understood in highly categoric terms, as they were during the period of the Cold War.

We cannot expect the "clearing away" effect of Leninism's extinction to be self-contained, a political storm with an impact conveniently limited to the confines of what used to be the Leninist world. On the contrary, the Leninist extinction of 1989 has hurled the entire world into a situation not altogether unlike the one described in the Book of Genesis. Central points of reference and firm, even rigid, boundaries have given way to territorial, ideological, and political confusion and uncertainty. We now inhabit a world which, while not "without form and void" like the primordial chaos in Genesis, is nonetheless a great deal more fluid than it was just a very short while ago. The major imperatives of this world, moreover, will be the same as those facing Yahweh in Genesis: "naming and bounding."

We must respond to a world that will be increasingly unfamiliar, perplexing, and threatening. Many kinds of existing boundaries will come under assault; many will change. The task will be to establish new national and international boundaries and to identify—"name" and "bound"—the new entities that result.

In his much discussed essay on "The End of History," Francis Fukuyama has taken the view that "the triumph of the West, of the Western idea, is evident first of all in the total exhaustion of viable systematic alternatives to Western liberalism."[1] His allowance for the "sudden appearance of new ideologies or previously unrecognized contradictions in liberal societies" is a throwaway. For him, Hitler, the Nazi revolution, and World War II were a "diseased bypath in the general course of European development." Similarly, his allowance that the "fascist alternative may not have been played out yet in the Soviet Union," is a liberal Goliath's view of a possible fascist David. "Exceptions" on the order of the Nazi and Bolshevik regimes do not prove the liberal "rule"—the former almost destroyed liberalism, and the latter had the nuclear weapons to do so.

Fukuyama is correct to observe that liberal capitalism is now the only politically global civilization, and to suggest that "the present world seems to confirm that the fundamental principles of sociopolitical organization have not advanced terribly far since 1806." But neither of these propositions can justify his Idealist, ahistorical assertion that liberal capitalist civilization is the absolute end of history, the definitively final civilization. Indeed, there are enduring reasons why liberal capitalist democracy will always evoke external and internal challenges, as I will later attempt to show.

Fukuyama's vision of history's culmination and my Genesis image are both exaggerations, of course. But if a theorist's only choice is what type of error to make, I offer mine as likely to prove more accurate in assigning meaning and more helpful in attempting to influence the world that we are about to enter. The global transformation of boundaries and identities that the Leninist extinction has set in motion is more apt to resemble the world outlined in Genesis than the stingy and static picture of things to come that Fukuyama presents.

Shifting Boundaries

The cataclysm that befell the Leninist world in 1989 can be understood as a kind of mass extinction. In paleontology, a mass extinction is defined as the abrupt and accelerated termination of a species that is distributed globally or nearly so. What separates it from other forms of extinction is its rapid and comprehensive character. Leninism has suffered the sudden destruction of its "genetic" or identity-defining features—those that provided each Leninist regime, and the Leninist "regime-world" as a whole, with a continuously recognizable identity across time and space. The concept of class war, the correct ideological line, the vanguard party as the exclusive locus of leadership, and the Soviet Union as the incarnation of revolutionary socialism have all been rejected in the Soviet Union itself, and Soviet support was withdrawn from the Leninist replica regimes of Eastern Europe. The momentous result has been the collapse of these regimes and the emergence of successor governments aspiring to democracy and capitalism but faced with a distinct and unfavorable Leninist legacy.

That legacy includes a ghetto political culture that views the state with deep-seated suspicion; a distrustful society where people habitually hoard information, goods, and goodwill, and share them with only a few intimates; a widespread penchant for rumormongering that undercuts sober public discourse; and an untried, often apolitical leadership, barely familiar with and often disdainful of the politician's vocation. Moreover, the Soviet-enforced isolation of the nations of Eastern Europe from one another has sadly reinforced these countries' long-held tendencies toward mutual ignorance, distrust, and disdain. All in all, this is not a promising foundation for liberal capitalist democracy.

The first to change among those boundaries and identities that for half a century have determined the world's political, economic, and military complexion will probably be territorial borders. The most immediate and obvious border problems involve the Soviet Union and parts of Eastern Europe. Demands for sovereignty in Georgia, Azerbaijan, Ukraine, the Baltic states, Moldavia, and Russia itself have created turbulence and tension in one of the world's two thermonuclear superpowers. The recent strains between Czechs and Slovaks show how widespread the potential is for shifts in borders and political identities within the old Leninist imperium. In fact, it may turn out that it was a great deal easier to contain a well-bounded and identified Soviet bloc than to prevent the current crises of boundaries and identities in the same area from spilling over into adjacent areas.

The potential disintegration of Yugoslavia could remake the map of southeastern Europe. The Macedonian question is not settled, and could entangle Serbia, Bulgaria, and possibly Turkey. In fact, given the current crises in the Persian Gulf, Soviet Central Asia, Bulgaria, and Yugoslavia, Turkey may emerge as a pivotal nation in a radically reshaped political region comprising parts of the Middle East, the Balkans, and Central Asia.

The Soviet Union's Central Asian republics, home to many of the USSR's more than 50 million Muslims, are demanding sovereignty. In a recent *New York Times* report, Barbara Crossette observed: "Central Asia is an old idea taking on new life not only in Pakistan but also in the Muslim world beyond the Middle East—as far east as China's Xinjiang region. . . . [A] process, however tenuous and exploratory, of rediscovering old cultural, historical, religious, and commercial bonds is underway, perhaps most of all in Pakistan, the nation in the middle."[2] This has stirred concern in India, which fears that it may one day find itself facing an Islamic bloc stretching from the Pakistani frontier to the edges of Europe.

The Leninist world of East Asia, too, may undergo border and political-identity changes. Leninist rule in China rests on the continued presence of its founding cadres, leaders who have the one thing that Eastern Europe's Leninist rulers lacked in 1989: confidence in their own political and ideological purpose. But neither the Chinese, the North Korean, nor the Vietnamese regime can any longer define that purpose in practical terms. All are drifting toward extinction. In North Korea, the death of Kim Il Sung will immediately raise the threatening issue of unification with the South. In China, the inevitable dying off of the communist gerontocrats will raise the threat of centrifugal regionalism.

For decades, the compelling reality of the Soviet-American rivalry gave substance and stability to formal territorial boundaries in the Third World. The influence of Washington and Moscow on their respective Third World clients, given each superpower's fear that a change in boundaries might aid its rival, helped to stabilize international borders. The Leninist extinction and America's consequent declaration of the end of the Cold War have changed all that. Old historical issues and frames of reference have reasserted their claims on the attention of many Third World elites. President Hafez Assad of Syria has a mural in his office depicting the Battle of Hittin, where Saladin won a crucial victory over the Crusaders in 1187. Assad values it because Hittin was "where the Arabs defeated the West." His frame of reference is one that promises to become more salient and consequential in a world without Leninism.

In coming to grips with the Leninist extinction's global impact we must be ready for chaos in some places, opportunities in others, and for the slim but persistent possibility that new civilizations might emerge.

New Ways of Life

The emerging international environment's primary characteristic will be turbulence of an order not seen during the Cold War. In this new world, leaders will matter more than institutions, charisma more than political economy. It is precisely at such times—when existing boundaries and identities, international and national, institutional and psychological, are challenged—that charismatic leaders offer themselves as sources of certainty and promise. We can expect their appearance, for William James's observation that societies "at any given moment offer ambiguous potentialities of development . . . leaders give the form"[3] is particularly true of Genesis environments.

Even charismatic leaders, to the extent that they are constrained to act in the context of existing state institutions, will be of real but only limited consequence; they may affect the distribution of power in a larger or smaller area, but will be powerless to institute truly epochal changes. It is also possible, however, that in a turbulent, dislocating, traumatic Genesis environment the dissolution of existing boundaries and identities can generate a corresponding potential for the appearance of genuinely new *ways of life*.

A new way of life consists of a new ideology that militantly rejects existing social, economic, religious, administrative, political, and cultural institutions. It calls for the creation of new and better ones (this invidious element is essential); a new political language that "names" and delineates the new way of life; a new and potent institutional expression; the emergence of a social base from which members and leaders can be drawn; the assignment and acceptance of a great historical task demanding risk and sacrifice; and finally, a geographical or institutional core area able to furnish resources equal to the task of creating a new way of life.

Some historical examples should make the argument more evocative. Liberal ideology asserted a new social ontology in which the individual was the basis of social identity and responsibility. Capitalism and democracy (as Karl Polanyi so brilliantly grasped)[4] required a new way of life, not the mere redistribution of power. Nazism and Leninism made ideological demands of the same order (though not, of course, of the same content).

All new ways of life depend on a new political vocabulary; Leninism is unimaginable without its talk of "the dictatorship of the proletariat," "the vanguard party," "the correct line," and "democratic centralism." Similarly, every new way of life—social, economic, political, or cultural—must be embodied in a novel institution and partisan pattern of authoritative behavior. Absolutism had the royal court; liberalism, the market and Parliament; Leninism, the Party and the Plan. For each new way of life there must be a social base uprooted from its previous identity, available for a new one, and drawn to the new ideology. From this base a new elite can emerge: royalist officials, ascetic capitalist entrepreneurs, Bolshevik cadres, or SS men.

For a new way of life to assert itself, a determined minority must completely identify with a mission—establishing the supremacy of the king; of free trade and the market; of the race and the Fuhrer; or of the Party and the *kollectiv*—for a critical period during which new elites, practices, organizations, and beliefs can crystallize.

I am not claiming that a new way of life will inevitably appear in response to Leninism's extinction, merely that the historical "clearing away" and attendant trauma associated with this momentous event could occasion such a development. In the next decade and beyond, an unusual number of leaders and movements will appear to press for some new way of life or the restoration of some bygone glory. Saddam Hussein's current attempt to rouse the Arab Muslim peoples is only the first effort of this kind. Most or even all of the aspirants will fail. But they will be both signs and causes of growing national and international disorder. All this, in a sense, does mean the end of history—the history of the last 45 or even 200 years. But it does not mean the inexorable assimilation of the world to the current Western liberal way of life, nor even the continued adaptive strength of the liberal West.

Liberalism and Its Critics

The growth of disorder and turbulence, the appearance of charismatic leaders and movements, and the possible evolution of new ways of life will occur in a political universe that may now be running on inertia, but which is for the moment still well delineated nationally and internationally. The proliferation of Genesis environments does not mean that developments will be either apocalyptic or unintelligible. Precisely because Genesis environments develop out of and in opposition to more delineated and "named" environments, the theorist is well positioned to grasp the interconnections and meanings of events. After the extirpation of Fascism-Nazism and the extinction of Leninism, what next? What developments are most likely in a world dominated by the liberal capitalist democratic civilization? I confidently predict one general trend.

Liberal capitalist democracy has aroused a heterogeneous set of opponents: Romantic poets, Persian ayatollahs, aristocrats, the Roman Catholic Church, and fascists. For all the real and massive differences that separate these diverse oppositions, one can detect a shared critique. Liberal capitalist democracy is scorned for an inordinate emphasis on individualism, materialism, technical achievement, and rationality. While the Roman Catholic preference for the family over the individual as the basic unit of society and the Nazi preference for the "race" differ radically as positive alternatives, there is a common negative theme: liberal capitalism is indicted for undervaluing the essential collective dimension of human existence.

Similarly, liberal capitalism has regularly evoked passionate criticism of its tendency to ignore or marginalize the human need for security, and its repression of spontaneity and expressive human action. But nothing has been more central to liberal capitalism, or more capable of eliciting opposition over the last 200 years, than its elevation of rational impersonality as the organizing principle of social life. Liberal capitalist democracy rejects the ethos of heroic striving, awe, and mystery that throughout most of history has been seen as raising man above the level of the brutes and the realm of iron necessity. This rejection has evoked criticism from various sources within liberal societies; it has also helped to arouse countermovements as perverse as Nazism and Stalinism.

But no matter how impressive liberal capitalist democracy's triumphs over the Catholic Church, the Fascist and Nazi movements, and now Leninism may be, these remain *particular* victories. Precisely because liberal capitalist democracy has a partisan identity, it cannot be or do all things equally. As long as the West embodies this partisan identity, it will regularly witness the rise of both internal and external movements dedicated to destroying or reforming it—movements that in one form or another will stress ideals of group membership, expressive behavior, collective solidarity, and heroic action. A major locus for such movements will be the Third World.

Beginning with India's independence in 1947, many opponents of the liberal West have looked upon the Third World as a source of promise. But the promise has yet to be realized: with the possible exception of Islamic fundamentalism, no new way of life has emerged anywhere in the Third World. No new ideology has been embraced by leaders who go on to create a new political vocabulary for, and recruit a new leadership stratum from, a mobilized social base that can populate innovative institutions, pursue historically extraordinary tasks, and draw from a powerful and prestigious core area. No London, Moscow, Mecca, or Rome has arisen in the Third World. Instead, one generally sees depressingly familiar examples of tyranny, corruption, famine, and rage in prenational settings. Even so, it would be premature to dismiss the Third World as a potential source for a new way of life; most of the ex-colonial world, after all, has been independent for only a few decades.

Movements of Rage

Yet even if no new civilization emerges from the Third World, developments there do not augur well for the adoption of liberal capitalist democracy. I want to examine three such developments: the continuing obstacles to democratic consolidation; wars between Third World countries; and, above all, movements of rage.

It is amazing to contemplate the facility with which Latin Americanists who quite recently were gloomily speaking and writing about the "breakdown of democracy" have begun to enthuse about the "transition to democracy"—not only in Latin America but, by unwarranted extrapolation, in Eastern Europe and the Soviet Union as well. Economic and social development in a nation places the question of democracy on the agenda, but an irreversible transition to democracy requires much more in the way of sociocultural and institutional preconditions. The history of Argentina bears perpetual witness to this. Poorer countries like the Philippines, where democratic political institutions are facades that do not match the country's social and cultural "constitution" or the military's political culture, will find the transition to stable democracy even harder to achieve. Even India's circumscribed and faulty but still substantial democracy is beset by growing threats of regional, linguistic, and religious conflict as the Congress Party-based pan-Indian generation of bureaucrats, officers, and politicians passes from the scene.

The Leninist extinction favors an increase in the number of wars fought between Third World countries. Many such countries have been left (courtesy of colonialism) with arbitrary borders and fictive national identities; absent the old Soviet-American rivalry, Third World irredentisms will flare up more often and more intensely. Their significance will vary, ranging from sad but peripheral cases like Liberia, with its civil war and consequent invasion by several divided West African nations, to the Iraqi invasion of Kuwait with its massive international repercussions. Saddam Hussein's annexation of his oil-rich neighbor is a case of a Third World leader attempting to create favorable new boundaries and political identities in what he sees as a disrupted, and therefore both promising and threatening, environment.

In the near future the most extraordinary Third World trend may be the rise and triumph of what I call "movements of rage." Although not yet grouped together by theorists, some such movements have already emerged: the Mulele uprising in the Kwilu province of Zaire, the Tupamaros in Uruguay, the Khalq in Afghanistan, the Khmer Rouge in Kampuchea, and the Shining Path insurgency in Peru. All are revolutionary movements with a Leninist or Maoist vocabulary but an ethos akin to the thought of Frantz Fanon. Their motivating spirit is nihilistic rage against the legacy of Western colonialism. These movements typically originate in resentments held by provincial elites—men and women who seethe with loathing for the culture of the metropolis, and yet at the same time feel enraged at being excluded from it. Their murderous ire is aimed at those who have been "contaminated" by contact with Western culture: those who wear ties, speak European languages, or have Western educations.

Movements of rage are nihilistic backlashes against failure: the failure of the Third World to create productive economies, equitable societies, ethical elites, and sovereign nations. They are desperate responses to the fact that nothing seems to work. The hoped-for magical effect of adopted labels like "one-party democracy," "Leninism," or (as is now becoming fashionable) "market capitalist democracy" has been and will continue to be a disappointment for most Third World countries. Movements of rage are violent nativist responses to the resulting frustration and perplexity.

One can question whether I have proved the existence of a new type of revolutionary movement, a Third World variant of fascism. Very few of these movements have come to power, and when they do (as in Afghanistan and Kampuchea), they self-destruct. So did the Nazi regime—at the cost of 50 million lives.

In any case, the failure of many movements of rage to come to power so far tells us very little about their potential in a post-Leninist world, unless one believes that the Leninist extinction is a self-contained event. The burden of my entire argument has been to challenge that assumption. In the new, more turbulent Genesis environments emerging in Leninism's aftermath, one cannot gauge the potential for future movements of rage by generalizing from their earlier failures.

Instead, one must imagine a Third World increasingly neglected by the United States and the Soviet Union except when a very clear and pressing emergency occurs in a strategic location; a Third World where aggression occurs more and more frequently; where nuclear-weapons technology is more widely dispersed; where the few democracies that have any standing (such as India) may fail; and where checks on emigration to the West remove a vital escape valve. In this far from ideal world, movements of rage might indeed become a significantly disruptive international force, especially if one appears in a country like Mexico.

The Long March to Democracy

The Leninist extinction is not a surgical historical strike that will leave the liberal regimes of the West and their Third World allies unaffected. All horizons, including the West's, will be dramatically affected.

Yet does not the worldwide rush toward liberal capitalist democratic idioms, policies, and institutional facades refute this claim? And what of the shift by socialist parties to positions that differ insignificantly from their historic capitalist antagonists; the tentative moves toward a multiparty system in African socialist regimes; the belief by many East Europeans in the market's miraculous quality? These are not illusory phenomena; they are real. But how significant and persistent will they turn out to be? If one interprets these phenomena in developmental rather than static terms, then their significance also resides in the predictable surge of anger that will follow the equally predictable failure (in most cases) of the market and electoral democracy to produce sovereign, productive, equitable nations in the greater part of Eastern Europe, the former Soviet Union, and the Third World.

It would be more accurate to think of a "long march" rather than a simple transition to democracy. Not every route has to be a copy of a prior Western one; alternative courses will be possible, but exceptional. In the maelstrom of the Soviet Union and Eastern Europe, one must expect bishops, generals, and demagogues to be as prominent as entrepreneurs, intellectuals, and democrats. In a Third World ridden with failure and wracked with frustration, one must be prepared for rage. Finally, one must also take note of the emerging worldwide conflict between liberally oriented "civics" and insular "ethnics," a conflict that directly calls into question the value and status of liberal democratic individualism even in the West.

No amount of optimism about the twenty-first century should be allowed to obscure the significance of the nineteenth-century insight that political forms are integrally related to cultural and social patterns. It would be a shame if, with the defeat of the Leninist organizational weapon, Western intellectuals replaced it with a superficial notion of democratic institution building.

Democracy remains a possible outcome, though one that is historically rare and whose birth is usually painful. Those who wish democracy well should remember this, and make a patient effort to endure the "long march" that lies ahead.

NOTES

1. Francis Fukuyama, "The End of History?" *The National Interest* 16 (Summer 1989): 3-18.

2. Barbara Crossette, "Central Asia Rediscovers Its Identity," *New York Times*, 24 June 1990, E3.

3. William James, *The Will to Believe* (New York: Dover Publications, 1956), 227-8.

4. Karl Polanyi, *The Great Transformation: The Political and Economic Origins of Our Time* (Boston: Beacon Press, 1965). See especially chapters 3-10.

23.
WHY DEMOCRACY CAN WORK IN EASTERN EUROPE

Giuseppe Di Palma

Guiseppe Di Palma is professor of political science at the University of California at Berkeley. His publications include To Craft Democracies: An Essay on Democratic Transitions *(1990), and* The Central American Impasse *(1986), coedited with Laurence Whitehead. His article is based on papers presented at the Conference of Europeanists in Washington, D.C. and the 1990 meeting of the Italian Political Science Association.*

The revolutions of 1989 may have rung down the curtain on communist rule in Eastern Europe, but did they also set the stage for the establishment of stable multiparty democracies? Can the nations of Eastern Europe imitate the successful transitions to democracy that have taken place in southern Europe, Latin America, and elsewhere over the past two decades? What lessons might these earlier instances of democratization hold for scholars and East European political practitioners in the 1990s? Most analyses of postcommunist Eastern Europe have dwelt more on doubts and fears than on the grounds for hope. It may be useful, therefore, to balance the picture by taking a second and more hopeful look.

Students of democracy have recently been faced with a series of unprecedented and momentous events. Yet even when there were clear signs of impending change, we have been unable to see these events coming. Every time, we have played down their significance and counseled prudence in assessing their novelty. When called upon to forecast, we have repeatedly opted for pessimism or taken refuge behind qualifications and "on the other hand" disclaimers. Almost every time, things have worked out differently—and generally better—than we had expected. And every time our pessimism was confounded, we have discovered new reasons why the next stage in the unfolding of events should not be as easy as the last.

In defense of this persistent pessimism, it might be argued that the transitions in Eastern Europe face greater difficulties than those that have taken place in southern Europe and elsewhere. But of course, these earlier transitions were also greeted with a great deal of pessimism. We should not let our memory be tricked by their eventual success. It is also worth noting that what is now cited as the main impediment to democratization in Eastern Europe (the double conundrum of how to "marketize" collectivist economies and how to privatize communist parties) was being cited little more than a year ago as the reason why there could not be a crisis of communism *tout court*. Yet the crises have occurred—and that was by far the most difficult (and important) step.

The grounds for this misplaced pessimism about transitions have not changed much over the years. With all due regard for the specifics of the East European case, the litanies of what could and would go wrong—in southern Europe in the 1970s, in Eastern Europe in the 1990s—are essentially variations on certain classic themes derived from an established literature about democratization.

The first theme is that attempts at rapid changes of regime are invariably traumatic, and prone to backfire. Even if democracy initially emerges, the trauma surrounding its birth can hamper its legitimacy and performance. Democracy is a matter of rules for mediating plural and conflicting interests; when it is introduced abruptly and against the wishes of some of the players, the "losers" will resist it and the "winners," lacking tested democratic organizations and personal experience, will be less than fully at ease with its methods. Thus consolidation is placed in doubt, while backsliding is an ever-present possibility.

The second and overarching theme is that the historically best, yet no longer available, path to democracy has been both gradual and linked to the emergence of favorable social, economic, and cultural conditions.[1] These typically include economic prosperity and equality; an economically diversified yet culturally, ethnically, and nationally homogeneous society featuring a large independent middle class; and a national culture which, by virtue of a penchant for tolerance and accommodation, is already well disposed toward democratic ways. By their very nature, accelerated transitions violate the double prescription: because they are fast, and because they occur in response to political contingencies that may have little to do with the self-propelled, slow-motion rise of auspicious conditions.

A related theme, which focuses on the importance of civil society, applies to the specific problems of postcommunist transitions. Most East European countries had little tradition of civil society before communism—they never developed the liberal, bourgeois class of citizens commonly associated with the flowering of civil society in Western Europe. Whatever nascent tradition of civil society may have existed before the war was wiped out by communism, which effectively abolished economic interests linked to class and suppressed other societal cleavages. The construction of a civil society can most surely be accomplished through the reconstitution of the market. But this situation presents a Catch-22. Because no market currently exists in Eastern Europe, there are no market-oriented classes with an objective interest in its reconstitution. Thus the advent of a market, and therefore of civil society itself, is in jeopardy.

Even if a market is successfully introduced, say the pessimists, the pressure to catch up with the rest of Europe will fuel populist expectations that East European economies will be too weak to meet, possibly giving rise to authoritarian backlashes. Thus the market and democracy itself may be subverted. Unfortunately, the only set of socially rooted interests unfrozen by the fall of communism has been conflicting nationalisms, whose tendency toward unruliness is likely to be exacerbated in countries preoccupied with their relative backwardness.

In addition, while East European dissenters bravely spoke the language of civil society in ways that hastened communism's fall and won the sympathy of world opinion, dissent is not synonymous with civil society. Behind the dissent there was no tradition of democratic political parties, organized interests, and distinct social groups. Dissent was the product of an undifferentiated social movement held together by intellectual justification and a common enemy; thus it is likely to exhaust itself once the transition is over.

Given the warning signs that line the path of democratization, an attitude of extreme caution or even of pessimism would seem appropriate in the face of the sort of willful, politically driven transitions that we have recently witnessed. In the immediate but decisive future, it would seem, the transitions in Eastern Europe will fail to achieve economic viability or the reconstruction of civil society, and will reactivate premodern national and ethnic cleavages. But is this all that can be said? Even if we concede that the transitions are saddled with the difficulties and risks just described, is it not more interesting to ask how they can nevertheless be made to succeed? For as we know, many of them outside of Eastern Europe have already succeeded.

The Communist Collapse

If we take our bearings only by the warning signs—and more precisely by the theories that justify them—it becomes hard to conceive how history can ever change. Although things do not change all the time, occasionally they do. Our age seems to me to be a time of change—a time when a new *zeitgeist* is born, when people and governments become convinced that things must and can change. Such moments are rare; the British historian H.R. Trevor-Roper speaks of them as the "lost moments of history." It would be unfortunate if we failed to take proper notice of them.

Thus I wish to offer a counterlitany for Eastern Europe, one that is based on the experience of successful transitions elsewhere, but which is also attuned to the case at hand. The surprise with which many analysts have reacted to the crises in Eastern Europe stems from an incomplete understanding of the old distinction between communist totalitarian (or posttotalitarian) dictatorships and right-wing authoritarian dictatorships. It is true that, other things being equal, the former are distinguished from the latter by their greater resilience and endurance. But we should not forget that communist regimes, by their very nature, are meant to endure for a purpose. They are goal-oriented in a way that authoritarian regimes are not. Communists in power do not see themselves as temporary *régimes d'exception*, but as representatives of a global and solidary alternative to an inalterably unjust international economic order. They do not exist to "catch up" within that order, but to scuttle it. By the same token, such teleological regimes also have a deep and ingrained concern about their identity and self-justification. Their legitimacy is less a matter of public support than a matter of fulfilling a theory of history. When such regimes fail in terms of their own goals—and when that failure is declared by their ideological hegemon, the Soviet Union itself—the resulting identity crisis can prove utterly devastating. The way is then open for unprecedented popular mobilization.

When right-wing dictatorships approach failure, we often witness pragmatic calculation and deliberate action on their part designed to fashion a way out (perhaps including democratization itself) of the crisis. Spain is the classic example. But when communist regimes fail *at long last* by their own exclusive criteria, calculation and protective action give way to dispirited retreat. Thus, what we have witnessed in Eastern Europe (Romania being the only exception) is an almost total collapse of moral confidence and political will. The communist regimes there lost faith in their own right to rule—their "Mandate of Heaven," if you will.

Hence the instantaneous and general mobilization of the people of Eastern Europe, something that has no equivalent in other democratic transitions. It was less the great popular mobilization that caused the abdication of the regimes—their refusal, for instance, to use force against their own people—than it was the other way around. But there was also another source of mobilization that we must take into account: the popular revolt against the particularly big lie (the excruciatingly perverse system of make-believe) in which Brezhnevite regimes trapped their own citizens.

The lie is well captured by Timothy Garton Ash:

> . . . by demanding from the ordinary citizens seemingly innocuous semantic signs of outward conformity, the system managed somehow to implicate them in it . . . [U]ntil almost the day before yesterday everyone

in East Germany and Czechoslovakia was living a double life: systematically saying one thing in public and another in private.[2]

Similarly Václav Havel:

> All of us have become accustomed to the totalitarian system, accepted it as an unalterable fact and therefore kept it running . . . None of us is merely a victim of it, because all of us helped to create it together.[3]

Thus as communist regimes finally abdicate and the implicating lie stands revealed, mass mobilization becomes cathartic. As Garton Ash puts it:

> In order to understand what it meant for ordinary people to stand in those vast crowds in the city squares of Central Europe . . . you have first to . . . understand what it feels like to live a double life, to pay this daily toll of public hypocrisy. As they stood and shouted together, these ordinary men and women were not merely healing divisions in their society; they were healing divisions in themselves. . . . People had had enough of being mere components in a deliberately atomized society: they wanted to be citizens, individual men and women with dignity and responsibility, with rights but also with duties, freely associating in civil society.[4]

A Counterlitany

Having said this much about the special features of communist crises, I wish now to present my counterlitany. Its *leitmotiv* is that democracy can emerge from a regime crisis as a simple matter of convenience or compulsion. In the process, political actors can learn to overcome objective and contingent impediments, as well as motives of personal resistance. Especially favorable conditions are not required.

Genuine democrats need not precede democracy. Democracy's rules, being a means for otherwise difficult mutual coexistence, may come to be embraced simply as an expedient "second best." They can be a matter of instrumental agreement, developed without a popular or elite consensus on fundamentals as the transition unfolds. In some cases, as Albert Hirschman has illustrated in many of his works on political development, new attitudes and beliefs may well develop only *after* political actors have embarked, perhaps unintentionally, upon new behavior (like calling for free elections).[5] Also, democracy may be chosen by default because other political options are impracticable or thoroughly discredited, not necessarily because it is considered intrinsically superior.

Considerations such as these should cast doubt on one of the grounds for pessimism about the prospects for democratization in Eastern Europe. If communist regimes have lost not just temporary clout and credibility but the very will to rule, then the question of what motivates incumbents (and opponents) to move toward democracy, though interesting per se, loses decisiveness. What is crucial is that they do move toward democracy, not *why*. Whether the move issues from conversion, calculation, or necessity, the results may be similarly effective.

A lack of familiarity with democratic rules and institutions is no hindrance either. Just as new behavior can modify beliefs and attitudes, behavioral skills can be learned with practice. How much practice? Taking its cue from the historical examples of democracies that emerged slowly from liberal oligarchy, democratic theory emphasizes the virtues of protracted, even generational, socialization. Yet I am impressed by the rapidity and eagerness with which political actors seem to have learned the ropes of the democratic game in recent transitions.

Nor is there anything particularly surprising about this alacrity. On the contrary, its absence would strike me as surprising. Since democracies have been around for quite a while, since the examples of how to succeed or how to fail are abundant, and since there is an investment in succeeding, any ambitious political actor who does not want to be left behind must be a quick study. Democratic Spain is the best, though hardly the sole example of effective learning. If Spain, why not Eastern Europe? Indeed, Eastern Europeans have already begun to look to Spain as a model. Nor should we forget that, committed as they are to the removal of all vestiges of communism, East Europeans have shown an equally strong commitment to the reconstitution of a diverse and tolerant community.

If aspiring democrats can learn the ropes, so also can incumbents change their tune—and possibly be rewarded for it, too. Vested institutional interests, such as the interest that incumbents have in their own incumbency, are not immutable. A regime transition is by definition a time when what Guillermo O'Donnell and Philippe Schmitter call "normal social science methodology"—scholarly reliance on enduring group interests, structures, and values to predict behavior—is no longer useful.[6] In the "destructured" context of transitions, these things may cease to work as valid predictors. Perceptions of interest change, class alliances may be suspended, institutional identities may lose their appeal, cultural values may no longer instruct. Except for a few die-hards, incumbents will be guided by their shifting perceptions of costs, benefits, and the behavior of others.

Once again, the reason why incumbents modify their behavior is of little moment. If nothing else convinces them to change, then stalemate, material and political costs that far exceed returns, and a collapse of goals and will may persuade them to give way. This seems to be the case in Eastern Europe.

Incumbents who modify their behavior in response to the predicaments I just described may not desire democracy, but may nonetheless back into it. They may believe that a few liberalization measures will suffice, only to discover the truth of Tocqueville's observation that oppressive regimes are in greatest danger precisely when they begin to relax their grip. The need for further reforms may become more compelling, and further reform may be initiated, if not by the same incumbents, then perhaps by other incumbents with more innovative dispositions. Thus, what starts as an effort by the old regime to rescue itself may take an unintended and quite different direction. Because East European regimes have suffered not merely a stalemate but a devastating failure of goals and will, this scenario may fit the region quite well.

"Given the spirit of abdication displayed by Eastern Europe's communist regimes ...the point of no return on the path to democratization is at hand in the region."

The more the reforms inch toward democratization, the more a bandwagon effect may take hold. More cautious members of the regime, reluctant at first to support reform, may find it harder and harder to stay on the sidelines. So even if tactical liberalization proves insufficient to rescue the regime, the mounting pace of reform may have rendered the option of retrenchment too costly to embrace. The lack of acceptable and workable conservative alternatives may play a part in creating such a bandwagon effect.

The availability of clear conservative alternatives seems absolutely essential for those who would arrest the momentum of democratization. Without them, there is too much risk of missing out on what could turn out to be the only game in town. Lacking alternatives to propose, regime hard-liners may grumble and denounce reforms but end up voting for them. It happened when the Spanish Cortes approved the *Ley para la reforma politica* in 1976. It is now happening in Eastern Europe and—most clearly and most tellingly—in the Soviet Union as well.

It follows from this that the likelihood of antidemocratic backlashes has been exaggerated. The record of military coups may seem ominous, but it does not take into account nonevents: cases where the military complied with reforms, where coup threats were not carried out, or where coups failed. Such nonevents often go unnoticed or make little impression. Still, they show that when backlashes become sufficiently risky, hard-liners, foot-draggers, and nostalgics may prefer to express their discontent not through armed revolt, but through the new political channels that democratization is creating. To borrow Hirschman's terminology, "voice" may replace "exit." Not surprisingly, the venting of "voice" will create an impression of instability and irresoluteness. We should, however, be able to separate impression from substance.

Given the spirit of abdication displayed by Eastern Europe's communist regimes, the apparent unavailability of East European armies for coup activities, and much else that I have argued above, it seems to me that—save for Romania—the point of no return on the path to democratization is at hand in the region.

Extreme discontent about economic hardships possibly brought about or aggravated by democratization will not normally be enough to turn people against democratization. Support for democratization also comes from an appreciation of democracy as a civic conquest: as *the* method for reconstituting a diverse political community. In the years between the two world wars, when democracy was most seriously challenged by totalitarian models, disaffection from democracy was not generally highest where its material performance was poorest. Disaffection was most severe where, for other reasons, alternative totalitarian models had made great inroads. By the same token, when democracy is on the rebound (as it is now), and when no other significant models are offered, democratic legitimacy need not be closely tied to what democracy can deliver in material goods. Research on Spain in the late 1970s and early 1980s shows that while confidence in democracy's economic performance ebbed over the years, support for the new regime was not affected by it. In Eastern Europe, where the people took to the streets not for bread but for political dignity, the prospects of democracy should not be linked simply to material performance.

Civil Society and the Market

When it comes to choosing between democracy and its alternatives, Eastern Europe is already reaching a point of no return; this does not, however, necessarily mean that democracy in Eastern Europe will have an easy life. We may agree now—although by no means would we have agreed some months ago—that at least in four East European countries (Poland, Hungary, Czechoslovakia, and what used to be East Germany) there is no prospect of a return to communism. We may equally agree now—but again, would not have agreed some months ago—that in the short run there is no significant alternative to democracy. But are the conditions present to sustain democracy in the long run?

We are told in this regard that civil society and the market are vital to democracy—that there can be no democracy without a civil society, and no civil society without a market. But this is the language of prerequisites, which implies sequential evolution over time. Even assuming that this is normally the case, the sequence may be reversed when overdetermining events deflect the course of history, as they are now doing in Eastern Europe. Under these circumstances, democracy emerges first as a conscious choice, made by aspiring democrats as well as many others. Once democracy has thus been chosen, its preservation demands the creation of a market; the creation of a market then becomes virtually inevitable. The conventional argument is that because in Eastern Europe we have not only a political transition but also a socioeconomic one, this double feat is especially difficult. We may as well argue the opposite. It is precisely the close and unprecedented connection between a political and a socioeconomic transition that, instead of jeopardizing both, may help the latter ride piggyback on the former.

Besides, the suggestion that Eastern Europe has hardly any market-oriented interests traps us in an intellectual corner. On the basis of such reasoning, the rise of the market in early modern Europe would be utterly inexplicable. Yet the comparative advantage of the market and bandwagon effects still won out over feudal resistance. Eastern Europe's advantage over early modern Europe is that it does not have to reinvent the wheel, for today everyone knows how the market works. Thus the decision for the market is largely a political one: not *whether* to introduce the market, but *how* to introduce it. The great desideratum now is to choose a process such that the inevitable losers, both from the old regime and society, will be few, unable to arrest the process, and eventually interested in joining the very market they now disdain. But these are policy matters; they presuppose the invalidity of the claim that in a marketless society nobody can desire the market.

The notion that without a market there cannot be a vital civil society also needs fine-tuning. Although true in the long run, it does not imply that the market must come first; in fact, civil society may be instrumental in preparing the cultural and associational terrain for a market. Again, the case of early modern Europe is suggestive. Some students of modern Europe see civil society as a product of the market, while others see the market as the offspring of a secularized civil society born from the cultural and religious ferment of the Protestant Reformation. Still others see modern civil society as a political reaction to bureaucratic absolutism. And yet another school locates the roots of both civil society and the market in the medieval legacy of religious, urban, and peasant associations.

In the case of communist and marketless Eastern Europe, the striking thing is the way that dissent, working against overwhelming odds, continued to cultivate the art of association as an existential response to communism. Can this art not be put to good use in an Eastern Europe now seeking the market?

In this regard, concerns that the civic legacy of dissent will quickly dissipate once communism is gone are also exaggerated. It may be true that, unlike their Western counterparts, democratic oppositions in Eastern Europe had no tradition of political parties, organized interests, and social formations behind them. But the dissidents of Eastern Europe did something that hardly any opposition to Western dictatorships did. Instead of building clandestine and conspiratorial organizations, they deliberately and successfully strove to build a fairly open and visible parallel society. Conceding this, some scholars such as Jacques Rupnik raise the question of how "practitioners of moral indignation [can] turn into professional politicians who can orchestrate the compromises of everyday life."[7] They can, for the expression of their indignation was anything but contemplative, involving instead some very practical collective behavior aimed at reviving public opinion as a critical and influential interlocutor of communist power. Poland is exemplary in this regard.

This raises another consideration concerning the supposedly spent legacy of dissent. There exist striking similarities between the political style of East European dissent and that of the emerging political movements of postmaterialist Western Europe. In both cases—and contrary to the classic case of movements at the dawn of mass politics—what these movements seek is less political recognition for some distinctive social groups and their associated parties than the recognition of issues that often cut across conventional social cleavages.

Do the new movements of Western Europe have a recognizable social and subcultural basis? Not any more than East European dissent does. Do they suffer from this? Apparently not. In the past, political mobilization rested on the strength of its social base; now it is coming to rest on individually available educational, intellectual, and informational resources. It is becoming "cognitive mobilization." Participation in competitive politics in Western Europe has become more a matter of personal choice and personal involvement.

Thus while Eastern Europe might suffer from its lack of partisan-organizational traditions, it may benefit from the opportunity to tap into a new style of West European politics that dissidence has in some ways already prepared it for. As the 40-year-old ice cap of totalitarian communism continues to melt, East European civil societies may draw special strength from a synergy of domestic impulses and foreign examples. So the legacy of dissent may not be in jeopardy after all.

The Legacy of Dissent

Though East European societies suffer from relative backwardness, the legacy of dissent may help them to escape the dire prophecies of the theorists of backwardness. By deciding to make civil society, rather than the state, the force behind Eastern Europe's regeneration, the dissidents have made an explicitly anti-Leninist choice. It is above all a cultural and indeed a moral choice, one that is very unusual in cases where intellectual mobilization against autocratic and retrograde rule has drawn its inspiration from advanced foreign models.

Most often in such cases, intellectual mobilization comes under the sway of chauvinistic and politically expedient desires to "catch up," which in turn lead to political, institutional, and social distortions unfavorable to the growth of a vital and differentiated civil society. In our case, however, dissidence has instead opted to speak in a selfless and typically Western civic language. It is a language that entrusts progress not to development policies and statism, but to the proper constitution of citizens' relations with one another. It is also a universal language.

What we may be witnessing in Eastern Europe, without quite realizing it, is the birth of a new structure of normative thought. Never in previous transitions to democracy has the proper constitution of civil society been made so central—not in southern Europe, not in Latin America, not even in the resistance to Fascism and Nazism.

The civic legacy of dissent may also endure because of the support that the East European civic revolutions have received from the rest of Europe, and from prevailing views favorable to democracy and a new cooperative European order. To be sure, the support that Europe lends should be more than merely moral. As Andrew Janos has suggested, new international regimes may yet help rescue new and weaker democracies from the vagaries of international economics and politics and from the traps of backwardness. Such was the case with postwar Western Europe, and with southern Europe in the 1970s. If placed in the context of a larger Europe, the new civic culture of Eastern Europe might even curb the threat of chauvinistic nationalism, which could otherwise be ignited by the political frictions to which backwardness gives rise.

NOTES

1. The best analysis of paths and conditions is in Robert A. Dahl, *Polyarchy: Participation and Opposition* (New Haven: Yale University Press, 1971). See also Samuel P. Huntington, "Will More Countries Become Democratic?" *Political Science Quarterly* 99 (Summer 1984): 193-218.

2. Timothy Garton Ash, "Eastern Europe: The Year of Truth," *New York Review of Books*, 15 February 1990, 18.

3. Cited in ibid., 18.

4. Ibid., 18, 21.

5. Albert O. Hirschman, *A Bias for Hope* (New Haven: Yale University Press, 1971), 321-25. Research on Spain shows that Spaniards who sympathized with the Franco regime are not necessarily hostile to the new democracy. Spaniards regard the two regimes as distinct experiences, and judge them on the basis of different orientations and expectations about government. See Peter McDonough, Samuel H. Barnes, and Antonio López Pina, "The Growth of Democratic Legitimacy in Spain," *American Political Science Review* 80 (September 1986): 735-60.

6. Guillermo O'Donnell and Philippe Schmitter, *Transitions from Authoritarian Rule: Tentative Conclusions about Uncertain Democracies* (Baltimore: Johns Hopkins University Press, 1986), Chapter 1.

7. Jacques Rupnik, *The Other Europe* (New York: Pantheon, 1989), 270.

24.
THE POSTREVOLUTIONARY HANGOVER

Leszek Kolakowski

Leszek Kolakowski, a leading critic of the Communist regime in Poland in the 1950s and 1960s, was expelled from the University of Warsaw in 1968 and emigrated to the West. He is a senior research fellow at All Souls College, Oxford University, and a member of the Committee on Social Thought at the University of Chicago.

The extraordinary events of the last two years in Central Europe have resulted in Himalayas of print, and it is hardly possible to add anything new or original. Nonetheless, I want to present a few thoughts concerning the postrevolutionary hangover in Central Europe. In fact, this hangover was unavoidable. There has never been a successful revolution (bloody or not) that has not produced massive disappointment almost at the very moment of its victory. This was inevitable because, in order to mobilize the amount of social energy necessary to overthrow a well-established order, people must have extremely inflated hopes—hopes that simply cannot be realized. The discrepancy between such expectations and the postrevolutionary reality is bound to be very large, yet prerevolutionary self-deceptions are a necessary condition of success.

It was predictable and predicted that in all the countries of Central Europe the unity of the democratic opposition, once cemented by a common adversary, would fall apart soon after the communist regime had been defeated. Distinct ideas, mentalities, and interests, which were previously more or less hidden, would come to the surface. There is nothing calamitous in this. Rather, it should be considered a return to what we may call normality in the Western sense. Alas, normality is still far away. In Poland, there are about 150 political parties, only a few of which have any electoral significance and none of which, it seems, has an impressive membership.

It was no less predictable and predicted that the obstacles in the path of economic reform would be immense, but how immense they would turn out to be could not have been predicted. The transition to a market economy with a substantial private sector is easier said than done. There has never been a historical precedent for this sort of transition, and everything had to be improvised on the spot. What was needed was no less than the rediscovery of money. The point was not simply to limit inflation, but to put into place mechanisms that would make it possible to know what things cost. Under the old command economies, prices were arbitrarily set by central planners; nobody knew the real cost of anything. Since the market is the only reliable source of information about prices, the freeing of prices was a fundamental condition of reform, but it had bad sides as well. The immediate results were a decline in most people's living standards and a rise in unemployment. Taxation measures designed to prevent an increase in wages provoked widespread discontent and strikes. Among Polish workers one may even hear voices claiming that things were better under the Communists, when there was no fear of unemployment. About politics they say, "We couldn't care less."

This does not mean, of course, that Poland or any other country in Central Europe is threatened by a mounting wave of communist sympathizers. The situation provides fertile ground, however, for all sorts of demagogues promising people that all social and economic problems can be solved in no time. Freeing prices was a necessary, but by no means sufficient condition of the transition. A great deal of national wealth, including large parts of industry and parts of agriculture, is still in the hands of the state. Ownership titles are often very unclear, as are legal rules dealing with business and privatization, which might frighten off foreign investors.

The denationalization process does not necessarily imply that everything must be privatized as a matter of rigid dogma. State-owned companies can coexist with a market economy, as the experience of Western Europe shows. The extent of state intervention is a contentious issue between movements with a more or less social democratic leaning and the die-hard Hayekians. It is certainly arguable that market forces themselves do not automatically solve all social problems.

The communist heritage survives not only in the economy and in political institutions, but in minds as well. The workers want to have shares in their companies' profits and to remove restrictions on profits, but they would also like to have guarantees against unemployment. The peasants want to have freedom of trade for their products, but demand that the state fix minimum prices for agricultural commodities and protect them from imports by high tariffs. The intelligentsia enjoys the regained freedom of speech and print, but also wants lavish state patronage of cultural goods.

All these conflicts can be solved only by more or less awkward compromises. One cannot have the best of both worlds. Above all, establishing a strong rule of law turned out to be less easy than expected after decades of a system in which the party leadership had been practically unrestrained by law. Again, everybody is for the rule of law, but it is easier said than done. One may reasonably hope that this messy state of affairs will eventually be put in order, but it will take years. Still, I do not believe that Poland or Czechoslovakia or Hungary is threatened with a kind of dictatorship as a solution for what might occasionally seem intractable chaos. Political vitality in these countries is too widely dispersed, and there do not seem to be dictators in waiting among the really important political elite.

"In a totalitarian or semi-totalitarian regime with an obligatory ideology, intellectuals can achieve a kind of socially privileged position that they cannot keep in a democratically ordered society."

Among the victims of communism's ongoing demise is the extraordinary alliance of workers and intelligentsia that was once embodied in Poland's Solidarity movement. This holy grail of democratic opposition was actually found in 1980 and functioned quite well during the military dictatorship and thereafter. It lost its old meaning, however, under the new conditions. Solidarity is still in search of a new identity now that its previous role as a broad civil rights movement encompassing all sorts of political, cultural, and economic grievances and aspirations has come to an inevitable end. In a totalitarian or semi-totalitarian regime with an obligatory ideology, intellectuals can achieve a kind of socially privileged position that they cannot keep in a democratically ordered society. In communist regimes, the workers can strike if the system is already weakened, whereas intellectuals can speak as individuals or small groups and make their voices audible and significant. They can contribute to the corrosion of the system by individual acts.

One can predict that this privileged role of intellectuals will end in the coming years with the return to normality. Professional politicians will probably replace writers, historians, actors, and professors in the political machinery. It needs stressing, however, that Poland, in contrast to other former Soviet protectorates, succeeded in creating not only a politically active class of intellectuals but a political worker elite as well, which might conceivably shorten the process of reconstruction.

I would like to conclude by making three polemical remarks that do not seem to be out of place. First, the present situation in Poland emerged from the long series of negotiations between the opposition and the Communist party and government early in 1989. At that time, there was a vocal minority of people both in Poland and elsewhere who were hostile to the very idea of negotiating and making deals with communists. This minority now believes that their resistance has been vindicated because communism collapsed anyway, and because the negotiations weakened the opposition by needless compromises and soiled it by dirty deals with the enemy. I consider this position wrong; today it reflects mainly the frustration of those whom the political process left behind.

It is true that in the years 1987-89 communist rule was clearly enfeebled, even though nobody could imagine the pace of its future disintegration. But the decisive moment in the disintegration of communism was the Polish elections of June 1989, only partially free for the parliament and entirely free for the upper chamber. The results of these elections were so shattering, so devastating that the Communist Party simply collapsed, and the first non-Communist government was formed. But the elections were a direct result of negotiations and could not have been organized in any other way. Without them the disintegration of communism would probably have been much more complicated and possibly bloody. As a result of the way the whole process began, Poland was left behind by other countries that followed it in a domino effect. They could benefit from their position as latecomers, whereas Poland was left for some time with a parliament in which 65 percent of the members were Communist nominees (even though hardly anybody among them would still define himself now as a Communist).

It is plausible to believe that Gorbachev's intention at the beginning was simply to replace particularly compromised and hated leaders like Ceauşescu, Honecker, or Husák by another and presumably more flexible team of so-called reform communists. Eventually, he probably realized that this would not work and that keeping the party in power, while perhaps feasible, would demand a price he was unable to pay: the total destruction of everything he was trying to accomplish in his own country. The 1989 "roundtable talks" in Poland set in motion the entire wheel of crashing changes. To say now that one should not have negotiated because communism broke down anyway is like saying, "You should not have killed the tiger because you see that the tiger is dead anyway."

Second, since Gorbachev first came to power in 1985 there have been those people who insisted that both *perestroika* and the changes in international communism were no more than a gigantic hoax designed to get U.S. troops out of Europe on the pretext that the Cold War had ended, leaving the continent ripe for Soviet domination. Everything, they averred, was planned in advance in order to keep communist power intact under the false light of *glasnost* and various pseudo-changes. Incredibly enough, there are still people who continue to assert this interpretation of events, which I think now borders on insanity. It is clear that nothing was planned in advance (or at least that whatever was planned went wrong), and that Gorbachev reacted to unexpected events in haste without knowing what would happen next; that there was no super brain that organized everything for the benefit of Soviet power, no cunning super magician who pulled strings and moved the puppets before the eyes of the dazed audience. The collapse of communism in Central Europe is *real*, and those who refuse to recognize this have a mindset that is a mirror image of the communist way of thinking. According to the communist doctrine of old, capitalism cannot really be reformed, only destroyed in a revolutionary cataclysm. So now communism, according to the doctrine noted above, cannot be changed and finally fall apart through bloodless pressure, but can only be crushed in a violent upheaval. To cling to this ideology now, I think, is a symptom of doctrinal blindness.

My final remark is directed at the army of Sovietologists who for years and years, starting with Khrushchev's time, kept repeating that the communist system was getting better and better every day. Whoever was in power or came to power at a given moment—Brezhnev or Andropov or Gorbachev—opened an era of great promise. Most Sovietologists, of course, stopped short of claiming that the Soviet system was a splendid model lighting a radiant pathway for mankind. They simply tried to convince us that the system was becoming more and more democratic, more and more pluralistic, and more and more rational with every passing night. Moreover, they were usually ill-disposed if not downright hostile to the emerging democratic opposition (or the dissenters) in the Soviet Union and its satellites because such movements, according to their theory, hampered the natural tendency of communism to democratize itself and placed obstacles in the path of the Soviet vehicle's rush toward glorious "convergence." These Sovietologists kept explaining to us—until quite recently—that there were not the slightest symptoms of instability, let alone of crisis or disintegration, in the Soviet Union.

But to dismiss some implausible interpretations of events is not to come up with a credible prediction for the future. We cannot avoid the temptation of playing fortune teller, but we know that we do not possess this most desirable gift. It is plausible to think that the coming years will not bring any radical solutions to the recently decommunized countries. Instead, these countries will keep riding down a very bumpy road without either perishing or finding perfection.

25.
AFTER THE MOSCOW COUP

Charles H. Fairbanks, Jr.

Charles H. Fairbanks, Jr., *research professor of international relations at the Paul H. Nitze School of Advanced International Studies of Johns Hopkins University, is working on a book on Soviet bureaucracy. His article, "The Suicide of Soviet Communism," appeared in the Spring 1990 issue of the* Journal of Democracy.

In the wake of this past August's failed coup, the issues in Soviet politics have become clearer. The confusions sown by Gorbachev's maneuvers and compromises have lost their power to obscure what is truly at stake. The vestiges of the old communist order tried to arrest the country's drift into catastrophe by closing off the democratic opening. The partisans of democracy rose up to stop them while the rest of Soviet society passively looked on.

The coup was the old communist elites' last-ditch bid to reverse their loss of power at "the center." But they did not rise in the name of communism or the Communist Party (CPSU); the documents they issued during their 70 hours of power make no references to communism, socialism, Marxism-Leninism, the masses, or most of the other familiar terms. None of the coup leaders was a member of the CPSU's Politburo or Secretariat, and neither the all-Union nor the Russian Party issued an official statement during the coup. While several Party structures were obviously involved in the putsch, the Party could no longer lead it. Gorbachev had forced the Party to give up its title to rule and its mechanisms of rule in February-July 1990.[1]

The elites that attempted the coup had long been restive, but by mid-1991 they had lost hope that Gorbachev would ask them to step in and take over, and their loyalty to him was gone. The betrayal of Gorbachev is indeed astonishing in extent. On Sunday, August 18, Gorbachev was general secretary of the CPSU, president of the USSR, commander-in-chief of the armed forces, and chairman of the Defense Council. Under the Leninist doctrine of democratic centralism, every one of the Party's 100,000 paid employees owed him obedience. In all of the Russian

Republic, not one of these officials is known to have come forward to defend him. As president, Gorbachev legally commanded millions of state officials, yet he was betrayed not only by his hand-picked defense minister, KGB chief, and prime minister, but by his own chief of staff, Valery Boldin, who had for years controlled both the information that reached Gorbachev and the documents that went from him to lower officials; by his vice-president, Gennady Yanayev, personally elevated by Gorbachev over the wishes of an unwilling Supreme Soviet; and by Anatoly Lukyanov, the leader of the Supreme Soviet, his protégé and college roommate. When the 21 members of the Cabinet of Ministers (outside the national security area), created less than a year ago by Gorbachev in the latest of his constitutional schemes, met to discuss the coup, only 2 opposed it, while 14 approved it unambiguously.

Of the governments of the republics, apparently so rebellious, only Russia, the three Baltic states, and Moldavia clearly resisted the first attempt to put the military behind the revival of the center. The Ukrainian and Byelorussian leaders initially expressed approval, while the leaders of the other republics (including the noncommunist presidents of Armenia, Georgia, and Kirghizia) equivocated until it became clear who would win. Some Russian local and provincial governments opposed the coup, and so did some of the coal miners and the people in the streets of Moscow and Leningrad. The opposition rallied behind Yeltsin, not Gorbachev. The first armed challenge left Gorbachev virtually alone.

Thus the coup made clear that the outwardly imposing political structure being renovated by Gorbachev was already rotting away beneath the surface. To tumble it down required only a puff of wind.

This fact is important in a way that goes far beyond the coup and its immediate effects. Modern states rest less on palpable things, like buildings and tanks, than on habits of obedience and accountability that link higher and lower officials in a governmental machine organized by laws and rules, and on the political culture that supports these laws and rules. During the coup, the ties that linked the parts of the government failed on a massive scale, just as they crumbled during the collapse of the Czarist regime and then the Provisional Government in 1917-18. What the coup made manifest was a growing disintegration of the state. Gorbachev has said, quite rightly, that *perestroika* is a revolution. In some revolutions, a new group simply takes over the old state apparatus; in others, the apparatus disintegrates and has to be rebuilt by the victors. It is clearer and clearer that the Soviet revolution is of the second type, the type that disrupts life much more fundamentally and offers far harder challenges to the new rulers.

The coup failed because it had weak, indecisive leaders who were neither communist nor anticommunist; because most of them were unwilling to kill; and because it had no active public support. But most of all, the coup failed because the institutions behind it were divided; the minister of defense and the chairman of the KGB gave orders, but their respective subordinates down through the ranks made their own decisions about whether to obey, to back Yeltsin, or to remain neutral (probably the most frequent response). Many changed their minds with the drift of events. Officials ranging from then-foreign minster Bessmertnykh to the chief of Gorbachev's bodyguard went into seclusion, using illness as an excuse. In many places, such as Leningrad, supporters of the two sides made private truces behind the backs of their nominal leaders. At the risk of oversimplification, one might say that the coup took place because of the disintegration of the state, and then failed because of the disintegration of the state. This disintegration (including that of the Party apparatus) is the basic condition under which democracy-building must now take place.

> *"...the coup took place because of the disintegration of the state, and then failed because of the disintegration of the state."*

We have been slow to see this because we have focused on the headlines about friction between the declining central government and the resurgent republics. In fact, similar tensions exist at the provincial level in most of the republics. In the Russian Republic, for example, many of the "autonomous" provinces (such as the Tartar republic) want to escape Russian control by becoming Union republics, while many purely Russian provinces are refusing to send food to other provinces or threatening to interrupt trade and communications within Russia until their various demands are satisfied. In Moscow itself, the reformist leaders of certain districts have claimed a right to disobey their fellow reformists in the larger city government. The coup and its failure showed similar breakdowns of hierarchy within bureaucracies located in one place. It is becoming a political war of all against all.

Given what is happening to the Soviet Union, it is worth asking whether we have paid enough attention to the problem of democracy-building under conditions of state disintegration. Most recent transitions to democracy have relied on basic continuities in civil bureaucracies and lower-to-middle-level political structures. These transitions were either very rapid or slow and controlled. If they were slow and controlled, new structures and habits had time to take root and grow. If change was rapid, as in Eastern Europe, the existing structures and habits could be transferred intact to the new regime. The East European cases are closer to the Soviet case than many others, but with important differences in the speed of the transition process, the size and relative ethnic homogeneity (in most cases) of the nation-state, and the degree of legitimacy enjoyed by communist rule. Eastern Europe's communist governments had so little legitimacy that they existed side-by-side with "counterstates," whether embodied in institutions like Solidarity and the

Polish Catholic Church or simply latent in the consciousness of society, as in East Germany, Hungary, and Czechoslovakia.

In the Soviet Union, the transition has been slow, but uncontrolled; Gorbachev's "revolution within the Revolution" turned into a revolution *against* the Revolution. The USSR has never had a real civil service (a little-known fact), and the rule of law is feebly developed. More generally, the Soviet governmental structure lacks the "fixed jurisdictional areas" attributed to the modern state by Max Weber, a lack traceable in part to the presence of parallel state and Party authorities for each area of public business. Only with *glasnost'* are we getting a sense of the "premodern" character of Soviet governance, of its disorganization, informality, and arbitrariness.[2]

These structures were failing in many areas as long ago as the Brezhnev era, and the current upheaval has weakened them even further. The collapse of the Union government and the CPSU has wreaked administrative havoc: the Union government (not the republics) ran most of the economy, while the Party apparatus was the real government in the provinces. Even before the coup, this growing administrative chaos was threatening to overwhelm the nascent drive toward democracy, and it will continue to imperil democratic development.

Breaking the Stalemate

Democracy does have significant resources, including the leadership of Boris Yeltsin, who emerged from the coup as the heroic standardbearer of liberty. He has become a champion of democracy and the market, but has the *apparatchik*'s frown and air of concentrated will—still regarded in Russia as the marks of a real leader. Yeltsin can vary, as the situation requires, between brutality, typified by his public humiliation of the newly rescued Gorbachev, and a sense of the practical: he knew that Gorbachev's original attempt to solve the nationalities problem through a union treaty would instead create endless difficulties. Yeltsin is particularly adept at anticipating shifts of public opinion and at framing issues to his advantage.

Yeltsin's greatest achievement was to wrest Russian nationalism from the grip of authoritarians and anti-Semites and make it work for the democratic side. Moreover, the cowardice shown during the coup by many of the leaders of the non-Russian republics bolsters the claim that "Russia saved the Union." Now the democratic cause seems to justify the stature that the Russians will inevitably have by virtue of their numbers and relative modernity.

The coup became a public drama that symbolically cemented the identity of the public (and the Russian nation) with democracy. Henceforth Russians will not be in the position of having their freedom handed to them by someone else. Yeltsin and the heroes who defended the Russian Parliament have given Russia the makings of a democratic history. The noble scene of Russians rallying around their parliament's "White House" and waving the old tricolor flag presents a sweet irony: the banner of the Emperor and Autocrat of all the Russias, designed by the cruel Czar Peter the Great, at that moment became a symbol of freedom.

All this is solid gain, but still more important is the occasion—eagerly seized by Yeltsin—that the coup provided to smash the power of the Communist Party apparatus and its remaining strongholds: the KGB, the Interior Ministry, the army, and the defense industries. Gorbachev engineered the suicide of the Communist Party, but refused to bury it. The CPSU, emptied of significant reformers, still clung obstinately to power. It could no longer be a force for change, but it could not be displaced as long as it maintained the charade that it was only one political party among many contending in the democratic process. The party benefitted from the fear prominent democrats had of lapsing into "neo-Bolshevism," a broad label that covered any political practices (from the use of illegal measures and violence to mere assertions of one's own correctness and one's opponents' error) that evoked the bad old days of Communist rule.

The coup broke the spell. Its leaders are under arrest; the Communist Party has been banned in Russia and some other republics, its publications shut down, its property sequestered and under legal assault. Some of these measures are questionable, and some are surely temporary. On balance, however, there can be no doubt that Yeltsin was right to break the stalemate in which the democrats had legitimacy but no power because the antidemocrats were exploiting democratic scruples in order to shield power gained through intimidation and violence. Few nations have ever won their freedom without resort to something resembling Yeltsin's means.

Perils and Opportunities

The debacle in which the coup ended has greatly increased the likelihood of a lasting democratic transformation in Russia. Yet enormous difficulties remain, including problems posed by the army; by the vestiges of the Communist Party apparatus; by Gorbachev; by ethnic tensions; by political culture; by the disintegration of the state; by the weakness of democratic political parties; and finally, by the acid test of performance.

The secret police can be destroyed, but no superpower can decree, as the ruler of Egypt did after a coup in 1882, that "the army is hereby dissolved." As the ultimate source of state power, the armed forces are dangerous in any situation of civil disorder. In the Soviet Union, they are also a sump into which surviving authoritarian attitudes are draining.

Military life requires discipline, and all democracies must face the problem of settling the relationship between a necessarily authoritarian military and its democratic environment. In the Soviet system, this problem lay dormant because communism militarized the whole of public life; the official press would speak of "the cultural front," and of fruit-growing as a "shock sector." As public life is demilitarized, the soldiers are finding themselves in a world more and more alien to their attitudes and aspirations. There is a cultural chasm between democrats, including Yeltsin, and the military. Military officers, who are among the few people in the USSR who move from place to place with their jobs, have a psychological investment in the Union as opposed to any specific republic or locality. Although the coup revealed surprising sympathy for Yeltsin in the officer corps, a democratic Russia will probably still have to confront the problem that Weimar Germany and post-World War II France faced: a military establishment temperamentally out of harmony with the democratic regime.

Thus we may not have seen the last of Soviet coups. And because this coup destroyed the weary establishment that headed the military and the security services, the next putsch may be conducted with more competence and less restraint. One has the impression that many of the colonels, like Viktor Alksnis of the "Soyuz" movement, are more radical than the generals above them. More than one modernizing country has seen the pattern of a tentative, limited intervention in politics by senior generals that opens the way for radical junior officers. Turkey in 1908-13, China in 1911-31, Japan in the 1930s, and more recently Syria and Iraq all display variations on this pattern.

The second problem is posed by the lingering vestiges of the Communist Party apparatus. In the big cities, the Communist Party will dwindle into a tiny fringe group. But in smaller cities, in the countryside, and in the Muslim republics, it will live on in local "mafias"—groups of powerful people linked by tribal, clan, or patron-client ties—even as it officially sinks out of sight. We do not know how successful Yeltsin will be in extirpating these mafias, which are thought to control 60 to 70 percent of the local government units in the USSR. The examples of western Sicily, of the Philippines, and of Central America indicate that it may actually become harder to root out such local mafias after their loss of formal political power. This problem will have consequences for national politics. In a democratic Russia, local machines will be useful for delivering votes, but ex-Communist bosses may prefer not to deliver them to democrats. We need to inform Soviet democrats about historical cases in which regions dominated by nondemocratic politics (the American South, the Italian *mezzogiorno*) were somehow incorporated into larger democratic systems.

Third, there is the problem of Mikhail Gorbachev, who has lost nearly all of whatever prestige he still retained at the time of the coup. If he declines the role of "constitutional monarch" and seeks instead to compete politically against Yeltsin, Gorbachev must look for support mainly in the non-Russian republics (where democracy is often weak and communism still not extinct) and from those who favored the coup. Gorbachev's sincere refusal to forswear "socialism" has already opened up this ominous possibility.

> *"The democratic opposition's success...should not blind us to the thinness of Yeltsin's actual support."*

Fourth, the many-headed nationalities problem will not be resolved by the independence of the republics. Ethnic tensions exist not only between republics, but within republics as well. The wrangling that is now going on between the republics and the weakening center is only Act I of the drama. Act II will pit Russia, now dominant and again asserting its claims to control the surviving structures of central authority and to revise borders, against most of the other republics plus the vestiges of the all-Union government. Interrepublican tensions will then become entangled with ethnic conflicts inside republics. Kazakhstan, for instance, is home to more Slavs than Kazakhs, but the latter were there first, and aspire to guide the republic's politics and culture. This situation is a ticking time bomb. If it has not thus far exploded, it is because the local political bosses, working within the rigid limits of communist politics, managed to cobble together political machines that combined Kazakhs and Russians in a delicate balance and hid ethnic tensions from view. It is not likely that such artificial solutions will long survive the extinction of communism or the advent of democracy.

A fifth problem is that of political culture. The democratic opposition's success, and the absence of visible public support for the coup, should not blind us to the thinness of Yeltsin's actual support. The brave crowds that took to the streets of Moscow and Leningrad (and at times dwindled, according to some observers, to only a few thousand) and the coal miners were Yeltsin's main resources. His call for a general strike failed (perhaps because of poor communications). Not even the Moscow Soviet supported the strike call, and even in the Kuzbass—the citadel of working-class democratic sentiment—only some of the mines were shut down. The events of late August established that the fraction of the public that is passionately engaged in politics belongs to the democratic camp. Yet nothing happened to contradict the longstanding impression that the bulk of the population is politically passive.

Sixth, there is the above-mentioned disintegration of the state to contend with. To carry out his policies and tackle the country's desperate problems, Yeltsin needs a reliable administrative machine. He lacks one now, and is trying to fill the gap by taking over institutions that belong legally to the Union. After the failed coup his efforts will proceed with less hindrance but will remain intrinsically difficult. Creating a state out of chaos is no easy task.

Seventh, Yeltsin does not have a party system to give him a solid footing in this political quicksand. The existing democratic parties are very small, and no one knows what will happen, in the new atmosphere, to the party that Shevardnadze, Yakovlev, and others were planning to launch before the coup. Without a strong party organization, Yeltsin will remain a charismatic leader orating in a void. The democratic world outside Russia has a responsibility to convey the experience of parties both to Yeltsin, who has preferred to stand above party, and to other democrats for whom party politics means dozens of tiny parties that in practice are little more than intellectual coteries.

Ultimately, any of these problems could turn deadly if Yeltsin fails to perform ably as a ruler—especially if he fails to turn the economy around. The coup plotters, after all, did make one point that was irrefutable: Gorbachev was leading the country toward catastrophe. A similar performance by Yeltsin is likely to provoke another coup. Yeltsin's administrative skill is largely untested, but it is clear that from now on he will have to bear the responsibility that until last August 18 rested with Mikhail Gorbachev. The credibility of democracy and the market hangs on the outcome. In a centrally planned economy the disintegration of the state means economic collapse, and Yeltsin has no good models to consult: even the so-called 500-day plan was less a real plan than a direction—windy, vague, typically Soviet. Yeltsin and his advisors must come up with new economic models not in the study, but while simultaneously creating a government in the midst of disorder and an atmosphere of continuing crisis.

All things considered, it is difficult to be very sanguine. The euphoria felt by many in the West after the coup collapsed is understandable, but deeply misguided: the coup was a symptom of profound and still unresolved problems. If Russia's transition to democracy does succeed, it will not be through a velvet revolution, but only through difficult decisions and strong measures. Yet perhaps we can learn from the coup. What seemed to be a disaster was also a tremendous opportunity that Yeltsin shrewdly seized. Similarly, the dreadful hardships and terrible perils ahead will also present opportunities to gain distance from the oppressive legacy of communism, to display new-found strengths, and to define Russia anew.

NOTES

1. Charles H. Fairbanks, Jr. "The Suicide of Soviet Communism," *Journal of Democracy* 1 (Spring 1990): 18-26.

2. See Charles H. Fairbanks, Jr., "Bureaucratic Politics in the Soviet Union and in the Ottoman Empire," *Comparative Strategy* 6 (1987): 333-62; and "Jurisdictional Conflict and Coordination in Soviet and American Bureaucracy," *Studies in Comparative Communism* 21 (Summer 1988): 153-74.

26.
IS CHINA READY
FOR DEMOCRACY?

Andrew J. Nathan

Andrew J. Nathan is professor of political science at Columbia University. He is the author of Chinese Democracy *(1985) and coauthor of* Human Rights in Contemporary China *(1986). This essay is an updated version of a chapter in his latest book,* China's Crisis: Dilemmas of Reform and Prospects for Democracy, *1990, © Columbia University Press, New York. Reprinted with the permission of the publisher.*

The Chinese Communist regime has always claimed that China already has, in the words of Deng Xiaoping, the "broadest democracy that has ever existed in history," and that Western-style "bourgeois democracy" is not worth having anyway. But a contradictory theme lies beneath the surface of such defensive rhetoric. Deng has often argued that "national conditions" (*guoqing*, a code word for backwardness) do not allow China to have as much democracy as it would like.

"In our construction today," Deng said in 1979, "we must do things in accordance with Chinese conditions and find a Chinese-style path to modernization. . . . Departure from the four basic principles [socialism, Marx-Lenin-Mao Thought, dictatorship of the proletariat, and party leadership] and talk about democracy in the abstract will inevitably lead to the unchecked spread of ultra-democracy and anarchism." Speaking to George Bush in February 1989, just before the Chinese government interfered with Fang Lizhi's attendance at the U.S. president's banquet, Deng said, "If we were to run elections among China's one billion people now, chaos . . . would certainly ensue. . . . Democracy is our goal, but the state must maintain stability."[1]

This self-critical view of their capacity for democracy is widespread among Chinese of all political persuasions. The events of 1989, however, raise the question of whether it has become outdated. In December 1989, Taiwan carried out the first multiparty elections in Chinese history in an institutional setting that, although guaranteeing an overall victory for the ruling party, nonetheless allowed intense competition and substantial gains by the opposition. On the mainland, the massive demonstrations of last spring revealed a passionate and widespread yearning for democracy. After nearly a century of struggling for democracy, have the Chinese created the conditions for it? How might the transition occur? What would Chinese democracy be like?

Since Taiwan is culturally Chinese, its experience may help suggest what a Chinese form of democracy would be like. But it is a much smaller, richer, and more cosmopolitan place than mainland China. Would the mainland have to reach Taiwan's level of development before it could think of beginning a transition to democracy?

Social scientists have identified no absolute threshold of development required to qualify a people for democracy, but China is now clearly above the minimum level in simple economic terms and far above it with regard to social development and communication facilities. China's gross national product (GNP) per capita in 1980 was already above the level found in the three poorest stable democracies of the 1970s. By the end of the century, the figure may match or exceed the level enjoyed by the eight poorest democracies in the early 1970s (India, Sri Lanka, the Philippines, Turkey, Costa Rica, Jamaica, Chile, and Uruguay in ascending order of wealth).[2]

China is far more industrialized than the other poor and lower-middle income countries as measured by the proportion of gross domestic product (GDP) attributable to industry (nearly 50 percent). China's urbanites constitute between 12 and 32 percent of the population, depending on the definition used. Most of China's villages have schools, however rudimentary. The level of literacy revealed by the 1982 census was as high as or higher than that of India and Turkey. In 1985 the government extended the period of compulsory schooling to nine years, a measure that should gradually raise the average level of education even higher. Mass communication in the form of wired loudspeakers, radio, television, and newspapers penetrates into virtually every village and effectively reaches illiterates and people living in deserts or on steppes, and rivers.

In addition, despite recent trends toward increasing concentration of wealth, China still has a relatively equitable distribution, which is generally considered a helpful condition for democracy. It also has strong police and military institutions, which are as necessary for keeping the peace in a democracy as in a dictatorship.

Chinese Political Culture

The doubts of Chinese about their own capacity for democracy, however, center not on communication facilities or literacy but on political culture. The popular 1988 television series *River Elegy* typified this view, arguing that China's ancient, peasant-based civilization would doom it to poverty and autocracy until it was replaced by a modern culture. "This broad yellow earth of ours cannot teach us what is the true spirit of science; the devastating Yellow River cannot teach us what is the true mentality of democracy," the narrator states. China is an example of Marx's "Asiatic mode of production":

> Myriad unmentionably insignificant individuals, ranked and amalgamated into a unity by a certain order, bearing up that ultimate supreme entity—doesn't this monolithic social structure resemble a massive pyramid? Therefore such things as democracy, freedom, and equality could hardly come to belong to an 'Asiatic' [civilization like China].

According to Su Xiaokang, the main author of the screenplay, "What is needed is a reconstruction of the Chinese people's cultural-psychological structure."

After the suppression of the democracy movement, *People's Daily* denounced *River Elegy* for insulting the Chinese people and belittling their achievements under socialism. Yet the series' view of China's national character as the seedbed of dictatorship was shared by the regime. For example, the party's official inquest into the Mao era, published in 1981, laid the blame for Mao's errors mainly on the national characteristic of feudalism:

> Our Party fought in the firmest and most thoroughgoing way against [feudalism], and particularly against the feudal system of land ownership and the landlords and local tyrants, and fostered a fine tradition of democracy in the anti-feudal struggle. But it remains difficult to eliminate the evil ideological and political influence of centuries of feudal autocracy. . . . This meant that conditions were present for the overconcentration of party power in individuals and for the development of arbitrary individual rule and the personality cult in the Party. Thus, it was hard for the Party and state to prevent the initiation of the "cultural revolution" or check its development.[3]

In placing the responsibility for authoritarianism on Chinese national character, both the party and the democratic intellectuals transferred much of the onus for an acknowledged catastrophe from the shoulders of those who wrought it to the backs of those who suffered it. They perpetuated the belief that the Chinese people must be profoundly transformed before they will be qualified for democracy. What outraged the party elders about *River Elegy* was not its pessimism about Chinese culture but its authors' usurpation of the party's self-assigned mission of enlightening the Chinese people and the Westernizing character of the enlightenment they wanted to offer.

No one has ever drawn up an authoritative list of the cultural prerequisites of democracy. One scholar argues that democracy requires widespread acceptance of such values as dignity, autonomy, and respect for others; belief in individual rights; trust, tolerance, and willingness to compromise; commitment to democratic procedures and values; public spirit; and nationalism, among others.[4] An influential study of the political cultures of five democracies identified a number of attributes conducive to stable democracy, including a relatively high degree of consensus on some basic political values (including nationalism, modernization, and the desire for order); widespread acceptance of the present constitutional order as legitimate; and a certain degree of alienation from politics that reduces expectations directed at the political system.[5]

The Beijing demonstrations of 1989 put many of these attributes on display. The people of Beijing evidently desire democracy and freedom. They are nationalistic and concerned about politics. They are wary of government. They showed a capacity for public spiritedness, spontaneous yet orderly cooperation, and tolerance.

Encouraging Evidence

These may only be impressions, but some scientific evidence exists to support them. In December 1988, four months before the Tiananmen Square demonstrations, a pilot study for a scientific national sample survey was conducted in Beijing by Shi Tianjian, a Columbia University graduate student. The study was designed to collect, among other things, the first set of reliable data on the political attitudes of Chinese citizens. In the pilot study, Shi's respondents showed extremely high levels of attention to political news in newspapers and on radio and television. Seventy-seven percent of the respondents said they were interested in politics.

The respondents also demonstrated strong aspirations for more democracy. In a question on the role that the National People's Congress ought to play, 65 percent felt it should either "convey the masses' opinions to the government" or "set laws and represent the citizens in supervising government," while only small numbers assigned it more passive roles or felt unable to comment. Seventy-two percent agreed with the statement that "democracy is the best form of government," and 79 percent disagreed with the proposition, "If we implement democracy in our country now it will lead to chaos." At the same time, the questionnaire revealed a reservoir of trust in the government; for example, nearly half the respondents said they would expect to receive fair treatment if they sought the help of a government organ.

The picture created by this survey and by the events preceding the crackdown on 4 June 1989 in Beijing suggests that the Chinese people are proud of their country, have substantial political interest and knowledge, and retain considerable faith in socialism and the Communist Party. They strongly desire more freedom and democracy (although their ideas of democracy are not very specific); they are cynical about how much their own voices count in their local unit or in politics generally; and they are normally reluctant to buck the system by demonstrating or appealing vigorously for their rights when these are abused. This pattern of attitudes combines elements of what have been described as "aspirant" and "deferential" political cultures. If these attributes characterize Chinese political culture, they bode well for the functioning of a future democratic politics in China.

Democracy has been defined as a system of institutionalized uncertainty: "it is the act of alienation of control over outcomes of conflicts that constitutes the decisive step toward democracy."[6] Such a transition begins when the ruling elite, or a substantial section within it, perceives that the potential advantages of giving up some control over outcomes outweigh the risks. As an example of the kinds of conditions under which this may happen, it may be useful to look at the democratizing transition taking place in Taiwan.

Democratization in Taiwan

When president and Kuomintang (KMT) party chairman Chiang Ching-kuo embarked on political reform in 1986, Taiwan had reached a high level of economic and social development and had a highly educated and politically sophisticated public. These conditions created a demand for political reform. But Chiang's decision to shift from slow liberalization to more rapid and fundamental democratization was based on the calculation that it was worth risking a loss of control over the pace of change in order to improve his regime's ability to deal with threats to its international survival and internal stability.

In the early 1980s, Taiwan was becoming increasingly isolated internationally and seemed to have no effective way to respond. The peaceful unification offensive of the People's Republic of China (PRC) had placed Taiwan's diplomacy on the defensive. In 1982, President Ronald Reagan, viewed by Taiwan as a staunch friend, agreed to a joint communiqué with the PRC committing the U.S. gradually to reduce arms sales to Taiwan. South Korea, Taiwan's major ally in Asia, showed increasing interest in establishing ties with Beijing. In early 1986, Beijing gained admission to the Asian Development Bank, presenting Taiwan with the riddle of how to maintain its own participation without accepting the status of a mere local government.

At home, a series of incidents suggested that the ruling party and the security apparatus were becoming inbred, arrogant, and complacent. Relatives of a jailed opposition leader were murdered in 1980 (the murder has never been solved); a visiting Taiwanese-American professor died in police custody in 1981; and in 1984, Taiwanese gangsters in California assassinated a U.S. citizen, Henry Liu, who had written a controversial biography of Chiang Ching-kuo. During the assassins'

American trial the following year it was revealed to the embarrassment
of the Taiwan government that the assassination had been ordered by its
chief of military intelligence. Also in 1985, the financial collapse of the
large Tenth Credit Cooperative and the related Cathay investment
company was linked to government officials, leading to the resignation
of the minister of finance. All these developments caused a loss of
international prestige that the regime could ill afford, and fed popular
support for the opposition. The opposition criticized the ruling KMT
more and more aggressively in the press and in the legislative *yuan*.
The Garrison Command responded by using its martial-law powers to
ban many opposition magazines, which made the regime increasingly
unpopular. Against this background it was not certain that the KMT
could perform well in important national elections scheduled for
December 1986.

The most serious threat, however, came from the unsettled succession.
President Chiang, a diabetic, turned 70 in 1979. By the mid-1980s, he
was visibly weakened, making fewer public appearances, going out in a
wheelchair, and limiting himself to short speeches. His heir-apparent, the
popular and able Prime Minister Sun Yun-hsuan, suffered a cerebral
hemorrhage in 1984. As matters stood, the ability of Chiang's successor
to consolidate power and take on the country's problems would be
hampered by conservative party elders and by the mainlander-dominated
military and security bureaucracies, groups that all retained much power.

In the 1980s, Chiang Ching-kuo began to make succession
arrangements, and political reform became part of them. In 1983, he
demoted the second most powerful man in his regime, Wang Sheng,
head of the military's political warfare department, to the post of
ambassador to Paraguay. The following year he chose Lee Teng-hui, a
native Taiwanese, as his vice-president and constitutional successor
should he die in office. Chiang appointed several new Taiwanese
members to the ruling party's Central Standing Committee, and exiled
his son, Chiang Hsiao-wu, a potential dynastic successor, to a diplomatic
post in Singapore. On the Republic of China's Constitution Day in 1985,
Chiang placed his personal prestige strongly behind a strictly
constitutional succession, adding that, so far as he was concerned, neither
a military man nor a member of his own family could conceivably
succeed him in office.

In addition to providing his successor with the political resources to
consolidate power, Chiang's reforms endowed the new leader with some
much-needed flexibility in policy matters. As probably the last
mainlander president of Taiwan and the last national leader in the Chiang
family line, Chiang Ching-kuo's unchallengeable legitimacy within the
Kuomintang enabled him to move Taiwan in the direction of native
Taiwanese rule and prolonged political separation from the mainland.

If these were Chiang Ching-kuo's calculations, his gamble paid off handsomely. The KMT performed well in the 1986 elections. Upon Chiang's death in January 1988, the constitutional succession went smoothly, and Lee Teng-hui was subsequently able to make himself a fairly strong president. In 1989-90, Taiwan enhanced its profile in the international arena by participating in the Asian Bank meetings in Beijing, establishing new formal economic ties with a number of West European and Soviet bloc countries, and gaining diplomatic recognition from the Bahamas, Grenada, Belize, and Liberia. As a result of giving up some of its control over the political system, the KMT has strengthened both its domestic authority and its international prestige.

The Crackdown in Beijing

In May 1989, Deng Xiaoping could have reaped benefits comparable to those gained by Chiang Ching-kuo by taking smaller risks. Deng could have authorized Zhao Ziyang to begin a dialogue with the students, allowed Zhao to renounce the controversial April 26 *People's Daily* editorial that labeled the demonstrations a "turmoil," directed the National People's Congress (NPC) to adopt the relatively liberal press and demonstrations laws that were already in draft, and ordered vigorous prosecution of corruption among the relatives of the top leaders. Deng could then have fulfilled his oft-stated intention to hand power over to Zhao and retired in glory, bringing the other elderly leaders along into retirement with him. These actions might have ended the demonstrations; solved the long-pending succession problem; bequeathed his countrymen a strong, popular leader with an unambiguous mandate; established a precedent for resolving social conflicts through peaceful legal procedures; ameliorated at least temporarily the legitimacy crisis that was the immediate cause of the 1989 troubles; and provided his successor with a surge of popular support that could have been used to push economic reform through its next, most difficult phase—price reform. These actions would have strengthened international confidence in China's stability and would have improved the prospects for both successful integration of Hong Kong into the PRC and peaceful reunification with Taiwan. Instead, Deng and his octogenarian colleagues opted for repression.

The repression of June 1989 has left in its wake a regime that is the weakest in PRC history. Its most powerful leaders are elderly, feeble, and lacking in intellectual flexibility. There is no clear successor. All the most powerful younger men in the regime—Li Peng, Jiang Zemin, Qiao Shi—are so badly compromised by the role they played in Deng's repression that maintaining them in power will be costly to the regime. The mix of personnel under the top leaders reveals severe factionalism. Numerous politicians formerly associated with Hu Yaobang and Zhao Ziyang remain in the central government and in the provinces, alongside others whose careers were patronized by the hard-line octogenarians. At a moment when the nation is wedged between the old system and the new and needs strong leadership, the political structure promises only a paradoxical combination of policy paralysis and frequent, unpredictable political realignments.

The repression has done nothing substantial to reverse the decay of social control that helped bring on the crisis of spring 1989. Propaganda about the "counterrevolutionary rebellion" seems unable to persuade many people. Coercive measures designed to reform the thinking of students will probably just increase their disaffection. The regime has arrested large numbers of participants in the April-June demonstrations, but it cannot restore the ideological fervor or the tight system of social controls that used to make possible Mao-style campaigns of mutual persecution. Control mechanisms that rely primarily on the police and cannot draw on voluntary cooperation are costly and relatively ineffective.

The crackdown is likely to make the economic situation worse. The regime is more divided than ever about the solutions to its economic problems, and even if it could formulate a clear policy it would not have the power to carry it out. Political demoralization makes it even more likely that enterprises and individuals will evade government policies whenever it seems to be in their interest to do so. The rate of foreign investment will probably decline, not only because of economic sanctions but because of concern about political risk. Inflation, one of the proximate causes of the 1989 crisis, is likely to increase because the regime lacks means to control the rate of investment, the money supply, or prices. Corruption, another major cause, will probably worsen because the government can neither move back to a planned system nor go forward to a market system. The trend toward economic federalism is likely to accelerate as the central government is increasingly unable to provide anything of economic value to the provinces in exchange for the taxes and regulations it imposes on them.

In short, all the problems that brought on the crisis are still there and are getting worse, while the means to deal with them are weaker than before. In addition, the government's international prestige has been damaged, and the prospect of obtaining Taiwan's reunification with the mainland is more remote than ever.

It is not surprising that a weak regime facing so many problems has been drawn to authoritarian policies. These have included reasserting direct control over foreign trade, financial institutions, major enterprises, and the grain supply; suppressing incomes and consumption; tightly controlling the propaganda media; concealing intraregime conflicts; and deterring autonomous political discussion. But the conditions for a Mao-style popular mobilization that could reestablish the legitimacy and effectiveness of the regime no longer exist; the most the authoritarian regime can achieve is repression. As long as it retains control of the armed forces, even an unpopular, inefficient, coercive regime can survive for many years, but it is unlikely to solve China's economic problems or win popular legitimacy. So it cannot be considered stable.

Prospects for a Democratic Transition

It is not easy, but it is possible and sometimes necessary for a weak regime to begin a transition toward democracy. Given the existence of a strong social demand for liberalization, it is probable that some groups within the regime will see sponsoring change in the direction of democracy as a way of gaining factional advantage. Even were it not the case that many of Zhao's followers remain high in the regime cobbled together by Deng Xiaoping since the repression, democratic reform would still present itself as a possible tactic to factions seeking to improve their power positions.

The opening for a new attempt at democratization could be created by Deng's death, by renewed social disorder, or by the fall of Li Peng as a result of rivalries within the regime. The chances for success will be greatest if a dominant faction uses democratization to try to solidify its power. But since rival factions are sure to lose from such a change, they will try to form a veto bloc. The weakness of authority inherent in a factionalized regime makes it possible that such a bloc will succeed. Devolution of power is easier for a strong leader like Chiang Ching-kuo whose personal authority overrides opposition in all sectors of the party and government, or for a new and popular leader like Mikhail Gorbachev who can use his political "honeymoon" to introduce policy innovations. But there is little likelihood that a strong leader will emerge in China after Deng dies.

A weak regime that tries to democratize under the pressure of economic stagnation and popular dissatisfaction faces a larger risk that political reform will spin out of control and lead to a rapid "deflation" of power. To make a successful transition under these circumstances, it is helpful to have a powerful external force to guarantee stability. In Poland in 1989, the silent, ambiguously threatening presence of the Soviet Union helped to persuade the factions in both government and opposition to work together for a smooth transition. It is possible that China's army will play the role of silent guarantor in its own country, just as in 1989 it emulated the repressive role that the Soviet army played decades earlier in Eastern Europe. It may be just as well, then, that the Chinese army shows no sign of splitting. Also, the patience and nonviolence of the democratic opposition in China, even if it is born of weakness, may prove as useful as the restraint shown by Solidarity in helping the regime to navigate a democratizing reform.

Such an attempt at transition might occur at any time, but it is impossible to set a deadline for it. The Chinese Communist regime is too entrenched to collapse: the ruling party and its army are still the only two large organized political forces in society. They have enormous vested interests to defend, and the struggles within them are over the distribution of power, not the regime's survival. The exile-led democratic movement is unarmed and divided on both goals and strategy. Even if the adherents of this movement took up arms, which is improbable, no foreign power is likely to offer assistance on the scale needed to overthrow the government. In fact, any foreign threat to China's perceived national security would make those in power less willing to take the risks of democratizing. Thus there seems to be little possibility that democratization will be forced on China from outside. The transition to democracy is likely to come from above when it comes, and to be hard, prolonged, complex—and inconclusive.

For when Chinese democracy begins to take shape, it may turn out to be a mixture of democratic and authoritarian elements, openness and secrecy, idealism and selfishness, turbulence and stability. It will be hard for Western and especially American observers to recognize as democracy, and far from satisfactory to the Chinese themselves as an end point of their political development. Democratic politics in China will have many characteristics of Chinese politics in the past, only they will occur in the open rather than in secret. Such politics may be characterized by moral and symbolic posturing, a stress on personal loyalty, frequent betrayals, extreme rhetoric, emotional intensity, fractionalization of viewpoints and organizations, moralization of political issues, and consequent difficulty in pragmatic compromise. The issues in a democratic China may not be all that different from those that have agitated Chinese politics earlier in this century—national pride and independence versus openness to the world, the clashing interests of the cities and the countryside, the degree of freedom to be allowed individuals who offend the mores of the national community in pursuit of selfish gain or notoriety, and the permissible degree of interference by the ruling party in administrative affairs, education, and the military.

To some extent the politics of Taiwan may serve as a preview, even though Taiwan and the mainland have very different political traditions and face different issues. Since political liberalization occurred in Taiwan, there have been carnival-like rallies and demonstrations, some featuring the throwing of rocks at the police. One opposition politician jumped on tables in the legislative *yuan* to grab the microphone and the neckties of elderly politicians of the ruling party. Numerous small opposition parties have been formed, and there have been constant joinings and defections among the opposition groups. Although self-immolation is not a Chinese tradition, two Taiwan independence activists burned themselves to death in political protests in 1989. Similarly, during the May 1989 protests in Beijing, more than a dozen demonstrators registered to burn themselves in protest against the government's failure to enter into dialogue, although none actually did so. It is not likely that democratic politics will be any less turbulent in China than in Taiwan.

Speculations on Chinese Democracy

The institutions of a democratic China will probably evolve from the present structure. The system will probably have a single supreme legislature like the National People's Congress, unicameral and not subject to judicial review. It may well have a single dominant party that stays in office permanently like those in Taiwan and Japan. This is most likely to be the Communist Party, which will enter the democratizing transition with enormous advantages in size, organizational sophistication, and control over resources that it can use to fight and win elections. Protecting the vested interests of party members and party-chosen bureaucrats will be high on the agenda of the politicians who engineer the transition.

The factionalized opposition will develop out of the existing satellite parties as well as some democratic organizations in exile acceptable to the Communists. Elections will be short and hard-fought, with manifestoes and personal attacks. A high proportion of the electorate will participate, but many of the voters will be mobilized on the basis of personal ties to the candidates or payoffs from political machines rather than issues. Some broad version of socialism will continue to be the official ideology, and few politicians will question it. The press, freed from government control, will be intensely partisan, with every journal serving the interests of some party, party faction, or social group. Readers will still have to read between the lines, and much of what they read will not be true. The military will continue to serve as a silent arbiter, its interventions kept as much as possible from the public eye, and will continue for a long time to owe its primary loyalty to the ruling party.

Although some of the exiled democrats advocate American-style federalism and separation of powers for China, I suspect that neither will be adopted: they are unfamiliar and would tend to divide power that will already be fragmented. China will continue to seek governmental efficiency through an ostensibly centralized system of undivided sovereignty. But the tug-of-war between the central government and provinces as big as European states will continue, and the center will probably weaken as the provinces grow stronger.

The international stake in China's course of development is large. In both Cambodia and Korea, the danger of war is substantial if China fails to play a constructive role: war in either place, especially Korea, could involve other powers, including the Soviet Union and the U.S. As one of the world's nuclear powers and a major arms supplier, China must participate in any successful disarmament arrangements. With one quarter of the world's population, China has an enormous potential impact on world food markets, on the population problem, and on the environment. If China does well, it can make a large positive contribution to world prosperity both as a producer and as a market. Otherwise, China will continue to pollute the earth and the atmosphere, will stunt the development of a quarter of humankind, and will be an unreliable partner in dealing with world security issues.

Although many countries fear a strong China, a weak China is even more threatening because of the damage it can do to itself and to the world. From now on, it is doubtful that an undemocratic China can be stable and strong. A more democratic system may give China more real stability than the cycles of repression and popular outrage that have shaken the country throughout the twentieth century. To be sure, previously hidden clashes of interest and personality would be visible, and no one would be in full control. But democratic institutions might provide peaceful and legitimate channels for resolving issues of power and policy; ways of forming a national consensus on important issues; a political environment that fosters economic growth; protection for dissent; and a means for the political system to continue to evolve without mass violence.

NOTES

1. These quotations come from *Selected Works of Deng Xiaoping (1975-1982)* (Beijing: Foreign Language Press, 1984), 171, 184 (with a slight retranslation from the Chinese text); and "Deng Xiaoping on Upholding the Four Cardinal Principles and Combatting Bourgeois Liberalization," *Beijing Review*, 17-23 July 1989, 22.

2. I am using the 1972 figures reproduced in G. Bingham Powell, Jr., *Contemporary Democracies: Participation, Stability, and Violence* (Cambridge: Harvard University Press, 1982), 36; and also, for the purposes of illustration here, his list of what were at that time democratic regimes. I am also using the World Bank's evaluation of China's per-capita GNP as standing at $300 in 1980 and aiming at $800 (in 1980 dollars) in 2000 in *China: Long-Term Development Issues and Options* (Baltimore: Johns Hopkins University Press, 1985), 21.

3. "On Questions of Party History," *Beijing Review*, 6 July 1981, 25-26.

4. J. Roland Pennock, *Democratic Political Theory* (Princeton: Princeton University Press, 1979), 239-53.

5. For the concept of civic culture, see Gabriel A. Almond and Sidney Verba, *The Civic Culture: Political Attitudes and Democracy in Five Nations*, abridged ed. (Boston: Little, Brown and Co., 1965).

6. Adam Przeworski, "Some Problems in the Study of the Transition to Democracy," in *Transitions from Authoritarian Rule: Comparative Perspectives*, eds. Guillermo O'Donnell, Philippe C. Schmitter, and Laurence Whitehead (Baltimore: Johns Hopkins University Press, 1986), 58, quotation slightly edited.

27.
LATIN AMERICA'S
FRAGILE DEMOCRACIES

Peter Hakim & Abraham F. Lowenthal

Peter Hakim is staff director of the Inter-American Dialogue. *Abraham F. Lowenthal* is executive director of the Inter-American Dialogue and professor of international relations at the University of Southern California in Los Angeles. Their essay draws in part on Chapter Four ("Democracy on Trial") of The Americas in a New World, the 1990 report of the Inter-American Dialogue, and on an earlier draft that will appear in a forthcoming volume to be published by the National Defense University.

The turn toward democracy in the Americas has been widely applauded in both the United States and Latin America. The Western Hemisphere, it is often said, is on the verge of becoming fully democratic for the first time in its history—with only Castro's Cuba now standing in the way. Some U.S. officials, present and former, give U.S. policy considerable credit for Latin America's democratic openings, while others think that the U.S. role was marginal at best. There is, however, little disagreement that the regional transition from authoritarian rule was spearheaded by Latin American opposition movements—parties, unions, women's groups, church officials, courageous political leaders, and plain citizens. And no one doubts that in recent years democratic politics has gained important ground throughout most of Latin America and the Caribbean.

Yet democracy in Latin America is far from robust. It is nowhere fully achieved, and it is perhaps most firmly established in those few countries where it was already deeply rooted and vibrant a generation ago. In most other nations, democracy is endangered by political and criminal violence, conflicts between civilian and military authorities, prolonged economic decline, and gross social and economic inequalities. Democratic institutions in much of Latin America remain weak—plagued by rampant corruption, political polarization, and growing public skepticism about government and politics. In some countries, democratic forms are still a facade; in others, they are precarious and vulnerable.

Latin American democracy today needs reinforcement, not premature celebration.

The Trend Toward Democracy

Latin America's democratic progress in the 1980s was real and significant, as encouraging in its way as the collapse of communist rule in Eastern and Central Europe. In country after country, military regimes and personalist dictatorships gave way to elected civilian governments. In the final months of the decade, Brazil held its first direct presidential elections since 1960 and Chile its first since 1970—thus bringing civilian presidents to office in every country of South America for the first time in a generation. Nicaragua's elections in February 1990 were the most open and competitive in that country's history, and elected civilian governments are today in place in every nation of Central America. At the beginning of 1991, Fidel Castro's regime in Cuba remains the only consolidated and unambiguously authoritarian government still ruling in Latin America.

Government office, if not always power, is now usually transferred peacefully from one elected president to another throughout Latin America. In recent years, incumbent administrations have yielded office to elected opponents in countries as diverse as Argentina, Bolivia, the Dominican Republic, Ecuador, Jamaica, Peru, and Uruguay—in some cases for the first time in memory. Not since 1928 had one democratically elected president succeeded another in Argentina before Carlos Menem replaced Raúl Alfonsín in 1989. In the face of economic crisis and terrorist threats, Peru has held three consecutive presidential elections for the first time in nearly a century. In economically traumatized Bolivia, frequent military coups have given way to three successive elections.

Even in countries where elections have remained flawed, important democratic gains have been registered. Although the balloting was marred by credible charges of fraud, Mexico held its most competitive presidential contest in more than a generation in 1988, and popular pressures are building for the further opening of Mexican politics. Despite severe restrictions on political participation in most Central American countries, elections have come to be accepted as the only legitimate route to office in that region. The 1989 presidential vote in Paraguay—called after a military coup ended Alfredo Stroessner's 35 years of dictatorial rule—was organized too hastily to be fairly contested; it did, however, allow opposition parties to campaign, express dissent, and begin mobilizing support. By nullifying Panama's national elections in 1989, General Manuel Antonio Noriega only underscored the massive popular repudiation of his regime. After several failed attempts to hold free elections in Haiti following the downfall of the Duvalier dynasty, an internationally supervised presidential vote finally took place in December 1990.

No longer is it commonly accepted that Latin America is somehow predisposed toward authoritarian rule, or that its culture is inherently antidemocratic. Year by year, it has become more evident that most Latin Americans embrace the fundamental democratic idea—that government authority must derive from the uncoerced consent of the majority, tested regularly through competitive and broadly participatory elections. It is striking that the commitment to building democracy has thus far even survived prolonged hyperinflation in Argentina, Bolivia, Brazil, and Peru; democratic institutions in many European nations in the 1920s and 1930s crumbled under similar circumstances.

It was not many years ago that self-proclaimed military "guardians" on the right and revolutionary "vanguards" on the left throughout Latin America openly expressed their disdain for democratic procedures—and could claim some significant following. In recent years, however, a wide spectrum of Latin American opinion has come to recognize the value of democracy: military officers and former guerrillas as well as intellectuals, corporate executives, small entrepreneurs, and religious leaders. But even as democratic ideals are now widely embraced, the practice of democracy remains very uneven across the region.

Costa Rica, Venezuela, Jamaica, and some of the smaller Caribbean countries have enjoyed uninterrupted democratic rule for more than a generation. Their political and civic institutions are relatively strong, human rights are respected, and civilian authorities exercise firm control over the armed forces. The prospects for sustaining vigorous democracy may be even more promising in Chile and Uruguay. Although they suffered years of military rule in the 1970s and 1980s and unsettling remnants from that period persist, the two countries boast long democratic traditions and solid representative institutions.

Elsewhere in the region, however, democracy is troubled—in some places, deeply so. The tasks of reinforcing and expanding democracy in the Hemisphere must begin with a sober appraisal of the severe challenges it faces.

Political Violence

In four countries—Colombia, Peru, Guatemala, and El Salvador—governments face insurgent threats to their effective control of national territory. Each of them confronts a vicious cycle of violence and counterviolence that, to varying degrees and in different ways, is undermining the institutions, procedures, and values essential to democracy. As long as the violence continues, democratic practice will remain truncated and precarious. The armed forces will intrude in political decisions, the authority of civilian leaders and institutions will be compromised, economic progress will be blocked, politics will remain polarized, and human rights abuses will persist at levels that destroy confidence in the democratic process.

Colombia continues to suffer repeated outbreaks of intense insurgent violence even as guerrilla activity overall has declined in the past several years. Sustained negotiating efforts by successive Colombian governments have led several guerrilla groups to stop fighting and enter politics. Two significant groups, however, continue to do battle, and the government has not been able to guarantee the security of the former guerrilla leaders who have become active politically within the democratic system. Nearly a thousand of them have been murdered in the past three years, including two presidential aspirants and scores of mayoral candidates. Their deaths, along with the kidnapping of many prominent citizens and the gangland-style killing of the leading candidate for president in the 1990 election, reflect the pervasive insecurity that besets Colombia. But insurgent movements are by no means the only menace to democratic politics in Colombia. A greater danger may come from the relentless violence of criminal drug organizations and paramilitary groups—often condoned or tolerated by national security forces—that operate in complex and shifting alliances with each other and with the remaining guerrilla fighters.

As devastating as the violence has been, Colombia's political institutions continue to demonstrate resilience and flexibility. The country's political leaders and most citizens remain committed to democratic rule, and the constitutional reform process now underway may strengthen that commitment. But democratic politics is being severely tested in Colombia, and its survival cannot be guaranteed.

El Salvador and Guatemala, in contrast to Colombia, lack established democratic institutions and traditions. After decades of almost uninterrupted military rule, elected civilian governments came to office in both nations in the mid-1980s amid prolonged guerrilla insurgencies. Since then, national and local elections have become somewhat more competitive, and have gained a significant measure of international approval. In neither country, however, are all major political constituencies represented at the polls, nor has democratic practice extended much beyond periodic and restricted elections. Civilian leaders have failed either to establish control over the armed forces or to end the violence that wracks both societies.

During the past decade of civil war in El Salvador, some 70,000 persons have died and hundreds of thousands have been displaced from their homes. Both the guerrillas and state security forces have been guilty of assassinations, random killings of citizens, and cruel violations of basic human rights. Neither side is now able to prevail by force of arms. The insurgent forces control large expanses of territory, but have little prospect of military victory. The army commands sufficient firepower to contain the guerrilla advances, but not to force their surrender.

The grim prospect of a destructive military stalemate, combined with the tempering of ideological passions both domestically and internationally following the end of the Cold War, may finally be propelling El Salvador toward peace. After a year of slow progress, UN-mediated negotiations supported by both the United States and the Soviet Union have in recent months produced some significant agreements between the guerrillas and the government that could well point the way toward a settlement. The obstacles to peace are still formidable, however. It is by no means clear yet whether the intransigence of hardliners on both sides can be overcome and the necessary compromises achieved. And even if a peace settlement is reached, the long years of fighting are bound to leave behind a bitter legacy of mistrust and division, making the task of building stable democracy daunting.

In Guatemala, more than 35 years of guerrilla violence and counterinsurgency have claimed the lives of over 100,000 civilians, while many thousands of others have been imprisoned, tortured, or displaced from their homes. By 1986, when the first civilian president in a generation came to office, the army controlled most of the countryside and appeared to have routed the guerrillas. But in the past two years, the rebels have regrouped their forces and resisted efforts to dislodge them from their strongholds. In recent months the guerrillas and the government have begun unprecedented face-to-face negotiations, but a peace settlement still appears a long way off, if it is possible at all.

The insurgency in Guatemala does not challenge governmental control, nor is it the central focus of national politics. But it has led to the persistent involvement of the armed forces in Guatemalan politics and to their continued repressive tactics in rural areas. The war is fueled by bitter ethnic and class divisions, which in themselves are a major obstruction to democratic progress. Electoral politics has meant little for Guatemala's impoverished indigenous majority, which has long been dominated by an urban minority of European ancestry. The 1990-91 elections, which were tarnished by violence among competing political parties, promise no immediate change. A profound process of national reform will be necessary to end the violence in Guatemala.

The Shining Path and Tupac Amaru insurgencies in Peru have become entrenched and virulent. With no apparent external support, the Shining Path has spread gradually through much of Peru since 1980. In the past five years, it has demonstrated a growing capacity to mobilize rural and urban support, disrupt the country's economy, intimidate local government officials, and inflict violence on a large scale. The Tupac Amaru movement is less powerful, but its targeted violence is also severely weakening the Peruvian state. Neither group has shown any inclination so far to enter peace negotiations with the government.

Some 20,000 deaths in Peru during the past ten years have been attributed to the guerrilla groups and the military forces battling them, and the killing is expanding. Both sides engage in pervasive human rights abuses. More than half of Peru's population has been placed under one form or another of emergency military rule. Democratic practice is more and more restricted to Peru's urban centers, and even there it is threatened.

The drug trade adds to the violence in Peru and complicates government efforts to control the guerrillas. The Shining Path finances itself partly by taxing drug traffickers and protecting peasant coca growers. Despite intense pressure from Washington, successive Peruvian governments have been reluctant to engage the army in the fight against the narcotics network because they are concerned that intensifying and militarizing the antidrug campaign will produce new recruits for the insurgents and expand the influence of the armed forces. President Fujimori has recently accepted U.S. support for such a military effort, but only as a condition for desperately needed economic assistance.

The Peruvian government is still freely elected, but it operates under restrictive and repressive conditions and with decreasing authority. Peru today is battling against national disintegration and mounting despair.

Strong Armies and Fragile Polities

Even where insurgents do not threaten, democratic rule is often challenged by armed forces that are not effectively subordinated to civilian control. Civil-military relations vary considerably from country to country in Latin America, but they remain troublesome nearly everywhere and are a source of serious tension in many nations. Constitutional democracy requires that all military forces be subordinate to the effective professional and political direction of elected civilian authorities. Today only a handful of Latin American countries—Costa Rica, Mexico, Venezuela, and the Commonwealth nations of the Caribbean—fully meet that basic condition.

In Guatemala and El Salvador, the military virtually defines the extent of civilian authority and influences most aspects of government policy. The armed forces of Bolivia, Ecuador, Honduras, Nicaragua, and Peru retain so much institutional autonomy that they are at best "conditionally subordinate" to civilian officials. Panama's security forces remain an active threat to democratic rule, despite the cashiering of more than 400 senior officials during a year-and-a-half-long effort to turn the army into a civilian-run police force. In Argentina, the armed forces have repeatedly confronted civilian authorities in the past several years, with debilitating effects on democratic institutions. Brazil has avoided such confrontations, but to some extent by making preemptive concessions to the military. In Haiti, military elements have operated for years as a rogue force. The army's move late in 1990 to prevent a coup by Duvalier loyalists, coupled with the new president's dismissal of most senior commanders, may point the way to a more responsible military, but hardly one that is securely under civilian direction.

In Chile and Uruguay, where civilians had seemed firmly in control until the armed coups of the early 1970s, military regimes have left a legacy of unresolved civil-military conflicts, some of them embedded in law. Chile's civil government operates within a series of legal restraints imposed by the armed forces before they left power. Former dictator Augusto Pinochet is still commander of the army and cannot legally be removed by Chile's elected president. Although the civilian governments of both Uruguay and Chile are gradually and skillfully asserting greater authority over their armed forces, the military's influence on policy remains strong in both nations.

Although direct military rule is now exceptional in Latin America, extensive military influence undermines the authority of elected civilian leaders, and the deterrents to further military intervention are still weak throughout the region. Until the armed forces are fully subordinate to elected civilian authority, democracy will remain at risk. In some places, armies may again seize power in the 1990s, but even where they do not, they will remain a significant obstacle to democratic advance.

Political violence and military incursions into politics are not the only obstacles to consolidating Latin American democracy. Effective democratic practice requires structured and dependable institutions, accepted rules of political conduct, and established judicial procedures. In their absence, politics can become personalized and erratic.

Legislatures and judicial systems in much of Latin America still lack the autonomy, stature, resources, and competence needed to carry out all of their constitutional functions fully. Courts are overburdened and their proceedings, both criminal and civil, are routinely delayed for years. Judges are, for the most part, poorly trained and paid, and they lack the funding to conduct investigations and administer justice effectively. In many places, judicial decisions are heavily influenced by political considerations, intimidation, or outright corruption.

Legislative systems face similar problems. Presidents, frustrated by delay and indecision, frequently resort to exceptional procedures to bypass the legislative process. In doing so, they debase the formal institutions of government, compromise legal norms, and undercut democratic legitimacy. This is especially troubling because there has been evidence in several countries—Brazil, Argentina, and Uruguay among them—that democratic institutions grow stronger when they are respected by all major political actors.

Except in a few nations, notably Chile and Uruguay, political parties in many countries of Latin America and the Caribbean have long lacked effective ties to regular constituencies and are often little more than vehicles for contesting elections and distributing patronage. They rarely offer coherent programs and are frequently manipulated to serve the personal ambitions of their leaders. For example Ecuador, with its array of small parties of constantly shifting loyalties, is plagued by these problems. So is the Dominican Republic, where old-fashioned *caudillismo* is combined with political opportunism. Democratic practice under such conditions is incomplete and crisis-prone.

Where political parties are weak, the media, particularly television, often exert a great and immediate influence on political choice, and sharp swings of public opinion are common. These factors contributed to the quick rise from obscurity to prominence and the subsequent election of independent presidential candidates without national party affiliation in Brazil and Peru. In both countries it has been difficult for the new and inexperienced presidents to govern without the organized support needed to forge legislative majorities and mobilize popular backing on policy issues.

Democracy in Latin America is also hampered by the lack of sustained citizen participation in political life. Although the waning of authoritarian rule sparked the emergence and growth of voluntary organizations in country after country, most nations of the region still lack a vigorous array of nongovernmental institutions through which the demands of ordinary people can be expressed, mediated, and consistently brought to the attention of authorities. In much of the region, trade unions, business groups, professional organizations, and civic associations remain weak and fragmented, and are too narrowly based to play effective political roles. In many countries, the press represents only a limited range of opinions, and does not serve as an effective check on corruption or the abuse of power.

Even in those nations with relatively strong political and judicial institutions, democratic governance is threatened when citizens stop participating actively in political life because of disillusionment, apathy, or a sense that they have been unfairly excluded or disadvantaged. Throughout much of Latin America today there is a growing distrust of politics. That voters in so many countries are casting their ballots for political newcomers reflects, in part, their low regard for established democratic leaders as well as their frustration with continued economic and social deterioration. Even more troubling, abstention from elections and skepticism about their significance are sharply on the rise. In some countries, growing emigration by professionals, entrepreneurs, and students is another manifestation of deep disaffection.

Economic Crisis

Each of these threats to democratic governance in Latin America—political violence, military incursions into politics, fragile institutions, and alienated citizens—has been greatly exacerbated by the region's economic crisis.

Since the debt crisis struck in 1982, the region has been mired in depression, its deepest and most prolonged ever. Per capita income has fallen by more than 10 percent for the region as a whole, and some countries have fared much worse—for example, in Peru, Argentina, and Nicaragua, per capita income has plunged 25 percent or more. In only two countries, Chile and Colombia, have living standards improved over the past ten years, though by very small amounts.

The cumulative effects of eight years of depression now pose severe obstacles to economic recovery and renewed growth:

- Latin America's debt burdens are enormous. Its aggregate debt today exceeds $420 billion, $100 billion greater than in 1982. Each year, Latin America pays out about $25 billion more in interest and principal than it obtains in new loans. That net outflow—amounting to 3 percent of the region's total output and more than 20 percent of its exports—deprives Latin American countries of the resources needed for investment and crucial imports. It also keeps budget deficits high, fuels inflation, and saps investor confidence.

- Record levels of inflation plague many countries. The average annual rate of inflation exceeded 1,000 percent for Latin America in 1990, more than 10 times higher than in 1982. Four countries—Brazil, Argentina, Peru, and Nicaragua—have been battling hyperinflation. Only Mexico, Costa Rica, and Bolivia have substantially reduced inflation from 1982 levels.

- Eight years of low investment—averaging some 16 percent of Gross Domestic Product (GDP) compared to 22 percent during the 1970s—have left Latin American industry with deteriorating physical plants, outdated technologies, and a lagging ability to compete internationally.

- More people than ever are trapped in poverty. Unemployment and underemployment are widespread in nearly every country. Wages have deteriorated badly, by 50 percent or more in some places. The quality of housing, medical care, and education has steadily worsened. Crime rates have surged. Life has gotten much harder in Latin America, and women and children are suffering the most.

- All of these economic ills have produced a devastating loss of confidence. Large numbers of people from all classes are leaving the region. Few countries are able to attract foreign investment, while domestic capital flight continues to drain resources. In country after country, economic distress has eroded the credibility of national leaders and reduced their capacity to govern.

Austerity has seemingly become a permanent fact of life in much of the region. In only a few countries are there solid prospects for sustained economic improvement anytime soon. Economic adversity is threatening Latin American democracy in several ways.

Worsening economic conditions help to sustain the Shining Path and other insurgencies. In some countries, economic "shock" treatments to halt rampant inflation have provoked outbreaks of violence. In Venezuela, more than 300 people died in riots protesting rises in the price of staple products. Food riots in Argentina contributed to President Alfonsín's decision to transfer power to President-elect Menem six months before the end of his constitutional term. Social and economic reversals were a main cause of Trinidad's violent uprising in July 1990. Other outbursts have occurred in Brazil and the Dominican Republic, and they can be expected elsewhere. In some places where large-scale group violence has not erupted, street crime and a pervasive sense of personal insecurity have become widespread, producing demands for order that are sometimes pursued at the expense of law.

Democratically elected leaders who have failed to stem economic decline have lost support and authority, thereby making it harder for them to institute and sustain the painful adjustments required for economic improvement. "Stop-and-go" policies, in turn, further damage economic performance and intensify political instability. In recent years, incumbent parties have only very rarely been able to retain office for more than one term. As one democratic leader after another loses support, the credibility of democratic rule itself is endangered.

Programs of market-oriented economic liberalization have become politically divisive. Even though such reforms have been widely adopted throughout Latin America and the Caribbean, they continue to face stiff resistance from many quarters. Economic reform programs in some countries have further concentrated income and wealth, and thus widened the already large gap between the rich and the poor. Social cohesion and political stability are put at risk as class divisions deepen.

If market strategies are unable to restore growth soon and to address such fundamental problems as poverty and inequity, advocates of alternative economic approaches are likely to gain increasing electoral strength. Politics then may become more polarized, and calls may intensify for restrictions to block opponents of current policies from power. In some countries, Argentina and Mexico among them, governments already seem tempted to circumvent or distort democratic processes in order to overcome opposition to their economic policies.

Requisites for Democratic Consolidation

It is not easy to make democracy work. Presidents must be strong enough to lead and command respect, but their power cannot be absolute. Legislatures must have the authority to curb executive power, but they must also be ready to cooperate and accept reasonable compromise. Courts must be independent, bound only to the rule of law. Political parties must be more than vehicles for protest or for winning elections; they must be able to represent their supporters effectively and formulate program and policy alternatives. It is proper for interest groups to serve their special constituencies, but they must also respect the rights and interests of others. Leaders and citizens alike must be willing to live with uncertainty and to accept unfavorable political outcomes that result from democratic procedures. Democracy draws its strength from a politically active populace and a multiplicity of representative institutions operating within legal and constitutional norms. Only a handful of Latin American countries can yet meet these standards.

With few exceptions, the countries of Latin America have achieved the first critical stage in the transition to democracy. Throughout the region, authoritarian regimes have yielded to elected governments. But elections—even where they are fully free and fair and are scheduled on a regular basis—are not enough by themselves to produce or sustain democratic rule. Few nations have yet managed to develop strong representative institutions that can maintain the rule of law, protect the rights of all citizens, effectively respond to popular demands, and give ordinary people a continuing, active voice in public policy decisions. Almost everywhere, progress toward meeting these and other vital requirements of democracy has been slow and painful, and some countries have, in fact, regressed in recent years.

For democratic institutions to take firm root and flourish in Latin America, four difficult challenges must be met.

First, the region's remaining internal wars must be ended. Democratic politics cannot thrive in settings where civil strife divides societies, expands the political role of armies, retards economic progress, and produces gross human rights abuses.

Second, the armed forces must be more effectively subordinated to the political control of civilian governments. In many nations this will require a profound rethinking of the mission and purposes of the military.

Third, many countries of the region have yet to curtail pervasive violations of human rights. Democratic practice and the rule of law cannot be consolidated unless the rights of political dissidents, minorities, and other vulnerable groups are respected and protected.

Finally, only a handful of nations have been able to restore economic stability and growth and to create opportunities for disadvantaged groups. Democratic institutions cannot thrive under conditions of prolonged economic hardship—when millions of citizens must survive without jobs, adequate shelter and nutrition, basic education, or much hope for the future.

Each of these challenges is daunting, even for those nations where democracy has begun to take root. They are not impossible to overcome, however. Acting individually and in concert, there is much that the countries of the Americas can do to protect, strengthen, and extend democratic politics in the 1990s.

Internal Wars

Direct negotiation between the warring parties is the best way to end Latin America's ongoing insurgencies. Nicaragua's decade-long war was resolved by a negotiated settlement, and the government and guerrillas now appear close to agreement in El Salvador. Negotiating efforts in Colombia have not yet stopped all guerrilla violence, but they have led several insurgent groups to lay down their arms and begin to compete politically.

A settlement can only be achieved, of course, when both sides—the guerrillas and the government forces—are prepared to make significant concessions for peace. But negotiations have a far greater chance of succeeding when they have the sustained and unambiguous support of many countries both within and outside the Hemisphere, including the external backers of the combatants. Peacemaking efforts by the UN and the Organization of American States can also play a vital role—as they did in Nicaragua and are doing in El Salvador.

Only the insurgencies in Peru now seem immune to a negotiated solution. The Peruvian government should keep open the future possibility of negotiations, but the immediate need is to design and implement a more effective strategy for combatting the guerrillas. Such a strategy must include far greater attention to remedying the economic deprivation and social injustice that are fueling the violence—and this, in turn, will require external financial aid, given Peru's desperate shortage of resources. It is also imperative that the armed forces stop their massive abuse of human rights, which adds both to the violence and to the appeal of the guerrillas. Destroying democratic values is no way to protect democracy.

Civil-Military Relations

There is no ready-made formula that civilian authorities can adopt to establish control over their armed forces. That task will remain difficult as long as civilian governments are weak and imbalances persist between fragile political institutions and strong military establishments. Lasting changes in civil-military relations will require basic shifts in the attitudes of Latin American officers that may well take a generation or longer to achieve.

Democratic leaders must maintain open communications with the armed forces, persistently seeking to build mutual confidence and to define an appropriate and agreed-upon mission for the military. They must also at times stand up to military officials and reject their intrusions into political affairs. It is crucial, in turn, for civilian politicians to resist the temptation to call on the armed forces to mediate political conflicts, endorse partisan causes, or promote particular candidates for office.

Military assistance programs from abroad must be designed to reinforce civilian control of the armed forces. Care must be taken not to aggravate the current imbalances between civilian and military institutions. Training programs in military strategy and other defense issues, like those offered at the Inter-American Defense College in Washington, should incorporate many more civilian participants in an effort to build civilian competence in Latin America to manage national security policy. In addition, the United States and other nations should make sure that efforts to fight the narcotics trade in places like Peru, Colombia, and Bolivia do not enmesh armies in political tasks and undercut civilian authority.

Human Rights

All nations of the Hemisphere, individually and together, can and must work harder to strengthen safeguards against human rights abuses. Stronger internal measures are urgently needed in many countries, some of which clearly require, in the first instance, stronger civilian control over military and police forces. National human rights offices, such as the one recently established in Mexico, can play an effective role in investigating, publicizing, and redressing violations—but they must be granted the authority, independence, and resources necessary to carry out their functions.

Latin American and U.S. leaders should also take action to broaden the mandate and expand the resources of the three official inter-American institutions responsible for protecting human rights (i.e., the Inter-American Commission, Court, and Institute), all of which are making significant contributions. The network of nongovernmental organizations that professionally and objectively monitor human rights should also be supported. Democratic governments should not provide economic or military assistance to regimes that systematically violate basic human rights.

Wherever there is the danger that national elections will be marred by fraud, manipulation, or violence, the inter-American community should stand ready to provide electoral monitors and other needed assistance. When such assistance is made available on a multilateral basis with respect for the host nation's sovereignty and laws, it can build confidence in the electoral process and increase prospects that the outcome will be accepted as fair by all parties. In 1990 alone, internationally monitored elections in Nicaragua, Chile, and Haiti constituted decisive steps toward political opening in those countries.

Economic recovery

The resumption of economic growth, combined with concrete measures to alleviate poverty and inequity, would contribute most to restoring confidence in democratic rule in Latin America. The task of economic recovery is largely up to each country—and most of the region's countries are struggling to restructure their economies and make them more productive. They are taking action to curtail budget deficits and bring inflation under control, giving new emphasis to extending trade and foreign investment, and turning toward markets and private enterprise.

The countries of Latin America, however, still need help from outside. External debt burdens continue to frustrate economic recovery and growth in all but a few countries of the region. The recent agreement among the United States and other industrial countries to slash Poland's debt was based on that country's enormous needs, its determined efforts to restructure its economy along market lines, and its commitment to building democracy. Most nations of Latin America meet all three criteria and deserve the same relief that was extended to Poland.

Perhaps even more than debt relief, Latin America requires open markets for its products and access to investment capital. The United States and other industrial countries should redouble their efforts to achieve a successful conclusion to the Uruguay Round of GATT negotiations, and Washington should move forward with its declared intention to strengthen hemispheric trade links. Even under the best of international circumstances, however, no Latin American country will be able to recover its economic vitality and address the needs of its people unless it takes the necessary measures to put its own house in order.

The hard fact is that it will take years of struggle to secure democratic stability in most countries of Latin America. There will be setbacks—even outright failures—in some places. Even where progress is made, democratic institutions will remain vulnerable for decades to come. The democratic idea has been gaining important ground in the Western Hemisphere, as in other regions of the world, but vigorous and consolidated democratic rule is still to be achieved. That is the challenge of the 1990s.

NOTES

The authors gratefully acknowledge the helpful comments on earlier drafts of Bruce Bagley, Julio Cotler, Liliana De Riz, Samuel Fitch, Manuel Antonio Garretón, J.A. Guilhon Albuquerque, Frances Hagopian, Jonathan Hartlyn, Bolívar Lamounier, Scott Mainwaring, Cynthia McClintock, Gabriel Murillo, Kenneth Sharpe, and Francisco Weffort.

28.
AFRICA: THE REBIRTH
OF POLITICAL FREEDOM

Richard Joseph

Richard Joseph, *professor of political science and director of the African Governance Program at the Carter Center of Emory University, is the author of* Democracy and Prebendal Politics in Nigeria: The Rise and Fall of the Second Republic *(1987). This article has benefited from the research assistance of Amy Poteete.*

For the vast majority of Africans, colonial rule is now something known mainly from history books. What they know from experience is postcolonial rule, with its single parties, military regimes, presidents-for-life, extensive security establishments, and glaring inequities. For these populations, a virtual miracle is taking place: the consummation of what is now widely called "a second independence." This time the autocrats to be overthrown emerged from their own societies, with assistance from some of the very countries and international institutions now rejoicing at their removal.

The democratic movement has moved so swiftly and on such a broad front that these reflections must be provisional. As Table 1 indicates, there are now 25 countries in Africa, or approximately half of the states on the continent, that can be classified as either democratic or moderately to strongly committed to democratic change.[1] The number of firmly authoritarian states has continued to shrink, with only Equatorial Guinea, Djibouti, Libya, Malawi, Sudan, and Swaziland still meriting inclusion in that category. The pace of change, moreover, is still accelerating; it is conceivable that by 1992 the continent will be overwhelmingly democratic in composition.

The scale of the African transformations rivals that of the revolutionary upheavals of 1989 in Eastern Europe. What has caused these massive changes? What new models of political organization have emerged? Who are the agents of change? What difficulties have they already encountered, and what great challenges lie ahead? These are some of the questions to which we will try to give preliminary answers.

Table 1 — Types of African Political Systems

ESTABLISHED DEMOCRACIES	EMERGING DEMOCRACIES*	DIRECTED DEMOCRACIES**	CONTESTED SOVEREIGNTY
Botswana	Benin	Egypt	Ethiopia
Gambia	Cape Verde	Morocco	Liberia
Mauritius	São Tomé &	Zimbabwe	Somalia
Namibia	Príncipe		Western Sahara
Senegal			

REGIMES IN TRANSITION - DEMOCRATIC COMMITMENT

Strong	Moderate	Ambiguous	AUTHORITARIAN
Congo	Angola	Algeria	Djibouti
Côte d'Ivoire	Burkina Faso	Burundi	Equatorial Guinea
Gabon	Guinea-Bissau	Cameroon	Libya
Nigeria	Mali	Central African	Malawi
Zambia	Mozambique	Republic	Sudan
	Niger	Chad	Swaziland
	Rwanda	Comoros Islands	
	Sierra Leone	Ghana	
	South Africa	Guinea	
	Togo	Kenya	
	Tunisia	Lesotho	
	Uganda	Madagascar	
		Mauritania	
		Tanzania	
		Zaire	

*Nations in the process of institutionalizing democracy.
**Systems in which formal institutions and practices of constitutional democracy are present, but in which the extensive powers of the ruling elite limit political participation.

Source: *Africa Dēmos* (July 1991), published by the African Governance Program of the Carter Center of Emory University.

The Kenyan scholar Peter Anyang Nyong'o captured the twocontrasting perspectives on the democratic movement in Africa when he observed that the movement appears "homegrown from the point of view of its advocates and foreign-imposed from the point of view of the defenders of the single-party regime."[2] Indeed, complaints about the imposition of external models of democracy on Africa now seem to come mainly from either officials and apologists of the embattled regimes or unswerving ideologues. Most advocates of democracy, on the other hand, are pleased that foreign governments and international agencies are at last supporting the struggle for political pluralism and withdrawing their support from autocrats and dictators.

Although the democratic movement in Africa first burst into the headlines in 1990, it is not exactly new, nor is it merely an echo of events elsewhere in the world.[3] Students of Africa can trace the roots of its democratic movements to individuals and organizations that have been harshly repressed for decades. Anyang Nyong'o notes that "pressure for democracy" has been evident in all African countries since independence.[4] Long-banned parties and associations as well as long-exiled individuals are now returning to help fulfill the original democratic promise of the anticolonial struggle.

Even where the independence process itself was not hijacked outright, as in Cameroon, a drift toward authoritarianism often set in, triggering decades of political instability, military interventions, and economic decline. Many African governments had lost their popular legitimacy long before the rest of the world, especially their patrons in the West and East, were prepared to acknowledge that occurrence.

At an international conference in July 1991, President Quett Masire of Botswana recited an African proverb that is highly applicable to the continent's democratic movement: "Slowly, slowly, an egg grows feet and walks." The embryo of renascent African democracy has been slowly growing feet despite the prevalence of authoritarian rule. Many groups and individuals that are now fearlessly confronting their governments have defied them surreptitiously for years. Achille Mbembe has eloquently described the alternative institutions and values that survived under the authoritarian carapace of most African countries.[5] The existence of this underground culture explains why, when the people decided that the time had come to move against their oppressors, they were able to do so in such a resolute and comprehensive manner.

Another point not sufficiently acknowledged is the antiapartheid struggle's role as a catalyst of the contemporary democratic movement in Africa. African governments long castigated the oppressive policies of South Africa's apartheid regime while indulging in similar practices themselves. But as President de Klerk was forced to peel away layers of repressive laws, comparable states of emergency, censorship laws, and human rights violations in black African countries became ever less defensible. As the parallels were drawn, there emerged a continent-wide democratic movement that accorded no immunity to any form of oppression, whatever the race, religion, or ideology of the perpetrators.

Seven Models of Transition

By their very nature, democratic transitions involve variety and creativity. One of the central features of the African democratic movement has been the resurrection of the principle of self-determination. It is the African people who are determining the contours of the transition process and the structures of the newly democratized systems. From the columns and research files of *Africa Dēmos*, we can identify seven basic models of transition. Given the speed and fluidity of events, it is not surprising to see some countries shifting categories or, at times, even spanning more than one.

1. *The National Conference.* The classic case in this category is the virtual civilian coup that took place in the West African republic of Benin over ten days in February 1990. It resulted in President Mathieu Kérékou's removal from effective control of public policy, the establishment of a transitional government, and the formulation of guidelines for multiparty elections. A year later came a similar meeting in the Republic of Congo, which dragged on for over three months but led to a similar outcome. Other countries where the government has been confronted with consistent demands for a sovereign national conference include Togo, Niger, and Madagascar. The Mobutu regime in Zaire repeatedly postponed the start of its national conference, while President Paul Biya of Cameroon has put up as much resistance as did presidents Gnassingbé Eyadéma of Togo and Ali Saibou of Niger before they both began yielding to relentless popular pressure.

2. *Government Change via Democratic Elections.* It had often been remarked that no African country, excluding the island of Mauritius in the Indian Ocean, had experienced a change of government via elections in the postindependence era. This is no longer true, although only island states have so far held free elections without an intervening national conference to displace the authoritarian regime. Between January and March 1991, the Portuguese-speaking West African island nations of Cape Verde and São Tomé & Príncipe witnessed the removal of single-party governments via popular balloting. The subsequent March 1991 election in Benin, which led to Kérékou's defeat at the hands of interim president Nicéphore Soglo, demonstrated that the democratic movement in Africa had come of age and could perform that most critical of tasks, the peaceful replacement of one government by another through general elections. In October 1991, Zambia is expected to become the first English-speaking African country during the current wave of democratization to undergo political renewal via multiparty elections.

3. *Co-opted Transitions.* Africa has always had elections—the 1980s even saw a boomlet of studies, mostly by French-speaking scholars, on "elections in noncompetitive systems." These studies sought to devise a methodology for examining the supposed positive dimensions of these elections despite their denial of real competition, openness, and verification.

Many of the African leaders who have encountered popular challenges, including Denis Sassou-Nguesso in Congo and Didier Ratsiraka in Madagascar, have pointed unavailingly to their recent overwhelming reelections (albeit in noncompetitive contests) as reasons why they should be allowed to complete their renewed terms. Others like Félix Houphouët-Boigny of Côte d'Ivoire and Omar Bongo of Gabon acted in time to allow multiparty elections. With control over the media and electoral machinery and ample financial resources, they were able to trounce their opponents at the ballot box and stay in power despite widespread charges of fraud. Ironically enough, President Bongo of Gabon, where the opposition won significant legislative representation, exudes more confidence than does Houphouët-Boigny of Côte d'Ivoire, where the opposition controls only 12 of the National Assembly's 175 seats. Several of the Ivorian opposition parties (most of which control no legislative seats) are calling for a more genuinely democratic transition via a national conference, and are seizing every opportunity to mount popular demonstrations to this end.

Were it not for the strength and determination of the opposition, and the absence of reliable external support, many leaders such as Eyadéma and Mobutu might also have succeeded in hijacking the transition. An interesting variation on this model is the case of Senegal, where President Abdou Diouf made the bold move of inviting leaders of the major opposition parties to join his government. All but one accepted—including Abdoulaye Wade, leader of the Parti Démocratique Sénégalais (PDS), who was briefly detained after his party denounced the legislative elections of February 1988 as fraudulent. Paradoxically, Abdou Diouf has refurbished the democratic image of the country's political system by broadening his government to include some of the opposition parties rather than following the more common method of democratizing the regime by subjecting it to more political competition.

4. Guided Democratization. This model, once widely praised, has now lost much of its luster because of the faster pace and greater breadth of other transitions. In such cases, represented most notably by Guinea and Nigeria, a military regime retains virtually complete control of the process, and the transitions are complex and deliberately prolonged. In October 1989, well ahead of the democratic upheavals in most other countries, President Lansana Conté of Guinea declared his intention to transfer power to a multiparty system. Since then, however, the process has lost credibility despite a referendum approving a new constitution and the February 1991 introduction of a transitional regime that includes civilian representation.

In the case of Nigeria, while there is considerable cynicism about President Ibrahim Babangida's unpredictable style of leadership, he has stayed in control of the transition process since seizing power from General Mohammed Buhari in an August 1985 palace coup.[6] Local councils with elected members from the two permitted parties are already in place, with elections for control of the 21 state governments expected later this year. Presidential elections will follow in mid-1992. The planned transfer of power at the federal level, once promised for October 1992, might not take place until early 1993.

While lacking the popular enthusiasm, heated debates, and drama usually associated with past electoral periods, the Nigerian transition still enjoys some credibility because of the well-known complexities of Nigerian politics and society. Periodic adjustments notwithstanding, the basic program of transition has followed the guidelines laid down in 1986. In Guinea, the Conté government has decreed a five-year transition starting in 1991, after which elections will be permitted. Even then, as in Nigeria, it will be on a two-party basis (which could subsequently be expanded in Guinea to include more parties). Nigeria's president Babangida has accorded himself more than eight years in power based on a plan to bring a stable Third Republic into being as well as to restructure the economy. President Conté now seems to be attempting the same maneuver, though he is likely to have more trouble holding the opposition at bay.

   5. *Recalcitrance and Piecemeal Reforms.* The list of regimes determined to stare down their critics and resist basic reforms grows shorter with each passing month. The overthrow of President Moussa Traoré in Mali on 20 March 1991, after clashes between the security forces and the democratic movement cost hundreds of lives, rudely reminded Africa of the Tiananmen Square option. Fortunately, Traoré's military colleagues deposed him and granted opposition demands for a transitional government charged with planning a national conference to reintroduce multiparty democracy. Mauritania belonged squarely in this camp until President Ould Sid'Ahmed Taya's April 1991 decision to permit multiparty elections. Similarly, Jerry Rawlings of Ghana, whose Provisional National Defense Council (PNDC) will be ten years old in December 1991, has reluctantly agreed to convene a constitutional assembly leading to multiparty elections. Rawlings, however, continues to heap abuse on the democratic movement and will no doubt seek new ways to foil his opponents as they continue to press their demands for a complete transfer of power and a break with the PNDC's autocratic style of governance.

   Another regime that has shown considerable recalcitrance while granting piecemeal concessions is the government of Cameroon, where Paul Biya has lifted press restrictions, permitted opposition parties to operate, and granted amnesty to political prisoners. Nevertheless, the opposition is dissatisfied with these reforms and insists on a national conference that would supplant Biya and his party. The unswerving hard-liners among the recalcitrants are found in such countries as Malawi, Kenya, and Sudan. In Malawi, no democratic breeze has been allowed to disturb the cloistered system of aging President Hastings Kamuzu Banda. President Daniel arap Moi of Kenya has made minor concessions to his domestic and external critics by releasing a few prominent detainees and instituting such reforms as the abolition of "queue voting" and the restoration of judicial tenure. President Moi has not budged, however, in his rejection of demands for multipartism or any other changes that would require the regime to relinquish its absolute control. In Sudan, meanwhile, the military regime of Lieutenant General Omar Hassan Ahmed El Bashir, which does little to disguise its alliance with the fundamentalist National Islamic Front, refuses to open the door to meaningful negotiations with the Sudan People's Liberation Army or to permit the country's established political parties to operate.

6. *Armed Insurrections Culminating in Elections.* In several African countries, including South Africa, determined armed struggles have been waged. Among the salutary consequences of the worldwide democratic movement is the way it has facilitated the resolution of these conflicts through peaceful elections. The reduction of Cold War tension made possible the transfer of power to a democratically elected government in Namibia and its accession to independence in March 1990. Global detente also facilitated the unbanning of the African National Congress and its affiliated organizations by President de Klerk of South Africa, as well as the Estoril Accord on Angola that provides for October 1992 elections involving the former warring parties.

There are other countries in which democratization may provide the exit from armed conflict. The National Resistance Movement of Yoweri Musevini in Uganda, after overthrowing the despotic rule of Milton Obote in 1986, introduced a quasi-democratic system. Musevini has not yet permitted competitive multiparty elections, though he has introduced many ancillary features of a democratic system, such as freedom of the press, respect for human rights, and an ombudsman. In Rwanda, President Habyarimana has responded to an armed insurgency that began in late 1990 by agreeing to introduce a multiparty system and other reforms. In Ethiopia, despite the insurgents' rhetorical commitment to Marxism, a July 1991 meeting aimed at establishing a provisional government also approved a charter that includes the key liberal democratic freedoms of expression, assembly, belief, and association. Multiparty elections are promised in a few years. Similarly, concerted efforts are under way in Liberia to end the armed insurgency of the National Patriotic Front of Liberia (NPFL) and to resolve the contested national leadership through free elections. If African governments become replaceable via the ballot box or amenable to change by peaceful means, there should be a corresponding decline in the resort to armed struggle.

7. *Conditional Transitions.* The greatest fear of the democratic movement in many African countries is that the ruling regimes will find pretexts for cancelling or postponing the transition toward democracy. In most cases, popular pressure is so strong that the government dares not renege on concessions. The cases in which governments have been able to interrupt democratic transitions have usually featured overt threats to the regime that also imperil the democratic aspirations of the people. This option is clearly seen in countries like Algeria and Tunisia, with their strong Islamic fundamentalist movements.

In both countries, the government has moved to arrest members of these movements. Algeria's Front Islamique du Salut (FIS) seems to have precipitated army repression in late June 1991 by launching demonstrations on the eve of elections. President Ben Ali of Tunisia had earlier moved to dismantle his country's threatening Ennahda movement with widespread arrests of its militants on national security grounds. In both countries, the government has publicly reaffirmed its commitment to democratization, although fulfillment will likely depend on the electoral prospects of the fundamentalists. Several other countries, including Nigeria, have potentially significant fundamentalist movements that could challenge and destabilize transitional governments and their successors.

A Workshop of Democracy

Richard Sklar's characterization of Africa as "a workshop of democracy" aptly describes a continent that promises to be among the world's exciting arenas of democratic experimentation in the decade ahead.[7] As mentioned earlier, the decades of authoritarian rule following independence inspired Africans to devise methods of communicating and acting outside the reach of the state's repressive agencies. Such informal networks drew on institutions and customs that owed little to either colonialism or its Africanized successor regimes. The current movement is able to build on these incipiently democratic institutions while developing others in response to prevailing circumstances.

The most notable innovation thus far is the national conference, which was first used in Benin. Though it is unclear who in that country first advanced the idea of such a meeting, the appropriateness of the national conference as a means for peacefully reconstructing discredited political systems is indisputable. These popular gatherings have been so comprehensive in scope that we cannot do them justice here, but a few features are worth underlining. The first is that they represent the emergence of a new political order in the midst of the old, with the new assuming sovereign authority, insisting on the binding character of its decisions, and gradually turning its predecessor into an empty shell. Once the call for a national conference goes up, the offers of beleaguered leaders to negotiate with the opposition are summarily dismissed. Indeed—and this is especially true in French-speaking Africa—democratic movements that settle for anything less than a national conference are now being viewed as having blundered. "Who says democracy says national conference" has become the watchword of many of Africa's democratic activists.

A second notable feature is the way the national conferences aim to achieve comprehensive representation for what are called *les forces vives*—meaning, roughly, the manifold groups and institutions of civil society. Scores of political parties and civic associations are represented, with participants usually numbering in the thousands. Because of the difficulty of reaching agreement on who should be included, the conference planning committees often become arenas of contention, as in Niger and Zaire, with repeated postponements a common result. Leading exiles are often invited back, some after many years abroad, to assist in the political rebirth of the nation.

In addition to relegating the head of state to an honorific position while transferring his powers to a conference-appointed executive, the meetings have also become places where the misrule and abuses of past and present governments can be exposed. Such exercises in collective catharsis may go to extremes, as happened in Congo, but there is no denying their therapeutic value. Representatives of all sectors of these societies can finally discuss charges and countercharges that could not be aired under the old repressive systems, and thus gain some hope of putting poisonous acrimony behind them. Some conferences have even subjected high officials to public interrogation. In both Benin and Congo, the conferences concluded with national leaders acknowledging their failings. One leader, President Sassou-Nguesso of Congo, even assumed responsibility for his predecessors' errors. The several national conferences that began in mid-1991 will tell their people—often through televised sessions and other media—more than the most assiduous journalists in the United States could learn about their government's misdeeds by invoking the Freedom of Information Act.

One feature that has characterized the national conferences, as well as the democratic movement generally, is the leading role of religious organizations and church leaders. Roman Catholic prelates presided over the national conferences in both Benin and Congo, where Bishop Ernest Nkombo was also appointed to head the body charged with implementing the transition plan that the conference formulated. In several countries, including Madagascar and Zambia, church leaders have served as vital intermediaries between the regime and its opponents. When governments grow highly intransigent, as was once the case in Zaire and is now the case in Kenya, religious organizations have kept up the pressure with well-publicized sermons and pastoral letters. In this regard, the contemporary democratic movement is following the trail blazed during the antiapartheid struggle by redoubtable religious leaders like the Reverend Beyers Naude and Anglican Archbishop Desmond Tutu.

The amazing successes of the national conferences have provoked reactions from leaders like Eyadéma in Togo, Mobutu in Zaire, and Ratsiraka in Madagascar. After reluctantly agreeing to such conferences, these leaders have resisted opposition demands to accord them sovereign status, employing a variety of tactics (including the use of military force) against the opposition. This final test of wills will decide whether the national conference movement continues to prevail, or whether more leaders will go down with their regimes (as in Mali) rather than accept merely ceremonial status. In any case, it is unlikely that these embattled leaders can stem the rising democratic tide.

In addition to mass rallies, street demonstrations, and strikes, other measures have been introduced in Togo, Madagascar, and Cameroon to pressure governments by shutting down essential services. A new term has joined the political vocabulary of Cameroon: the "ghost-town campaign." Using the support of taxi and truck drivers to block or slow commercial traffic, such campaigns have succeeded in halting economic activity in selected locales for as long as the demonstrators wished. In Cameroon, where the national soccer team's exciting performance in the 1990 World Cup tournament attracted international praise, the red card that referees use to banish unruly footballers from the field has been used by demonstrators to decide who should be allowed to pass through their roadblocks. Faced with potential anarchy, Paul Biya of Cameroon must choose between a peaceful leave-taking via the national conference and continued resistance to the inevitable transfer of power.

At one time, it seemed that the freedom to organize political parties, so long denied in many African countries, would result in the proliferation of minor parties spawned by contentious and mutually suspicious regional, religious, or ethnic groups. Although splintering tendencies are still observable, for example in Zaire, what is most striking is the extent to which opposition parties and groups have leagued together to bargain effectively with governments. Certainly this has been the case in the Central African Republic, Togo, and Madagascar. In Zambia, the diverse Movement for Multiparty Democracy (MMD) converted itself into the country's leading political party under the same name as soon as President Kenneth Kaunda conceded that he could not win a referendum on single-party rule. The collaborative tendency among opposition groups is now so apparent that African autocrats' usual arguments about the unifying power of their rule have been discredited. What is being made clear is how parochial the authoritarian governments had become, with their class and ethnic favoritism (especially toward the head of state's own group), and how broad-based and transethnic are the movements opposing them.

Democratization and Economic Restructuring

The upheavals that Africa is now living through are rooted in a series of overlapping, albeit sometimes contradictory, social struggles. At the most obvious level, there is a revolt against regimes that have enriched a tiny class of "political aristocrats" while consigning most of their fellow citizens to misery and deprivation. Most of the old political systems decisively lost their legitimacy because their economic performance, and hence distributional capacity, became hopelessly inadequate.

The economic dimension of these revolts can be glimpsed in the multiplicity of social groups that have taken part in direct actions aimed at bringing down single-party regimes. Popular demonstrations have often boasted a diverse array of participants, ranging from the unemployed to civil servants and teachers, with every possible social category in between. In some countries, such as the Congo and Zambia, strong trade union federations have added their organizational capacity and resilience to the democratic movements. The comprehensiveness of the rejection of authoritarian regimes should not blind us, however, to an even more general consideration.

In recent decades, most of Africa has become subject to a kind of dual governance. As African states became increasingly ineffective at promoting economic development, the international community assumed control of their economic policies through the imposition of structural-adjustment programs devised by the IMF and the World Bank. The overseas development agencies of the major industrial countries also participated in and strengthened these arrangements. Africa thus found itself under two overlapping forms of international economic domination: a world trading system, now directed by transnational companies, into which the continent has been integrated for centuries as a supplier of raw materials and primary agricultural products; and the operations of international financial institutions aiming to stabilize the continent's declining economies, restore financial solvency, and re-ignite economic growth.

African governments, like most regimes in the developing world, have long railed against the inequities of the global trading system. Yet their efforts to break out of it, often through state-led development schemes, have mostly failed. The hardships resulting from economic decline, and then from the austerity measures mandated by structural adjustment programs, were initially blamed on the international financial agencies. Eventually, such complaints were no longer fully convincing; Africans began to hold their authoritarian governments increasingly responsible for economic failure, for glaring inequities in how the burdens of austerity were shared, and for the humbling loss of national sovereignty to the Bretton Woods institutions and other foreign agencies.

What implications do such observations hold for the future of the democratic movement? Replacing authoritarianism with democracy will not fundamentally change Africa's economic situation. The developed countries will remain preoccupied with each other and with the USSR and Eastern Europe. The problems of debt relief, investment, and access to overseas markets that so vitally concern Africa will still be treated peripherally and inadequately. Moreover, the international financial agencies will continue to insist on the fulfillment of signed agreements promising reforms in economic policy.

The authoritarian African state, which had gradually become an instrument for implementing externally formulated economic policies, is now decayed. Its more democratic successors will eventually come into direct confrontation with the same global financial institutions. Speaking at an important conference on "The Prospects for Africa in the 1990s" held at the British House of Commons in June 1990, Secretary General Salim Ahmed Salem of the Organization for African Unity warned, "While Africa must democratize, our efforts will be hamstrung by the nondemocratic international economic system in which we operate." There is likely to be an increasing contradiction between the expanded voice of Africans in the formulation of their governments' policies and the minimal voice that these same governments will enjoy in influencing the operations of the global economic system.

Two questions follow: First, to paraphrase political scientist Atul Kohli, "What economic reform strategies are compatible with democratization?" It has often been remarked that the implementation of structural adjustment programs depended heavily on the authoritarian nature of African governments.[8] What is not known is how these same policies "can be implemented in the context of democratic politics."[9] The second question is whether, if African countries succeed in subjecting development policies to "democratic evaluation," the neo-imperial pattern of global decision making will undergo a commensurate adjustment.[10] International agencies that are increasingly outspoken in their calls for democratization in Africa must urgently address such questions. They have recognized that the authoritarian nature of the African state is a central part of the problem.[11] How will they respond to an African *dēmos* whose ideas about economic restructuring differ from those of the World Bank, the IMF, and their affiliates?

Challenges and Opportunities Ahead

People in many African nations have watched their standards of living drop steeply in recent years. In some cases, real earnings have fallen back to independence-era levels. Unless the new democracies can restore economic growth, they will face direct challenges from the very social forces that are currently undermining authoritarianism. At the time of the 1983 elections in Nigeria, one letter-writer to a newspaper bluntly exclaimed: "Many people have stopped bothering themselves with classifying African regimes as democratic or otherwise. . . . I am one; I tell you, all these noises about 'democracy' and 'democratic' are mere luxuries to the sufferers."[12] The new democracies will face the heightened expectations of their supporters. While they may be able to gain some breathing space to try and revive collapsed economies, the international community must be prepared to make generous assistance available to them, beginning with the cancellation of burdensome, unpayable debts that were contracted by corrupt, inept, and undemocratic governments.

The emergent democracies will also have to address issues connected with democratization that go beyond the restoration of multiparty elections. Nigerian social scientist Ayesha Imam has pointed out that the state alone has not been responsible for denying basic rights—there are also "crisscrossing networks of oppression" to be found in the economic, cultural, and religious spheres.[13] There is already evidence of attempts to undo such networks within the broader movement for democracy—with regard, for example, to the rights of women who remain very weakly represented in African politics. Women in some countries have become alert to the opportunities that the democratic movement gives them to assert their special claims. A public demonstration by women in Niger, for example, ensured that they would be given adequate representation on the committee that planned the national conference. Throughout the continent, there are other marginalized groups and societal forms of oppression based on race, ethnicity, class, and caste that the democratic movement must address.

Africa must also avoid a reenactment of what happened after independence, when authoritarian regimes demobilized many associations that had played important roles in the anticolonial struggle. The heightened levels of democratic awareness and activism that make the national conferences possible cannot be sustained indefinitely. On the other hand, the business of governing cannot be left entirely to governments as before. Autonomous action by civic associations is needed if democracy is to flourish.

No matter how attractive their constitutional and institutional innovations, African democracies must prove that they can do a better job of governing than their predecessors. One promising aspect of current transitions is the accession to office of individuals of proven administrative skill. Many such persons are being drawn from international agencies such as the World Bank and various UN bodies, reversing the "brain drain." Benin, Côte d'Ivoire, Congo, and Mali are among the countries that have looked to such organizations as a source of new leaders. In countries where new officials have tended to be home-grown, as in Algeria and Gabon, they have also fit a more technocratic mold. As the reconstructed governments pursue a more managerial and less partisan style of leadership, the new political parties must avoid excessive political jousting. So far, the signs are promising. The struggle for democracy is generating an awareness of common interests and a shared fate that could undergird the needed coalition governments. Revulsion at the ways in which authoritarian governments have favored particular sectional groups while claiming to champion national unity, as well as at the persistent greed of ruling groups in the face of deepening austerity, have inspired renewed commitment to social equity. Yet such commitments can be sustained only if there arise organizations and institutions capable of pressing the claims of all *les forces vives* of society, especially those that have suffered systematic exclusion in the past.

Finally, Africa has to end the tyranny of armed force, whether it appears in the form of soldiers grasping after wealth and privilege via military rule, or in that of advocates of some noble cause or other who cannot abide the delays and complexities of democratic contestation. There are tens of millions of refugees and other displaced persons in Africa today. Angola, Ethiopia, Mozambique, Somalia, and the Sudan have all sacrificed entire generations on the altar of armed conflict. Parents in some countries connive to get their children into military academies rather than regular schools because the armed forces seem a surer route to power and wealth. In others, entire villages empty at the approach of military recruiters seeking youths to defend lost causes. Such madness must cease. The democratic movement in Africa must be a humanistic one that lends renewed meaning to the integrity of the human person and the need for tolerance and accommodation. Above all, Africa needs peace. If peace is shown to be one of the first fruits of the democratic movement, many others will follow in time.

NOTES

1. This classification was devised by *Africa Dēmos*, a bimonthly publication of the African Governance Program of the Carter Center of Emory University.

2. Peter Anyang Nyong'o, "The One-Party State and Its Apologists: The Democratic Alternative" (Paper delivered at a conference on "Thirty Years of Independence in Africa," Windhoek, Namibia, May 1991), 3.

3. See Claude Ake, "Rethinking African Democracy," *Journal of Democracy* 2 (Winter 1991): 32-44.

4. Anyang Nyong'o, "The One-Party State and Its Apologists," 4.

5. Achille Mbembe, *Afriques indociles* (Paris: Éditions Karthala, 1988).

6. Larry Diamond, "Nigeria's Search for a New Political Order," *Journal of Democracy* 2 (Spring 1991): 54-69.

7. Richard Sklar, "Democracy in Africa," *African Studies Review* 26 (1983): 11-24.

8. Richard Joseph, ed., "Beyond Autocracy in Africa" (Working Papers of the Inaugural Seminar of the African Governance Program, Carter Center of Emory University, February 1989).

9. Anyang Nyong'o, "Development and Democracy: The Debate Continues," *CODESRIA Bulletin* (Dakar, Senegal) No. 2 (1991), 12.

10. Thandika Mkandawire, "Further Comments on the 'Development and Democracy' Debate," *ibid.*, 11.

11. International Bank for Reconstruction and Development, "Sub-Saharan Africa: From Crisis to Sustainable Growth" (World Bank, Washington, D.C., 1989).

12. B. Olusegun Babalola, cited in Richard Joseph, *Democracy and Prebendal Politics in Nigeria: The Rise and Fall of the Second Republic* (Cambridge: Cambridge University Press, 1987; Spectrum Books, Nigeria, 1991), 159.

13. Ayesha Imam, "Democratization Process in Africa: Problems and Prospects," *CODESRIA Bulletin* (Dakar, Senegal) No. 2 (1991), 5.

29.
UNCERTAINTIES OF
A DEMOCRATIC AGE

Leszek Kolakowski

*Born in Poland in 1927, **Leszek Kolakowski** was professor of philosophy at the University of Warsaw from 1950 to 1968. During that period, he emerged as one of the leading internal critics of the Communist regime in Poland and was denounced by Communist Party chief Wladyslaw Gomulka. Following the student unrest of 1968, he was expelled from the university and left Poland for the West. Professor Kolakowski currently divides his academic year between Oxford University, where he is a senior research fellow at All Souls College, and the University of Chicago, where he is a member of the Committee on Social Thought. He has written more than 30 books, including the renowned three-volume study* Main Currents of Marxism *(1978). The recipient of numerous awards, he was chosen in 1986 to deliver the 15th annual Thomas Jefferson Lecture by the National Endowment for the Humanities of the United States.*

Leaving aside the historical vicissitudes of the word *democracy* and all kinds of spurious and fraudulent usages of it ("socialist democracy," "people's democracy," "Islamic democracy"), we may say that this concept, as usually understood, includes three components.

First, we think of a set of institutions aimed at assuring that the power and influence of political elites correspond to the amount of popular support they enjoy.

Second, we have in mind the independence of the legal system from the executive power; the law acts as an autonomous mediating device between individual or corporate interests and the state, and is not an instrument of ruling elites.

Third, we think of enforceable barriers built into the legal system that guarantee both the equality of all citizens before the law and basic personal rights, which (though the list is notoriously contestable) include freedom of movement, freedom of speech, freedom of association, religious freedom, and freedom to acquire property.

These three components are not necessarily linked; they may exist separately—both conceptually and as a matter of historical experience. The principle of majority rule is insufficient if we are to make a distinction between democracy and ochlocracy, the rule of the mob. The principle of majority rule does not by itself constitute democracy; we know of tyrannical regimes that enjoyed the support of a majority, including Nazi Germany and Iranian theocracy. We do not call democratic a regime in which 51 percent of the population may slaughter the remaining 49 percent with impunity. Neither are the first and second components sufficient without the third, as we can easily imagine a regime in which enforceable and predictable legal rules operate without assuring either equality or personal rights.

Continuing Threats to Democracy

As much as all of us who are committed to liberty welcome the worldwide movement that aims at the establishment or restoration of democratic institutions in communist countries, in military dictatorships, and in other forms of tyranny, we had better not imagine that the cause of freedom is now safe and its victory imminent. For there are a number of factors that now and in the foreseeable future will continue to threaten democratic institutions.

First among them is the enfeebled, but still living, force of Sovietism. We notice, of course, the deep crisis of totalitarian institutions: the increasing reassertion of civil society in communist countries; the economic, social, and cultural bankruptcy of "real socialism"; and the collapse of the ideological legitimacy of Soviet-type systems. But the time is not yet ripe for the last rites. The accelerated changes, indicating that the rulers themselves have lost confidence in the vitality of their regimes (the clearest symptom of decay), have lasted only for a short time, and their outcome is by no means certain. There are rational grounds to expect that *perestroika* in the Soviet Union will fizzle out, and this might result in a political regression whose character and scope it would be vain to speculate upon. Imperialist expansion has been built into the very ideological foundations of the Soviet regime, and the unambiguous renunciation of this expansion would require an ideological transformation that is difficult to imagine. The only potential rival of Marxism-Leninism—Great Russian chauvinism—would bring a mortal danger to the empire if it were established as the official doctrine, as it would inevitably inflame even more all the nationalisms of the non-Russian population. And we do not know what might happen if the ruling party faced a real threat of being removed from power. It is much too early to write the obituary of communism.

A second source of antidemocratic energy is the growth of malignant nationalism all over the world. Patriotic feelings are not in themselves incompatible with a democratic outlook, insofar as they mean a preferential solidarity with one's own nation, the attachment to national cultural heritage and language, and the desire to make one's nation better off and more civilized. (Patriotism wants to make the nation clean; nationalism, to whitewash it, as Chesterton says.) Nationalism is malignant and hostile to civilization when it asserts itself through belief in the natural superiority of one's own tribe and in the hatred of others; if it looks for pretexts, however silly, to expand into others' territories; and above all, if it implies an idolatrous belief in the absolute supremacy of national values when they clash with the rights of persons who make up this very nation. There is no need to prove that this kind of rapacious and potentially totalitarian nationalism is increasing in various parts of our globe.

A third antidemocratic factor is religious intolerance and theocratic aspirations. To be sure, the theocratic tendency, which naturally does away with the separation of the state from religion and establishes an ideological despotism, is most clearly and most dangerously active in Islamic countries, where there are reasons to expect that it will grow. Islamic countries, however, make up a large segment of mankind; while none of them is fully democratic in the Western sense, they differ significantly in the degree of intolerance. We also notice an increase in theocratic aspirations among some Israeli Jews. Analogous tendencies in Christianity do not seem strong or dangerous for the time being, but their seeds are quite alive and occasionally display their vitality.

A fourth menace to democracy comes from terrorism and criminal violence. The danger is not that terrorists and drug dealers will take over power in civilized states, but that they might compel democratic governments to combat them—presumably with popular consent—through measures that violate democratic rights. Nobody, of course, opposes security checks at airports, and we naturally assume that these are no more than a trivial nuisance, a small price to pay for the relative safety of travel. But strictly speaking, these checks imply that each of us is treated, without any grounds, as a suspected terrorist. What if the efficient fight against terrorists and criminals were to require not only large-scale unwarranted searches but preventive killings, the suspension of the principle "innocent until proven guilty," the growth of vigilante organizations, and so on? We might accept such measures under duress when we feel they are needed to defend democracy, but we should not pretend that they would leave the health of democracy intact.

The fifth, and potentially the most important, danger to democracy might come from the long-term changes that are affecting virtually all parts of our planet. The rapid pace of economic growth during the postwar decades has produced—both in the rich and in the poor countries—a mentality of endless expectations. Somehow we have gotten used to the hope that each of us is going to have more and more of everything in the indefinite future and to the firm belief that this is what each of us deserves. But these hopes are bound to end up in bitter disappointment, at least for the overwhelming majority of the world's people.

Overpopulation, shrinking resources of agricultural land and of water, and ecological catastrophes will certainly compel mankind in the near future to devote more and more effort and money to repairing the damages already inflicted on our environment and to warding off further calamities. This will not only lead to growing restrictions imposed on our freedom of movement and property rights. It will result, above all, in a dampening of our hopes for "more and more" and, indeed, in the demand that we recognize that we have enough, or even that we must manage with less, limit our wants, and accept a more modest life. The amount of frustration, irrational rage, and aggressiveness that these imperatives are going to cause will be enormous, and will affect the poor and the rich alike. For the degree of frustration depends not on the absolute level of satisfaction, but on the distance between this absolute level and our subjective needs, and our needs can and do expand indefinitely along the endless spiral of greed. It is hard to predict what ideological expression or other channels this frustration might find, but in order to tame it and to prevent society from plunging into chaos or falling prey to a lawless tyranny, it is likely that many undemocratic restrictions will be needed.

Widespread misery is fertile ground for the successful demagogy of totalitarian movements and for the temptation to "solve" social problems by means of military dictatorship. We have seen this many times, especially in Latin America and in Africa. If the relatively rich countries will be compelled to lower human expectations—even without causing real misery—it can only add to the danger.

This is not to say that the cause of freedom is lost; we have enough evidence to conclude that people need not only security but freedom as well. But we must also never forget that freedom is always vulnerable and its cause never safe.

INDEX